THE MELTING POT AND BEYOND
ITALIAN AMERICANS IN THE YEAR 2000

THE MELTING POT AND BEYOND
ITALIAN AMERICANS IN THE YEAR 2000

Proceedings of
the XVIII Annual Conference of the
American Italian Historical Association

Held at the Biltmore Plaza Hotel, Providence, Rhode Island

November 7—9, 1985

Edited by
Jerome Krase and William Egelman

Brooklyn College
Brooklyn, N.Y.

Iona College
New Rochelle, N.Y.

The American Italian Historical Association
1987

Volume XVIII in the series of Annual Proceedings of the American Italian Historical Association

LIBRARY OF CONGRESS CATALOG CARD NUMBER:
ISBN: 0-934-675-18-X
ISSN: 0743-474X

Published in the United States of America by
The American Italian Historical Association
209 Flagg Place
Staten Island, New York 10304—1148

CONTENTS

PREFACE

The American Italian Historical Association's Eighteenth Annual Conference was held in Providence, Rhode Island November 7—9, 1985. Its main theme, "The Melting Pot and Beyond: Italian Americans in the year 2000," was designed to stimulate thought not only on the past and present condition of Italians in America, but also on their future. The theme played on the title of Daniel P. Moynihan and Nathan Glazer's work on the continuing significance of ethnicity and race in American social and political life. (1) We felt it was important to ascertain how much Italian Americans had changed or progressed since their early settlement in the American colonies and their mass migration to the United States at the turn of the century. We also wised to consider how the character of subsequent migration has changed and in what direction Italian Americans were going. A sub-theme of the meetings was the Italians of Rhode Island, recognizing that this state has the greatest concentration of citizens who trace their roots back to Italy of any state in the union. In recognition of the outstanding achievements of Rhode Island's Italians, the first two chapters of this volume chronicle the political careers of John Pastore and Luigi De Pasquale. The stories of these two men parallel the social and political development of the states Italian American population.

Although the conference could not possibly consider all the ramifications of the issues raised by the conference themes, at the meetings over a one-hundred participants presented their views on Italian American life, past, present and future in forms ranging from standard paper readings to film, video and painting. The papers presented here have been selected from a pool of over seventy submitted for consideration. As chapters in this volume they are loosely arranged in the following order; politics, research methods, immigration, religion and education, literature and art, and local life.

Of special note is the publication in this volume of the 1985 Vincent Visceglia Prize winning essay by Wallace P. Sillanpoa, "The Poetry and Politics of Arturo Giovannetti." This prize is awarded to the best paper presented at the Annual Meeting. The Selection Committee this year was chaired by Gary Mormino and included the Conference Co-chairmen and the A.I.H.A. Editorial Selection Committee.

The 18th Annual Meeting of the American Italian Historical Association set new records for number of participants, registrants, grants and revenues raised. In addition, the local and national publicity generated greatly enhanced the prestige of our organization and the recognition of the importance of our endeavors to collect and disseminate knowledge on the Italian American experience. For this success we are indebted to many individuals and groups and most especially the people of Rhode Island. Not everyone who assisted in the organization of the Conference and the publication of the Proceedings can be cited here. Even the following limited acknowledgements are considerable.

First and foremost in our minds for crediting the success of the Annual Meeting and this Proceedings are the Italian Americans of Rhode Island. They were represented in many ways at all levels of conference planning and participation. We especially thank the Consortium of Italian American Organizations of Rhode Island composed of the Italian American Historical Society of Rhode Island, The Italo-American Club, Itam Vets, Sons of Italy of Rhode Island, United Italian Americans and the Verrazano Committee. They were ably represented on our Local Arrangements Committee by Louis DiCarlo, Joyce Fratantuono, Anthony Leone, Joseph Muratore, Arthur R. Russo, Carmela Santoro, Remo Trivelli and Ronald L. DiOrio of the Rhode Island Governor's Policy Office. The help of Paula Colicci of the Rhode Island Chamber of Commerce was also invaluable.

From its inception the idea of an American Italian Historical Association annual meeting in Providence was supported by Governor Edward D. DiPrete of Rhode Island and Mayor Joseph R. Paolini Jr. of Providence as well as the A.I.H.A.'s own Peter Sammartino, who also represented the National Italian American Foundations at the early stages of planning.

The Providence meetings was exceptional in many ways, not least of which was the involvement of the Connecticut Italian Teachers Association and the Rhode Island Teachers of Italian. These organizations presented two large sessions which were an important part of the conference program. In addition, a tour and reception for participants was provided by the John Carter Brown Library of Brown University. Substantial assistance and support for the meetings came from Iona College and the University of Rhode Island who were especially helpful in the early stages of planning and preparation.

Our task of putting together the Providence conference was made substantially easier by the continual efforts of A.I.H.A. Conference Committee members Frank Cavaioli, Salvatore LaGumina and Anne Marie Ricitelli. Constant encouragement and support was also provided by Constance DeVito Egelman and Suzanne Nicoletti Krase.

Selecting papers for inclusion in the Proceeding was a difficult process. We therefore are greatly indebted to the A.I.H.A. Editorial Selection Committee composed of Phillip Cannistraro, Michael Tropea and Diana Cavallo and chaired by Richard Juliani.

The most important aspect of the A.I.H.A.'s annual meetings is insuring that the best and most representative papers presented are published in our Proceedings; a series now eighteen volumes in length. These volumes represent in many ways the history of recent scholarship on the Italian American experience because of their continuity. They also have focused on many areas of Italian American life not even alluded to in standard "ethnic studies" publications. They have consistently included articles which have broken new ground and have opened new avenues of investigation. Many times they have chronicled not only what people would like to know but also what they might not wish to hear about.

Since our Proceedings are vital to our existence as an organization and as individual scholars, we are most thankful to the Italian American Cultural Exchange Commission of the Rhode Island Heritage Commission and the Economic Development Council of Rhode Island for their generous support which made the timely publication of these Proceedings possible.

1. *Beyond the Melting Pot*, Cambridge, Mass.: The M.I.T. Press, 1963.

Jerome Krase, Brooklyn College
William Egelman, Iona College

March 2, 1987

Chapter **1**   **JOHN PASTORE, ITALIAN-**
AMERICAN POLITICAL PIONEER
Salvatore John LaGumina
Nassau Community College

On occasion the American political landscape produces individuals who
are the embodiment of ethnic politics, that is individuals who, while
commanding broad general popular appeal, are nevertheless also perceived
in particularistic mono-ethnic terms. One can think of Governor Herbert
Lehman of New York, Mayor Thomas Bradley of Los Angeles, Mayor Fiorello
H. LaGuardia of New York City and President John F. Kennedy, among others,
who fit this U.S. description in the last few decades. The subject of this article
is an Italian-American whose achievements in political life admirably qualify
him for inclusion in this circle.

Dapper, dimunitive and dynamic, John Orlando Pastore occupies a singular
and extraordinary position in the constellation of Italian-American political
luminaries. If being the first of an ethnic group to attain two of the most coveted
positions in the body politic qualify a person for distinction, then Pastore rates
a higher acknowledgement than most others in the ethnic group who may be
better known. Accordingly, Fiorello LaGuardia, arguably the most famous
of all Italian-American political figures and a man of immense popularity, never
achieved a position higher than that of mayor of New York City; never receiving
nomination to the governorship of his state nor to the august ranks of the United
States Senate. Although Geraldine Ferraro was nominated as the Democratic
candidate for Vice-President, the highest elective position she held was a
member of Congress. Governor of New York Mario Cuomo may yet make
history as a major party candidate for the Presidency, but that is for the future
to determine.

The Pastore saga began in the town of Sant'Arcangelo, province of Potenza
near Naples, where John's parents were born. Upon emigration to this country
in 1899, his father Michele settled on Balbo Avenue in the heart of Providence's
Little Italy, known as "Federal Hill". There, in contrast to the majority of

his fellow countrymen, he quickly utilized his Old World tailoring skill, opened up a shop in the family home, and as business prospered, moved the family to better living quarters. Success was short-lived, however, because in 1916, while young John was only nine years of age, his father died leaving four youngsters and a wife, then expecting her fifth child. Difficult days were surely ahead for the Pastore family which was forced to move back to the original Balbo Avenue apartment. When his mother went to work as a seamstress, John, as the second oldest son, assumed his share of work in the house; minding his younger brother and sisters, tidying up in the kitchen, cleaning the bedrooms and cooking for the family. Although life of comparative deprivation, it did not, however, engender despair. "We were a very poor family but a very happy family. We wanted for nothing more than what we had and we said our prayers every time was partook of the little bit that we did have."[1]

Federal Hill, where John was born in 1907 and where he spent his childhood years, was an authentic ethnic neighborhood in which an immigrant people could pursue social and economic goals amidst the welcome strains of the familiar language of their ancestors, the inviting aroma of their delectable foods, and the comforting support of their faithful institutions. Neighbors could be friendly and understanding, however, the Pastore family resolved not to be dependent on handouts and charity, no matter how well-intentioned. Erminia Pastore concluded that although a widow, she could lead her family to a position of middle-class respectability. "Make yourself liked; make people respect you," was her oft-repeated admonition. One road to achieve the goal of respectability among Providence's Italian-Americans was through a fastidious appearance. In the case of John Pastore, the trait, honed almost to a fault as a youngster, became his trademark for the rest of his career. Immaculately dressed from head to foot, John strove for a level of sartorial splendor which rendered his a legend in his time as he exercise meticulous care over the ties he wore and the whiteness of his dress shirts. Elegant in his wardrobe appearance, he became even more celebrated as a public speaker, spending numerous hours preparing speeches in order to obtain perfection — a self-imposed training which brought universal acclaim even to the extent of being compared with such senatorial giants of oratory as John Calhoun, Henry Clay and the inimitable Daniel Webster.[2]

Instinctively, but appropriately for Puritanically-oriented New England, the Pastore family subscribed to the hard-work ethic, deeming it validation of a life well-lived. In John's case necessity conjoined with preference; he began to work at the age of 9, running errands for a clothing store during his grammar school days and operating a foot press in a jewelry shop after school while attending Classical High School. John experienced deep disappointment upon graduation because although he had gained admission to two Ivy League colleges, dire family economic circumstances precluded his attendance. "I cried myself to sleep when I graduated from high school because I could not go to college." But this proved to be a temporary detour as he proceeded to take Northeastern University-sponsored law classes in a nearby Y.M.C.A. facility. "And while my friends went to dances and on dates, I studied."[3] Passing his bar examinations, he worked briefly as a lawyer before entering public life.

A brief summary of Rhode Island political history is helpful at this point. Simply put, control of politics overwhelmingly was in the hands of the Republican Party and the Yankee elites in the late nineteenth and early part of the twentieth centuries. The domination of the "establishment" spawned a mid-nineteenth century xenophobia in the form of a rampant anti-Catholicism especially hostile to the fast-growing newcomer population.[4] As new ethnic groups began to challenge the old order hegemony, the establishment resorted to such dubious tactics to maintain control, that it prompted a muckraking political analyst of the Progressive era to remark, "The political condition of Rhode Island is notorious, acknowledged and it is shameful.[5]

For years the Republican organization controlled Rhode Island's political destiny by outright malapportionment in the state legislature which gave rural towns excessive influence over cities into which the newly-arrived were moving.[6] Demographic changes of the late nineteenth century saw the ethnic composition altered by the influx of Irish, French-Canadians, Portuguese and Italians reduce the old Yankee stock to 30 percent of the total state population, did not, however, presage an immediate shift in political power. The old Yankee oligarchy continued to exercise clout until the 1930's when the Irish began to emerge, *via* the Democratic Party. Having established themselves as important wielders of political influence, Irish ascendancy was not inclusive — it refused to share power with other groups such as the Italians. Thus, although both parties began the process of absorption virtually simultaneously, Republican Yankees went further than the Democratic Irish in giving up their committee memberships to the newcomers.[7] So pronounced was the exclusion that it prompted more sensitive Irish-American political leaders to decry the discrimination. For example, in 1930, the North Providence Democratic Party Chairman resigned in protest over his party's failure to extend proper recognition ot the sizeable Italian population locally and simultaneously urged a rectification by calling for the addition of Luigi DePasquale to the ticket for Lieutenant-Governor.[8] DePasquale was in fact one of the pioneer political leaders of Providence's Italian-American community. The son of immigrants who enjoyed a modicum of business success, Providence-born Luigi became a lawyer in 1913 and soon opened a law practice. At the time Italians in Federal Hill and surrounding areas were growing communities displaying overwhelming proletarian and provincial characteristics. Political activities, such as they were in the 1910's, saw Federal Hill send Republicans to the City Council and the state House of Representatives. In 1916 DePasquale, who became the first of his nationality to represent his district as a Democrat, quickly became an advocate for the rights of his fellow ethnics.[9] Although under his leadership Rhode Island Democrats, including Italians, began to effect a degree of solidarity by the end of the 1920's, it was the emergence of the New Deal that finally enabled them to attain meaningful political voice, specifically the 1934 elections which saw state Democrats headed by Governor Francis Green reorganize state government.

1934 also was to be an important year for John Pastore. Only three years after being admitted to the Rhode Island Bar, the 27 year old Italian-American newly-enrolled Democrat gained the support of the local Italian ward leader and proceeded to run and win a seat to the Rhode Island State Assembly. This launched Pastore's career as a machine-made product of the hard-nosed Providence ward politics, however, in this instance devoid of the negative stereotypes usually associated with political machines. Regarded as a consistent, if unspectacular, partisan loyalist in the Rhode Island House of Representatives, he nevertheless gained valuable back-seat experience by articulating issues of the day and fostering the impression of a dependable and able figure.[10]

In 1938, as an assistant to the state Attorney General, he finally began to come into his own. Within a couple of years he was prosecuting most of the state's cases and was thereby thrust into a position where he could demonstrate his courtroom prowess as an intense prosecutor whose powerful voice charmed many including Elena Caito, whom he later married. During this period Pastore became a member of the Providence Charter Revision Committee. In 1944, at the age of 37, he ran a successful race for Lieutenant Governor and was sworn in as the first statewide Italian-American officer-holder of a largely ceremonial, but nevertheless, prestigious post.[11] Fortune continued to smile favorably because with a year, upon the resignation of Governor McGrath, who became Solicitor-General of the United States, Pastore was elevated to the governorship. At age 38, as the youngest governor ever for the state of Rhode Island and of course the first chief executive of Italian descent for the entire country, he ushered in a new era of political emergence of the ethnic group. Whether or not it was a matter of pure luck, as Pastore explained his rise, there is no gainsaying its timeliness. Pastore attained his vaunted position at a time when Italian-Americans were being stirred politically throughout the nation.[12] The 8 members of Congress of Italian heritage represented a doubling of any prior period; and furthermore, with the popularity of figures like Mayor Fiorello LaGuardia of New York City and other individuals, the ethnic group was on the verge of greater political power. The emergence of a second generation now ready to take its place as active political participants coincided with a fading negative impression associated with Italy's early wartime status.

Evidently Rhode Island was ready for the Pastore phenomenon. Indeed in recognition of his inimitable oratory, his deliberate effort to consider both sides of an issue, and his pugnacity, he was regarded "the most refreshing thing that has ever happened here."[13] He was well-described as a study in paradox, at once impulsive as a hare, yet as deliberate as a tortoise. As governor he was required to weed out corruption in government before it became a debilitating scandal, and simultaneously he tackled a myriad of economic and political issues. He proposed measures in behalf of anti-pollution, fair employment, mild tax-raising, and salary increases for state employees. His administration was credited with introducing the primary system in Rhode Island — not an altogether minor achievement for a state that was notorious for its limitations on democratic participation on the part of the electorate. As astute political participant/observer Matthew J. Smith has remarked, "Rhode Island did not experience any kind of political, social or economic reform during the so-called Progressive era."[14] Even the "Bloodless Revolution" of 1935 which saw Democrats finally oust the old Republican oligarchy from state control and which resulted in a revamping of the entire machinery of state government did not, however, mean reform of a political apparatus which continued its retarded nature. Against this background the adoption of a primary law in 1947 was of some significance. Indeed Pastore rated this as one of his major accomplishments.[15]

Like other parts of the nation Rhode Island was compelled to confront presures to remove rent controls in the post-war era. Enacted against a background of concern over scarce housing, federal laws had put a lid on rent charges. However, pressures to allow the free market to function in an unhindered manner worked to remove federal involvement and thus the problem was thrown into the laps of state and local governments. Pastore was very clear where he stood on the matter — for continued rent control. In testifying before the House Banking and Currency Committee that was considering legislation to terminate control, Pastore appealed for a one year continuation in order to avoid a "catastrophe".[16] Although his rhetoric sounded alarmist, he was ever the pragmatist and supported proposals to extend controls for six months in the spirit of a "practical man".

Pastore's voice was raised also in behalf of economic development in recognition of the changing industrial atmosphere. Rhode Island, along with other New England states, was then experiencing the loss of traditional industries such as textiles. Accordingly this was the subject of concern for the governor who excoriated industrialists whose exodus from the local area put undue strain on the economy by re-locating in lower wage-paying areas of the south or Puerto Rico denouncing them as "unworthy of being called Americans." An inveterate New England booster, the "Little Firecracker" proved a constant advocate of the region's agricultural, industrial and recreational advantages. His boosterism was so infectious that in January 1949 he was elected chairman of the New England Governors Conference, becoming chief spokesman for an imaginative plan to promote the industrial needs of the area. Although strongly endorsed by the majority, two negatives votes of Republican New England governors effectively killed the plan.[17]

By 1949 Pastore was attracting considerable attention outside the state. He was a valuable asset in rallying Democratic votes in nearby states and also a respected voice within Catholic circles, even while he displayed the temerity to chide fellow co-religionists on the requirement that they extend tolerance to others if they demanded tolerance for themselves.[18]

Clearly by 1950 Pastore had earned the support of Rhode Island Italian-Americans, an endorsement vividly reflected in the gubernatorial elections of 1946 and 1948. By the end of the 1940's the ethnic group had become fairly well absorbed in state politics as indicated by political scientist Elmer Cornwell's analysis of their membership in party machinery. Whereas three decades previously Italian-American committeemen could be found only in the scattered areas of high Italian concentration, by the 1960's they were beginning to appear as committeemen in wards with no significant Italian population.[19] Pastore was the beneficiary of the emergence of his fellow ethnics in party ranks as well as their ascendancy economically, attracting both Republican and Democrat Rhode Island Italian-Americans who provided him with a slim victory in 1946.[20] By 1948, his second race for the governorship, he had become the favorite not only of his fellow ethnics, but Rhode Island as a whole, receiving the backing of the largest plurality in state history. No sooner was the election over that he set his eyes on the national level, specifically a United States Senate seat where he would be able to deal with challenges not just from a small state or region, but of the entire nation, indeed the world. In November 1950 his ambition was fulfilled generously via a lop-sided 183,725 to 114,084 sweep which rendered him the biggest vote-getter in Rhode Island history.

Unlike some governors who had difficulty adjusting to the Senate, John O. Pastore was immediately at home quickly mastering its rules and in a quiet, unassuming manner, began his trek up the legislative ladder. He served as a member of the influential Appropriations Committee, the Commerce Committee and the Joint Committee on Atomic Energy, becoming chairman of the latter.

Over the course of a twenty-six year tenure as a Senator, Pastore naturally was participant in some of the most mementous issues to come before Congress — far too many to lend themselves to meaningful consideration in a brief summary of his career — therefore only a review of the highlights of that career will be attempted.[21] As a member of a minority Pastore demonstrated intense interest in civil rights, proving to be staunch advocate of legislation designed to advance the basic rights of black people — a concern which formed a cornerstone of the Lyndon B. Johnson administration. Upon assuming the presidency, Johnson resolutely prodded the nation towards an extension of civil rights which won him deserved praise for launching a Second Reconstruction.

The centerpiece of the movement was the Civil Rights Act of 1964 which outlawed discrimination in public accomodations, required equal access to public facilities and authorized the withdrawal of federal subsidies from institutions that evinced prejudice. The latter point, particular bone of contention, elicited spirited reaction on the part of southern senators who were prepared to filibuster the measure to death.[22] Thus the issue in the Senate was drawn with various individuals emerging as leaders among the proponents and opponents of the bill. Into this breach came Senator Pastore who, in his grandiloquent manner began the first line of defense of Title VI, the punitive feature of the bill, emphatically asserting that the time had come to get the federal government "out of the business of subsidizing discrimination."[23] As Senator Edmund Muskie put it, "When we needed to pass the 1964 Civil Rights Act, he was there as floor leader." Pastore's fulminations, along with the vigorous backing of other key senators served to guide the measure succesfully through Congress with Title VI intact.

Among the senator's greatest accomplishments were his pioneering efforts in behalf of public communications. Becoming Chairman of the Senate Communictions Sub-Committee in 1955, the formative years of the industry, he was in a position to alert Americans to the dire consequences of television violence. Presiding over committee hearings on the relationship between juvenile delinquency and television-portrayed aggression, he came out strongly against violence, however, not at the cost of free speech, therefore in 1962 he opposed a pre-screening procedure.[24] However, int he light of continued public outcry over the incidences of violence and sex in television programming, he changed his mind and endorsed a pre-screening procedure advocated by the Television Code Review Board. This board, one must hasten to add, was not a government agency but rather, a creation of the broadcasters themselves and thus constituted voluntary self-regulation. Pastore is to be credited with writing the bills which eventuated in laws making possible educational television and the public broadcasting system. It was not surprising therefore, to note that he was called the "Father" of Public Television. As one senator summed up his work: "Almost every critical piece of legislation dealing with communication matters can be traced to the hand of John Pastore. They include the Educational Television Facilities Act of 1962, the Public Broadcasting Act of 1967, and the Communications Satellite Act of 1962."[25]

Sharing a concern with most Americans over the need to reform campaign spending, in 1971, Pastore guided the first spending and disclosure bill through his chamber as the Senate passed the first bill of that nature in half a century. Designed to limit amounts that candidates running for federal office could spend on radio, television and other media, the bill did not take effect immediately because of a threat of a Presidential veto. The intent of the bill was of course admirable: to give the public an accounting of the source of campaign funnds — the very disclosure in itself constituting an advance in fostering public confidence in the integrity of the electoral process.[26]. In 1972 an even stronger version of the bill became law thereby vindicating his role as a pioneer in campaign spending reform because he introduced the concept of public financing for presidential elections. His work in this regard caused Senator Edward Kennedy to laud him for taking "national elections off the custom block and restore them to the people."[27]

Asked what he considered his most important accomplishment while serving the country as senator, John Pastore readily cites his role in enacting the nuclear ban treaty.[28] Nor is he alone in this assessment since virtually all his colleagues affirm this as perhaps his greatest feat.[29] By the 1960's Americans had developed a growing fear about nuclear proliferation, a fear heightened during the John F. Kennedy administration as the nation encountered several foreign policy crises. A legislator who saw that atomic energy could prove a boon to mankind if used wisely, Pastore accordingly, provided the essential leadership in forging an international legal mechanism designed to prevent a nuclear holocaust. In 1955, Republican President Dwight Eisenhower appointed him a United States delegate to the United Nations in which capacity he helped draft the United States resolution which led to the first International Atomic Energy Agency. He also led the Senate floor fight to ratify the Limited Nuclear Test Ban Treaty in 1963. As Chairman of the Joint Committee on Atomic Energy, Senator Pastore acquired a reputation as a world-wide expert in the field whose counsel was sought by both Democratic and Republican presidents.

Under his able leadership the Joint Committee on Atomic Energy addressed a wide range of complicated issues. Ever alert, he constantly demonstrated a relentless passion to get to the core of a problem rather than be deflected by peripheral matters. Thus, in one meeting which delved into the resignation of three General Electric nuclear engineers over safety concerns, Pastore repeatedly questioned the experts on the subject and the possible alternatives to insure safety, simultaneously stressing the need to keep the public informed. It was this kind of sensitivity which deeply impressed his colleagues.[30] The genuiness of his concern led Pastore in 1967 to propose a resolution calling for the enactment of a treaty to develop a sane nuclear policy. Accordingly he became the undisputed leader in the floor fight to ratify the Nuclear Non-Proliferation Treaty which won bipartisan support in 1969.

Although not a publicity seeking politician, his acknowledged brilliance, his eloquent oratory, and his genuine affability brought him to the attention of such an increasing number of Americans that in 1964 he became a national figure of such commanding stature that he was considered for nomination to the vice-presidency. Clever political professional President Johnson hinted that the Rhode Island Italian-American was indeed among several under contemplation for the national ticket that year in a move that probably was a political ploy to keep others off guard since he had apparently already settled on Senator Hubert H. Humphrey. Nevertheless, if Pastore was not to be the

Democratic vice-presidental nominee, he was destined to play a critical part in the political world of 1964. Clearly he was respected by President Johnson who praised his talents. "That Johnny Pastore, he's tremendous; sometimes I think he can do anything."[31] Johnson in fact called upon him to do two very specific things: serve as temporary chairman of the Democratic National Convention and give the keynote speech to his fellow Democrats. As temporary chairman Pastore was certain to remain faithful to the liberal Johnson agenda on civil rights as evidenced by his resolve to seat black Mississippi delegates. It was as keynote speaker, however, that Johnson showed his political acuity because he selected the man who was the party's most scintillating orator, one,

> who can wind stems with the best of them. He is a champion in rough and tumble debates, belts out speeches from the Senate floor without text or notes, all the while flailing about like a bantamweight going for the K.O.
>
> Pastore may well be the star performer in a show that might be notably lacking in drama.[32]

And indeed Pastore's keynote peroration was a forceful and inspiring demonstration worthy of a great stentorian legacy impressing the common and influential men and women alike displaying a Democratic partisanship, Pastore skillfully deflected a focus on dissension, declaring emphatically that the enemy lay outside the convention hall in the shape of Republicans.

> No matter how much the factions within the Republican Party stumble over one another trying to define the word "extremism" to the American people, the union of responsible Republicans and reactionaries is absolutely irreconciliable.
>
> As far as I am concerned, extremism is akin to fanaticism . . .
>
> What is the clear choice?
>
> Do they mean the choice to renounce the Nuclear Test Ban Treaty and begin testing again in the atmosphere and further contaminate the air?
>
> Do they mean a change in our social security system making it first voluntary then weaker and weaker until they destroy it?
>
> Do they mean the repeal of the minimum wage law?
>
> Do they mean to weaken the unions in America under the pretext of their so-called right-to-work law?
>
> Do they mean we should withdraw from the Atlantic Alliance and stand alone after spending billions and billions of dollars to make our Allies strong?
>
> Do they mean we should withdraw from the United Nations and fight over our problems rather than talk about them?

Do they mean the end of President Johnson's fight against poverty?

Do they mean to turn the clock back 32 years and erase all the social reforms we fought so hard to obtain?

What does the Republican candidate choose to have anything mean at any given moment?[33]

His vocal and emotional energy brought thousands of dozing Democrats to their feet and for one of the few times in his career a national audience saw him at his dynamic and articulate best. Johnson was especially pleased citing the speech as most influential. "My barber told me it made him proud to be an American."[34] The presentation thus helped kick off an effect winning campaign.

On occasion other colleagues called upon him to use his natural oratorical gift in their behalf. Senator Metcalf of Montana, for example, revealed that his state's Democratic Central Committee, upon learning that the Rhode Islander was vacationing in the western area, turned to him for help as a speaker in a desperate effort to fight off the challenging Republicans. "He graciously consented and that night gave a rousing speech that helped me in my campaign that year as much as any one thing."[35]

John Pastore's work in the Senate received acknowledgement not only from his colleagues, but also from the Rhode Island electorate which repeatedly supported him by huge margins including a whopping 83 percent to 17 percent for his Republican opponent in 1964. His popularity reached such proportions that to receive the Republican nomination to contest him was of the most dubious value — he was one of only eight senators to run ahead of the president that year.[36] Such a remarkable demonstration of endorsement for the Democrat illustrated how major a shift had occurred in Rhode Island during Pastore's own lifetime. Whereas Republicans had always elected their men to the Senate in Pastore's youth, it now regularly elected Democrats. Any objective assessment concluded that Pastore could have continued in that body indefinitely; this his retirement announcement in 1976 met with some surprise since it would bring to an end a truly illustrious career. The time had come, however, after forty-two years of public service including twenty-six years in the senate (only six senators had served longer) to spend more time with his wife, children and grandchildren. That he relinquished his authority and seniority prerogatives while still a capable and effective legislator, renders the decision even more meaningful.

Pastore's story is a true Horatio Alger Italian-American record. It reveals a proud sense of patriotism and devotion to his country while simultaneously ever mindful of his ethnic origins. As he so simply yet eloquently put it, "to understand me and to understand what motivates me you must understand my background and my beginnings because no matter how much we live we cannot separate ourselves from the lessons that we have learned from the very beginning of our lives.'' His beginnings were of course steeped in the milieu of Italian culture transplanted to the United States. His parents emigrated in the hey-day of mass immigration to America and his growing up impressionable years were in an authentic Little Italy reminiscent of so many others from which millions of the first and second generation sprang. It is no wonder that Italian-Americans honored him as a pioneering figure who literally opened new doors, who by his dedication and committment won universal acclaim and thereby rendered a little easier the paths of other Italian-American men and women who aspired to serve in similar capacities. Although a junior senator to Pastore by 22 years, Senator Pete Domenici of New Mexico, the second Italian-American elected to that body, readily made the connection

> My father and Senator Pastore's father both came from Italy. They came, I suspect, for very similar reasons — to enjoy the freedoms of a great nation. They came to be more than they had been. They came to create and work and to do something for their neighbors and for their Nation. They came, because they knew that America was a place where the humblest person could rise to great heights.
>
> . . . It has been men like John Pastore who have kept alive the dream that was in the minds of millions of immigrants to this land.[37]

Likewise Congressman Mario Biaggi of New York, spoke for many when he said:

> In addition to John's leadership position in the Senate, he is also a leader in the Italian-American community. He has been one of our most articulate and respected national spokesmen throughout his many years of public life. In the past year, he was instrumental in working with myself and other members of the Italo-American congressional delegation in establishing the Italian American Research Foundation which honored Senator Pastore at a dinner September 16.[38]

The foundation to which Biaggi referred came to be known as the National Italian American Foundation, and constituted the first major presence of an Italian-American umbrella organization headquarted in Washington, D.C. On September 16, 1976 thousands who were present at the foundation dinner paid tribute to the first of their nationality to achieve the august position of United

States Senator. For a people with historic Romanic roots, from which the term Senate is derived, it was an appropriate time of special pride and encouragement.

It might be regarded as understandable but excessive hyperbole when Senator Robert C. Byrd hailed the retiring Pastore as a man whose " . . . story is one that ought to be told and retold from the pulpits, from the desks of professors, and from the forums of politicians over and over again, . . . "[38] However, considering his historic career as the first of his ethnic group to attain a state governorship and a United States Senate seat, it is not an exaggeration to hold him up as a desireable model for the Italian-American community. Recognized as one of the finest orators in Senate history, his marvelous eloquence compelled colleagues to stop and listen whenever he spoke. And even on the last day he had to same electrifying effect moving his fellow senators to tears, while fighting to hold back his own tears when he issued his farewell. Many years later, still exquisitely dressed and finely groomed, he could still hold an audience enthralled. Thus this outstanding Italian-American public servant justly deserves a high place in the accounts of Italian contributions to the United States.

Footnotes

1. Stephanie Bernardo, *The Ethnic Almanac*, Garden City, 1931, p. 458. *Tributes To The Honorable John O. Pastore of Rhode Island in the United States Senate Upon The Occasion of His Retirement From The Senate*, 94th Cong., 2nd Sess. Doc. 94—277, United States Government Printing Office, Washington, D.C., 1976. p. 58.
2. *Tributes To The Honorable John O. Pastore*, p. 58.
3. *Tributes To The Honorable John O. Pastore*, p. 58.
4. See Duane Lockard, *New England State Politics*, Princeton, 1959, pp. 172—208
5. Lincoln Steffans, "Rhode Island: A State For Sale," *McClure's Magazine*, Vol. XXIV, February 1905, No. 4 pp.
6. For further evidence of Republican domination see William G. McLoughlin, Rhode Island, New York, 1978, p. 149.
7. Elmer E. Cornwell Jr., "Party Absorption of Ethnic Groups: The Case of Providence, Rhode Island," *Social Forces*, Vol. 38, No. 3. (March 1960), pp. 205—10.
8. Erwin L. Levine, *Theodore Francis Green: The Rhode Island Years, 1906—1936*, Providence, 1963, p. 113.
9. Joseph R. Paolino Jr., *An American Italian: The Life and Times of Luigi DePasquale (1892—1958)*, Paper delivered at American Italian Historical

Association Conference, November 9, 1985. DePasquale's interest in the nomination for lieutenant governor was said to be based on a desire for ethnic group recognition rather than for his own personal success. See also E.L. Levine, *Theodore Franics Green*, p. 131.

10. Samuel Lubell, "Rhode Island's Little Firecracker," *Saturday Evening Post*, November 12, 1949, pp.

11. Although possessing little real power, the lieutenant-governorship was a highly-coveted position that political professionals even were willing to change party allegiance in order to attain it. Christopher Del Sestor, for example, was a Democrat who turned Republican because of disenchantment with the Democratic Party who had chosen Pastore for that position instead of him. See Matthew J. Smith, "Rhode Island Politics 1956—64: Party Realignment", *Rhode Island History*, Vol. 35, May 1976, pp. 49—62.

12. Lubell, "Rhode Island Firecracker," *Saturday Evening Post*.

13. Lubell, "Rhode Island Firecracker," *Saturday Evening Post*.

14. Smith, "Rhode Island Politics 1956—64," *Rhode Island History*. Pastore continued to do battle with the state legislature over practices which reflected poorly on state government such as his opposition to overly generous monetary perquisites. See Duane Lockard, *New England State Politics*, Princeton, 1959, p. 220.

15. John Pastore Telephone *Interview*, September 12, 1986.

16. The New York *Times*, March 9, 1950.

17. The New York *Times*, January 29, 1949.

18. The New York *Times*, March 15, 1950.

19. Cornwell, "Party Absorption of Ethnic Groups," *Social Forces*.

20. Lockard, *New England State Politics*, p. 200.

21. For other issues in which pastore played a significant part see, *Congressional Record*, 88th Cong., 2nd Sess., pp. 10134—5, 89th Cong. 1st Sess., pp. 24562—3.

22. This topic is discussed in Eric Goldman, *The Tragedy of Lyndon Johnson*, New York, 1969, pp. 67—70.

23. The New York *Times*, April 8, 1964. See *Congressional Record*, 88th Cong., 2nd Sess., p. 13700 for further explication of the implications of the measure.

24. *America*, Vol. 20, April 12, 1969, p. 440.

25. Tribute To The Honorable John O. Pastore, p. 22.

26. Herbert Asher, *Presidential Elections and American Politics*, Homewood, Illinois, 1980, p. 280.

27. *Tributes To The Honorable John O. Pastore*, p. 39.

28. Pastore *Interview*,

29. *Tributes To The Honorable John O. Pastore*, passim.

30. *Tributes To The Honorable John O. Pastore*, p. 45.
31. Harold Faber, edit., *The Road To The White House*, New York Times, New York, 1965, p. 114. *Time*, August 7, 1964, p. 19. Pastore enjoyed such high stature that he figured prominently in the selection of the Democratic Senate leadership becoming a formidable contender for Senate Whip in 1965. See Lady Bird Johnson, *A White House Diary*, 1970, p. 215.
32. *Time*, August 7, 1964. Faber, *The Road To The White House*, p. 108.
33. *Congressional Record*, 88th Cong. 2nd Sess., pp. 21751—2.
34. Goldman, *The Tragedy of Lyndon Johnson*, p. 210.
35. Tributes To The Honorable John O. Pastore, p. 56.
36. Paul Tillet et. al., *The National Election of 1964*, 1966, p. 203. Michael Barone, Grant Ujifusa and Douglas Matthews, *The Almanac of American Politics 1979*, New York, 1975, p. 766.
37. *Tributes To The Honorable John O. Pastore*, p. 11.
38. *Tributes To The Honorable John O. Pastore*, p. 16.

Chapter **2**

AN AMERICAN ITALIAN: THE LIFE AND TIMES OF LUIGI DE PASQUALE (1892—1958)

Joseph R. Paolino, Jr.
Mayor, City of Providence

Introduction

The story of the Italians in America is one of the great epics of our time. Forced by a thoroughly dismal life in Italy to seek better times elsewhere, millions of *contadini* left Italy to seek their fortunes. Their destinations: the new worlds of North and South America.

The rural folk who ended up in the great cities of the United States certainly began lives as strange as any they could have imagined. They left a semi-feudal world of rigidly defined social roles for the freewheeling society of America. Certainty was swapped for uncertainty; rural despair for urban hope.

When a large topic like mass migration of a people from one continent to another is studied, it is often helpful to study some of the individual men and women who were part of that movement. The meanings of the great events covered can be given a vividness which the examination of tables of statistics can never convey.

One life which is work studying in the context of the Italian-American experience in Rhode Island is that of Luigi DePasquale (1892—1958), an eminent lawyer, politician, and judge.

Luigi DePasquale was one of the very first of the second generation Italian-American born in the country. The child of immigrants, he was a product of the American culture he was raised in; yet he was also influenced by and passionately interested in his Italian heritage.

The story of Luigi's rise to prominence is one that was to be repeated hundreds of thousands of times. During his lifetime, Italians went through the transformation from put-upon (and often despised) immigrants to citizens who were productive and respected in the community. They went from pawns in other people's political games to positions of leadership and honor.

Luigi DePasquale was a leader of his people and a leader in the larger community. His successes paved the way for later generations of Italo-

Americans. His was the prototypical Italian-American success story.

This paper will briefly describe his life in the context of his times and, by doing so, give life to the story of millions of other Italian-Americans as they strove first for acceptance and later for leadership and prominence in the American community they wholeheartedly joined.

Emigration of the Italians

The last third of the nineteenth century was a time of great dislocation in Italy. Southern Italy, especially, suffered as the consolidation of the Kingdom of Italy and the coming of industrialization upset ancient patterns of life.

In Southern Italy, there were simply too many people attempting to live off too little land. More and more of the *contadini* found it difficult to make a living beyond the subsistence level. Every member of the family worked long hours just to have enough to eat.

The population of Southern Italy grew by more than 25 percent in an economy that could not keep up. The *contadini* were faced with a stark choice: stay and live a life of grinding rural poverty, or leave for the opportunities and uncertainties of the Americas.

Millions chose to emigrate. Many thousands of *contadini* came to Providence, Rhode Island. Two of them were the parents of Luigi DePasquale.

Luigi's Roots and Youth

Italian emigration to the United States, virtually unknown before 1880, began in earnest during that ninth decade of the Nineteenth Century. Luigi DePasquale's mother and father, from the provinces of Benevento and Foggia, respectively, were part of an early trickle which later became a flood.

Luigi's family became established quite nicely. Antonio Luigi went into business for himself, while Maria stayed home and raised the family.

In Milford, young Luigi received the first fruits of life in America: a public education. He was a good student who did not have to leave school to help support the family. He graduated from Milford High School in 1909.

Luigi entered the law school at Boston University in the fall of 1909 (this was a common practice then.) Once again, he was a successful student. After four years of study, Luigi DePasquale received his law degree; shortly thereafter, he passed the bar exam on his first try. He was a lawyer, a professional man, and the family celebrity.

Young Luigi now had to set up his law practice. He did legal work in Milford, including successfully defending a man accused of murder; but city lights beckoned. The particular city in question was Providence where he was born and where he had family.

By 1914, Luigi DePasquale was in Providence living in his rented rooms in Federal Hill and practicing law in partnership with Anthony Pettine.

Young Luigi's Providence

In 1914, Providence was a thriving industrial city. The boosterism of its business community was second to none as businessmen claimed for the state's capital city the titles of "Gateway to Southern New England" or the "Premier City of Southern New England." Though Providence was at the beginning of a long economic decline, no one would have disputed that the businessmen's pride was justified in the years before World War I.

By 1914, the Italian community of Providence was large and well established. Federal Hill then, as now, was the largest and best known Italian neighborhood. There were also significant Italian colonies in the North End and Silver Lake.

These Italians were mostly laborers, factory operatives, or homemakers. In a typical pattern, the *contadini* clustered in urban recreations of their old villages. Among the first generation, there was very little sense of an Italian, as opposed to a village identity.

The Italian-Americans of Providence, if they had any political affiliation at all, were identified with the Republican Party, then the very dominant party in the city and the state. In 1914, Federal Hill sent Republicans to both the city council (then bicameral) and the State House of Representatives.

It wasn't long before Luigi DePasquale changed all that.

Luigi Chooses a Party

It isn't unusual for a young lawyer to break into politics. The two professions have been intertwined since ancient times. It probably came as no surprise when the twenty-four year old lawyer was nominated for Federal Hill's seat in the General Assembly in 1916.

What may have caused some eyebrows to rise was his choice of political party: the Democrats. In a Republican ward in a Republican state, it might have seemed to some a strange way to launch a political career.

Luigi, a young man of idealism and principle, probably found the Democratic Party a more hospitable home. The Democrats, led by President Woodrow Wilson, were at the beginning of their historic swing from a southern based party advocating state's rights and Jeffersonian ideals (and, therefore, implicitly anti-urban) exemplified by the long leadership of that great prairie populist, William Jennings Bryan, to a progressive party with a more urban orientation which could be an instrument for social change.

With the Republicans divided into progressive and conservative wings which engaged in a fierce fight for the soul of the party, the left wing of the GOP might have held some appeal for Luigi.

In Rhode Island, however, the progressive wing had never been much in evidence. The state was in the grip of a Republican machine which was as backward and venal as any in the country. The state's longtime Republican boss, General Charles Brayton, had only recently died. His very effective machine still lived.

Thus, Luigi's choice was probably inevitable. For a young man on the make, there was probably another factor which made the Democracy appealing: as the perennial minority party, it offered a much quicker trip up the ladder than the GOP.

Luigi Gets Ahead

Luigi campaigned energetically and with great charm. There was some surprise when he won the election by nine votes. In January 1917, he took his seat in the House. He served there for four eventful years, becoming a leader of the State Democratic Party in the process.

It didn't take Luigi long to fling himself into the arena. He took progressive stands on eliminating the property requirement, a device which limited voting for city and town councils to property owners. Not incidentally, this kept the Republicans in control, even when there was a nominally Democratic administration.

Representative DePasquale advocated reform in the regulation of public utilities, a Workmen's Compensation Law, and public ownership of the streetcar system. While he took a special interest in the problems of Italian-Americans, he was an advocate of the rights of all oppressed minorities. DePasquale was, in particular, an advocate for the rights of black Americans. At a legislative hearing, Representative DePasquale proclaimed:

> To despise a man regardless of his intellect and his character, simply because his face is black, is a crime against civilization . . .

> Race prejudice and race hostility present a serious problem, and a solution cannot be had by depriving citizens of their privileges and of their rights as guaranteed under the Constitution.

This was an unusual position for an Italian-American Democrat to take during the late teens and early twenties. It was not especially popular, and there was no political advantage in it for Luigi at all. That did not deter him from doing the right thing.

Ironically, it took Representative DePasquale some time to become reconciled to votes for women. When he did, however, it was forcefully and with the hope that the newly enfranchised women would be a force for good in the politics of Rhode Island.

Luigi DePasquale was on, as we would say today, the "Fast Track." At the start of his second term in the House, he was elected deputy floor leader of the Democrats, a position which brought him a measure of fame. In the midst of his busy poltical routine and law practice, he still found time to serve on a committee which welcomed the Italian war hero, General Diaz, to Providence as well as to pursue his avid interests in signing, motoring, and an assortment of social clubs. In the early 20's, Luigi also found time to marry Marie Michard.

Luigi's diligence brought spectacular dividends. In 1920, he was named a delegate to the Democratic National Convention, a singular honor for a twenty-eight year old lawyer who had barely shed his novice's status.

To top it off, DePasquale was nominated later that year for Congress in the second district. Luigi campaigned vigorously, keeping to a busy schedule of speeches at a series of party rallies. He made such a mark during his campaign, and his opponent, an incumbent, was so unpopular, that the latter was forbidden by his party leadership to appear in public so as to keep the unfortunate contrast with Luigi DePasquale to a bare minimum.

Unfortunately for Luigi, he had the misfortune to be running as a Democrat in a Republican state in what was perhaps the worst year for the Democratic party in the twentieth century. From the top of the ticket to the very bottom, the Democrats were soundly beaten in Rhode Island. Luigi DePasquale was one of the victims of his electoral disaster, losing to his opponent by a large margin.

The 1920's

The twenties were not good years for the Democrats in Rhode Island. Out of office nationally and equally powerless at the state level, these were years which offered little prospect of satisfaction to an ambitious young politician. Luigi, however, did not shirk his duty to this party. No sunshine patriot, he accepted election after the 1920 election as Treasurer of the Democratic State Committee.

In politics, like baseball, there is always a next year. The Democrats set about preparing for the election of 1922. In Rhode Island, the Republicans, arrogant after their unprecedented huge victory of 1920, were ripe for a fall. This, and the economic recession of the early twenties were enough to push the Democrats to victory in the state election of 1922. Luigi was very active in the campaign. A Democratic governor (William S. Flynn), lieutenant governor, and attorney general were elected. It was the first such victory since well before World War I. The new attorney general appointed Luigi DePasquale one of his assistants. Since the Rhode Island attorney general is the prosecutor for the entire state, Luigi became, in effect, an assistant district attorney.

The 20's were a contentious time in the state. The Republican old guard was, though they didn't know it, breathing their last as they fought a determined rear guard action against the Democrats who were determined to translate their electoral majority into actual control.

The ultimate source of Republican control was their perpetual lock on the State Senate. The Democrats could elect a governer here or there and occasionally win control of the House, but they never could gain a majority in the Senate where each municipality had exactly one vote. Hence, Little Compton was the equal of Providence; tiny Richmond cancelled out the City of Pawtucket.

This was a sore point with the Democrats. They were determined to achieve a more fair apportionment of the Senate. To achieve that end, they staged what amounted to a two-year filibuster in the Senate, holding up all other business as they attempted to force the Republican majority to place the measures they wanted on the ballot.

The GOP would have none of it. The situation became first tense and then ugly as the filibuster wore on. At the point of highest tension, the situation broke as a thug commissioned by the Republican State Chairman tossed a bromine gas bomb into the Senate Chamber (June 19, 1924.) The session broke up, and the GOP Senators used the opportunity to flee the state. They spent the rest of 1924 in exile in a hotel in Rutland, Massachusetts.

While this story had its farcical elements, it did not conceal the reality of a partisan struggle which was as bitter as any in the country. Confident that they had flushed out their opponents into betraying their fundamental bias against the working people, the Democrats prepared to wage their campaign on the issues they had dramatized in such an unforgettable way.

For whatever reason, the public, basking in on the new prosperity of the Coolidge years, did not seem too interested. The Democrats were rejected at the polls, leaving them in precisely the same situation they were in after the rout of 1920.

Rise to Power I

Amidst the wreckage, Luigi DePasquale once again stepped forward. He was made chairman of the Democratic State Committee. This was a momentous decision because, under the new chairman's stewardship, the Democrats embarked upon the course which would eventually lead them (and Luigi himself) to real power in the state.

The party, under his leadership, contested the 1926 election. With no big issues and the good times in full swing, the Democrats predictably lost.

1928 was different. Chairman DePasquale, as well as the rest of the Democratic Party, found the presidential candidacy of New York Governor Alfred E. Smith powerfully appealing.

In 1928, Al Smith was the premier Democrat in the country. In the governorship for all but two years since 1919, Smith had contested the presidential nomination at the exceptionally nasty Democratic Convention of 1924. Though he had been forced to withdraw his candidacy after one hundred ballots, he had not withdrawn his hopes.

Governor Smith was an urban version of William Jenning Bryan, the "Great Commoner." A product of the streets of the lower East Side of New York (he and the Brooklyn Bridge grew up together), he was a personable young man who drifted into the lower ranks of Tammany Hall.

Tammany realized it had a promising prospect on its hands. It wasn't too long before Al was nominated and elected to serve in the State Assembly at Albany. There, Smith established a record which impressed both Democrats and Republicans alike. He became so prominent that, in fifteen years, he went from freshman assemblyman to Governor of the State of New York. It was a remarkable rise.

Smith was a man who championed and praised the immigrants who were the newest Americans. Where most American politicians, particularly in the Republican party, praised the immigrants in an empty, ritualistic way, Al Smith praised them and sounded as if he meant it.

Smith was an urban Catholic and proud of it. He identified with the working man and woman and championed their cause. Rhode Island, with its disunited urban Catholic majority, found him attractive. Under the leadership of Luigi DePasquale, the Rhode Island Democrats united behind the New York governor's candidacy. At an enthusiastic state convention opened by Luigi DePasquale, the party instructed its delegates to the National Convention to support Al Smith. Luigi was named one of those delegates.

Foundation For The New Deal

Though DePasquale and the rest of the Democrats couldn't know it, by this action they were laying the foundation for the future New Deal coalition and their own power.

Prior to 1928, the ethnic groups were kept divided by combination of clever Republican strategy and old fashioned heavy-handed intimidation. The cleverness came in when the Republicans would nomiate safely conservative ethnics for office. They were particularly successful with the candidacies of Aram Pothier, a French Canadian American who achieved prominence as a businessman and who was elected governor in the years befor the war.

The GOP, in a bind, called him out of retirement to run for governor in 1924. He was as popular with the French Canadian voters as ever and won. He was re-elected the following year.

Through this method, the Republican kept the Irish, Italians, and French Canadians from uniting. The lack of unity on the art of these different groups kept the Democrats out of power.

The intimidation was equally effective. Rhode Island was one of the most industrialized states in the nation. The industrialists were solidly Republican and not at all shy about offering some friendly guidance about how to vote. It was expected that casting a Republican vote was a condition of employment at many mills and factories. It is not surprising that most workers, who needed their jobs more than they needed a Democratic president or governor, complied.

For years, these tactics made the GOP virtually unbeatable.

Al Smith's candidacy upset the applecart. He was as attractive to the average ethnic Catholic Rhode Islander as he was to the Democratic leadership. DePasquale and the other party leaders were certainly right when they sensed the potential which the Smith nomination represented.

The proof was in the votes. While 1928 was to prove to be a dismal year for Al Smith, it was the turning point for the Rhode Island Democrats. Al Smith carried the state by a narrow margin, the first time the Democrats had accomplished that feat in a two-way race since before the Civil War. The state ticket lost by a small percentage.

This made Rhode Island part of a national trend. The Republicans were slowly losing their grip on the nation's urban centers. In 1920 and 1924, the GOP carried the twelve largest cities in the United States by a combined total of over one million votes. In 1928, they lost the same combination of cities by a little over ten thousand votes.

Luigi DePasquale retired as State Chairman after the 1928 election. As he travelled up to the State House on January 2, 1929 to cast one of the State's five electoral votes for Governor Smith (DePasquale had been nominated as presidential elector), he could take some satisfaction in the Democratic Party's breakthrough in the election. Still, the party could not quite put together enough votes to win actual power in the state.

It took a national disaster — the Great Depression — to finally put the Democrats over the top.

Rise To Power II

The Depression finished the work that Al Smith began. Misery was so widespread that voters flocked into the Democratic column.

In 1932, the Democrats of Rhode Island presented a powerful ticket to the voters of Rhode Island. Franklin D. Roosevelt was at the top, pledging a "New Deal" for the American people. For governor, the Democrats nominated Theodore Francis Green, a Yankee Democrat who had toiled in the political vineyeards much longer than Luigi DePasquale (Green had first run for governor in 1912.)

Luigi had not vanished from the scene. He spent 1932 in a very intense fight against a rival political faction on Federal Hill which was, in turn, part of a nasty intra-party fight featuring the Democratic mayor of Providence against the Democratic city chairman.

Luigi, siding with the mayor who had a reputation for good government, he headed a slate of candidates which was beaten in a party caucus conducted in a blatantly fraudulent manner. Indignant, Luigi cried fraud and challenged the results. He pressed his case all the way to the State Supreme court which agreed with him and threw out the results. Unfortunately, his slate, running under an independent label, still lost the election. The mayor, however, was renominated and re-elected by a record majority.

Green, meanwhile, led the Democrats to their greatest victory in living memory. The Party swept all five general offices as well as all the Congressional seats. They won a majority in the State House of Representatives. The Senate remained stacked for the Republicans. This gave the GOP a veto over the Democratic program which they weren't shy about using. This meant that Green and the Democrats were still not really in control.

In 1934, the Democrats presented themselves to the electorate. With Green once again on top of the ticket, the Democrats easily won. They picked up seats in the Assembly and actually came within two votes of winning control of the Senate.

One of the new Senators was Luigi DePasquale. By this time, the apportionment of the Senate had changed slightly. Instead of one seat, Providence had four. Given his standing in the community and with the Italo-Americans, DePasquale was nominated by his party and easily elected.

The new Assembly took office on January 1, 1935. This time, they were not to be denied. In the course of that day, the Democrats, acting with unity and discipline, seized control of the Senate by refusing to seat two Republicans Senators and replacing them with the two Democrats who had been declared defeated.

The new Democratic General Assembly proceeded to reorganize state government, passing an omnibus bill which gave effective control of the government to Green and the Democrats. Hundreds of Republican office holders were dismissed in the process.

Just to make sure the whole business stood up, the Democrats fired the entire Supreme Court and elected a new panel which was expected to uphold the legality of what the Democrats had done. The Republicans would spend most of the next fifty years in the wilderness.

Senator Luigi DePasquale, after nearly twenty years as a leader of the perpetual minority, was suddenly part of the governing elite. He didn't have to wait for long to receive his reward for his labors and his endurance.

Judge DePasquale

Toward the end of the 1935 session, Senator DePasquale was named a justice of the Sixth District Court. He was the first Democrat ever named to this court. On June 22, 1935, the new judge presided for the first time. It was the start of a judicial career which spanned twenty-three years and thousands of cases.

Luigi DePasquale was a forceful, distinctive personality as a politician. He was no less so as a judge. He had a profound respect for the law and expected all who came before him to share that respect. He was known to send home defendants who he considered improperly dressed with instructions to dress up. He was stern with lawbreakers when he thought the circumstances demanded it. On one occasion, his own son-in-law was brought before him for a traffic violation. The Judge thought the offense was severe enough to warrant a twenty dollar fine. He was also very hard on people who cheated the state unemployment and Worker's Compensation funds, which he thought was plain theft against the honest working people and businessmen of the state.

The Judge, nonetheless, remained a compassionate and humane man. When he thought the circumstances warranted it, he would show mercy. Sometimes, when forced to impose a fine which the defendant could not pay, Judge DePasquale would, through a bailiff, loan the unfortunate man or woman the cash to pay up.

When Luigi DePasquale took his oath as a judge, he did not, however, end his advocacy and support for the causes he believed in. The Judge never stopped promoting the goal of racial and ethnic harmony. He continued to speak out against racism and anti-semitism. In a light vein, St. Patrick's Day was as big an event in his court as it was in the Irish wards. He would halt business to pass out green carnations and extolled the role of the Irish in making America. The Judge liked to say that while Columbus discovered America, "Casey steered the boat."

For ten years, Judge DePasquale presided over Juvenile Court where he handled thousands of cases. He took an active interest in the welfare of these young offenders. For over thirty years, he held an annual dinner, the proceeds of which benefited disadvantaged youth.

He had his own very decided opinions on keeping youth on the straight and narrow path. He was a strong believer in religious training as a means of instilling moral values in children. He once estimated that 75 percent of the people who came before his court had not had this education. The cause and effect seemed obvious to him. Judge DePasquale also believed that a good way to keep teenagers under control was to restrict their mobility. He would advocate raising the driving age above the age of sixteen.

Judge DePasquale was a teetotaler who was nonetheless a "wet" during prohibition. Though he saw nothing wrong with the use of alcohol in moderation, he was nevertheless deeply affected by the misery caused by alcoholism. He saw it just about every day in the endless parade of alcoholics that passed through his courtroom.

The Judge had an enlightened attitude towards the disease of alcoholism at a time when many were still inclined to dismiss the alcoholic as morally deficient. He was a supporter of a greater role for the state in dealing with the disease and was instrumental in getting the state to establish a division of alcoholism.

On April 30, 1958, Judge Luigi DePasquale suffered a heart attack while presiding over his court. He died on May 3rd. He was much beloved and universally respected, both for personal qualities and his distinguished career. When his funeral mass was held, the church was absolutely packed with everyone from the highest dignitaries to the most humble citizens of Federal Hill.

An American Italian

Luigi DePasquale felt a strong identification with his Italian nationality. This made him a fairly typical second generation Italo-American. As a rule, second generation immigrants felt little, if any, of the old ties to the village or province from which their parents hailed and still felt attached to.

This village orientation was one factor which retarded the progress of Italians for some time. Where groups like the Irish, English, French, Germans, Jews, etc. maintained a national identity which transcended regional differences once they got off the boat, the Italians felt no such thing.

This meant that the immigrants were not a cohesive block. Established politicians found that old country rivalries were transplanted to the States. In the ensuing atmosphere of suspicion and distrust, it was easy to keep the Italians disunited and out of positions of influence. One faction was always ready to "knife" another at an election. This sort of behavior violated a basic rule of American politics: for an ethnic group to achieve power, it must first achieve unity.

Eventually, that unity was achieved. The original immigrants gradually died, taking their ancient grudges and hatreds to the grave. The ones who remained started to see how futile these petty rivalries were. The younger generation, fairly oblivious to the old disputes, was quick to agree.

After World War I, the Sons of Italy was formed (Luigi DePasquale was a member) with the view of forging that sense of an Italian community which had eluded their fathers in the old country. In Rhode Island, Luigi DePasquale was one of the leaders who helped make the Italian community.

Luigi was proud of his Italian heritage and took an active interest in Italian affairs. He was active in organizing relief efforts for Italian victims of World War II. His work eventually won him a decoration by the Italian government. Yet, he was an American first. He believed in America because he saw what it did for him, his family, and so many other refugees from dozens of old countries. He was critical of the United States only when it denied its promised opportunities to its own citizens through discrimination or tried to bar potential immigrants, such as Italians, through restrictive immigration laws.

Luigi DePasquale not only wanted everyone to have the benefits of what America offered, he was also insistent that everyone accept its responsibilities. He thought that it was necessary for all newcomers to learn English as soon as possible. He demanded that everyone respect the laws and customs of the country that made so much possible. In short, he wanted full membership in the American community for all its citizens.

Luigi DePasquale was an American Italian. While he took pleasure in the great ethnic stew that was, and is, Rhode Island, he did not think those differences should divide people or alienate them. In his political career, he sought justice for all; in his courtroom, he tried to mete it out. To a great extent, he succeeded.

Conclusion

Luigi DePasquale was the prototypical Italian-American success story. As one of the first of the second generation Italo-Americans, he was a pace setter as a lawyer and political leader. By his example, he showed the way to his compatriots.

Yet, he was more than an example worth emulating. If he were merely another successful man, his story would not command our attention.

Luigi DePasquale was more than an ethnic leader. He transcended ethnic lines to become a leader of the whole community. This is his true significance to us today.

In part due to his efforts, the Italian-Americans found common purpose, first with each other and later with other ethnic groups. The presidential candidacy of Governor Al Smith, which Luigi enthusiastically supported as chairman of the Democratic Party, was the vehicle through which this unity was first realized.

Once together under the banner of the Democratic Party which had become the party of dynamic social change, it was only a matter of time before this coalition of diversity achieved true power in the state. Once they achieved that power, the individuals involved could progress from token positions in an established rural-based Yankee power structure to leading positions in a new regime which they themselves created.

This is the promise of America: the government goes to the majority, but minority rights are to be respected. In Rhode Island, the promise was kept. The Democrats won control of state government in the thirties. Luigi DePasquale, one of the people who made this possible, saw his service to the community acknowledged and rewarded by his appointment to the bench where he served with honor and distinction.

This, then, is what the life of Luigi DePasquale teaches us: while we all are entitled to, and should, take pride in our respective ethnic heritage, that pride should not become a wall which separates one part of the greater community from another.

When that road is taken, the result is distrust, disunity, and despair. Luigi DePasquale understood this; that is why he emphasized the necessity of being an American first. He knew that only by adopting American values and by burying the feuds and rivalries of the old country (whichever country that was) could the new Americans find success and fulfillment in their new country.

This is the lesson of the life of Luigi DePasquale. It is a lesson which is important today as the newest wave of Americans reach our shores from Latin America and Asia. They must be allowed to realize their aspirations to membership in the American community just as, two generations ago, the Italian-Americans demanded their rightful place.

Luigi would approve. We best honor his memory and his ideals by upholding our newest citizens' rights to achieve what we have achieved.

Chapter   **3**   **DOING RESEARCH IN AN
ITALIAN VILLAGE**
Michael A. LaSorte
State University of New York at Brockport

Needing additional data for a study on turn-of-the-century emigration, I decided in September of 1984 to go to a southern Italian village to look at the communal archives and to do some unstructured interviewing and observation. Because this was my first attempt at field research in Italy, I thought it wise to review some of the published Italian village studies done by American scholars in order to anticipate the problems that I would encounter. I found little useful information. In some instances the investigators discussed briefly the problems of the cooperation of villagers and access to archives or what alternatives were taken when the desired information was not available. But little systematic attention was given to the consequences of these problems on the data received or the interpretation of the data. Rather than recognize that questions such as access and cooperation have significant consequences for any study, they were often treated as minor irritants peripheral to the research project. Also insufficient consideration was given to the problem of language or cultural differences; and even less to methodology, particularly in regard to the dilemmas of reliability and validity. I had to conclude that there has been little interest in the accumulation of detailed information on the day-by-day experience of research. This in spite of the fact that the American scholar conducting research in Italy confronts a research environment in variance in significant respects with that found in this country.

This paper attempts to address some of these issues through an examination of my own experience during a three-week period spent in Alberone (a fictitious name), a southern Italian village of 10,000 inhabitants situated several miles inland from the seaport city of Taranto. I make no claims that my experiences or circumstances were typical; on the contrary, it became obvious to me that the person doing the research, and where it is done, are crucial variables in every step of the research process.

I selected Alberone for the same reason that others selected their villages — convenience. Filippo Sabetti[1] did his study in Camporano, Sicily, as a result of a fortuitious encounter with the village mayor while in Palermo and a caution from colleagues to steer clear of certain villages where there was perceived danger. Rudolph Bell[2] made his choices based on the advice of an in-law and a student of his whose uncle was the mayor of a village. Donna Gabaccia[3] chose to study Sambuca because the archives were accessible and, for Sicily, well organized. Robert Evans[4] looked for a congenial village with an available house, and Charlotte Chapman[5] selected hers because a native she befriended in Chicago had friends there. In my case I know more about Alberone than any other place in Italy. I had visited the village previously three times over the past twenty years, knew its history and knew that I would be given a cordial reception on my arrival and a place to stay rent free. Most importantly, an elderly aunt of mine lived there, a woman with a keen interest in village life who was active in village affairs and who counted among her close friends many of the village *notabili*. I felt that she would be an ideal intermediary between myself and the village institutions and its inhabitants.

Although one can appreciate the necessity of selecting a village for reasons of access, anticipated cooperation or comfort, it is important to keep in mind that these criteria make the selection process purposive, not random, thereby severely limiting the scope of the data. The study's conclusions cannot be said to hold for all villages or most villages. In fact the limits of any generalizations deriving from such study results are not a known factor because those villages not considered for selection for reasons of hostile natives or sparse documents or whatever find little or not representation in the current literature on Italian villages.

On the morning of the 22nd I arrived in Alberone and talked with my aunt, describing what I wanted. At first she refused to believe that material on migration existed in the municipal archives. I was prepared for that one. Pietro Lippolis, an Alberone native, in a 1961 publication, had culled emigration data from the municipal registers, for 1900 to 1910, showing that 2695 townsfolk had been granted passports for travel abroad.[6] (And I knew that this material existed in other communes. William Douglass[7] made use of a series of books, *Libri dei Passaporti*, that he discovered in the archives of a sourthern Italian hilltown.) Once convinced, my aunt went to work on her sources. On the morning of the 24th I was introduced to a schoolteacher, whose hobby was local history and who knew the assessor. He also doubted that the emigration books existed. Once he was convinced, he promised to conduct me the next morning to the municipality. But that was after he suggested that he would mail copies of the emigration sheets to me after I returned home. It seemed an easy solution but I felt an incorrect one. I told him that I preferred working through the books myself. My thoughts at that moment were that he was putting me off in order to avoid doing something of no value to him. That evening the schoolteacher returned to tell me that he suspected the material was not processed or catalogued and remained in dustry boxes someplace. My response to him that I did not mind dust and that I was accustomed, if not expecting, to work with unorganized material had no effect. *Non preoccuparti*, don't worry, he said. I am still looking into the matter. His promise of that morning that he would escort me to the municipality was forgotten.

On the morning of the 25th, Tuesday, the schoolteacher reported that all of the municipal records had been burned in a fire in 1930. I found that curious since I had assumed that Pietro Lippolis had gathered his emigration data from the Alberone archives in the 1950s, well after the alleged fire. However, I was not certain, and the story about a first was plausible. Documents are fragile and are subject to destruction from many causes. In 1798 Alberone was sacked and the records were scattered, making it impossible for scholars to say much about the village before that date. Robert Evans had difficulty gathering historical data in a Venetian village because the local archives had been burned in a 1943 fire. But despite the possibility of a fire, I remained skeptical and said as much to my aunt. Her reaction supported what I was hesitant to say. *Chiacchiere!* Lies! she said. She did not recall a fire in 1930. But more to the point, she confided to me, you have to understand these bureaucrats. The bureaucracy soaks up money like a blotter soaks up ink, giving nothing in return. Those placed have their own ways of doing things and are geniuses at doing nothing. We are dealing here with *La Mafia Bianco*, she continued, a subculture more insidious than the Sicilian *La Mafia Rossa*. *La Mafia Rossa* only kills, she told me, while *La Mafia Bianca* seeks to confuse and to procrastinate with the aim of arrogating authority unto itself. Her statement reminded me of the observation of Luigi Barzini, who wrote that "in all of Italy there is a lower-case mafia."[8] The code of this mafia writ small cannot be violated without disastrous effects, for it is a guide on how to get things done.

As an outsider I really could not evaluate the validity of this notion. But if true I would have to conclude that in the end I would only be able to get from them what they chose to give to me. As the days progressed I began to believe that this included everyone in the village. What I was seeing and hearing were only the tip of the village iceberg and what lay beneath I could only imagine. Many of those with whom I spoke, not surprisingly, expressed cynicism about the workings of the Italian bureaucracy, even at the village level where officials are not that far removed from those they serve. Many were quick to say that civil servants were lazy, good-for-nothing types who take their jobs because they were incapable, unlike themselves, of productive labor. I was introduced to the village librarian as a case in point.[9] When I talked to the school superintendent he remained neutral on the question of a conspiracy to keep me away from the records; his attention was diverted at that moment to the fighting of a vicious headcold. The archpriest told me that he had used the current emigration books to develop a mailing list for the

Alberonesi working abroad and did not think that any older books existed.

The 26th and the 27th passed without word from the schoolteacher. But I kept stirring the pot and by Friday, the 29th, my aunt became agitated and decided to get to the bottom of the issue. By now it had become for her a matter of family honor and community pride. Her American nephew was not going to be treated in this high-handed manner. She leaned on the schoolteacher with the result that I saw him that afternoon. He had talked with the clerk at the Assessor's Office and had been told that I could see the immigration and emigration books for 1934 to the present. Was I interested? I said yes, for by this time I wanted to follow this drama through to its ultimate conclusion. The schoolteacher made an appointment with the clerk for the next morning at 10:30. At 10:15, while I was preparing to leave, the schoolteacher appeared at the door to notify me that the clerk wanted an opportunity to organize the files so that my search would be untroubled. The appointment was set back to Monday morning, October 1. I could sense that this appointment would not be broken, and it wasn't.

I arrived at the building and met the clerk, who was very correct in his behavior and appeared only too anxious to accommodate me. The phrase *una bella figure* came to mind: He struck me as being very concerned that I not think him either a cafone or incompetent. Two sets of large books were placed on the desk before me. The first, from 1934 to the current date, was a chronological listing of Alberonesi who had left the village; the second, covering the same time period, listed those who had moved into the village. The information for each person included date, name, destination or origin, and sex. The books were in excellent condition, with no evidence that they had needed any organizing or dusting off. I worked in the clerk's office for one week, during which time I asked a number of discrete questions about other material. I did not press on any of my questions for I was there as a guest nor did I overstay my welcome. At one point the clerk showed me a large ledger of certificates of births from 1885. And other similar ledgers existed. I did not probe as to why these had survived the alleged fire of 1930.

With time the clerk's rather cool and correct attitude softened. Perhaps he realized that I was not a bad fellow after all and not a threat to him. When I left he was profusely apologetic that I could not get what I wanted. They used oil lamps in those days, he told me. The village had electricity, of course, but is was during Fascism and everyone was forced to go back to using lamps (because the regime has so improverished the *Mezzogiorno*). Thus the lamps caused the fire with Mussolini a direct contributor. The question continues to linger in my mind: Did that fire happen and were the records destroyed? I am sure that I will never know, although I take comfort from John Briggs, who sought similar information in a variety of locales, and concluded: "Communal archives, unfortunately, are unprepared to receive scholars, and local officials often try to dissuade them from doing research in their records.

Anyone contemplating work in these collections must be ready to face rebuffs and, if admitted, to sift through piles of unorganized and unindexed material. These archives are spotty, having been decimated by neglect, natural disasters, wars, and Red Cross scrap-paper drives. yet the rewards can be very great for these who persist.''[10]

The operative word is ''persistence'', but even that will not solve the basic problem of comprehension. I know it is a cliche to say that when the Italian American goes to Italy he is shocked to find that he is not Italian. But it happened to me this time in a much more profound sense than before because a I went deeper into the village structure and culture I had increasing difficulty in understanding what was going on around me. Even with my knowledge of the village idiom (which I, and others, have found can be a valuable asset) I knew that much was happening that I could not clearly comprehend. Or I should say, because I had a degree of familiarity from my background and previous visits that someone else might not have, I was perceiving more and understanding less.

Other researchers have talked about the problems of getting access to data, soliciting cooperation, and combatting suspicion and bureaucratic inertia. These are real problems but I think that they are acute problems and much more solvable than the chronic dilemma of the comprehension of a foreign culture. As a foreigner you never know whether you got it right or not and when to cease gathering information.

When Burton Clark decided to study the Italian academic structure he discovered quickly that the bureaucracy consisted of several levels, and his attempts to go beyond the surface reality were met with much frustration. ''The early days in the field confirmed that anyone attempting to penetrate the Italian university system would face a curious setting. At first glance, much was on the surface, laid bare in formal rule. On second glance, practice was heavily shielded in unspoken and confidential ways. And where was power to be observed? Knowledgeable professors sent the researcher to the central agencies in Rome to walk the bleak corridors and knock on the doors of officials. There, equally knowledgeable Italians turned the visitor around and pointed the way back to the offices of the professors. The crossroads of decision were confusing, so shaded that most participants were unsure from day to day what was going on and where to go to find out. Thus there seemed some point to the stereotype of the system as veritable chaos.''[11]

The Italian bureaucracy is a reflection of the Italian culture in general. And the Italian culture keeps its secrets well. Gavin Maxwell, an Englishman who spent several years in Sicily, eventually came to realize that what he had grasped about Sicilians was inconclusive and subject to an array of interpretations. As he writes in the prologue of his book, *The Ten Pains of Death*, ''. . . at the end of my third year I was still, to most of my acquaintances, a stranger, to be trusted with only a little of the truth either about themselves or anyone else.''[12] (Maxwell) My relationship with my aunt has been of this nature. I was "blood" but I was still a stranger, for I belonged to another generation and I came from the other side of the Atlantic. Because we have been in correspondence over the past thirty years and she knows of my academic interests, I have gotten more from her than other relatives. But I have no idea what remains to be known. If she did not want to talk about something, it was never broached, no matter how much I persisted. Outside the family she was always circumspect, and, although a woman of strict integrity, was not above creating false impressions if the situation warranted it.

My spoken Italian was adequate for everyday social intercourse but was far from adequate when it came to detailed expositions of my research aims and especially on those occasions when I had to speak rapidly and effectively in order to impress or to convince. My forced reliance on my aunt and the schoolteacher for the opening of channels of communication severely limited my options. I have had to conclude that the village informant is a poor substitute, as is a fluent spouse or colleague, for it removes the researcher at the mercy of another's interpretation without being able to test and retest the ground at first hand. Without a deeper understanding of the finer distinctions imbedded in the language and the culture, I could not make the connection between what people said and what people meant, nor could I guess at what was left unsaid.

On the basis of my own experiences and these of others, I must say that the view of the outsider contains many restrictions. Unless that view is very perceptive, the product will be little more than superficial. I think Carl Levi's book *Christ Stopped at Eboli*[13] fails because he remains the critical outsider, whereas Giuseppe Bufalari's work *La Masseria* is a much more profound view of southern folkways because of his superior grasp of *contadina* life.[14] Edward Banfield's concept of amoral familism is problematic for many reasons, one being that he developed it after only a superficial and indirect contact with the subject matter.[15]

Few village studies can compare with the work of A.L.. Maraspini[16] who achieved a remarkable understanding of Pugliese cultural imperatives and the way in which they are actually implemented under the varying conditions of concrete reality. Nor can many compare with Ann Cornelisen's work, which shows an insight rare in village studies.[17] This insight is purchased at substantial effort — that of becoming an insider. Without the insider's perspective the necessary insight will not be developed, with the result that much of the interpretive potential of archival/interview/observational data will be lost.

The future is very bright for village research by Americans in Italy. A sufficient literature has already established a firm groundwork for the next generation of scholars.[18] Unlike the past when few Americans of Italian heritage entered the social sciences, with the coming years a growing number will be found directing their substantial intellectual energies to the enterprise. This can only be beneficial, for these young scholars will bring with them, in addition to their superior academic training, an accumulation of experience and insights from their ethnic backgrounds that will give them the advantage of quicker and deeper access to the subject matter. The provincialism that is implicit in a specific ethnic identification will, of course, be a detriment to the research project until it can be correctly conceptualized and placed into the proper perspective. This can be achieved by developing an appreciation for the complexity of Italian village life through preliminary forays into the field and a thorough review of the Italian literature. Although Alberone and the surrounding communities share much in the way of a common regional culture, studies currently being produced by local scholars reveal significant variations that have endured up to the present day. Both these scholars and their research, much of which appears in publications with limited distribution, should be fully consulted prior to the development of the research design. The design should also anticipate documenting the expressive and methodological aspects of the research, both neglected areas. An objective and comprehensive village literature would require no less.

Footnotes

1. Filippo Sabetti, *Political Authority in a Sicilian Village* (New Brunswick, N.J.: Rutgers University Press, 1984).
2. Rudolph M. Bell, *Fate and Honor, Family and Village. Demographic and Cultural Change in Rural Italy Since 1800* (Chicago: University of Chicago Press, 1979).
3. Donna R. Gabaccia, *From Sicily to Elizabeth Street. Housing and Social Change Among Italian Immigrants, 1880—1930* (Albany, N.Y.: SUNY Press, 1984).
4. Robert Evans, *Life and Politics in a Venetian Community* (South Bend, Ind.: University of Notre Dame Press, 1976).
5. Charlotte G. Chapman, *Milocca, A Sicilian Village* (Cambridge, Mass.: Schenkman, 1971).
6. Pietro Lippolis, *Le murge dei trulli* (Roma: De Luce Editore, 1961).
7. William A. Douglass, *Emigration in a South Italian Town* (New Brunswick, N.J.: Rutgers University Press, 1984).
8. Luigi Barzini, *The Italians* (New York: Antheneum, 1965).
9. For a useful discussion of Italian distrust and cynicism towards government employees and authority, see Lola Romanucci-Ross, ''Italian Ethnic Identity and its Transformations,'' in George De Vos and Lola Romanucci-Ross (eds.), *Ethnic Identity* (Palo Alto, Calif.: Mayfield, 1975).

10. John W. Briggs, *An Italian Passage: Immigrants to Three American Cities, 1890—1930* (New Haven: Yale University Press, 1978): 335.
11. Burton R. Clark, *Academic Power in Italy* (Chicago: University of Chicago Press, 1977): 2.
12. Gavin Maxwell, *The Ten Pains of Death* (New York: Dutton, 1960).
13. Carlo Levi, *Christ Stopped at Eboli. The Story of a Year* (New York: Farrar, Straus, 1947).
14. Giuseppe Bufalari, *La Masseria* (Milano: Lerici, 1960).
15. Edward C. Banfield, *The Moral Basis of a Backward Society* (Glencoe: IL1.: Free Press, 1958).
16. A. L. Maraspini, *The Study of an Italian Village* (Paris: Mouton, 1968).
17. Ann Cornelisen, *Women of the Shadows* (New York: Random House, 1970); *Strangers and Pilgrims. The Last Italian Migration* (New York: Holt, Rinehart and Winston, 1980).
18. Other relevant works not already metioned include, Thomas Belmont, *The Broken Fountain* (New York: Columbia University University Press, 1979); Anton Block *The Mafia of a Sicilian Village, 1860—1960* (New York: Harper and Row, 1974); Constance Cronin, *The Sting of Change. Sicilians in Sicily and Australia* (Chicago: University of Chicago Press, 1970); John H. Davis, *Land and Family in Pisticci* (New York: Humanities, 1973); Feliks Gross, *Il Paese. Values and Social Change in an Italian Village* (New York: New York University Press, 1973); David I. Kertzer, *Family Life in Central Italy, 1880—1910. Sharecropping, Wage Labor, and Coresidence* (New Brunswick, N.J.: Rutgers University Press, 1984); Joseph LoPreato, *Peasants No More. Social Class and Social Change in an Underdeveloped Society* (San Francisco: Chandler, 1967); Sydel Silverman, *Three Bells of Civilization. The Life of an Italian Hill Town* (New York: Columbia University Press, 1975).

Chapter **4**   **PLACES, COMMUNITIES AND**
REGIONS IN THE AMERICAN
ITALIAN STUDIES —
TERRITORIAL COVERAGE
Joseph Velikonja
University of Washington

Recent years have witnessed an increasing number of studies on Italian Americans. Many of them are duly recorded in bibliographical inventories. These meritorious achievement, nevertheless, when examined from territorial perspective, reveal an uneven coverage of the vast continent.

My own bibliographical efforts of almost a quarter century, from a bibliography of 1963[1] to more recent surveys of 1977[2] and 1985[3] consistently sought to ascertain the territorial and regional coverage of studies on the presence and achievements of Italian immigrants in the United States. These reviews were aimed at geographers and historians to alert them that the objects of investigation — the Italian-Americans — are at their doorsteps and that very few areas or communities have ever been exhaustively investigated and documented. This review is the fourth in a series of assessments. It recognizes significant new contributions as well as persisting inadequacies.

The recording of Italian experiences in the United States is now in its third period: the first embraced the turn of the century and the height of immigration; the second coincides with the New Deal era, often characterized as a period of ethnic demise, when the studies aimed to record the ethnic existence at the verge of predicted disappearance; the third is the period of "ethnic revival and revivalism", triggered by the energy of the Civil Rights movement, spilled over to include other ethnics and expanded during the bicentennial celebrations.

In spite of the sizeable volume of national, regional or local ethnic studies, numerous *lacunae* remain in the territorial coverage. The common view that there is little to be added to the already recorded patrimony of ethnic history under closer scrutiny gives way to the discovery of large gaps in the recordings of temporal sequences and in their geographic territorial coverage. In this review I refer only to the published evidence of the Italian Americans in the United States, comparing and contrasting the research results of the most recent decades. The review is neither complete, nor exhaustive, primarily due to the difficulty in verifying numerous ethnic reportings in local, state and regional publications that do not enter into conventional bibliographical inventories.

Immigrant experiences fit into the general model of migration mechanism. Contemporary geographical studies acknowledge the significance of the historical process in population movements and present it within the framework of time-geography. A scheme of geographical studies of migration, originated by Lee[4] and adopted by Mangalam[5] can be further refined to account for the time dimension. Origin and destination are discretely defined territorial entities, linked by the intervening distance that the immigrants cover in their journey. Considering the time sequence, the departure is followed by transit, and by subsequent arrival and accommodation. The time-space line of the immigrant begins at the point of origin and changes direction with departure, moves laterally to the destination and continues to run downward at the destination. The migrant moves from the society at origin and joins the society at destination.

This scheme does not show anything new, except that the second generation immigrants, i.e. the children of immigrants, start without a direct association with the area of origin and therefore do not carry the same structural characteristics as the immigrants themselves.

The graph should be further expanded by parallel links between origins and destinations portraying subsequent migrations from the same area to the

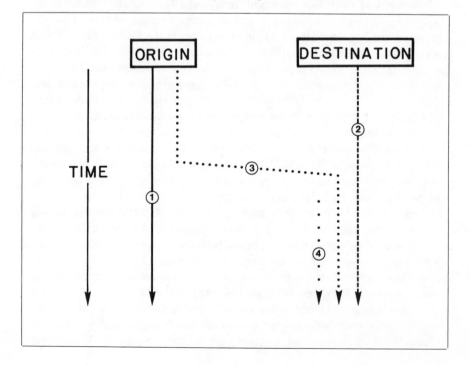

same destinations, but not having the same time-space experiences as the previous migrants. This particular aspect is rarely an object of investigation in ethnic migration studies.

The present paper is only a fragment of immigrant assessments. it only deals with the complex system of migrant distribution at destination, using the *Italian* label to identify the ethnic group and separate it from the large immigrant population as well as from the large native population in the United States. Neither is the purpose of this paper to assess the United States destination in competition with other alternative destinations, nor is the intention to analyze the content of various studies. The territorial coverage or lack of it prompted this review.

The East Coast receives the most attention in Italian American migration studies. The Atlantic seaboard has remained the dominant destination of Italian immigrants for more than a century. Even the most recent 1980 Census finds the majority of people with the Italian ancestry in the Atlantic Coast states. Nevertheless numerous Italian clusters in the region have escaped recording and lack local histories or analyses.

While there is an evident correlation between the distribution of Italian-Americans and the existence of researchers "in the field" who did and still do produce regional assessments, there is also a correlation with the territorial distribution of the Italian ethnic press. It should be noted, that individual researchers cover only selected items. The consequence of the uneven coverage of the United States is the skewed stress by which the East Coast Italian-American experience is accepted by historians, sociologists and anthropologists as *the* experience that is generically valid for all Italian immigrants regardless of their destination or of their time of arrival. Any different experience is presumed to be an anomaly or an aberration that deviated from the established norm.

I have been saying for many years to the researchers of the American immigration history that there is a wide world west of the Appalachians; it even spans for many miles west of the Mississippi River; the presence and contributions of the Italian-Americans in the west is generally unknown and only seldom recorded. Some gaps have been filled in the last ten years due to the efforts of a few individuals, but there is still much more to be done.

The review of recently completed studies[6] and of ongoing research[7] prompted this supplement. the announced "ongoing research projects" tend to take their time and the results are not available either for review or scrutiny until publication. Zimmerman's statement regarding my research promises much more than I will be able to deliver in the forthcoming ten years or so. I am nevertheless thankful for her generosity.

The Italian-American studies are well represented in each of the major regions: Northeast, Midwest, South and the West (Table I). When, however, we try to refine the regional scheme and use, for the sake of convenience,

Table I
Italian-American Studies — Regional Survey

	Velikonja 1963	Cordasco-LaGumina 72	Pane 1908—76	Velikonja 1976—83	Zimmerman 1985	Ph.D. 1976—85
New England	29	23	12	16	4	6
Middle Atlantic	93	70	38	65	24	21
East North Central	33	39	15	22	8	3*
South Atlantic	6	8	2	13	4	1*
East South Central	0	8	0	1	1	0
West South Central	24	17	4	13	3	1
West North Central	9	6	2	19	0	2
Mountain	4	12	2	8	1	2
Pacific	17	32	8	17	10	6
Others & unidentified	13	18	1	3	1	7
Total	228	233	84	177	56	48*

*The total of 48 includes on title that is counted both in East North Central and in South Atlantic.

Sources listed on Table II.

states as the units, the coverage is less satisfying. If we go even further and use smaller units such as cities, communities or specially designated areas, major gaps appear on the map. This in itself is not surprising. In 1980 — 76 percent of the U.S. population lived on 16 percent of the land that encompasses the metropolitan areas. The Italian immigrants are concentrated there (over 90 percent); the search for an Italian presence outside of the metropolitan areas is less productive.

Bibliographies seldom list studies by locational grouping. The alphabetical listings by authors or titles, by subjects or by dates of publication is inadequate for ascertaining the regional and locational coverage. The summary provided here refers to six bibliographical listings; my own bibliography of 1963[8] which included 228 references in the regional coverage; Cordasco-LaGumina's bibliography of 1972[9] has 233 items; Pane's inventory of doctoral dissertations completed between 1908 and 1976[10] includes 84 studies that can be identified by the region. This inventory is supplemented by my survey of the 1975—1983 studies[11], Zimmerman's 1985 review of research in progress[12] and the 1976—85 list of completed doctoral dissertations[13]. The most recent period is given separate attention. In general, only a few items published in 1986 are recorded in this review.

All these bibliographies reveal a paucity of studies outside the Atlantic Seaboard. It would require a much more elaborate analysis to provide detailed documentation. The duplication of listing in the six inventories gives undue accent to some areas. It is nevertheless possible to discern that the studies reflect the spatial distribution of population of Italian ancestry in 1980. The discrepancies are more evident in details than in aggregate areas.

Considering first the three earlier listings (Table II), which cover the period prior to 1976, only 13 of the contiguous states are represented in all three inventories (California, New Mexico, Colorado, Missouri, Nebraska, Louisiana, Michigan, Illinois, New York, Pennsylvania, New Jersey, Connecticut, Massachusetts); 13 states appear in one of the three listings and 13 in none of them (Nevada, Wyoming, North Dakota, South Dakota, Iowa, Kansas, Oklahoma, Kentucky, Tennessee, Georgia, South Carolina, New Hampshire and Maine).

Somewhat broader coverage is evident in more recent assessments: those recorded in my 1976—83 report, in the inventory of 1976—85 dissertations, and in the "research in progress" report by Diana J. Zimmerman. The coverage shows again the consistently large representation of states in the Atlantic, Eastern Midwestern States, Louisiana, Arizona and California; eleven states are listed in each inventory embracing Massachusetts, Rhode Island and Connecticut; the states of New York, New Jersy, Pennsylvania and Illinois, Michigan, Louisiana, Arizona and California. None of the three lists covers Maine, New Hampshire, Vermont, North and South Carolina, Georgia, Tennessee and North and South Dakota, Kansas, New Mexico and Idaho.

REGIONAL COVERAGE

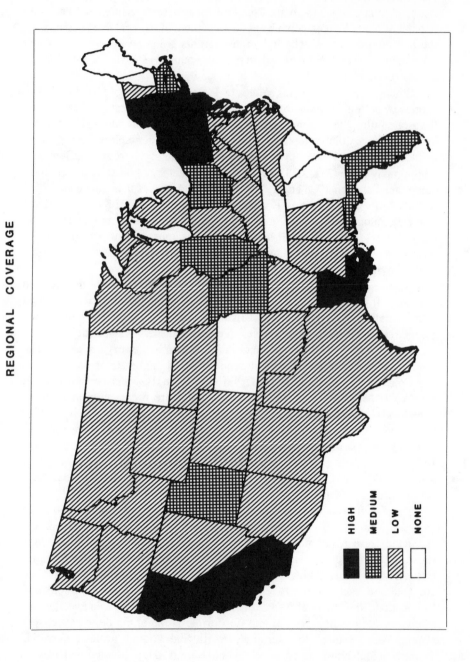

Table II
Italian-American Studies — Survey of Title Citations

	Velikonja 1963 (a)	Cordasco-LaGumina 72 (b)	Pane 1908—76 (c)	Velikonja 1976—1983 (d)	Zimmerman 1985 (e)	Ph.D. 1976—85 (f)	New Titles (g)
New England							
Maine	-	-	-	-	-	-	-
New Hampshire	-	-	-	-	-	-	-
Vermont	2	1	-	-	-	-	-
Massachusetts	17	11	9	8	1	2	2
Rhode Island	-	4	2	2	1	2	2
Connecticut	10	7	1	6	2	2	-
Middle Atlantic							
New York	68	47	26	43	17	17	9
New Jersey	12	7	2	5	4	2	1
Pennsylvania	13	16	10	17	1	2	2
East North Central							
Ohio	2	3	1	5	-	1*	-
Indiana	-	-	1	1	1	-	-
Illinois	24	30	11	11	3	1	1
Michigan	4	3	2	3	3	1	-
Wisconsin	3	3	-	2	1	-	-

Table II (Cont'd)
Italian-American Studies — Survey of Title Citations

South Atlantic							
Delaware	–	–	–	1	–	–	1
Maryland	–	1	–	3	1	1	–
D.C.	–	–	1	–	1	1	–
Virginia	–	–	1	1	–	–	–
West Virginia	3	1	–	–	–	1*	–
North Carolina	1	–	–	–	–	–	–
South Carolina	–	–	–	–	–	–	–
Georgia	1	–	–	–	–	–	–
Florida	–	6	–	8	2	–	1
East South Central							
Kentucky	–	–	–	–	–	–	–
Tennessee	–	–	–	–	1	–	–
Alabama	–	3	–	1	–	–	–
Mississippi	–	5	–	2	–	–	–
West South Central							
Arkansas	8	–	–	1	–	–	1
Louisiana	16	12	4	8	1	1	2
Oklahoma	–	–	–	2	–	–	–
Texas	–	5	–	2	2	–	1
West North Central							
Minnesota	–	2	–	1	–	–	–
Iowa	–	–	–	3	–	–	–
Missouri	8	2	1	14	–	1	1
North Dakota	–	–	–	–	–	–	–

Table II (Cont'd)
Italian-American Studies — Survey of Title Citations

South Dakota	-	-	-	-	-	-	-
Nebraska	1	2	1	1	-	1	-
Kansas	-	-	-	-	-	-	-
Mountain							
Montana	-	2	-	1	-	-	-
Idaho	-	1	-	-	-	-	-
Wyoming	-	-	-	1	-	-	-
Colorado	3	2	1	1	-	-	-
New Mexico	1	2	1	-	-	-	-
Arizona	-	4	-	2	1	1	1
Utah	-	1	-	3	-	1	1
Nevada	-	-	-	1	-	-	-
Pacific							
Washington	-	1	-	1	-	-	1
Oregon	1	1	-	1	-	-	2
California	17	30	8	15	10	6	-
Alaska	-	-	-	-	-	-	-
Hawaii	-	-	-	-	-	-	-
Others/non-identified	13	18	1	3	-	7	6
	228	223	84	177	56	48	35

*total of 48 includes one title listed in Ohio and in West Virginia

Table II (Cont'd)

Italian-American Studies — Survey of Title Citations

Sources:

(a) Joseph Velikonja. *The Italians in the United States: Bibliography.* Carbondale: Southern Illinois University, Occasional Papers I (1963).

(b) Francesco Cordasco and Salvatore LaGumina. *Italians in the United States: A Bibliography of Reports, Texts, Critical Studies and Related Materials.* New York: Oriole Editions (1972).

(c) Remigio Pane, "Sessant'Anni di Studi Americani Sugli ItaloAmericani," *Bolletino* 5 (Firenze: Comitato Italiano per la Storia Americana, 1976): 64—92.

(d) Joseph Velikonja, "Italian Americans in the East and West: Regional Coverage in Italian American Studies, 1973—1983," in Lydio F. Tomasi (ed.) *Italian Americans: New Perspectives in Italian Immigration and Ethnicity.* New York: Center for Migration Studies (1985), 141—172, 419—421.

(e) Diana J. Zimmerman, "Ongoing Research on Italian Americans in the U.S.: A Survey," in Lydio F. Tomasi (ed.). *Italian Americans: New Perspectives in Italian Immigration and Ethnicity.* New York: Center for Migration Studies (1985): 173—192.

(f) Ph.D. Dissertations listed in Appendix.

(g) Items listed in References.

Combining the two sets, no studies have been recorded for: Maine, New Hampshire, South Carolina and Georgia, Tennessee, Kansas, North and South Dakota, and the detached states of Hawaii and Alaska. In six combined inventories, the states of Kentucky, Wyoming, Idaho and Nevada are present with one citation each, and Delaware, Virginia, Washington and Oregon with two.

My earlier assessment that, "The regional inventories demonstrate significant coverage of the eastern United States, especially the state and communities in New York, Connecticut and Rhode Island with less comprehensive portrayal of Massachusetts, New Jersey and Pennsylvania,"[14] should be modified by stressing the lack of studies of Massachusetts communities except for Boston, lack of an adequate survey for Connecticut, and total absence of upper New England states and communities of Maine, Vermont and New Hampshire. The past ten years have seen significant expansion of regional and local studies of communities in the states of New York and Pennsylvania, but the field is far from being exhausted. The assessments both of economic contributions and the survival of cultural heritage in smaller communities of the region is still mission. Rudnicki's dissertation of the Manufacturing Heartland[15] is an attempt of broader scope, that should be followed by additional explorations. Vermont, the hotbed of radicalism, with prosperous Italian communities in the quarry country, is virtually unrecorded. The agricultural seasonal and permanent labor of the Italians in New Jersey received attention in general population studies due to Rudy Vecoli.[16] Dennis J. Starr's study and bibliography of the Italians of New Jersey just appeared.[17] The hundreds of the Italian mining communities in Pennsylvania and West Virginia are seldom touched. There are studies of major cities and major city clusters (Pittsburgh, Philadelphia, Baltimore); the rural, or non-metropolitan clusters received moderate attention. Even the Mohawk River Valley, from Albany to Buffalo, including such Italian communites as Rome, Syracuse, Utica, and Schenectady, have generated less attention than their numerical size would warrant.

The Midwest seems to be adequately covered until we realize that Ohio is represented by earlier studies of Cleveland and by shared attention of Steubenville, Ohio, with Weirton, West Virginia, in Richard P. Lizza's dissertation. No investigation in progress is reported for the state. Indiana is surfacing with the efforts of James J. Divita, and Kentucky appears for the first time in the promised investigation of Louisville by a doctoral study.[18] It is hoped that the studies of Russell M. Magnaghi[19] will fill a major gap in the investigation of the Italians in the Upper Peninsula of Michigan.

The state of Illinois extends beyond the city limits of Chicago; communities outside of Chicago have hardly been touched. For the upper Midwest Vecoli's research on Minnesota Italians[20] leaves numerous topics uncovered. The labor historians as well as geographers of social structures ought to build parallel studies to those completed for the Scandinavians and Poles. Some investigations have been completed in unpublished surveys.

The South is in general less represented. The combination of smaller numerical presence of the Italians in the region and the recency of investigative efforts contribute to scanty attention. The well known exceptions are the studies of New Orleans, Louisiana, and Tampa, Flordia.[21] The share of the Italians in the new wave of Florida migration is presumed but not investigated. What Martinelli has done for Arizona,[22] of Montgomery, Alabama clusters, a study of the Italians in Memphis, both covering the controversy of church relations, the newspaper publication efforts, and community survival would add significant chapter to historical geographical coverage.

Belfiglio's recent writing puts Texas on the map but does not exhaust the topic. Nor do the local studies of Oklahoma complete the inventory. Colorado is surprisingly neglected. The rich history of the Italian contribution and the honorable survival of the second and third generation would give an excellent opportunity to local investigators to complement the studies of Colorado and Utah by Notarianni.[24]

The absence of Kansas is incomprehensible, be it for the Italian presence in the Kansas Southeast, or in Kansas City, Kansas, or in the scattered farming clusters throughout the state, a spillover of the Colorado and Utah industrial colonies.

The presence of Italians in Montana is unrecorded. I quote my observation:

> The The Meagerville in Butte, Montana [is] described by Rolle vanished with the open pit mine, now closed. The Italians — Where are they now?[25]

And where are any studies of Helena, Butte, and Anaconda? With the closing of mines and smelters, the evidence and the documents are destined for disposal.

Similar comment applies to the study of the Idaho Panhandle. Only local pamphlets proudly display pictures of the Italians in mining communities and enthusiastically refer to the Cataldo Mission, built by Father Ravalli; but the documentation stops there. The Basks in Idaho are presumably more attractive for the state archivists and historians.

Fortunately Cofone,[26] in a series of articles, put Nevada on the map, partially filling one gap. Oregon is represented by a study of South Portland.[27] This leaves Washington to be tackled. The California coverage has not improved in recent years in spite of a series of excellent studies on San Francisco. Who will analyze Fresno and Sacramento, Stockton and Crescent City, Bakersfield and San Jose and dozens of others?

The Providence conference of The American Italian Historical Association in 1985 further confirmed the earlier assessment: Seven of the 48 identifiable titles of papers of the conference dealt with local or regional experiences. Of these, papers on Oswego, New Haven and two on Texas reached beyond New York City — and as an irony, research on Rhode Island was only marginally represented. Smith's published dissertation (1985) partially fills the gap.[28]

The most recent publications demonstrate greater territorial spread and better coverage. They also present reassessments of earlier findings in greater depth and more thorough analysis. Comparative studies with other ethnic groups are more common; comparative analyses of Italian experiences at different destination are still rare. Samuel Baily continues his pioneering work with the New York-Buenos Aires comparison.

Further progress is evident in the publication of ethnic experiences in national and international scholarly periodicals, a phenomenon that was a rarity in the past. The quality of research is recognized in the fact that a greater number of doctoral dissertations are being published by academic publishers.

The prevailing trend in doctoral dissertations demands theoretical and conceptual contributions, while master's level work often consists of empirical and inventory compilations. The masters' theses that contain a wealth of empirical information remain unpublished, unrecorded and unrecognized.

Futhermore, bibliographers make mistakes. Cordasco[29] lists a study of West Virginia with studies of the West; in my 1963 bibliography[30], two studies on New Haven are placed in Massachusetts. The 1975 bibliographical guide[31] characterizes my 1963 list as "A bibliography of famous Italian Americans"; this is not what I intended and did 25 years ago.

From the standpoint of geography, the practice of sociologists and anthropologists of hiding the locations of their investigations is deplorable: imaginary cities, neighborhoods and regions, unidentified location with invented labels and undisclosed areas, intentionally or unintentionally assume a universality of phenomena, therefore making a claim that what occurs at one place is equally valid for any other place.[32] This method has been ingrained in numerous studies related to ethnicity, going back to the Dillingham Commission reports[33] where, in detailed analyses especially of the American West, the locations often remain unidentified. Geographers' predilection for studying phenomena at locations is not an idiosyncracy, but a basis of thorough and lasting research. Geographical studies normally define places, areas and regions of investigation. Geographers may be blamed for their gross generalizations, but their local, locational and regional studies do not presume universality or uniformity. "You studied one, you studied them all" is not quite the guiding principle in geographical research.

Herbert J. Gans writes in *Contemporary Sociology*[34] as a response to Micaela Di Leonardo, that "the domination of ethnic studies by ethnic insiders is harmful, not only because of possible conflicts of interest and intellectual blindness, but also because the greater the domination, the greater the likelihood that outsiders will be ever less welcome.''

Being an "ethnic" myself, I accept the blame for whatever idiosyncracies I have committed. Not being an Italian-American, nor a historian, I nevertheless often find myself as a welcome outsider in the circle of Italian-American historians.

I take strong exception to the statement reported in the *New York Times*[35] made by Francis A.J. Ianni of Columbia University at the conference on Societies in Transition: Italians and Italian-Americans in the 1980s, October 13, 1985 at Temple University-Balch Institute for Immigrant Research; where he said: " . . . Italian-Americans are not an ethnic group but rather are individuals who have taken on characteristics that people from Italy supposedly share . . . These characteristics came from myths created both by the American society into which they came, and by themselves.'' I also disagree with Humbert Nelli's comment, reported in the *NY Times* article, that Dr. Ianni's theory is "the most novel and thought-provoking idea of the entire conference.''

Accepting Ianni's formulation and Nelli's observation would remove Italian-American experiences from historical and geographical investigations and place them in the realm of speculative psychology. Such statements are counterproductive for scholarly research.

In the last ten years, two dissertations in geography (Torrieri, 1982); Rudnicki, 1979) have dealt with the Italians. The earlier decade is not much better. For geographers, Gans' warning of the danger of studies by ethnic insiders is not applicable, nor is there any rush of geographers — outsiders willing to research the Italian or other 'ethnics' of European roots. The argument has not been exhausted. As a response to my inquiry to Wilbur Zelinsky regarding the inadequacy of ethnic representation in the marvelous Atlas he helped co-edit,[36] he wrote that the inadequate coverage is a result of unavailability of proper material. A recent publication by Russel L. Gerlach on Settlement patterns in Missouri[37] is a modest attempt to recognize the European roots of Missouri population.

The most recent review of theses and dissertations in geography lists only one master's thesis that refers to Italian Americans.[38]

I conclude with a comment for geographers:

Geographers have made a negligible contribution to Italian-American studies; two doctoral dissertations in geography in ten years and not a single article on Italian Americans in any of the major American geographical publications. It never fails to amaze me that major research-oriented geography institutions sit in the middle of the ethnic mosaic of the American population without noticing it. My own search and research is viewed as a peculiar idiosyncracy of a somewhat unorthodox "foreigner", who, on top of the persistent demand for field verification, bothers with such population groups as the Italians.

The rare enthusiasts among the American geographers have a long agenda. If they do not do it, the investigation will not be done.

Footnotes

1. Joseph Velikonja. *The Italians in the United States: Bibliography.* Carbondale: Southern Illinois University, Occasional Papers I (1963).
2. Joseph Velikonja, "Territorial Spread of the Italians in the United States," in S.M. Tomasi (d.). *Perspectives in Italian Migration and Ethnicity.* New York: Center for Migration Studies (1977), 67—84.
3. Joseph Velikonja. "Italian Americans in the East and West: Regional Coverage in Italian American Studies, 1973—1983." in Lydio F. Tomasi (ed.) *Italian Americans: New Perspectives in Italian Immigration and Ethnicity.* New York: Center for Migration Studies (1985), 142—172, 419—421.
4. Everett Lee, "A Theory of Migration," *Demography* 3 (1966):47:57.
5. J. J. Mangalam. *Human Migration: A Guide to Migration Literature in English.* Introduction. Lexington: University of Kentucky Press (1968): 1-20.
6. Velikonja, footnote (3)
7. Diana J. Zimmerman, "Ongoing Research on Italian Americans in the U.S.: A Survey," in Lydio F. Tomasi (ed.). *Italian Americans: New Perspectives in Italian Immigration and Ethnicity.* New York: Center for Migration Studies (1985):173—192.
8. Velikonja, 1963, footnote (1)
9. Francesco Cordasco and Salvatore LaGumina. *Italians in the United Staes: A Bibliography of Reports, Texts, Critical Studies and Related Materials.* New York:Oriole Editions (1972).
10. Remigio Pane, "sessant'Anni di Studi Americani Sugli ItaloAmericani," *Bolletino* 5 (Firenze: Comitato Italiano per las Storia Americana, 1976):64—92.
11. Velikonja, 1985, footnote (3)
12. Zimmerman, footnote (7)
13. Appendix to this review.
14. Velikonja, 1985, 147.
15. Rudnicki's dissertation listed in the Appendix.
16. Rudolph J. Vecoli. *The People of New Jersey.* Princeton: Van Nostrand (1965).

17. Dennis J. Starr. *The Italians of New Jersey: A Historical Introduction and Bibliography*. Newark: New Jersey Historical Society (1985).
18. Zimmerman, 179.
19. Zimmerman, 178.
20. Rudolph J. Vecoli, "The Italians," In June Holmquist (ed.) *They Chose Minnesota. A Survey of the State's Ethnic Groups*. St. Paul: Minnesota Historical Society (1981):449—471.
21. The most recent is: Gary R. Mormino and George E. Pozzetta. *They Chose Minnesota. A Survey of the State's Ethnic Groups*. St. Paul: Minnesota Historical Society (1981):449—471.
22. Most recently a chapter in William C. McCredy, (ed). *Culture, Ethnicity, and Identity*. New York: Academic Press (1983), "Beneath the Surface: Ethnic Communities in Phoenix, Arizona", 181—194.
23. Jeffrey Lewellen, "Sheep Admist the Volves: Father Bandini and the Colony of Tontitown, 1898—1917," *Arkansas Historical Quarterly* 14 (1986): 19—40. to be noticed also: Louis Guida's *Italians in the Delta*. Thirty minute documentary, first shown in New York on November 12, 1986.
24. Philip F. Notarianni, "Rise ot Legitimacy: Frank Bonacci as Union Organizer in Carbon County, Utah," *Rendezvous* 19 (1983):67—74.
25. Velikonja, 1985, 152.
26. Three articles by Albin J. Cofone were published in the *Nevada Historical Society Quarterly* between 1982 and 1984.
27. William Toll, "Ethnicity and Stability: The Italians and Jews of South Portland, 1900—1940, "*Pacific Historical Review* 54 (1985):161—189.
28. Judith E. Smith. *Family Connections: A History of Italian and Jewish Immigrant Lives in Providence, Rhode Island, 1900—1940*. Albany: State University of New York Press (1985).
29. F. Cordasco, footnote (9).
30. J. Velikonja, 1963, footnote (1)
31. C.M. Diodato, J. Coleman and J.F. Balletutti. *Writings on Italian-Americans*. New York: Italian American Center for Urban Affairs (1975): 46.
32. The unidentified locations are analyzed in the dissertations of Karen Curtis, Christine Casey, C.H. Edson, Richard L. Leveroni, Leon Allen Page III.
33. William Paul Dillingham. *U.S. Immigration Commission, 1907—1910 Reports*. Washington: Government Printing Office (1911). 41 volumes.
34. Herbert J. Gans, "Ethnicity, Ideology, and the Insider Problems, "*Contemporary Sociology* 14 (1985):302—304.
35. Fred Ferretti, "Conferees Urge Italian-Americans to Forge Close New Links to Italy," *The New York Times* October 14, 1985.
36. John F. Rooney, Wilbur Zelinsky and Dean R. Louder. *This Remarkable Continent*. College Station, Texas: Texas A&M University Press (1982).

37. Russel L. Gerlach. *Settlement Patterns in Missouri. A Study of Population Origins, with a Wall Map* Columbia: University of Missouri Press (1986).
38. Susan Jane Pineo. The Geography of Viticulture in Sonoma County. M.A. Thesis. University of California — Davis (1985).

References

Alba, Richard D.
"The Twilight of Ethnicity Among Americans of European Ancestry: The Case of Italians." *Ethnic and Racial Studies* 8 (1985): 134—158   *GENERAL*

Alba, Richard D.
"the Twilight of Ethnicity Among Americans of European Ancestry: The Case of Italians." in Richard D. Alba (ed.). *Ethnicity and Race in the U.S.A. Toward the Twenty-Firsty Century*. London, Boston, Melbourne and Henley: Routledge & Kegan Paul, 1985: 134—158.   *GENERAL*

Baily, Samuel L.
"Patrones de Residencia de los Italianos en Buenos Aires y Nueva York: 1880—1914." *Estudios Migratorios Latinoamericanos* 1 (1985): 8—47.   *NY*

Belfiglio, Valentine (1983)
"Montague: An Italian Folk Island in Central North Texas. *"Panhandle — Plains Historical Review* 56 (1983): 33—48.*TX*

Body-Gendrot, Sophie
"Luttes de Classe et Luttes Ethniques dans le Lower East Side a Manhattan." *Revue Francaise de Science Politique* 32 (1982): 973—999.   *NY*

Buonanno, Michael
"Becoming White: Notes on an Italian — American Explanation of Evil Eye." *New York Folklore* 10 (1984): 39—55.   *NY*

Brumberg, Stephan F.
"Going to America, Going to School; the Immigrant — Public School Encounter in Turn-of-the-Century New York City." *American Jewish Archives* 36 (1984): 86—135.   *NY*

Calice, Nino
"Il Fascismo e L'Emigrazione Lucana negli USA." *Studi Storici* 23 (1982): 881—896.   *GENERAL*

Calomiris, Ellen
"Conflict, Cooperation, Acceptance: The Italian Experience in Delaware." *Delaware History* 20 (1983): 269—290.   *DE*

Cetti, Luisa
"Donne Italiane A New York e Lavoro a Domicilio

Cofone, Albin J.
      "Reno's Little Italy: Italian Entrepreneurship and Culture in
      Northern Nevada." *Nevada Historical Society Quarterly* 26 (1983):
      97—110.   *NV*
Cofone, Albin J.
      "Italian Images in Northern Nevada Writing." *Nevada Historical
      Society Quarterly* 27 (1984): 260—267.   *NV*
Dillon, Richard
      North Beach. The Italian Heart of San Francisco. Novato, CA:
      Presidio Press, 1985.   *CA*
Fasce, Ferdinando
      "Immigrazione Italiana e Fabbrica USA: il Caso Scovill
      (1915—1920)." *Studi Storici* 26 (1985): 5—27.   *CT*
Femminella, Francis X
      (ed). *Italians and Irish in America.* Staten Island, N.Y.: AIHA,
      1985.   *GENERAL*
La Sorte, Michael
      La Merica. Images of Italian Greenhorn Experience. Philadelphia:
      Temple University Press, 1985.   *GENERAL*
Lewellen, Jeffrey
      "Sheep Amidst the Wolves: Father Bandini and the Colony of
      Tontitown, 1898—1917." *Arkansas Historical Quarterly* 14
      (1986): 19—40.   *AR*
Lothrop, Gloria Ricci
      "Uno Squardo al Passato: A Backward Look at an Italian
      Household During Depression Days." *Pacific Historian* 27.4
      (1983): 38—47.   *CA*
Magnaghi, Russel M.
      "Louisiana's Italian Immigrants Prior to 1870." *Louisiana History.
      The Journal of the Louisiana Historical Association* 27 (Winter
      1986): 43—68.   *LA*
Model, Susane
      "A Comparative Perspective on the Ethnic Enclave: Blacks,
      Italians, and Jews in New York City." *International Migration
      Review* 19 (1985): 64—81.   *NY*
Mormino, Gary Ross
      *Immigrants on the Hill. Italian — Americans in St. Louis,
      1882—1982.* Urbana and Chicago: University of Illinois Press,
      1986.   *MO*
Mormino, Gary R. and George E. Pozzetta
      *The Immigrant World of Ybor City. Italians and Their Lation
      Neighbors in Tampa, 1885—1985.* Urbana and Chicago: University
      of Illinois Press, 1986.   *FL*

Notarianni, Philip F.
        "Rise to Legitimacy: Frank Bonacci as Union Organizer in Carbon
        County, Utah." *Rendezvous* 19 (1983): 67—74.   *UT*
Orsi, Robert Anthony
        *The Modonna of 115th Street: Faith and Community in Italian
        Harlem, 1880—1950*. New Haven: Yale University Press, 1985.*NY*
Quadagno, Jill S.
        "The Italian American Family." in Charles H. Mindel and Robert
        W. Habenstein. *Ethnic Families in America. Patterns and
        Variations*. Second Edition. New York — Oxford: Elsevier, 1981:
        61—85.   *GENERAL*
Roche, John Patrick
        "Social Factors Affecting Cultural, National and Religios
        Ethnicity: A Study of Suburban Italian-Americans." *Ethnic Groups*
        6 (1984): 27—45.   *RI*
Scarpaci, J[ean] Vicenza
        "Labor for Louisiana's Sugar Cane Fields: An Experiment in
        Immigrant Recruitment." *Italian Americana* 7.1 (1981): 19—41.
                                                                     LA
Simons, William, Patti Samuel and George Herrman
        "Bloomfield: An Italian Working Class Neighborhood." *Italian
        Americana* 7.1 (1981): 103—116.   *PA*
Smith, Judith E.
        *Family Connections: A History of Italian and Jewish Immigrant
        Lives in Providence, Rhode Island, 1900—1940*. Albany: State
        University of New York Press, 1985.   *RI*
Starr, Dennis J.
        *The Italians of New Jersey: A Historical Introduction and
        Bibliography*. Newark: New Jersey Historical Society, 1985.*NJ*
Swann, Michael M.
        "Ethnic Population Change and Patterns of Spatial Readjustment
        among Local Businesses: The Italian Area of Syracuse, New York,
        1960—1970." *Syracuse University, Department of Geography
        Discussion Papers* 46 (1978).   *NY*
Taylor, P.A.M.
        "Ethnic Success: Boston's Italians." *Immigrants and Minorities*.
        2 (1983): 64—77.   *MA*
Tebbets, Diane
        "Food as an Ethnic Marker." *Pioneer America Society Transaction*
        7 (1984): 81—88.   *GENERAL*
Tirabassi, Maddalena
        "Prima le Donne e i Bambini: Gli International Institutes e
        l'Americanizzazione degli Immigrati." *Quaderni Storici* 17 (1982):
        853—880.   *NY*

Toll, William
> "Ethnicity and Stability: The Italians and Jews of South Portland, 1900—1940." *Pacific Historical Review* 54 (1985): 161P189.*OR*

Vecoli, Rudolph J.
> "The Formulation of Chicago's "Little Italies." in Ira A. Glazier and Luigi De Rosa (eds.) *Migration Across Time and Nations. Population Mobility in Historical Contexts.* New York, London: Holmes & Meier, 1986: 287—301.
>
> [same published earlier in *Journal of Ameican Ethnic History* 2.2 (1983): 5—20.]   *IL*

Yancey, William L., Eugene P. Ericksen and George H. Leon
> "The Structure of Pluralism: 'We're all Italian Around Here, Aren't We, Mrs. O'Brien?' " in Richard D. Alba (ed.) *Ethnicity and Race in the U.S.A. Toward the Twenty-First Century.* London, Boston, Melbourne and Henley: Routledge and Kegan Paul, 1985: 94—116.   *PA*

Ph.D. Dissertations
1976—1985

Aleandri, Emelise Francesca
> A History of Italian-American Theatre: 1900—1905.
> City University of New York, 1984   *NY*

Balancio, Dorothy Marie Cali
> The Making and Unmaking of a Myth: Italian American Women and Their Community.
> City University of New York, 1985   *NY*

Capozzoli, Mary Jane
> Three Generations of Italian American Women in Nassau County, New York 1925—1981.
> Lehigh University, 1985   *NY*

Carlin, Marianne Beck
> Education and Occupational Decisions of the Children of Italian and Polish Immigrants to Rome and New York, 1900 to 1950.
> Cornell University, 1978   *NY*

Casey, Christine
> Ethnic Identity and Self-Esteem in Second and Third Generation Polish and Italian Sixth Grade Children.
> Columbia University Teachers College, 1985.   *EAST COAST*

Cinel, Dino
> Conservative Adventurers: Italian Migrants in Italy and San Francisco.
> Stanford University, 1979   *CA*

Cohen, Miriam Judith
>
> From Workshop to Office: Italian Women and Family Strategies in New York City, 1900—1950.
> University of Michigan, 1978   *NY*

Crispino, James A
>
> The Assimilation of Ethnic Groups: The Italian Case.
> Columbia University, 1977   *CT*

Curtis, Karen
>
> I Can Never Go Empty-Handed: Food Exchange and Reciprocity in an Italian-American Community.
> Temple University, 1984   *NORTH EAST*

De Marco, William Michael
>
> Ethnics and Enclaves: The Italian Settlement in the North End of Boston.
> Boston College, 1980   *MA*

De Sena, Judith Noel
>
> The Dynamics of Neighborhood Defense: A Sociological Account of Greenpoint, Brooklyn.
> City University of New York, 1985   *NY*

Di Leonardo, Micaela
>
> The Varieties of Ethnic Experiences: Kinship, Class and Gender Among Italian-Americans in Northern California.
> University of California, Berkeley, 1981.   *CA*

Edson, C.H.
>
> Immigrant Perspectives on Work and Schooling: Eastern European Jews and Southern Italian, 1880—1920.
> Stanford University, 1979.   *UNKNOWN*

Fichera, Sebastian
>
> The Meaning of Community: A History of the Italians of San Francisco.
> University of California, Los Angeles, 1981   *CA*

Fortuna, Giuseppe
>
> Recent Italian Immigrants in Queens, New York.
> City University of New York, 1981   *NY*

Furio, Colomba Marie
>
> Immigrant Women in Industry: A Case Study, The Italian Immigrant Women and the Garment Industry, 1800—1950.
> New York University, 1979.   *NY*

Giordano, Paul Anthony
>
> The Italians of Louisiana: Their Cultural Background and their Many Contributions in the Fields of Literature, the Arts, Education, Politics, and Business and Labor.
> Indiana University, 1978   *LA*

Hutchens, Nancy Cheryl
> Recent Italian Immigrants in Brooklyn: Their Social World.
> Rice University, 1977   *NY*

Killinger, Charles L., III
> Gaetano Salvemini and the United States. A Study in Italian Antifascism.
> The Florida State University, 1985   *GENERAL*

Leveroni, Richard Laurence
> Italian Folktales and Italian-American Ethnic Identity. State University of New York at Albany, 1984.   *NO LOC.*

Lizza, Richard Patrick
> Some Dimensions of the Immigrant Experience: Italians in Steubenville, Ohio and Weirton, West Virginia, 1900—1930.
> West Virginia University, 1984.   *OH-WV*

Mamone, John Robert
> Italian and Puerto Rican Male Social Bonds in School, Factory and Community.
> Rutgers University, 1978.   *NJ*

Martinelli, Phylis Cancilla
> Ethnicity in the Sunbelt: Italian American Migrants in Scottsdale, Arizona.
> Arizona State University, 1984.   *AZ*

Model, Suzanne Windholz
> Ethnic Bounds in the Work Place: Blacks, Italians, and Jews in New York City.
> University of Michigan, 1985.   *NY*

Mormino, Gary Ross
> The Hill Upon the City: An Italo-American Neighborhood in St. Louis, Missouri, 1880—1955.
> University of North Carolina, 1977.   *MO*

Notarianni, Philip F.
> Tale of Two Towns: The Social Dynamics of Eureka and Helper, Utah.
> University of Utah, 1980.   *UT*

Page, Leon Allen III
> Effects of Bilingual Home Language Environment on Metalinguistic Ability of Second, Third and Fourth Grade Italian-Background Children.
> State University of New York at Albany, 1983.   *NO LOC.*

Pascucci, Robert Russell
> Electric City Immigrants: Italians and Poles of Schenectady, New York, 1880—1930.
> State University of New York, Albany, 1984.   *NY*

Passero, Rosara Lucy
> Ethnicity — The Men's Ready-Made Clothing Industry,
> 1880—1950: The Italian Experience in Philadelphia.
> University of Pennsylvania, 1978.   *PA*

Peroni, Peter Aloysius, II
> Chambersburg: Its Enculturative Process.
> Rutgers University, 1977.   *NJ*

Roche, John Patrick
> Ethnic Attitudes and Ethnic Behavior: Italian-Americans in the
> Rhode Island Suburban Communities.
> University of Connecticut, 1977.   *RI*

Rudnicki, Ryan
> Peopling Industrial America: Fromation of Italian and Polish
> Settlements in the Manufacturing Heartland of the United States,
> 1880—1930.
> The Pennsylvania State University, 1979.   *NORTH EAST*

Sansone, Carmela
> The Relationship Between Ethnic Identification and Self Acceptance
> in Third Generation Italian-Americans.
> New York University, 1983.   *NY*

Scherini, Rose Doris
> The Italian-American Community of San Francisco: A Descriptive
> Study.
> University of California, Berkeley, 1976.   *CA*

Schwartz, Laura Anker
> Immigrant Voices from Home, Work and Community: Women
> and Family in the Migration Press, 1890—1938.
> State University of New York at Stony Brook, 1984.   *CT*

Simboli, Ben James
> Acculturated Drinking Practices and Problem Drinking Among
> Three Generations of Italians in America.
> University of California, Berkeley, 1976.   *CA*

Smith, Judith Ellen
> Remaking Their Lives: Italian and Jewish Immigrant Family, Work
> and Community in Providence, Rhode Island 1900—1940.
> Brown University, 1980   *RI*

Spengler, Paul Albert
> Yankee, Swedish and Italian Acculturation and Economic Mobility
> in Jamestown, New York from 1860 to 1920.
> University of Delaware, 1977.   *NY*

Stack, John Frances Jr.
> The City as a Symbol of International Conflict: Boston's Irish,
> Italians and Jews, 1935—1944.

University of Denver, 1977.   *MA*

Stephenson, Sally S.

Michael A. Nusmanno: A Symbolic Leader.

Carnegie-Mellon University, 1978.   *PA*

Stibili, Edward Claude

The St. Raphael Society for the Protection of Italian Immigrants, 1887—1923.

University of Notre, 1977.   *NY*

Terwillinger, Marlene P.

Jews and Italians and the Socialist Party, New York City, 1901—1917.

The Union for Experimenting Colleges and Universities, 1977.*NY*

Thabet, Jamal Saeed

Work Goals and Job Satisfaction: A Cross-Cultural Study of Italian-American, Polish-American and Expatriate Yemeni Nationals.

United States International University, 1985.   *MI*

Torieri, Nancy Karen

Residential Dispersal and the Survival of the Italian Community in Metropolitan Baltimore, 1920—1980.

University of Maryland, 1982.   *MD*

Tricarico, Donald

The Italians of Greenwich Village: The Social Structure and Transformation of an Ethnic Community.

New School for Social Research, 1980.   *NY*

Venditta, Patrick Louis

The Americanization of the Italian-American Immigrants in Omaha, Nebraska.

University of Nebraska, Lincoln, 1983.   *NE*

Venturelli, Peter Joseph

Acculturation and the Persistence of Ethnicity in a Northern Italian-American District.

University of Chicago, 1981.   *IL*

Vitone, Samuel Francis

Community, Identity and Schools: Educational Experiences of Italians in San Francisco from the Gold Rust to the Second World War.

University of California, Berkeley, 1981.   *CA*

Chapter 5

THE POSITION OF ITALIAN AMERICANS IN CONTEMPORARY SOCIETY

Richard N. Juliani
Villanova University

My purpose is to present a very broad overview of the position of Italian-Americans within American society at the present time. While much of the information is positive and gratifying to report, other aspects are somewhat negative and unpleasant to convey. For unlike many other areas of research, the study of ethnicity, especially for those of us with strong personal identification with our subject matter, often is clouded by the projection of our own treasured values, memories and feelings.

In attempting to assess the current position of Italian-Americans, three principal dimensions must be addressed. The first set of issues includes the demographic, geographic and ecological parameters of Italian-Americans as a part of the American population. How many are there? In what states and regions of the nation do they live? In what kinds of communities do they live? The second set of topics involves the position of Italian-Americans in the stratification system of the United States. How are they distributed in regard to economic class, social status and political power? Finally, the third set of problems concerns their cultural location and social acceptance in regard to their assimilation as Americans. How much of their Italian origins still determines their behavior? How are they seen and accepted by the rest of American society? To be sure, these questions are not independent of one another, but frequently overlap with each other. Indeed, the interaction among these properties and conditions provides major propositions for students seeking to unravel the complexities of ethnic life in pluralistic societies.

Estimates of the current Italian-American population have sometimes reached a figure as high as 20,000,000 individuals.[1] Unfortunately, once such numbers have been published, they often receive wide acceptance. More reliable techniques of determining the size and composition of the population generate a substantially lower total of Americans with Italian origins. A special study of ancestry and language by the Bureau of the Census in November, 1979, reported 11,751,000 Americans to have Italian ancestry.[2] These individuals represented about 6.6% of the total U.S. population. Of this total, 5,641,000, or about 48% of them, reported themselves as having multiple ancestry, that is, they were part Italian, while 6,110,000, or about 52% of them, identified themselves as being entirely Italian in ancestry. The 1980 Federal Census provided somewhat different figures, reporting 12,183,000 Americans, or 5% of the total population, as having Italian ancestry. Of this figure, 5,300,000, or 44% had mixed ancestry, while 6,883,000, or 56% were entirely Italian in ancestry. These distinctions make it a bit difficult to compare numbers and the rank of Italian-Americans with other ancestry groups within the American population. But we can note that in contrast to the roughly 12,000,000 Italian-Americans, slightly more than 49,000,000 persons were entirely or partly of German ancestry; slightly more than 40,000,000 persons Irish or part-Irish, and more than 49,500,000 persons English or part-English. After these very large components, of the American population, the Italian-Americans can be found in numbers more comparable to the 21,000,000 Afro-Americans, 14,000,000 Scottish-Americans, 13,000,000 French Americans, 12,000,000 Hispanics, 10,000,000 American Indians, 8,000,000 Polish Americans and 8,000,000 Dutch-Americans.[4]

While Italian-Americans are found, of course, as residents of all 50 states, they are substantially concentrated in the Northeastern states. Italian-Americans comprise about 5.4% of the national population, but nearly 45% of all Italian-Americans live in the Middle Atlantic states. In other words, while only one in 20 Americans has Italian origins, almost one of every two Italian-Americans lives in New York, New Jersey or Pennsylvania, comprising about 12% of the population of these states. Another 15% of the Italian-American population lives in New England where they represent 16%, an even larger proportion of the total population of the area. In contrast, although 18% of all Italian-Americans live in the Midwest, they represent only 3% of the entire area. The remaining Italian-American population is almost equally divided between the South and the West and represented relatively small proportions of the total number of residents in both regions.[5]

Although some settled in rural areas in earlier periods of immigration to the United States, Italians overwhelmingly chose to pursue the industrial opportunities of more urbanized areas.[6] Italian-Americans retain this great preference for urban America. The 1980 Census showed that more than 90% of those Americans who were entirely Italian in ancestry lived in metropolitan areas, the 1979 Special Report showed that over 58% of them in SMSA's of 1,000,000 or more, and over 20% of them in the central cities of such areas.[8] Even those individuals who were only part Italian in their ancestry also reported comparatively high proportions of urban residence. Of the groups for which the Census Bureau provided data, only Hispanic and Polish Americans were anywhere near as urban as the Italian-Americans.

Generational and age data also provide interesting information on Italian-Americans. Of the more than 6,110,000 Americans of entirely Italian descent in 1979, only 42.7% were third generation Americans, that is, born in the United States of native born American parentage, the lowest proportion of any reported group, slighly below Hispanics and Poles, but substantially below the English, French, German, Irish and Scots. A similar pattern again prevails among those who are only part Italian in their ancestry. Another 44.1% of the entirely Italian population were second generation Americans, that is, native born but with at least one foreign born parent. Here the Italians slightly exceed the Poles, but greatly surpass all other groups for whom data were given. Finally, slightly over 13% of the entirely Italian population were first generation Americans, that is, themselves foreign born. Here, while the comparable Hispanic figure exceeded 30%, the Italians were greater than any other group.[9] Data gathered by the National Opinion Research Corporation for a five year period, 1975 to 1980, were not greatly different from those figures of the Census Bureau.[10] These figures indicate the relatively recent migration of Italians to this country compared to other European descent groups, but also suggest the diminishing migration of Italians in recent years.

The age structure of the Italian-American population contains similar features. Among Italian-Americans who identify entirely as Italian in origin, the median age is 42.3 years. This is nearly eight years above the median for all single ancestry Americans and even more than for such relatively youthful populations as Afro-Americans, Chinese Americans, Filipino Americans and Hispanic Americans, but not quite as high as the aging populations of Czechoslovakian, Hungarian, Polish, Russian and Swedish Americans. The Census Bureau data show 16.3% of those Americans who are entirely Italian in their origins to be 65 and over; 16.2% between 55 and 64; and 14.4% between 45 and 54; for a total of nearly 47% over 44 years of age. At the other end, about 25.4% of these Italian-Americans are below the age of 25 and another 28.1% are between 25 and 44 years.

The material position of Italian Americans within our society today can best be understood by their levels of achievement in regard to income, occupation and education. In these areas, Italian Americans have reached far greater levels of success than many other ethnic groups. These results are especially impressive when viewed against the historical conditions under which Italians arrived. First, although such information was often put to discriminatory uses, it was nevertheless true that during the period of mass imigration from the 1880's to the early 1920's, Italians did tend to arrive with rather modest levels of literacy, education and economic skills.[13] In addition, along with other members of the so-called ''new immigration,'' Italians were the victims of a series of oppressive actions, including even violence, by private individuals and groups as well as by local, state and federal government. It is also important to note the often cited research finding that Italians frequently intended to return to their native country and did so more than any other immigrant groups.[13] This intention also meant that they were willing to accept short-term gains as temporary migrant workers in the United States which often took the form of economic positions and conditions without any favorable implications for succeeding generations. Consequently, upward mobility was very limited for the first two generations of the Italians experience in the United States.[14]

In the third and fourth generations, however, Italian Americans have exhibited a formidable shift toward the middle class in their income, occupation and educational levels. In fact, Italian Americans are now equal to or above the average for white ethnic populations. Since the 1950's the Italian American levle of income has increased more than that of any other white ethnic group except the Jews. The level of Italian-American income today exceeds the national average. The median income of Italian American families exceeds all other groups except for Americans of Scottish or of German origins, two groups with a considerable older history as Americans.[15]

The levels of occupational attainment for Italian Americans have not risen as fast, however, as these striking income figures. Considerable research has reported the tendency of previous generations of Italian American children to enter the labor force at an early age in order to contribute to family income.[16] This tendency, of course, also reduced the length of education for these children and removed them from the opportunity for higher level jobs in later years. In many cases, Italian American boys simply pursued the same unskilled and semi-skilled occupations as their fathers. In more recent years, especially since the end of World War II, later generations appear to have moved increasingly toward white collar and professional careers. Despite this newer pattern of upward mobility, Italian Americans are still more concentrated in the working class then most other white ethnic groups. Moreover, the mobility of Italian Americans toward the middle class may be largely the result of structural changes in the American economy which have reduced the number of lower level jobs while increasing higher level, white collar positions.

The close relationship between occupation and education is clearly reflected in the similarity of the historical patterns of these variables for Italian Americans. As in the case of occupations, immigrants and their children tended to reach only very limited levels of education. But the great increase in the years of schooling completed by the third and fourth generation Italian Americans places them at almost the same levels as other white ethnic groups.[17] Viewed within an economic context, these sudden and dramatic changes raise some question about the common contention that Italian immigrant families traditionally placed a low value on education, but that has now changed in later generations. It is now an equally plausible hypothesis that economic necessity provided the determining force to earlier, low levels of attainment, and that these constraints have now been removed.

The social status position of Italian Americans can perhaps be discerned by changes in "social distance" ratings. First defined and used in the mid-1920's, "social distance" refers to the degree of intimacy that people are willing to allow in their relations with the members of other groups.[18] The scales usually range over a number of specific situations including: as persons to be excluded from my occupation; as neighbors; as fellow club members; and as close kin by marriage. Sociologists have applied these scales at least five times from 1926 to 1977 in their attempts to describe how social status has changed in the U.S. during more than fifty years.[19] Although the results show remarkable consistency overall during this period, some specific groups have made striking changes. The Russians, for example, moved the greatest number of positions, falling from a rank of 13th in 1926 to 29th in 1977. Other large changes were made by the American Indian who rose from 18th place in 1926 to 17th in 1977. The Italians were the only other group making a large change, rising from the 14th rank in 1926 to 5th in 1977. It is interesting to note that the Italians first fell in 1946, perhaps as a result of the position of Italy in the recently concluded world war, then rose in 1956, but achieved a very significant climb over the next two decades. By 1977, only Americans, English, Canadians and French ranked higher in the expressed attitudes of American respondents to social distance items.

It is important to remember that there is a complex relationship between actions and attitudes and that individuals are not always consistent in these matters. Despite the relatively high position of Italians in the social distance scales, prejudice and discrimination remain important issues for Italian Americans. American society has witnessed the end of the harsh treatment sometimes inflicted on Italians as immigrants in the 19th and early 20th centuries, but lesser forms of prejudice and discrimination against Italian Americans appear to persist in the United States today. A stereotype, shared by the mass media and our own personal acquaintances, that emphasizes organized crime, spicy foods, flashy clothes, strong emotions, great sexuality, physical appearance and violence remains all too familiar.[20] An important recent study of the image of Italian American presented by television showed that negative portrayals were twice as common as positive ones; that Italian Americans were disproportionately involved in crime; that they commonly had poor speaking habits; and that they were often comical or foolish characters.[21] Despite Daniel Travanti's portrayal of Captain Furillo, the more regular media image of Italian Americans was captured by Laverne DiFazio, Arthur Fonzarelli, Louie DiPalma, and Vinnie Barbarino. Motion pictures such as *The Godfather* and *The Godfather II* and television commercials such as for Godfather Pizza and, more recently, Subaru, contribute to the reinforcement of these images. Although we need more research on the role of the media in particular and the persistence of anti-Italian prejudice and discrimination in general, it seems that this area remains a significant source of irritation for Italian Americans. The National Commission on Social Justice on the Order Sons of Italy in America has launched a major effort to identify and to combat these problems and has achieved some commendable successes in convincing advertisers to correct stereotypical portrayals of Italians and Italian Americans. One systematic attempt has been made to determine how Italian Americans themselves felt about the extent of these problems.[22] This study found that Italian Americans believed that actual discrimination against them was declining much faster than prejudicial attitudes. But the same research also reported that Italian Americans in higher level positions were more likely to report discrimination as well. The author concluded that discrimination might not be a problem as long as Italian Americans remained in their working class positions, but became expressed when they attempted to move into middle class situations. Along with the ''social distance'' studies, the media problems suggest that Italian Americans have been ostensibly well accepted in American society, but that some lingering forms of prejudice are also evident.

Power, the third major dimension of social stratification, refers to one's capacity to determine the action of other persons. In a society such as ours, power is ordinarily related to position within either the government or private corporations. For any ethnic group, social power is reflected in the number of its members who hold high ranking positions within these institutions. As with occupations and education, the first two generations of Italian Americans experienced little success in regard to power, and more recent generations have begun to achieve more important positions. In the case of politics, it was again in the years after World War II that major changes occurred. From only four Italian American in Congress in the 1930's and only eight during the next decade, the number has reached 34 members at present.[23] The first Italian American member of the Senate was elected in 1950 and the first cabinet member was appointed in 1962. The political mobility of Italian Americans reached, of course, a new peak with the nomination of Congresswoman Geraldine Ferraro as the Democratic party Vice Presidential candidate in the 1984 election. But in contrast to the euphoria of many supporters of the Ferraro campaign, the degree of Italian American political attainment at the highest levels of the federal government remains low. In particular, despite the efforts of Italian American pressure groups, the failure to secure an appointment to the U.S. Supreme Court remains a significant disappointment. On the other hand, Italian Americans have achieved greater political success in elected and appointed positions in local and state government, particularly in areas with large Italian American populations such as New York, New Jersey, Massachusetts, Connecticut and Rhode Island.[24] Perhaps the considerable success at present by Italian American politicians at these lower levels holds great promise for another burst of upward mobility at the federal level in the very near future.

The situation for Italian Americans in regard to corporate power has been very similar to their experience with government. Despite again some well-publicized individual cases such as Lee Iaccoca, empirical studies show that the ethnic origins of American business leaders remain overwhelmingly northwestern European and Protestant and that Italian Americans remain far underrepresented in positions of corporate power in comparison to their proportion of the general population.[25] It is important to add that many prominent Italian Americans in business, such as Gino Paolucci, Edward J. DeBartolo, and Frank J. Pasquerilla achieved success as individual entrepreneurs rather than as M.B.A. holders climbing ladders in the corporate world. In short, despite the publicity given to individuals like Ferraro and Iaccoca, Italian Americans as a group may have far less power in government and industry than is at first believed.

Social mobility and cultural assimilation are clearly related experiences. The levels of attainment by Italian Americans within the stratification system provide basic information for some interpretation of their degree of assimilation. As previously noted, in terms of occupation, income and education, Italian Americans have reached comparable levels of achievement as the general population. They have also begun to enter the upper levels of power in many institutions, but remain far behind the dominant WASP group in this regard. Social researchers generally agree that alongside of these significant achievements in the stratification hierarchy, Italian Americans have also experienced a great deal of cultural assimilation, or acculturation, that is, the adoption of the patterns of thought and action of the dominant cultural group.[26] In other words, with their rising levels of attainment, Italian Americans have also become generally Americanized. These changes, however, are strongly related to generational differences. Although the children of immigrants often retained some food customs and language traits, by the third generation almost all of the traiditonal culture is replaced by American patterns of thought and action. The loss of the original language is regarded as a particularly significant marker of this cultural transformation. Social scientists regard upward mobility as a powerful determinant of acculturation, arguing that as Italian Americans move from the working class to middle class occupations and neighborhoods, they also become indistinguishable from other Americans at the same class level.

Assimilation, however, has another important dimension. Social scientists also regard structural assimilation as an important measure of a group's position within a pluralistic society. In contrast to acculturation, or becoming like the dominant culture, structural assimilation refers to the extent to which the members of any group are accepted by the dominant society.[27] In a discussion of racial groups, we often use the concept of integration to express this issue. In this regard, we have already seen that Italians, and presumably Italian Americans, have been the beneficiaries of a sizeable positive change in "social distance" rankings. The rising levels of attainment in the stratification system also indicates greater acceptance of Italian Americans by others. But we have also seen that the mobility of Italian Americans falls somewhat short at the upper levels of governmental and corporate hierarchies. In addition, research that focuses on the more personal forms of contact, such as patterns of residence and intermarriage, also suggests that the acceptance of Italian Americans may be limited. Journalists and scholars continue to note the persistence of italian American neighborhoods. While their ethnic homogeneity and cohesion have often been exaggerated, it is also apparent that class and generation may be the more important determinants of these neighborhoods. The future of these neighborhoods is an important question. In regard to intermarriage, numerous studies have shown that younger Italian Americans increasingly marry not only outside of their ethnic group, but also outside of the Catholic population.[28] Despite these findings, the full acceptance of Italian Americans, especially at the upper levels of our political and economic institutions and in the more intimate forms of social relationships, remains incomplete.

All of this brings us finally to the question of what is happening in the most fundamental sense to Italian Americans as an ethnic group, and by implication what is the future of ethnicity in general in a society such as our own. In the late 1960's and the 1970's, mainly in reaction against assimilation as a theory and as an ideology, Michael Novak vigorously argued and Andrew Greeley attempted to show with empirical data that ethnicity remained an important factor in our lives.[29] These proponents of the "new ethnicity" insisted that pluralism had survived in America and that regardless of class position, groups such as Italian Americans continued to have distinctive patterns of values, behavior and relationships. The late Geno Baroni sought to use that perspective to forge a new civil rights coalition uniting Blacks and white ethnic groups. Some critics now argue that this position was mainly a white working class response, disguised behind ethnicity, to perceived black economic and political gains, and that the "new ethnicity" has already disappeared.[30] Some influential social scientists and historians maintain that the ethnicity of Italian Americans as well as the members of other white ethnic groups is being continually reduced as they move into the middle class. To put it quite simply, the more they attain, the less they are Italian American. With each generation, this process continues on an irreversible course. According to this view, ethnicity is a function of class position, and being an Italian-American depends upon being a member of the working class.[31] A middle class Italian American is a sociological contradiction. Paradoxically, the same view also holds that with the reduction of ethnicity as an influence in our lives, social class becomes a stronger determinant of our patterns of thought and action. Furthermore, the adherents of this interpretation maintain that ethnicity is not entirely eradicated, but becomes limited to personal identity and some relatively trivial, occasional forms of cultural expression. Ethnicity is no longer a decisive determinant of any important aspect of our lives, but is reduced to "symbolic ethnicity," merely the vestigial reenactment of the past, and we have now entered the "twilight of ethnicity."

Another perspective contends rather naively that Italian Americans as a group have attained full opportunity, if not actual success, in their struggle to achieve and to be accepted in American society. In a recent address before the Supreme Council of the Sons of Italy, former U.S. Attorney General Benjamin Civiletti declared that ". . . we have come of age . . ." and further declared:

> There is an entry at every level of society, in every echelon . . . industry, commerce, education in our finest institutions where you find Americans of Italian descent at the top, as the chancellor, the president, the vice president, the chairman . . . there is no position, there is no rank, there is no sacred American society (sic) from which Italo-Americans are excluded, or as to which they cannot aspire with some competent or reasonable effort of achievement.[32]

This interpretation appears to be a case of a badly informed speaker or one who has placed before his audience that which he thinks it would most like to hear and to believe rather than anything based upon sound research and reflection.

My own conclusion is that Italian Americans at the present time are experiencing great levels of personal success, but that they do remain victims of usually subtle, but occasionally blatant, forms of rejection and disparagement. In particular, their success itself sometimes provides the license to others for derogatory portrayals which Italian Americans are asked to tolerate with a good sense of humor. At other times, the rejection takes even more serious forms, such as at the top levels of corporations, among those Americans who remain a bit uncomfortable with others who are just a little bit different. But in addition to these problems of our society, a separate set of issues may be found on the part of our academic colleagues. The association of ethnicity and class has been far too simply drawn, and scholars may have created their own stereotype of the Italian American subculture as an exclusively working class experience. It is not clear that membership in the middle class precludes serious and meaningful expressions of ethnic group membership, that is, personal values, patterns of behavior, and interpersonal relationships that go beyond merely "symbolic ethnicity." At the risk of taking an "ad hominem" swipe at some of my colleagues, it is possible that many of them have not adequately resolved their own sense of ethnic identity and their own relationship to their ethnic origins. If this is the case, their analysis of ethnicity may be a projection of their personal lives. It also seems that they fail to recognize the extent to which the core culture of American society and the social patterns of the dominant group are not ethnically neutral, but clearly reflect the ethnic origins of earlier arrivals to the United States. In short, upward mobility may not necessarily eradicate ethnicity, but generate newer forms of it, and we must be alert and imaginative enough to recognize these possibilities.

Footnotes

1. Richard Gambino, *Blood of My Blood*. Garden City, New York: 1974. p. 115. Gambino actually says that ". . . their number is unknown for certain," but then he cites an estimate of more than twenty million and proceeds to discuss its distribution by generation. This figure is also prominently displayed beneath the title of Gambino's book on its dust cover.
2. U.S. Bureau of the Census, *Ancestry and Language in the United States: November 1979*, Current Population Reports, Series P-23, No. 116. Washington, D.C.: U.S. Government Printing Office, 1982. p.7.
3. U.S. Department of Commerce, Bureau of the Census, *General Social and Economic Characteristics*, United States Summary, PC 80-1-C1. Washington, D.C.: U.S. Government Printing Office, Table 76.
4. These figures are based on both the special report for 1979 and the 1980 Census.
5. U.S. Department of Commerce, Bureau of the Census, *General Social and Economic Characteristics* . . . Table 234; Richard D. Alba, *Italian Americans*. Englewood Cliffs, New Jersey: Prentice Hall, p. 115.
6. Robert F. Foerster, *The Italian Emigration of Our Times*, Cambridge, Mass.: Harvard University Press, 1924.
7. U.S. Department of Commerce, Bureau of the Census, *General Social and Economic Characteristics* . . . Table 76.
8. U.S. Bureau of the Census, *Ancestry and Language* . . . p. 10.
9. U.S. Bureau of the Census, *Ancestry and Language* . . . pp. 10—11. Figures from the CPR Report for November, 1979, rather than the 1980 Census, because the earlier data allow comparisons with a greater number of other ethnic groups.
10. Alba, p. 114.
11. U.S. Bureau of the Census, *Ancestry and Language* . . . pp. 8—9. Again, the CPR Report is used because of the greater number of possible comparisons.

12. Joseph Lopreato, *Italian Americans*. New York: Random House, 1970.
13. Eugene Schuyler, "Italian immigration into the U.S.," *Political Science Quarterly*. IV (1889) P:481; Imre Ferenczi, "An Historical Study of Migration Statistics," *International Labor Review*, XX (1929) PP:356—384; and Imre Ferenczi, in *International Migrations*, Vol. I, edited by Walter F. Willcox, New York: National Bureau of Economic Research, 1929.pp. 390—393, 472—474.
14. Thomas Kessner, *The Golden Door*. New York: Oxford University Press, 1977.
15. U.S. Bureau of the Census, *Ancestry and Language* . . . p. 12; Martin N. Marger, *Race and Ethnic Relations*. Belmont, California: Wadsworth, 1985, pp. 105—106.
16. Alba, pp. 32, 61—62; Foerster, pp. 324—5, 348—9, 336.
17. U.S. Bureau of the Census, *Ancestry and Language* . . . p. 10.
18. Carolyn A. Owen, Howard C. Eisner and Thomas R. McFaul, "A Half-Century of Social Distance Research: National Replication of the Bogardus' Studies," *Sociology and Social Research* 66 (October, 1981) pp. 80—82.
19. Owen et al. pp. 84—98.
20. Marger, pp. 109—112.
21. S. Robert Lichter and Linda Lichter, *Italian-American Characters in Television Entertainment*. Prepared for The Commission for Social Justice, Order Sons of Italy in America, May, 1982.
22. James A. Crispino, *The Assimilation of Ethnic Groups*. Staten Island, New York: Center for Migration Studies, 1980. pp. 118—120; see also Marger's discussion of this study, pp. 111—112.
23. "Italian-Americans on the Move," *Sons of Italy Times* Philadelphia (August 20, 1984).
24. Marger, p. 106.
25. Marger, pp. 108—109
26. Alba, pp. 133—145
27. Alba, pp. 145—150; Milton M. Gordon, *Assimilation in American Life*. New York: Oxford University Press, 1964.
28. Alba, pp. 145—150
29. Michael Novak, *The Rise of the Unmeltable Ethnics*. New York: Macmillan, 1972; Andrew M. Greeley, *Why Can't They Be Like Us?* New York: Dutton, 1971.
30. Stephen Steinberg, *The Ethnic Myth*. New York: Atheneum, 1981.
31. Herbert J. Gans, "Symbolic Ethnicity: The Future of Ethnic Groups and Culture in America," in *Majority and Minority*, edited by Norman R. Yetman and C. Hoy Steele. Boston: Allyn and Bacon, 1982.
32. "We Have Come of Age . . ." *OSIA News* (December, 1984).

Chapter **6**   # THE ITALO-ALBANIAN-AMERICAN EXPERIENCE: A BIBLIOGRAPHIC SURVEY

Richard Renoff
Joseph A. Varacalli
Nassau Community College

Introduction

"Italian-Greek-Albanian-American" is a confusing hyphenation that requires explanation. An Italian-Greek-Albanian-American is not usually a person of quadruple ancestry although in individual cases this is possible. Rather this ethnic group arose from something which preceded a mass migration to America. The first section of our paper therefore is a survey of the origins, history, and present state of this group. Subsequent sections will explain the images of them to be found in American publications, and our predictions concerning their situation in the year 2000 A.D.

History

There is an ancient connection between Albania and Italy. Present-day Albanian territory was first populated by the ancient Illyrians in antiquity but was conquered by the Romans in 167—168 B.C. and remained a Roman colony until 395 A.D. when the territory came under Byzantine hegemony.[1] It was to the byzantine rite version of Christianity that the Albanians were converted during the fourth century but some in the North became Latin rite Catholics during the Middle Ages.[2]

The Turkish invasion of Albania was to give the Greek (Byzantine) rite in Italy and Sicily an infusion of vitality through migration. Greek rite Catholics of Greek descent had dwelt in Calabria and Sicily since ancient times. Even following the Great Schism between the Eastern and Western churces they had remained in communion with the Pope of Rome.[3] Assimilation, conversion, and pressure from local Latin rite priests and prelates were leading to the near extinction of the rite. After approximately 1448, Albanian refugees from Turkish expansionism settled in Calabria, Sicily, and other parts of italy. They were to eventually merge with the Italo-Greeks already there but as recently as the mid-eighteenth century a distinction was made by church officials between Italo-Greeks and Italo-Albanians.[4]

Other than the recensions of the Albanian language spoken and written in Italy and Sicily, the chief institution perpetuating a distinction between the Italo-Albanians and Italians was the Greek (Byzantine) rite. (A similar phenomenon took place among the Greeks under Ottoman rule where the Turkish *millet* system enabled the Orthodox religion to conserve Greek culture when there was no Greece and among the Carpatho-Rusyns who maintained the Greek (Byzantine) rite while under Habsburg rule.)[5] Although, for the Italo-Albanians, the liturgical language was Greek and many Latin customs were adopted, the Byzantine rite and some particular rites such as baptism by immersion and crownings at marriage served as boundary maintaining mechanisms. In fact, some important Italo-Albanian intellectual leaders were priests, most notably, Giovanni Francesco Albani who became Pope Clement Xi (1700—1721.)[6]

Professor Stavo Skendi in his, *The Albanian National Awakening, 1878—1912*, has discussed the crucial role of the cultural intelligentsia in this pan-Albanian movement. Among the possible causes of this movement were the increased consciousness of greater Italy among Italians during the period of Italian unification and the desire of Italian politicians to influence events in Albania. (Garibaldi's son, Riccotti, even proposed that an Italo-Albanian expeditionary force be sent to Albania.) Skendi notes that this movement evidently spread to some Italo-Albanians of the new world. However, certain Albanian politicians were not especially warm toward the Italo-Albanians for they considered them too Italianized.[7]

Skendi's work is in keeping with a theme discussed below in our section on images of the Italo-Albanians: a culturally tenacious people who have resisted Italianization. His stress on the role of the intelligentsia in organizing the political movement aligns him intellectually with those who believe a consciousness of cultural traditions is a necessary condition for political unity.[8]

Italo-Albanians formed a small portion of the economically motivated migration from Southern Italy and Sicily. The push and pull factors of this migration have been extensively discussed elsewhere and are beyond the scope of our paper.[9] Nonetheless, it behooves us to cite Father Fortescue's impression that the Albanian villages of Calabria appeared poorer than others in that province:

> Except perhaps at Lungro, all the Albanian Villages of Calabria give the impression of great poverty. All Calabria is a poor land; want of water, natural barrenness of the soil, and the economic difficulties of South Italy combine to make it so. But even in a poor district these Albanian villages stand out as poorer than any.[10]

Economic deprivation explains why many Italo-Albanian villages were reported as heavily depopulated due to emigration.[11]

Observers of Italian and other immigration patterns have noted the phenomenon called "chair migration", the tendency of people to settle in the same neighborhoods as their relatives, friends, and fellow villagers.[12] An example of an Italo-American community that is almost completely homogeneous by village of origin is Westbury, New York's migrants from Durazzano (near Naples,) recently studied by Professor Salvatore J. LaGumina.[13] Our supposition is that Italo-Albanians settled near other Italo-Albanians and quite possibly people from their own village.

Andrew J. Shipman (1857—1915), the leading American scholar of Eastern rite Catholicism of his generation, noted these locations of Italo-Albanians: Manhattan's Little Italy, the rest of New York City, Long Island (probably Inwood) and Elizabeth, Newark, and Jersey City, New Jersey.[14] To these can be added communities in Bayonne, New Jersey; Brooklyn (Bensonhurst), Oceanside and Utica, New York; Madison, Wisconsin; New Orleans, and Sacramento, California.[15] Somewhat surprisingly, few Italo-Albanians settled in Boston, the cultural and political center for Albanian-Americans.[16] This might indicate a feeling of affinity with Italians rather than Albanians.

A Greek (Byzantine) Catholic chapel for Italo-Albanians was founded in 1906 on Broome Street in New York's Little Italy. Ministered by Father (*Pappas*) Ciro Pinnola (1867—1946), a married priest who had migrated from near Palermo in 1904, the congregation moved to Stanton Street in 1906, its church being called, Our Lady of Grace. According to Shipman, writing in 1909 in *The Catholic Encyclopedia*, the flock numbered approximately 400.[17] Father Pinnola labored among his people for over forty years and also set up missions in Brooklyn and Long Island.[18] According to John DeMeis, editor of the *Newsletter of Our Lady of Grace Italian Byzantine Rite Catholic Society*, Pinnola received very little support from New York's Roman Catholic hierarchy.[19]

Neither have Italian-American scholars been kind to Italo-Albanian-Americans. An examination of the indices of some of the leading general histories (Lopreato, 1970; Iorizzo and Modello, 1980; Alba, 1985; Amfitheatrof, 1973; Rolle, 1980) and local area studies (Cumina, 1978 on San Francisco; Gabaccia, 1984 and Tricarico, 1984 on New York City; Nelli, 1970 on Chicago; and Nelli, 1970 on Chicago; and Schiro on Utica, 1940) and Tomasi (1975) indicate the virtual nonexistence of references to Italo-Albanian-Americans.[20] Put crudely, the "official" image of Italo-Albanian-Americans on the part of Italian-American intelligentsia is one of "no image" and presumably one of no importance.

Content Analysis of The Images of Italian Albanians

Andrew J. Shipman (1857—1915) was an American lawyer who defended Greek (Byzantine) Catholic interests during the trusteeship litigations with Orthodox Christians. Long a benefactor of Eastern rite churches, he wrote numerous articles about them for publications such as the Jesuit periodical, *America, The Catholic World*, and *McLure's Magazine.*[21] Most of these were compiled in a memorial anthology published in 1916.[22] Two essays dealing with Italo-Albanians are discussed below.

Shipman emphasizes two themes which we find recurring in the literature on Italo-Greek-Albanians and for that matter Eastern Catholics in general. The first is antiquity.

In mythology it is common to point to a godly or otherwise charismatic ancestor of one's tribe or an exhalted founder or one's way of life. For example, Armenian Christians claim that their ancestors were converted by St. Andrew and Ethiopian Christians claim St. James. It is not surprising that Shipman cites the missionary endeavors of St. Paul at Syracuse and Reggio, Calabria and points out that Greek was the language of the New Testament, the early disciples, and the Fathers of the Church.

In the context of the Albanian emigration following the Turkish invasion of their homeland Shipman presents some background information on the Albanian people. a language older than the Greek, customs pre-dating the Hellenic, Albanian claims to be the original inhabitants of the Greek peninsula, bear witness to the antiquity of the albanian people. A corollary theme is that the Albanians sustained their ancient practices despite Bulgarian, Greek, and Turkish pressures. Unlike other writers, Shipman does not feel the Greek rite would have necessarily died out in Italy had it not been for the albanian influx. Still, he points out that when he wrote his essay the Italo-Albanians were becoming Italianized.

The second theme is the Italo-Greek-Albanians as a bridge between Eastern and Western Christians. Shipman's Roman Catholic orientation is evident when he states:

> Thus, from the early stages of Christianity down to the time of the schism of the East and the West, the Italian-Greeks of the south of Italy looked towards Constantinople and its oriental rite.

> Greek was their language and their from of Christian worship, while the Latin rites and the Latin language were in a measure strange to them. Nothing concerning the faith was involved in this — they were Catholics and continued in the unity of the faith with the Roman Church — but it involved the external manifestation of that faith. They were, as I have said, and I use the expression

> advisedly today, all Catholics; for that word connotes at once universality and unity, and one cannot conceive logically of a Catholic separated from the centre of unity. At the same time, however, they were Greek Catholics and not Roman Catholics, inasmuch as they used the Greek and not the Roman liturgy and worship.[23]

While he lacks the condescension of other Latin rite authors who have written on Eastern rite Catholics, he does seem to be explaining to Western Catholics that the Italo-Greek-Albanians are truly Catholic.

Latinization is a common accusation which comes form the Orthodox opponents of Uniatism. While not directly confronting this issue, Shipman does argue that the Italo-Greek-Albanians kept their ancient usages much more steadfastly than the Romanian and Ruthenian Byzantine Catholics. Among the Eastern customs that were retained are the Greek-style vessels and vestments and the unshaven faces of the priests. In contrast, the Ruthenian priests of that era wore Roman cassocks and a hat that was neither Greek nor Roman and did not wear beards. Most significantly, the disputed clause *filioque* (and the Son) had not been inserted into the Nicene Creed among the Byzantines of Italy.

Still, the western Gregorian Calendar had been adopted and the priests did not chrismate (confirm) infants, a practice forbidded of Ruthenians in America shortly after Shipman wrote this article. He did not mention the dispute among the Italo-Greek-Albanians over leavened versus unleavened (*azyme*) communion bread nor Holy Communion for infants which is disputed in some Uniate groups. In the opinion of the present writers, Shipman exaggerated a bit the paucity of Latinizations. For example, statues rather than icons could be found in their churches and they had adopted certain Roman feasts.

Shipman's article contains some statistical information that cannot be found elsewhere. He not only estimates the number of Greek Catholics in Italy, but divides them ethnically into Albanians, 93,000; Greeks, 31,200; and Slavs, 30,000. These data, the historical material, and the descriptions of the Italo-Greek-Albanian religious customs make this article extremely informative.

Shipman's essay, "Greek Catholics in America," was written in 1909 and appeared in 1913 in *The Catholic Encyclopedia*.[24] It is mostly devoted to the Ruthenian Greek Catholics, but also contains a brief history and description of the customs of "Italian Greek Catholics."

Staunch supporter of the Eastern rites that he was, not surprisingly Mr. Shipman advocated an increase in the number of "Greek" rite priests in America. His essay was written a few years after the arrival of Father Ciro Pinnola in New York whose missionary activities in the area of that city are amply described. A pragmatic reason for supporting this rite was the influence of ideologies like Protestantism and socialism among these people.

A theme implied in Shipman's 1904 article which is made explicit in this essay is the prejudice and discrimination encountered by Greek Catholics in America. He points this out in the section on the Ruthenians and calls the Italian Greek Catholics ''neglected.''

Shipman gave an estimate of 20,000 Italian Greek Catholics living in America.

****

Greek Catholics in Italy were the subject of the essay ''Italo-Greeks'' by U(mberto) Benigni (1862—1924) in the *Catholic Encyclopedia*, (1913).[25] This article is mostly a factual account of the history and settlement patterns of the ''Italo-Greeks.'' A useful distinction is made between three different historic communities of Greek Catholics: 1) the vestigal communities of Byzantine Greeks; 2) Greek colonies of mainly Orthodox Greeks in maritime commercial centers such as Naples, Venice, and elsewhere; 3) the descendents of the Albanians (and some Greeks) who fled the Turks during the 1400's. There is also an exposition of some aspects of canon law and papal policy toward this rite.

****

However objective his treatment of the historical and sociological information, for Msgr. Benigni, the Latin rite is the norm — the standard against which other rites should be evaluated. Married priests of the Greeks were an obstacle to the attempt to eliminate married Latin priests during the reign of Pope Gregory VIII (1073—1085). According to Benigni, he and subsequent popes recognized the integrity of the rite. When he points out that a Greek rite wife may pass to the Latin rite, but not the reverse and that the children of mixed marriages belong to the Latin rite, he approves of these practices.

The following quote indicates his evaluation of the Latin as superior, ''The Holy See has always endeavored to respect the rite of the Italo-Greeks; on the other hand, it was only proper to maintain the position of the Latin rite.''

Adrian Fortescue (1874—1923), a distinguished English liturgist, published in 1923 by far the longest, most comprehensive study of the Italo-Greek-Albanians that has ever appeared before or since.[26] It is based upon meticulous scholarship, using sources in several ancient and modern languages and upon his observations during his travels to Calabria and Sicily. This opus gives credence to the statement in his biography in *The New Catholic Encyclopedia* that no one in England knew as much about Oriental liturgies. Fortescue's monograph, *The Uniate Eastern Churches*, is not only a magnificent *tour de force* on the Italo-Greek-Albanians, it is still the best reference work on this topic.

Within the descriptions of their churches, monasteries, and villages and amid explanations of canon law and history one central question weaves through the work: Is and will the integrity of this rite be maintained? As for the present (1923), and recent past, Fortescue found them far more Latinized than Shipman seemed to suggest in 1903. This is a major disagreement between these two authors which we do not think can be attributed to the passage of time. Fortescue did, however, have some cause for optimism about the future of this rite. In the following paragraphs the differences between Fortescue and Shipman will be noted as well as some of Fortescue's other observations.

Shipman, it will be recalled, found them much less Latinized than the Romanians and Ruthenians. For Fortescue, the basis for comparison is not another contemporary rite, but some pure Greek rite that existed in the past and may reemerge in the future.

The Latinizations which Fortescue reported are *azyme* (unleavened) bread, which he calls "a very grave matter (p. 181)," the Gregorian Calendar — "a small point (p.181)," Roman feasts (e.g., Sacred Heart, St. Joseph, and several others), Latin vestments, no Confirmation by priests, no *iconostases*, the presence of side-alters, Benediction of the Most Blessed Sacrament, shaven priests, and Roman cassocks. And, we mentioned above, a Latinization with monumental emotional, symbolic, and theological implications. Fortescue says the Italo-Greeks have added the *filioque* to the Nicene Creed. Shipman suggested they had not; in his words, "were allowed" to omit it and had "never altered" the Creed!

Fortescue noted that under Pope Leo XIII (1878—1903) a movement against these Latinizing tendencies began, fueled in part by a desire for union with the Orthodox churches. It started at Grottaferrata during the 1880's where "everything now is crupulously Byzantine (p. 182)." Fortescue, writing in 1923, reported this as spreading "through-out the Italo-Greek churches" and Parsons (1971, see below) found perhaps fewer Latinizations during the Post Vatican II era than either Shipman or Fortescue had found but nonetheless many were present.

To clarify the presence or absence of the *filioque* we suggest that Mr. Shipman was basing his statement upon what occurred at either Grottaferrata or at the Greek College in Rome where a purer Greek rite was practiced. In far award Calabria and Sicily where Rev. Fortescue traveled, the official efforts of the Popes to eliminate Latinizations had not penetrated into the folkways of the local priests and people.

****

"Manhattan's Eastern Catholics: The Italo-Greek-Albanians" by Gerard B. Donnelly, S.J. was one of a series of articles by him on Manhattan's Eastern rite communities appearing in the Jesuit magazine, *America*, early in 1936.[27] Father Donnelly's explanation of the differences between the Byzantine and Latin liturgies is accurate and thorough. Interestingly, he notes that the *filioque* is omitted from the Creed, that Communion for the faithful is under two species, and eight other differences.

After noting the estimate by another priest that several hundred thousand Italo-Greek-Albanians reside in America, he quotes the (unnamed) pastor of

Our Lady of Grace Church on Stanton Street who estimates 35,000 living in the New York Metropolitan area. However, regular parishioners numbered "less than 200."

Much of the article deals with the neighborhood and the physical characteristics of the church. Does it lack an *iconostasis* because of poverty or Latinization? He doesn't say.

Donnelly, like several previous and subsequent authors, feels compelled to stress that the Byzantine rite is truly Catholic and amusedly notes that the "papist baiting phrase, "Thine is the Kingdom' " is chanted at the end of the *Our Father*.

Donnelly's over-riding non-theological theme is the poverty of the church and its neighborhood. Extreme poverty in the Italo-Greek-Albanian villages of Calabria was described by both Fortesque and Lewis following their travels. According to Father Donnelly the poverty in new York creates a vicious circle because it deters people from attending services which in turn increases the poverty. Furthermore, Latin rite Catholics in the neighborhood are suspicious of Our Lady of Grace Church. There is a tinge of a perception of the Byzantine rite as exotic in this highly favorable article. Borrowing the phraseology of the popular song about the Bowery he say that the " strange liturgy and language" of the Byzantine rite are a good reason to visit the Bowery.

****

Donald Attwater (1892—1977) was certainly a most distinguished expert on Eastern Churches of his generation within the English-speaking world. Editor of several British periodicals and for a time contributing Editor for the American journal, *Commonweal*, he probably wrote more articles, books, and dictionaries on the Christian Orient than any other English language writer. This was mostly accomplished long before ecumenism was fashionable.[28]

Seven pages, regrettably, are all he devoted to the Italo-Albanians ("Italo-Grees") in his 232 page, *The Christian Churches of the East: Churches in Communion with Rome*.[29] Most unique about this chapter is his treatment of the tension between Latin rite prelates and the Italo-Albanian priests and people plus the various Latinisms which entered the rite of these people, e.g., Roman feasts, statues instead of icons, and devotions such as Benediction of the Most Blessed Sacrament. Mr. Attwater's book has much to recommend it as an authoritative introduction to the Eastern churches.

****

An Anglican scholar, Rev. Stephen C. Parsons, visited some parishes in the Greek Catholic diocese of Lungro, Calabria in 1969 and returned to this area in 1971 as well as to the Greek Catholic Diocese of Piani degli Albanese, Sicily. Reports on this visit appeared in *Eastern Churches Review*, a journal with an ecumenical editorial board published at Oxford.[30]

These reports address three issues that are virtually perennial in discussions of Italo-Greek-Albanians: the degree of Latinization, the Greek (Byzantine) rite as a mark of Italo-Albanian ethnic identity, and the Greek (Byzantine) as a bridge church. Parsons found many Latin rite borrowings such as holy water fonts, rosaries, "ostentatious tabernacles," and the absence of an iconostas in virtually all churches. Furthermore, the older clergy have little or no understanding of Byzantine theology. Among the younger clergy there is a renewal of interest in Byzantine theology and the study of Albanian culture and language.

The laity has not shared in the interest in things Albanian. Most comprehend the liturgy better in Italian and in two villages, Mezzoiuso and Palazzo Adriano in Sicily, no Albanian has been spoken for over a century. Here Greek and Latin rite churches co-exist. Parsons emphasizes the Greek (Byzantine) rite is a mark of Albanian identity, but hopes it will be more, something authentically Eastern Christian.

Parsons hopes "to see something appear which is neither predominately Eastern or Western, but which draws on the richness of both traditions." In the opinion of the present writiers, it is diffuclt to foresee this pleasing Orthodox critics of the concept of Eastern churches united with Rome.[31]

****

Professor Francis Dessart, Professor at the Institute des Hautes Etudes Economiques et Sociales in Brussels, emphasizes the attachment of Albanians in the diaspora to their homeland manifested in self-identity, language, and other forms of cultural maintenance and religious affiliation.[32] However, he says little about the Italo-Albanian-Americans except that their immigration was economically motivated and mostly permanent. Factors accounting for the conservation of Albanian culture are the Church because it is not at present dependent upon the Italian Latin rite hierarchy and uses Albanian in the Liturgy and the intelligentsia.

The intelligentsia (lay and religious) produced a cultural awakening in the nineteenth century in the form of a literarcy movement which became better known in Albania than in Italy. Profesor Dessart argues that the Italo-Albanian poets wrote in a purer (more Albanian) form of the ancestral language than that spoken by the peasants or upper class. At present, numerous publications in Albanian regularly appear prompting Dessart to term the cultural situation "not unfavorable."

Dessart stresses the cultural role of what Florian Znaniecki called the "men of letters."[33] Contrast the ethnic consciousness of the Italo-Albanian intelligentsia with that of other Greek (Byzantine) Catholic groups, the often magyarophile or russophile Carpatho-Rusyns and the often francophile Melkite Syrians! Comparative research might be done on these groups.

Paucity of space makes it difficult to summarize Dessart's carefully worked-out, conceptually clear, painstakingly documented, and informative article.

****

Pope John Paul II met with Italo-Albanian leaders in the cathedral church of Santa Maria della Ammiraglio (or della Martorana) in Palermo on November 21, 1982.[34] His message contained three themes that have been presented elsewhere: "constant attachment to the Chair of Peter," meaning at least while on Sicilian soil they were never Orthodox; a retention not only of the Greek (Byzantine) rite but also the Albanian language and customs; and the Greek (Byzantine) rite — the Holy Father said "Greek" — as a bridge between the Catholic West and the Orthodox East. Once again, then, we find the theme of a culturally tenacious ethnic group.

Five themes that recurred are: the Italo-Albanian Rite as a bridge between the Eastern and Western churches, Italo-Albanian religion as a boundary maintaining mechanism, pluralism within the Catholic Church, Latinization of the Italo-Albanian Rite, and the long-standing maintenance of Italo-Albanian culture. The latter two have implications for our conceptual scheme which is discussed immediately below.

The Future of Italian-Albanian Americans: Some Possible Scenarios

Around the time of the end of the mass migration of Southern Italians to the new world, there were some villages where Albanian was still spoken while the people had embraced the Latin rite, other villages had Italianized in language while retaining the Greek (Byzantine) rite, still others retain both their ancestral language and rite.

On the basis of this situation we are able to suggest four categories based upon language and religion. These characteristics may be used as indicators of the degree of retention of Italo-Albanian culture and are useful heuristic devices for the study of individuals and villages.

Our first "ideal type" will be called "Pure Albanian." He (or she) retains both the Albanians language and the Greek (Byzantin) rite. The second type, an individual who speaks Albanian, but does not attend a Greek (Byzantine) rite church, will be called "Albanian-speaking Latin Catholic." The third called, "Italianized Greek Catholic," speaks Italians but attends the Greek (Byzantine) liturgical celebrations. The fourth, called "Assimilated Albanian," speaks Italian and attends Latin rite services. The typology may be depicted as follows:

Religion

Language		Greek	Latin
	Albanian	Pure Albanian	Albanian-speaking Latin Catholic
	Italian	Italianized Greek Catholic	Assimilated Albanian

Of course, this typology does not present all concrete cases. The person in a mixed rite marriage who variously attends Mass in both rites, the former Albanian speaker who has migrated to a city such as Palermo and forgets his or her mother tongue, the villager who prefers the Greek (Byzantine) rite but attends Latin rite Mass because there is no Greek priest in the village; all these represent aberrations from our pure types. Nevertheless, these ideal types should prove extremely useful for studying past, present, and future trends in Italy and America.

Numerous ethnic groups have become extinct or nearly extinct. At present, the ways of life of such non-literate groups as the Ainu of Hokkaido Island, Japan and the Kung (Bushmen) of the Kalahari desert of southwestern Africa are eroding markedly. In America and Europe such small groups as the Cajuns and Creoles of Louisiana, the Germans of Texas, the Sorbs (Bends) of East Germany are dwindling and a Greek (Byzantine) rite group the Carpatho-Rusyns of Czechoslovakia, (analogous to the Italo-Albanians) are losing their identity and assimilating in both Europe and America.[35] Lest one think small size is a necessary condition for disappearance, not the assimilation of the once large "Scotch"-Irish-Americans.

What will be the fate of the Italo-Albanians in America? Are they already in what Professor Richard Alba calls the "twilight of ethnicity?"[36] To illuminate this question we have developed eight possible scenarios for the year 2000 A.D. which are presented in the paragraphs below.

Scenario One: "The Ideal Case"

A highly desirable scenario for preservation of Italo-Albanian-American culture in the year 2000 A.D. would be the presence of community institutions which function to support and perpetuate Italo-Albanian culture and provide opportunities for interaction with other Italo-Albanians. A Byzantine rite church would reinforce the link between the Italo-Albanian ethnic identity and this minority religion. Ethnic businesses, mutual aid societies, and nationalistic societies would fulfill analogous functions.

Religion's indispensible function should be stressed. In pluralistic America, the church became the most durable institution reminding one of the homeland and its way of life. As Oscar Handlin has so beautifully written, "A man holds dear what little is left. When much is lost, there is no risking the remainder."[37]

Italo-Albanian newspapers would be sold and distributed. Ideally, at least one paper would be religious and function to solidify the symbolic connection between religion and national identity. The press would also foster cultural transmission, language maintenance, and national identity. Language maintenance would not only be the provenance of the home, but foreign language schools whether government funded, molded on the parochial schools, or meeting after school hours or on Saturday will have been expressly designed for this purpose.

In such a neighborhood it would be possible for many individuals to spend the entire day interacting only with Italo-Albanians. This would be facilitated because apartments, houses, and tenements would be inhabited by immigrants (and their children) from the same village. Others would interact with outsiders only at work. Such a neighborhood would be institutionally complete — a sort of village with a city.[38]

In summary, Italo-Albanian language, religion, cuisine, and other cultural traits would be transmitted and strong feelings and perceptions of national identity would persist. Parring a large scale immigration from the Italo-Albanian villages of the *Mezzogiorno* this will not occur.[39] Most Italo-Albanians trace their descent to the economically motivated immigration of the turn of the century. If during those years they were (at best) only partly successful in founding and maintaining such neighborhoods, the cultural heterogeneity, impersonal relations, and physical mobility anticipated in 2000 A.D. will make the emergence of this favorable situation well nigh impossible.

Scenario Two

However important the religious and other community institutions are for promoting culture and identity, the emotional and practical significance of language should be emphasized. An Austrian writer, Karl Kraus, has called language the house in which the human spirit lives.[40] Some have argued that language is the *sine qua non* of nationalist movements.[41]

Our second scenario posits the absence of a church and other community institutions, but the presence of *language* and other forms of cultural maintenance in the home coupled with the presence of national consciousness. The absence of a church may not be as bad as it seems because the notion of a territorial parish is not crucial in the Byzantine rite; indeed, Father Ciro Pinnola ministered (theoretically) even to Italo-Albanians in New Jersey and Pennsylvania. Language (and dialect) would in such a situation become the chief symbols of ethnic identity. In fact Joshua Fishman indicates that for the second generation language retention is a major cause of ethnic self-identification.[42] This scenario would depend upon the retention of Italo-Albanian dialects in Italy and or America. There is some evidence that this is occurring among the elite in Calabria and Sicily, and among dialectologists in Italy and Albania. However, a premium is also placed upon a knowledge of Italian and our long term prognosis is not sanguine barring a large scale migration from Italy to the United States.

Scenario Three

Religious and other neighborhood ethnic institutions can function not only to transmit culture but also as a boundary maintaining mechanism to set the

Italo-Albanian-Americans apart from others. Few Irish immigrants spoke any language except English yet viable Irish neighborhocds persisted for decades.

The tiny Carpatho-Rusyn-American group has maintained a distinctive church organization, separate fraternal societies, and its own press even though its language is transititonal between Slovak and Ukranian.

The above scenario (the third) exists on a small scale at present. A handful of ethnically conscious Italo-Albanian-Americans in the New York metropolitan area attend Byzantine rite Catholic churches of other ethnic groups. However, the Italo-Albanians are the only Catholic Eastern rite group without a church organization of their own. If ethnic identity and culture are to be conserved it is imperative that one is established.

Scenario Four

It is logically possible for an ethnic group to have language maintenance, an ethnic church and other neighborhood institutions yet possess a confusion in the minds of individuals and disagreement among factions concerning ethnic identity. Analagous to the Italo-Albanians because of their Greek rite religion, the Carpatho-Rusyns of Czechoslovakia had a national church to which ninety-five percent of the people at least nominally belonged during the inter-war period but identified themselves variously as Rusyn, Russian, Slovak, Ukranian, and even Hungarian.[43]

Our fourth scenario would find a relatively homgenous Italo-Albanian language, one church organization but with several competing ethnic identities. One faction, called Albanian-American, might identify with the ancestral homeland, Albania, a second with Italy and call its members Italo-American (of the Greek rite); a third, a local or provincial orientation would consider itself Italo-Albanian-American. If we base a prognosis upon the assimilation process that has actually occurred since the mass migration from the *Mezzogiorno* which began around 1900, the second faction — the Italo-Americans of the Byzantine rite — appears more likely than the other two to be dominant. The actual fact is that most Italo-Albanians whose ancestors were Greek rite have become nominal or practicing Catholics of the Latin rite.

Scenario Five

During the 1970's at the peak of the so-called "ethnic revival" successful lobbying by Euro-ethnic leaders led the United States Bureau of Census to include a question on ethnic self-identification in the 1980 Census form. The question, called "Ancestry" was phrased, "Print ancestry with which this person identifies."[44] As a result, a projected 83 percent of all Americans identified themselves as members of an ancestry group with about 140,000,000 Americans reporting themselves to be members of such highly assimilated ethnic groups as English, Irish, and German.[45] Clearly, it is not only theoretically but also empirically possible to identify oneself as a member of an ethnic group yet neither speak nor understand the ancestral tongue nor live in an ethnic neighborhood.

Our fifth scenario then is ethnic self-identification as Italo-Albanian-American but without language maintenance and without an ethnic neighborhood. In 1980, 38,658 persons identified themselves as being at least partly of Albanian ancestry,[46] but how many of these are Italo-Albanians is impossible to determine. If a large scale immigration from Europe occurs before 2000 A.D., it will diminish the likelihood of scenario five. This is because significant numbers of immigrants would attempt to reproduce their old world way of life in America.

Scenario Six

The authors know of no past or present institutionally complete neighborhood in which *both* language maintenance and a national identity were absent. If one engages in wild speculation one could imagine, however, an Italo-Albanian neighborhood with ethnic businesses, a church, fraternal societies, etc. but with Italian (or English) as the spoken language and a confusion over or even a denial of ethnic identity. Like scenario one it necessitates a large scale migration from Europe.

Scenario Seven

"Ideal typically" this scenario consists of language maintenance without an ethnic neighborhood and with no ethnic consciousness. Similarly, some Carpatho-Rusyns have maintained their language in their homes and in its written from yet lack an identifiable neighborhood and are *confused* over ethnic identity.[47]

For the Italo-Albanians confusion seems unlikely. An Italo-Albanian-American *patois* might conceivably exist in 2000 A.D. without an ethnic neighborhood. Rather than a confused identity what is more likely is a *denial* of Italo-Albanian ancestry. On the other hand, were an Italo-Albanian ecclesiastical jurisdiction established, this could provide a favorable situation for foreign language schools which (as Joshua Fishman has found) function to increase ethnic awareness.[48]

Scenario Eight

Scenario eight would be the total (cultural, social, and marital) assimilation of this ethno-religious group.

Footnotes

1. Nicholas C. Pano, *The People's Republic of Albania* (Baltimore: Johns Hopkins P, 1968) 113—14
2. Michael Lacko, "Albania" *The New Catholic Encyclopedia*, 1967.
3. Donald Attwater, The Christian Churches of the East, Volume I: Churches in Communion With Rome (Milwaukee: Bruce, 1961) 66.
4. Adrain Fortescue, *The Uniate Eastern Churches: The Byzantine Rite in Italy, Sicily, Syria and Egypt*, ed. George D. Smith (New York: Benziger, 1923) 102. On the migration see, Attwater 66; Fortescue 115—24; and M. Petta, "Italo-Albanian Rite," *The New Catholic Encyclopedia*, 1967.
5. W. Lloyd Warner and Lee Srole, *The Social Systems of American Ethnic Groups* (New Haven: Yale UP, 1945) 157—58; Paul Robert Magocsi, *The Shaping of a National Identity: Subcarpathian Rus, 1848—1948* (Cambridge: harvard UP, 1978) 178—87.
6. For his biography see C. B. O'Keefe, "Clement XI, Pope," *The New Catholic Encyclopedia*, 1967. Neither the above biography nor the one in *The Catholic Encyclopedia*, 1913 ed. mention his Albanian descent. It is noted in Francis Dessart, "The Albanian Ethnic Groups in the World: A Historical and Cultural Essay on the Albanian Colonies in Italy," *East European Quarterly* 15 (1982): 475.
7. Stauro Skendi, *The Albanian National Awakening, 1878—1912* (Princeton: Princeton UP, 1967) 213—37.
8. For example Paul R. Magocsi, "The Role of Education in the Formation of a National Consciousness," *East European Quarterly* 7 (1973): 157—65.
9. Robert F. Foerester, *The Italian Emigration of Our Time* (Cambridge: Harvard UP, 1919) 47—126; Joseph Lopreato, *Peasants No More: Class and Change in an Undeveloped Society* (San Francisco: Chandler, 1967) 43—64.
10. Fortescue 163—64.
11. Norman Douglas, *Old Calabria* (London: Secker, 1923) 179.
12. John S. MacDonald and Leatrice MacDonald "Chain Migration, Ethnic Neighborhoods and Social Networks," *Millbank Memorial Fund Quarterly* 42 (1962): 82—97.
13. Salvatore J. LaGumina, "The History of Westbury's Italian-American Community," *Ethnicity in Suburbia: The Long Island Experience*, ed. Savatore J. LaGumina (Garden City, NY: Nassau Community College, 1980) 47—59.
14. Andrew J. Shipman, "Our Italian Greek Catholics" ed. Conde B. Pallen *A Memorial of Andrew J. Shipman: His Life and Writings* ed. Conde B. Pallen (New York: Encyclopedia Press, 1916(119. On Inwood see,

Salvatore J. LaGumina, *From Italy to Long Island: The Social History of an Ethnic People*, forthcoming.

15. John DeMeis, personal interview, 23 June 1985. On the New Orleans community see, Bret A. Clesi, "the Arbreshe and Contessa Entellina," *Liria* 1 March 1984: 4; 15 March 1984: 3; 15 April 1984: 12.

16. Federal Writers' Project, *The Albanian Struggle in the Old World and the New* (Boston: The Writer, 1939) 79—81; Dennis Lazar Nagi, "Ethnic Continuity As It Applies to a Less Visible National Group: The Albanian Community of Boston, Massachusetts," Ph.D. Diss., Rensselaer Polytechnic Institute, 1982, 59—72.

17. Andrew J. Shipman, "Greek Catholics in America," *The Catholic Encyclopedia* 1913.

18. Pinnola was originally from Mezzoiuso. For his obituary and a brief biography consult, *The Catholic News*, 30 January 1946.

19. John DeMeis, personal interview, 23 June 1985.

20. Joseph Lopreato, *Italian-Americans* (New York: Random, 1970); Luciano J. Iorizzo and Salvatore Mondello, *Italian-Americans*, (Boston: Twayne 1980): Richard D. Alba, Italian Americans: *Into the Twilight of Ethnicity* (Englewood Cliffs, NJ: Prentice 1985); Erik Amfitheatrof, *The Children of Columbus: An Informal History of the Italians in the New World* (Boston: Little, 1973); Andrew Rolle, *The Italian-Americans: Troubled Roots* (New York: Free 1980); Deanna Paoli Gumina, *The Italians of San Francisco, 1850—1930* (Staten Island, NY: Center for Migration Studies, 1978); Donna R. Gabaccia, *From Sicily to Elizabeth Street: Housing and Social Change Among Italian Immigrants*, 1880—1930 (Albany: State U of New York P. 1984); Donald Tricarico, *The Italians of Greenwich Village: The Social Structure and Transformation of an Ethnic Community* (Staten Island, NY: Center For Migration Studies of New York, 1984); Humbert S. Nelli, *Italians in Chicago, 1880—1930: A Study in Ethnic Mobility* (New York: Oxford UP, 1970); George Schiro, *Americans by Choice* (Utica, NY: Thomas J. Grifith, 1940).

21. For Shipman's biography see, J. D. Morrison, "Andrew Jackson Shipman," *The New Catholic Encyclopedia*, 1967.

22. See no. 14 above.

23. Shipman, *Memorial* 107.

24. See n. 17 above.

25. U. Benigni, "Italo-Greeks," *The Catholic Encyclopedia*, 1913.

26. See n. 4 above.

27. Gerard B. Donnelly, "Manhattan's Eastern Catholics," The Italo-Greek-Albanians," *America* (28 March 1936): 589—96.

28. For Attwater's biography consult, P. F. Mulhern, "Attwater, Donald," *The New Catholic Encyclopedia Supplement: Change in the Church*, 1979; also, *The Times* (London), 5 February 1977: 16.

29. Attwater 65—71.
30. Stephen C. Parsons, A Visit to the Greek Catholics of Calabria," *Eastern Churches Review* 3 (1970): 190—193; "Notes on a Further Visit to the Greek Catholics of Italy," *Eastern Churches Review* 3 (1971): 432—33.
31. Thomas Hopko, "Reflections on Uniatism," *Diakonia* 3 (1969): 300-11; Alexander Schmemann, "A Response," *The Documents of Vatican II*, ed. Walter M. Abbott (New York: America, 1966) 387—88.
32. Dessart 469—84.
33. Florian Znaniecki, *Modern nationalities: A Sociological Study* (Urbana: U of Illinois P, 1952) 25—29.
34. *L'Osservatore romano* (English Edition), 13 December 1982: 4.
35. Pavel Macu, "National Assimilation: The Case of the Rusyn-Ukrainians of Czechoslovakia," *East-Central Europe*, 2 (1975) 101—31.
36. Alba 159—75.
37. Oscar Handlin, *The Uprooted: The Epic Story of the Great Migrations That Made the American People* (Boston: Little, 1951) 117.
38. Raymond Breton, "Institutional Completeness of Ethnic Neighborhoods and Personal Relations of Immigrants", *American Journal of Sociology* 70 (1964): 193—205; on a similar theme see, William Foote Whyte, "Social Organization in the Slums," *American Sociological Review* 8 (1943): 34—39.
39. Despite sympathetic legislation, passed by the Congress, and sponsored by Italian-American leadership, allowing liberal immigration for victims of the November 1980 earthquake in Southern Italy, few Italians chose to immigrate to America.
40. Quoted by Peter L. Berger and Brigitte Berger, *Sociology: A Biographical Approach* (New York: Basic, 1972) 75.
41. Magosci, *Shaping of National Identity* 130.
42. Joshua Fishman, "Ethnic Community Mother Tongue Schools in the USA: Dynamics and Distributions," *International Migration Review* 50 (1980): 235—47.
43. Magosci, *Shaping of National Identity*, 105—129, 182.
44. US Dept. of Commerce, Bureau of the Census, *1980 Census of Population, Ancestry of the Population by State: 1980*, Supplementary Report, PC80-81-10 (Washington, D.C.: 1983) 9.
45. US Dept. of Commerce 112.
46. US Dept. of Commerce 112.
47. Paul Robert Magosci, "Carpatho-Rusyns," *Harvard Encyclopedia of American Ethnic Groups*, ed. Stephan Thernstrom (Cambridge: Harvard UP, 1980) 200—210.
48. Fishman, 235—47.

Chapter 7

LETTERS FROM SICILY AND THE RECONSTRUCTION OF AN IMMIGRANT PAST

Frank P. Vazzano
Walsh College

For many of us whose forebears were only recent immigrants to America the recognition of our ethnicity has been, at best, subliminal. We were, of course, aware of our distinctiveness but only coincidentally through special customs observed during holidays and from exotic dinner fare at other times. More recently, however, in the historical profession at least, we ethnics have become somewhat chic and, perhaps more important, profoundly curious about our European origins. That inquisitiveness has been augmented by a concern that ours is the last generation commonly to have either foreign-born parents or grandparents, those invaluable links to a time and place so different from our own.

Curiously, Mario Puzo's glamorization of Sicilian criminality in the United States evoked my initial adult interest in my Sicilian heritage. *The Godfather*, to me, was not so intriguing because of its ennoblement of a number of gangsters whose national heritage I accidentally shared. Rather, its allure emanated from its frequent descriptions of simple facets of Sicilian life. In one passage, for instance, Puzo described the gustatory delight in a breakfast of salami and fresh-baked Italian bread.[1] That description, mundane though it is, prompted a flood of personal recollections, for Puzo had recounted something intrinsic to my life for as long as I could remember. How many times as a child I had enjoyed a similar repast. After reading Puzo, I realized such a meal was not peculiar to one family but was likely indigenous to an entire island nation whose traditions I carried even to the kitchen table.

More significant in the recognition of my heritage were my grandfather's absorbing tales of the land he had left as a young man. They included accounts of the miraculous origins of the church in his native Gangi, Sicily; a happy story about the rare snowfall that occasioned a four-day celebration in his village; and the revelation of the macabre Sicilian custom of interring deceased parish priests, sans coffins, in church cellars. What interesting stories they were, but to an already incredulous young boy that is all they were, just stories.

Those accounts were, however, buttressed by other childhood experiences. As a small boy I often sat transfixed on my grandparents' porch while my Sicilian-born relatives and their compatriots spun out one rich story after another. Their dialect crackled through many a pleasant summer evening, but occasionally the voices lowered and wary eyes turned in my direction. The message, clearly understood, was that the conversation would now touch on those travails that forced a generation to leave its native land. Evidently relieved of their apprehensions by my tender years, the "old-timers" would discuss tragedies so nearly unspeakable that I knew never to ask about them. How compelling one of those stories was: the young man, estate steward to someone these transplanted Sicilians called *il Barone*, was brutally murdered, leaving behind a widow, four daughters and a young son. Although my relatives never made specific accusations, I knew the crime was the diabolical work of *la Mano Nera*, the Black Hand (the term Mafia was never used). In some fashion, although I cannot remember how, I correctly gathered that this steward to the *Barone* was my great-grandfather, my grandmother's father, faceless and almost nameless to me but certainly most painfully vivid to her.[2]

Inspired by Alex Haley's massive search for his roots, I was moved in the late 1970s to search for documentary evidence of my own origins. Some of it, fortunately for me, was as near as my grandfather's old trunk tucked unobtrusively into a corner of our attic. Its contents included sepia-toned photographs of scarcely identifiable kin, most of them males in poses and costumes so exaggerated that they appear more comic than heroic. Another find, an old army document, my grandfather's, disclosed my great-grandfather's name, Antonio, and that of his wife, Gaetana, *nee* Spitali. The tattered military record revealed that my grandfather could read and write, no small accomplishment in a Sicily that in the early twentieth century was just emerging, for all practical purposes, from the twelfth century.[3]

The trunk surrendered still another small but fascinating documentary treasure, a post card my grandfather sent form New York City to his wife who had remained in Gangi until he could afford her passage. His words, considering that they were transmitted from husbandd to wife, are stiffly formal, illustrative of a culture in which not even marriage eroded the immense deference to women that was expected of an honorable man: "Affectionate greetings from your spouse Vazzano Francesco. In New York on the 16th of January. En route to Chicago."[4]

Terse though it was, this card had special meaning to its recipient, my grandmother. Clearly, since it reposed in my grandparents' American effects, my grandmother not only saved it for some six or seven years in Gangi, she made certain that it crossed the Atlantic with whatever other meager belongings she and her three children could carry in steerage. How desperately she must have clung to this small keepsake, perhaps thinking by holding it close the conjugal link to her husban, interrupted by so much time and distance, would endure.

Nothing in my grandfather's trunk, exposed more about these immigrants' pasts than did a number of letters from relatives who remained in Gangi. The addressed envelopes, for instance, tracked the family's movements in America, while postmarks added a helpful chronology. My grandfather had often talked of his early experience in Chicago; those experiences now had a setting, 2721 Emeral Avenue, his first American address. I excitedly traced his subsequent moves. By February 1918, he was living in Lorain, Ohio; by May 1921, his wife and three children had joined him in Amherst, Ohio. From there, in 1922, it was back to Lorain, which became the family's permanent home.

The Sicilian letters also revealed how the immigrants had fired the imaginations of those at home with assurances of ready work and easy money. America was itself a panacea for life's ills, particularly the poverty that likely provoked the first family members to immigrate. Naturally the early immigrants could help pay for the passage of those eagerly anticipating a similar journey. The latter were not afraid to ask, either: "Above all else, we want help with finances, because you know how things are here for us . . . respond immediately [and] I can make my plans."[5]

Such importuning may not have been so crude as it appears. To the Gangitani their American kin seemed wealthy indeed. One letter, from a mother in Sicily to her daughter (my grandmother) in America, conveys an obvious enthusiasm for the daughter's most recent purchase, a clothes wringer to lighten her toil on laundry day.[6] The same writer was also taken by reports of the good food in America, a subject of great interest to her since she no longer had any teeth.[7] America promised a solution even to the dietary problems of the toothless.

But the link between the old life and the new, between America and Sicily, ran two ways. Promising though their new existence was, the immigrants clearly could not and chose not to forsake their pasts. Frequently their adherence to the old was demonstrated in the simplest ways: an urgent request for treasured tools left behind during a hurried departure;[8] the trans-Atlantic shipment of Sicilian-made headache powders, the only effective remedy for my grandmother's persistent affliction.[9] American curatives, for reasons likely more psychological than physical, simply did not work.[10] And, the exchange of hand-sewn linens and napery perpetuated memories of households far away.[11]

The Sicilian letters expose the strong emotional bonds between the immigrants and their family still in Gangi. Indeed, it is then that the missives are most eloquent. Their language is poignant, even powerful, growing all the more so as the writers realized that the separation, certainly vast, was also likely permanent.

Much of the evocative power of the letters stemmed from intensely personal experiences that in ordinary times would have been shared, for instance by husband and wife, but in the extraordinary circumstances of separation had to be endured alone. This was never better evidenced that in a letter from Giuseppina Vazzano, still in Sicily, to her husband, Francesco, in which she describes the birth of their second child, a daughter, the day before:

> My Dearest Husband, With the present letter I will let you know that thanks to God I gave birth to a beautiful baby girl, beauty that only God can give. Thankfully there was no difficulty, but you can't believe how I wanted you at that moment of birth.[12]

The new mother then compared her baby to the couple's first-born, a son about twenty months old: "She is beautiful but not as robust as Nino. She is too delicate." She continued with a description of age-old sibling rivalry: "The family and I burst out laughing because Nino didn't want to look at her and shook his fists."[13]

Impatient for acknowledgement of the happy news, Francesco Vazzano's brother Giuseppe sent a scolding letter to the Emerald Avenue address about five weeks later:

> I'm writing you this letter . . . because your wife and the whole family don't know what to think about your great silence . . . I'm not saying that you might be somewhat negligent, especially toward your wife, but your maximum silence makes me have such sad thoughts. Answer quickly.[14]

Giuseppe Vazzano's concern over his brother's failure to write was trifling compared to the poignancy of subsequent missives describing family sadnesses in Sicily. My grandmother's sister, Maria Carmel Blando, her sensibilities intensified by the still recent death of her husband and by wartime separations form other loved ones, was the family amanuensis one February day in Gangi. Describing the despair in the household, she wrote:

> Dearest Brother-in-Law, . . . in my heart and in everyone's heart anguish, desolation, discouragement reign. In our house this this year pain after pain have been accumulating, tear upon tear . . . Our brother [in military service], after a few days which flew by like the wind, has left again for whatever destiny has in store for him . . . How our house is now abandoned. Your letters do give solace, your warm and vibrant words fill our hearts with a little happiness and comfort.[15]

The letter writer was visited by the recipient's brothers that same day. The latter were obviously saddened by the separation from their brother. Maria Carmela Blando's words once again are eloquent to the point of pathos:

> Also your brothers are in great agony over you. This day they made us cry with their sentimental words about you. Your absence makes us sad . . . if you were with us we would be greatly comforted, and surely you would be a companion to our tears.[16]

The greatest poignancy was reserved, however, for the letters of Maria Santa Naselli, the aging mother who knew, after their departure for America, that she would never again see the faces of her children or those of her beloved grandchildren, Ninuccio, Peppinella, and Tanina. Her loneliness is haunting, her description of it almost spectral:

> Dearest Ninuccio of my heart, You can't believe how I long for you and your dear little sisters. I would love to hear those sweet words you used to say in my ear. When I go out I look left and right because I hear your voice but see no one.[17]

The writer worried that her two granddaughters had forgotten her and wondered if they still called for their "Mamuzza," their affectionate name for her.[18]

The marriage of Maria Santa Naselli's youngest daughter in 1926 deepened her longing for those in America. In October she lamented:

> Imagine how my heart is aching thinking that of so many children, I am now left alone. In eight days my dear Felice will no longer live at home, and I'll be alone without consolation. If I had you with me, Felice's departure wouldn't seem so brutal . . . But distance obstructs all our desires, for God has given us this crude destiny which divides us, one world from another.[19]

Twelve years later, still another letter to America, parts of which are nearly poetic, demonstrated that the passage of time failed to dull her sense of loss or weaken the familial bond: "Blood always needs to touch some of its own blood," she wrote.[20] No Sicilian needs an explanation of her meaning.

The extant correspondence ends with this 1938 piece. The family matriarch, Maria Santa Naselli, died on September 6, 1948, tended at the end by her daughter Anna who had returned to Gangi from New York City for what became the final visit with her mother.[21] Death took members of the American branch of the family, too, in succeeding years, but some remained to illumine and animate the Sicilian texts. Their memories are bright, their recall sharp. How much more the letters say because of their commentaries.

Still, my fragments detailing a few immigrant lives are, to most, trivial. But in combination with the bits and pieces that millions of us could amass they assume a monumental significance. I am left with a handful of letters, an army record, some faded photographs, a copy of a speech by some obscure minister in Mussolini's government, and a wealth of childhood recollections. These remnants of the past are not the stuff of some Sicilian charnel house; they are the things of which a substantial part of history is and remains to be made.

Footnotes

1. Mario Puzo, *The Godfather* (Greenwich, Conn.: Fawcett Publications, Inc., 1969), p. 100.
2. The details have been verified by one of the two surviving children. Interview with Anna Serio, nee Blando, Canton, Ohio, June 11, 1980.
3. Libretto Personale di Zazzano Francesco Paolo, distretto militare di Cefalu, 1911.
4. Francesco Vazzano to Giuseppina Vazzano, January 17, 1914, Author's Personal File.
5. Santo Blando to Giuseppina and Francesco Vazzano, December 4, 1922, Author's Personal File.
6. Maria Santa Naselli to Giuseppina Vazzano, May 15, 1921, Author's Personal File.
7. *Ibid.* This translation proved especially interesting. The letter writer used the word ganghe (literally, little rocks) instead of denti (teeth). A second translator, a native of Gangi, read the passage and immediately remembered that in the patois of the village ganghe meant teeth. Interview with Josephine Dargo, *nee* Vazzano, Lorain, Ohio, May 12, 1985.
8. Maria Santa Naselli to Giuseppina Vazzano, May 15, 1921, Author's Personal File.
9. Maria Santa Naselli to Giuseppina and Francesco Vazzano, December 4, 1922, Author's Personal File.
10. Interview with Josephine Dargo, Lorain, Ohio, May 12, 1985.
11. Maria Santa Naselli to Giuseppina and Francesco Vazzano, October 1926, Author's Personal File.
12. Giuseppina Blando Vazzano to Frencesco Vazzano, dated March 1, 1914 but postmarked February 28, 1914, Author's Personal File.
13. *Ibid.*
14. Giuseppe Vazzano to Francesco Vazzano, April 5, 1914, Author's Personal File.
15. Maria Carmela Blando to Francesco Vazzano, postmarked February 17, 1918, Author's Personal File; Interview with Josephine Dargo, Lorain, Ohio, April 6, 1985.

16. Maria Carmela Blando to Francesco Vazzano, postmarked February 17, 1918, Author's Personal File.
17. Maria Santa Naselli to "Ninuccio" Vazzano, May 15, 1921, Author's Personal File.
18. *Ibid*.
19. Maria Santa Naselli to Giuseppina and Francesco Vazzano, October [?] 1926, Author's Personal File.
20. Maria Santa Naselli to Giuseppina and Francesco Vazzano, June 7, 1938, Author's Personal File.
21. Interview with Anna Serio, New Hyde Park, New York, July 14, 1985.

Chapter **8** FILLIPPO MAZZEI'S VIRGINIA
PEASANTS
Glenn Weaver
Trinity College

Filippo Mazzei was certainly one of the most intriguing characters ever
to have lived in Virginia. Although his stay in the Old Dominion was a mere
five years, his influence was tremendous, and his presence was felt long after
he had returned to Europe.

Mazzei was born in 1730 at Poggio a Ciano, Italy, to a moderately
prosperous bourgeois family. After deciding against the priesthood as a
vocation, he studied medicine in Florence, practiced medicine in Myrna,
Turkey, and engaged in commerce in London, where he imported Tuscan wines
and foodstuffs and acted as an informal agent of Leopold I, Grand Duke of
Tuscany, with whom his friendship was on a first name basis.

In 1773, he came to Virginia, with the encouragement of Benjamin
Franklin, Thomas Jefferson, and several other wealthy Virginians. There he
started an experimental farm to introduce new vegetables to the colony and
established a vineyard and winery.

The Virginia Assembly made a generous grant of land, and to provide
financial backing for the farms which Mazzei named "Colle," Jeffereson and
Mazzei formed a "Company or Partnership for the Purpose of raising and
making Wine, Oil, agruminious Plants and Silk." Shares were sold at L50
sterling each, and among the 35 shareholders were Lord Dunmore, the Royal
Governor, with four shares, Thomas Adams, George Washington, and Thomas
Jefferson with one each, and Mazzei with four.[1]

The Grand Duke gave permission to recruit ten "peasants" to carry on
the farm work, and several were soon enlisted, although not all of them were
from Tuscany. Included in the group of men, who ranged in age from 18 to
40, were a Genoese farmer, two men from Lucca, one of whom was married
and had a small child, and a young tailor from Piedmont to take care of the
workmen's clothes and serve as Mazzei's house steward.[2]

Hardly had the final preparations to sail been made, when the "peasants" fell victim to a rumor that in America meteors fell with such frequency that it was unsafe to work in the fields. Several of the "peasants" refused to go on board, and Mazzei had to recruit others. One of these was Vincenzo Rossi, a twenty-year-old farmhand whom Mazzei designated as foreman. On September 2, 1773, however, Mazzei's somewhat reconstituted party sailed from Leghorn. On shipboard were Rossi, two farmers from Lucca, another from Genoa, and the tailor. Others sailed for Virginia later, arriving during the spring or summer of 1774.

We cannot be certain as to how many "peasants" were brought to Virginia by Filippo Mazzei, for the official Virginia records are silent so far as ship lists are concerned, and even Mazzei himself gave us little direct indication as to their number and even their names. Writing his memoirs at the age of eighty, Mazzei mentions his "peasants" in only the broadest of terms, with few references to individuals. In his memoirs, Mazzei referred to "six young Tuscans who had not yet (when he was setting up operations at Colle) arrived with my things."[3]

Our concern here is with both the whole company of peasants and with such individuals among them as can be safely identified. The story of the group (both Mazzei and the "peasants") is simply told. To be sure, the agriculture experiment and the workers involved attracted much attention, and Colle soon became something of a Virginia showplace. Planters from all sections of the colony visited the farm, where they admired the agricultural skills and diligence of the farmers, and where those Virginians who pretended to a smattering of the Italian language tried out their linguistic skills in conversations with the peasants.

Colle flourished for a while, and Mazzei's horticultural efforts resulted in the introduction of new strains of flowers, fruits, and vegetables, and, consequently, new elements in the American diet. Thomas Jefferson, Mazzei's neighbor was so impressed by Mazzei's skill and that of his co-workers that he proposed an expanded immigration from Italy.[4] Mazzei took up the idea and urged the "peasants" to write to friends in Italy urging them to come to Virginia.

Jefferson found the Italians to be diligent workers and model citizens of a republic. In fact, Jefferson was so pleased with his Italian neighbors that on August 30, 1778, he wrote to Richard Henry Lee, a Virginia representative in the Continental Congress:

> Emigrants (sic) . . . from the Meditteriane would be of much more value to our country in particular than from the more Northern countries. They bring with them a skill in agriculture and other arts better adapted to our climate. I believe that had our country been peopled thence we should now have been further advanced

in rearing (sic) the several things our country is capable of producing.

Jefferson then urged Lee to use his influence in the Congress to approach Mazzei in "procuring emigrants."[5]

But the whole operation at Colle collapsed in 1778, when the Continental Congress requisitioned the farm, with its modest dwelling, as a place of detention for Baron Riedesel, the German mercenary general who had been captured at the Battle of Saratoga. All but one of Mazzei's men chose to remain at Colle — temporarily at least — and the General tried, albeit without much success, to contine the operation of a working farm. In 1779, things at Colle went from bad to worse, when Governor Patrick Henry sent Mazzei on a diplomatic mission to the Grand Duchy of Tuscany. The diplomatic mission was a total failure, for Mazzei, despite his friendship with the Grand Duke, did not secure the loan which he had been sent to negotiate. Mazzei would not return to Virginia until 1783, and then only to see to the final disposition of his property and to collect monies due him from the Congress.

Furthermore, the four-year term of service under which the peasants had been engaged had expired in 1778, and although Mazzei would write later that he had left his men "all employed," they were actually left to fend for themselves. Jefferson became something of a patron of the Italian farmers, and for a while at least several of them lived at Monticello. Isaac Jefferson, one of Thomas Jefferson's slaves, was much intrigued with the Italians, and in a memoir dictated long after the events recounted, he described life at Monticello. There was, he said, "a tailor named Giovanni (who) . . . made clothes for Mr. Jefferson and his servants." There were also "Antoinine, . . . Francis, Madena and Belligrini, all gardiners." But what fascinated Isaac Jefferson most was his introduction to Italian cuisine. "The Italian people raised plenty of vegetables: cooked the most victuals of any people Isaac ever seen."[6]

But the Mazzei Italians did not remain at Monticello, for as Jefferson wrote in 1793, some of them had enlisted in the army, some took lands for themselves, and others found employment as gardeners by country gentlemen in the Virginia Piedmont. By that time, they were probably almost forgotten by Jefferson, then in Philadelphia as Secretary of State under the new Federal government. Jefferson's observations, however, were superficially correct, but the careers of several of the Mazzei Italians can be traced with greater precision. Also, the suggestion that some of the peasants worked for others may be offset by Mazzei's observation that, as of 1783, "So far as I could learn, there was not one person of the original group that went over (to Virginia) with me had not bought some property."[8]

Of the "Colle peasants," Vincenzo Rossi seems to have been Mazzei's favorite, perhaps because of his youth and energy,[9] and perhaps because he came from the same part of Tuscany as Mazzei. Rossi and Mazzei had a relationship unusual for eighteenth century Virginia employers and employees.

Mazzei had, almost from the time of his arrrival in Virginia, been a proponent of colonial independence, and in the event which in Virginia led up to the outbreak of the Revolution, Mazzei had been articulate in his support of revolt. After fighting had actually broken out with the Battles of Lexington and Concord in April, 1775, the rumor spread through Virginia that a British fleet was about to attack Hampton. Mazzei and Thomas Jefferson quickly joined an "Independent Company" of militia being raised in Albermarle County to march to Hampston's defense. Rossi, sensing that this was a time for high adventure, and, insisting to Mazzei that he be taken along and threatening to fight with a club if not given the use of Mazzei's extra gun, was enlisted as a private, the same rank as that of both Jefferson and Mazzei. The "company" was soon joined by Carlo Bellini, Mazzei's friend from Florence, who had just arrived in Virginia and who would later achieve fame as the first American professor modern language with an appointment to the College of William and Mary.

The volunteers marched bravely toward Hampton, soon to learn that no British attack was planned. Before the company was disbanded, however, it was assembled to hear a speech by Patrick Henry, who a year later would be elected governor of Virginia. As Mazzei later recalled the incident, Henry addressed himself particularly to the three Tuscans. Rossi, who understood hardly a word of English, found Mazzei an excellent simultaneous translator, and as Mazzei recounted the incident, "the eloquent expression on his (Rossi's) face indicated that at that moment he would not have swapped places with any great lord."[10]

Perhaps even before the Colle experiment had ended, rossi had both acquired a landholding of his own[11] and married. When Mazzei returned to Virginia in 1783, he found Rossi "living very comfortably with his wife and two small children. The older, who was six years of age, could read quite well, and the younger had just started going to school with his brother. Both were very well dressed."[12]

It would be pleasant to note that the Rossis lived happily ever after. Unfortunately, that cannot be said, for after 1783 they seem to disappear, as even their names do not appear in the decennial censuses beginning with 1790, nor does the name appear in land records or tax lists.

Although the Rossi's left no permanent mark in Virginia, such as certainly not the case with the family of Antonio Giannini, the senior member of the peasant group. Giannini, who came to Virginia with Mazzei's first contingent in 1773, was then twenty-six years of age, having been born at Fibbialla in the province of Lucca in 1747. Giannini was married to Marria Settima Modena of the same village, and at the time of arrival in Virginia, had one daughter, Catherine, then two years old. Family traiditon, one much doubted by by family genealogists, has it that the couple's second child (Nicholas) was born aboard ship.[13]

Giannini was a man of some education, as he wrote in a beutiful hand, and he soon became a sufficient master of the language to write in English as well as Italian. Giannini kept a regular correspondence with his father in Fibbialla and it is believed that he recruited by correspondence the Italians who came with the second group in 1774.

Even before Mazzei returned to Europe in 1779, Giannini had begun working for Thomas Jefferson at Monticello, as the two had, in October, 1778, entered into a contract whereby Giannini would undertake the care of the grape vines which had been planted at Jefferson's plantation. As Mazzei's plantation, Colle, was being divided, Giannini purchased a portion which he operated as a small farm.[14] In 1784, he acquired land on Buck Island Creek, some five miles southeast of Colle, and in 1792, he petitioned the Albermarle County authorities for permission to erect a mill on the property.[15]

There is some uncertainty as to whether Giannini ever operated a mill on Buck Island Creek, for as time went on, he became more and more involved with the goings on at Monticello and on his own small landholding nearby. When Jefferson went to Paris in 1785, as United States Minister to France, Giannini was placed in full charge of Jefferson's vineyards and orchards. Over the next few years, Giannini frequently sent American seeds for distribution to Jefferson's French friends, and Giannini was often sent French seeds and seedlings to be planted in the gardens at Monticello.[16] Indeed, it would seem that Giannini enjoyed this arrangement until his death some time after 1810.

Antonio and Maria Giannini had ten children — five sons and five daughters — all of whom married into the sturdy, Virginia, back-country yeomanry. Most of their children (and their immediate descendants) became small farmers, although one of his sons (Nicholas?) became a Baptist minister and changed the spelling of the name to "Gianniny"[17], one which has been retained by the "Nicholas Branch of the family. Although many members of the extensive clan remained in the Charlotteville area, one branch of the family located in Richmond when its members became involved in mercantile pursuits and dealings in real estate.[18]

Mari Giannini's brother, Francis Modena, was among the first arrivals of Mazzei's peasants in 1773. Although Thomas Jeffereson noted in 1799 that Modena had done "terribly well," probably meaning that he had acquired a landholding, we know little more about him other than that he worked at the carriage maker's trade and died in 1826. Descendants are still to be found in Fluvanna and Orange Counties, Virginia.[19]

Anthony Molina, apparently one of the younger members of the group, stayed on at Monticello for a while in Jefferson's employ. Jefferson noted that Molina was unhappy and wished to return to Italy.[20] Whether he ever returned to his homeland, or how he fared subsequently to Virginia, we do not know.

One Pelligrino (Christian name not known) also lived for a while at Monticello, spent some time in Philadelphia, and served briefly in the Continental Army.[21] It is assumed that the numerous Pelligrin family of West Virginia are descendants.[22]

The individual who presents the most difficulties in full identification is the Piedmontese tailor who came with the first contingent. Mazzei never identified him by name, simply referring, in his *Life and Wanderings*, to "my tailor." Isaac Jefferson noted that there was in Jefferson's employ "a tailor named Giovanni (who) . . . made clothes for Mr. Jefferson and his servants,"[23] and that certainly establishes his name, although it does not tell us whether this was his given name of his family name.

At any rate, "the tailor," or Giovanni, was a man of skill with his needle, and he attained considerable notoriety when he made Tuscan hunting jackets for Jefferson and his neighbors. The jacket, incidentally, became immensely popular with the Virginia Piedmont gentry. Mazzei was generous, and he allowed Giovanni to carry on his custom trade for "his sole profit."[24] Giovanni just missed an opportunity for even greater fame at the time the Albermarle Independent Company marched toward Hampton. Unfortunately, Mazzei, having permitted Rosi to accompany the expedition, felt obliged to leave the tailer in charge of his house, while Mazzei, Rossi, and Bellini enjoyed what seems to have been the time of their lives.[25]

In 1780, Giovanni accompanied Madame de Riedesel to New York. Jefferson reported at this time that Giovanni was then living at Monticello, "working for himself."[26] Also living at Monticello was Giovannini da Prato (or Del Prato) who entered the regular employ of Jefferson in January 1782. By that time, da Prato was married (whether to a Virginia woman is unknown, although certainly likely) and the couple were *both* parties to a verbal agreement with Jefferson.[27] In 1793, Jefferson gave da Prato 30 or 40 acres to work "on his own" at least three days a week. Jefferson noted at that time that da Prato was indeed "an excellent gardner and one of the most sober, industrious men I ever knew."[28] As late as 1812, da Prato was working for Jefferson on a day-to-day basis.[29]

The real success story among Mazzei's peasants was that of Giovanni Strobia. While most of the others of Mazzei's party were still in the Charlottesville area enjoying the hospitality and support of Thomas Jefferson at Monticello, Strobia was acquiring landholdings in widely-scattered parts of western Virginia.[30] Storbia soon set himself up as a merchant in Richmond, and his immediate success prompted Jefferson to write to Carlo Bellini in 1799 that "he (Strobia) got rich as a grocer in Richmond . . . (and) is in flourishing circumstances."[31] In fact, Strobia had indeed become a man of considerable consequence, serving for about two decades in the Virginia militia and rising to the rank of Captain. Mrs. Mary Strobia (presumably a Virginian by birth) was something of a feminist, as on April 13, 1793, she joined 37 other women in petitioning the governor of Virginia on behalf of one Angelica Barnet who was accused of murder.[32] Mary strobia died in 1795.[33] Strobia died in 1809, and the *Richmond Enquirer* carried the obituary: "Died on Friday evening last (March 19), after a long and painful indisposition, which he sustained with uncommon fortitude, John Strobia, in the 69th year of his age, and for 28 years a respectable inhabitant of this city . . . In his last moments he appeared perfectly willing to meet his Almighty Maker, and departed this transitory life without a single struggle!"[35]

Strobia's daughter, Catherin, married James Reat of Richmond, the ceremony being performed by the Reverend J. D. Blair, pastor of the leading Presbyterian congregation in the city.[35] One son, Francis Richmond (1787—1815), was first teller in the Bank of Virginia. Another son, John H. (1785—1856), married Ann Marie Lambert, daughter of Colonel D. Lambert, mayor of Richmond. John H. Strobia was employed by the city of Richmond as an "Inspector" or "Guager."[36] For most of his adult life, John H. Strober was a member of the famous elite militia company, the Richmond Light Infantry Blues, and upon his death in 1856, he was buried with full military honors by the Blues.[37]

Fillipo Mazzei's peasants provide us with an interesting case study of an ethnic group who found themselves in a part of the New World where immigrants from southern Europe were both rarities and minorities. Students of American immigration have always made much of the problems and difficulties encountered by such individuals and groups in the new social and cultural environment, but, in the case of Mazzei's peasants, none of the negative factors seems to have been present.

Each of the peasants seems to have been accepted for his own work, despite initial linguisitc barriers. Indeed, the foreign language of the farmers was evidently regarded as "quaint," and there is no record of any one of them being mentioned in any but the most complimentary fashion. And although these men were of peasant origin — and Mazzei never failed to emphasize this point — they seem to have been the very personification of the traditional middle-class virtues. Despite the fact that most of the group remained together for about two decades, they seem to have preserved little of their cultural heritage. There are, of course, those who would regard this as a case of rapid "Americanization," and this is not the time to argue whether or not this was totally desirable.

There was little intermarriage among the several Italian families, and that of Antonia and Maria Giannini, for example, had marriages with such Virginia yoeman families as Meeks, Pace, Haden, Hogg, Butler, and Tuggle.[38] Although most of the descendants preserved the original spelling, or reasonable variant thereof, of the family name, there is always the possibility, or probability, that there have been changes that obscure the Italian origins of descendants. It would be strange, for example, that the two sons of Vincenzo Rossi left no progeny.

Footnotes

1. Plan of Philip Mazzei's Agricultural Company, *The Papers of Thomas Jefferson*, Julian Boyd, *et. al.*, eds. (Princeton: University Press, 1950), I, 156—159.

2. The European aspects of the story can be followed in the two editions of Mazzei's memoirs: *Memoirs of the Life and Peregrinations of the Florentine, Philip Mazzei*, translated by Howard R. Marraro (New York: Columbia Univrsity Press, 1942), pp165ff., and *Philip Mazzei: My Life and Wanderings*, translated by S. Eugene Scalia and edited by Margherita Marchione (Morristown, NJ: American Institute of Italian Studies, 1980), pp196ff. The present writer has given a brief summary in "The Italian Presence in Colonial Virginia," in press with the Center for Migration Studies.

3. P. Pazzei, *Life*, p. 309.

4. Antohy F. LoGotto, *The Italians in America: 1496—1792*, (Dobbs Ferry, NM: Oceana Publications, 1972), p. 39.

5. Thomas Jefferson to Richard Henry Lee, August 30, 1778, *Virginia Magazine of History and Biography*, VIII (July, 1900), 115—116.

6. "Life of Isaac Jefferson of Petersburg, Virginia, Blacksmith, Containing a full and faithful Account of Monticello and the Family there . . . ," Slave memoir of Isaac Jefferson dictated to Charles Campbell in the 1840's, *William and Mary Quarterly*, 3rd series, VIII (October, 1951), 569, 573, 381.

7. Thomas Jefferson to Albert Gallatin, June 25, 1793, in *The Writings of Thomas Jefferson*, Andrew A. Lipscomb, editor-in-chief, 20 volumes (Washington: The Thomas Jefferson Memorial Association, 1903), I, ix.

8. P. Mazzei, *Memoirs*, p. 187.

9. In 1775 he was about 22 years of age and probably the youngest of Mazzei's workmen.

10. P. Mazzei, *Life*, pp. 216—217.

11. It is possible that Rossi was "on his own" without having spent time at Monticello. At least, he was not one of those remembered by Isaac Jefferson. See above.

12. P. Mazzei, *Memoirs*, p. 187.

13. The present writer is much indebted to Professor Omar Allan Giannini of the University of Virginia for most of the personal details of the Giannini family. Unless otherwise indicated, the information for this section of this study has been supplied by Professor Gianniny, a direct descendant through Nicholas, who probably born in Virginia in 1774.

14. Mazzei, *Memoirs*, p. 187.

15. Edgar Wood, *Albermarle County in Virginia*, (Charlottevill, VA: The Mickie Company, 1901), p. 360; Giovanni Schiavo, *Four Centuries of Italian American History*, (4th ed., New York: Vigo Press, 1957), p. 308.

16. Thomas Jefferson to A. Giannini, February 6, 1786, Jefferson Papers, Library of Congress; Antony Giannini to Thomas Jefferson, January 23, 1792, Jefferson Papers, Library of Congress.
17. Edgar Wood, *Albermarle County in Virginia* (Charlottesville, VA: The Mickie Company, 1901), p. 360.
18. See the various issues of the *Richmond Directory* for the mid-nineteenth century. The *Directories* for the period, incidentally, list an amazingly large number of Italian names, none of which can be traced to a pre-Revolutionary origin in the state. See also the Land Office Index in the Virginia State Library, Richmond.
19. Giovanni Schiavo, *Four Centuries of Italian-American History*, 4th edition, (New York: Vigo Press, 1957), p. 308; G. Wood, *Albermarle County*, p. 361; Land Office Index, Virginia State Library, Richmond.
20. Thomas Jefferson to Philip Mazzei, April 4, 1780, *Papers of Thomas Jefferson*, Boyd, ed., III, 342.
21. *Ibid.*; A.F. Guidi, "Washington and the Italians," in Richard C. Gorlick, Jr., Ed., *Italy and the Italians in Washington's Time*, (New York: Italian Publishers, 1933), p. 34.
22. Conversation with Rose Illick and Janet Salati, November 18, 1984.
23. See above.
24. P. Mazzei, *My Life and Wanderings*, p. 204.
25. *Ibid.*, p. 216.
26. Thomas Jefferson to Philip Mazzei, April 4, 1780, *Papers of Thomas Jefferson*, Boyd, ed., III, 342.
27. *Thomas Jefferson's Farm Book*, Edwin Morris Butts, ed., (Princeton: Princeton University Press, 1953), p. 159.
28. *Thomas Jefferson's Garden Book*, 203—204.
29. *Ibid.*, p. 493.
30. E.g.: 500 acres in Harrison County in 1788, and 1000 acres in Kanawha County in 1796. Land Office Index, Virginia State Library.
31. Quoted in G. Schiavo, *Four Centuries*, p. 308.
32. *Calendar of Viginia State Papers*, VI, 345.
33. *Marriages and Deaths from Richmond, Virginia, Newspapers, 1780—1820*, (Richmond: The Virginia Genalogical Society, 1983), p. 148.
34. *The (Richmond) Enquirer*, March 17, 1809.
35. *Marriages and Deaths from Richmond*, p. 148.
36. *Richmond Directory and Business Advertiser for 1850—1851*, p.
37. *Richmond Directory and Almanac for the year 1869*, p. 18.
38. Manuscript genealogy compiled by Omer Allan Gianniny, Jr., original in possession of the compiler, photocopy in possession of the author.

Chapter 9

SARDINIAN IMMIGRATION TO THE AMERICAS SINCE 1900 PROJECTED INTO THE YEAR 2000

Lina Unali
University of Rome
Franco Mulas
University of Sassari

In order to project Sardinian migration into the magic-mythical year 2000, it is useful to return to the beginning of the century when the Sardinian passage to America began.

At the end of the last century, Sardinian immigration was primarily directed toward South America, in particular Argentina and Brazil. In 1882, 36 families from Villacidro, a village in Southern Sardinia, embarked for South America to work in the plantations and in the construction of railways. This was the earliest recorded immigration. The study of the whole phenomena of Sardinian immigration is at an initial phase; moreover, we lack information except for the research we have been able to conduct ourselves.

From the first decade of this century onwards, the migratory movement, both toward the United States and South America has been constant, though occurring in different proportions and governed by a variety of rules. Since those early years North and South America are popularly distinguished as rich America, poor America. The capital of the first was often called *Nova Jolk*, while the capital of the second was called *Bonas Arias*. Migrating to one or the other often depended not only on immigration laws, but also on the immigrant's personal ability to sign his own name.

We can calculate that if the immigrants to the United States were about 3000—3500, including a high percentage of Calofortines, from the neighboring island of San Pietro (about 450), those migrating to South America may have been approximately 15,000.[1] This is still quite a limited number if compared with the multitude of European immigrants from all nations settling in South America before 1930, calculated at about 3,000,000.

The immigration to North and South America from the years 1900 to 1930 may be studied under a first formalizing set of antithetical patterns: industrial North America, agricultural South America. The words that are able to distinguish the different kinds of migration to North and South America at the beginning of the century were *agriculture* related to the South, particular to Argentina, and *industry* to the North, in particular to the United States. In Argentina even the people working in the few industries operating in the country at the time had the tendency to remember Argentina exclusively as an agricultural country. Although Sardinians were unskilled labourers, with a very low degree of specialization in any manual art or technique, the two words *agriculture* and *industry* serve not only to identify the kind of Sardinian occupation in the New World, but also their psychological and mental reaction to the different American milieus.

During our interviews, few Sardinians revealed the presence in their minds of images of the United States as an agricultural country with a vast and magnificent landscape. Instead, they approached the United States and afterwards remembered it in its urban aspects as an uninterrupted series of the city skylines and asphalt pavements. We have realized that in Argentina, on the contrary, even people who were engaged in industrial enterprises of various kinds remembered the country as mostly made of extended and beautiful fields, the dream of the shepherd, the planter and the farmer. The fertility and amplitude of the plains of the United States, the marvellous extention of its woods and ponds were psychologically neglected and fotgotten. America was not that. ''Yes, there was also countryside,'' were the words pronounced almost with anger by someone we had pressed for a declaration on the subject of the rural element of the United States.

An immigrant from Ovodda, Pietro Loddo, now 105 years old, described the Argentine land in the following manner: ''The countryside was better than here (in Sardinia). Over there Jesus Christ was born, the devil was born here, all stone. All is country there, without stone. I have never seen heaps of stone as there are here, not even one.'' Contrasted with Argentina, Sardinia appeared as a new version of Eliot's Waste Land where there is only stone and no water.

Much that can be said about the 1900—1930 immigration that might even be called *deep*, but also *granitic* immigration, so confined it was and definite in its contours, is connected with these two fundamental patterns. The Sardinians, for instance, normally shared the idea that the people from Argentina had no real wish or patience to to cultivate their fields, while in the United States they were under the constant impression that its inhabitants were fully absorbed in highly respectful and rewarding activities. Argentina was seen as almost feudal country in the hands of a group of enormously wealthy landlords, often described as running wildly on horseback, while in the United States the manager of industry (or *bosso*) led a life that, at least from the point of view of the hours of application and routine, was as intense as that of the humblest worker employed in the firm.

There was one difference between the mighration to North and South America that had little to do with that between agricultural and an industrial country arid was instead related to Sardinian history. Spanish was accessible to Sardinians not only in so far as Sardinian is like Spanish and Italian, but also because the immigrant could, to his great surprise, recognize in the sequence of words, traits that were much more similar to his own language than even to Italian. We refer to terms of very common use such as *apusentus* (rooms), *ventanas* (windows), *burro* (donkey), *triqu* (wheat), *mesa* (table). Some grammar characteristics, too, such as the *s* suffix for the plural, allow the Sardinian to use the Spanish words with confidence. It must have appeared almost a miracle to the immigrant. In reality Aragonese and Spanish dominations in the island lasting over several centuries made easy what might otherwise have been difficult communication between foreigners. Argentina was never really felt as a foreign country by the Sardinians. Also intermarriage began to occur soon after immigration.

Some immigrants to the United States studied English in evening classes, but very often English was substituted, especially in the first years by the language of gestures, synthetically presented by a returned immigrant from Bultei with the following words: "In the Ford Factory, when I have gone over there, what is your name they asked, then they continued using the words *this way* and *that*, all with gestures: this you carry here and this over there, and from there you take it here, they taught me how to do everything with gestures, amid all the noise that was in the factory."[2]

While the similarity between Sardinian and Spanish made easy the acquisition of terminology connected with the new type of life and occupation, in the United States many American words had to be given Italian form and sound in order to be used as a means of communication. Thus, for instance, the radiator of a car became known as *stima*, that vaguely resembles the English word *steamer*, but had nothing to do with the Italian word meaning esteem and estimation. The immigrants who acquired a fairly good knowledge of English were a very limited number. Among them Francesco Rombi, from Carloforte, whom we interviewed two years ago, was still fluent in English even after returning to Italy a number of years ago.

Immigration to Argentina was much easier than it was to the United States. The antithesis between Argentina *terra facile*, easy, accessible land and the United States *terra difficile*, difficult land, (a country requiring on the part of the foreigner a far more complex individual adjustment), must be further complicated by another model (or at least hypothesis of it), that partly modifies the preceeding one.

From interviews such as that of Pietro Loddo, Argentina seemed at times to suggest images of a feudal kind. "All day was a continuous giving," Pietro Loddo remembered referring to the way foreign manpower was exploited. Argentina often appeared as a land disproportionately divided between the wealthy who never engaged themselves in such a mean past time as work and of very poor people drinking mate all day long making no physical effort even to maintain themselves at the level of subsistence.

Working in the United States is instead not only presented a perfectly suited to everyone's capacity, rationally organized, well distributed during the day, but the whole of the nation is remembered as inflaming the immigrant with democratic and libertarian ideology. The mention of the great American liberty is in the mouths of every immigrant to the United States before 1930. The already mentioned Pietro Loddo, after mistaking the Statue of Liberty with that of Christopher Columbus has said: "There was written liberty for all." The concepts expressed by the word liberty remain one of the interpretive patterns of America and sometimes also a justification of the choice to remain there.

At this point we quote one of the few written documents that are available. In a letter of 1961, Domenico Arru, born at Pozzomaggiore in 1903 (he died in 1966) and immigrated in 1921, has written: "if, as I hope, you will take roots in very hospitable America, I assure you that as soon as I shall be free from what has become by now an oppressive work, through your kind invitation, I shall also satisfy my very old wish, that of experiencing again true liberty."[3]

Then came the Depression and immigrants to the North and South Americas greatly suffered from the consequences of it. During our interviews with them they most often showed the tendency, amid the expression unbearable suffering and discomfort, to simplify the causes of the catastrophe always ascribing everything that had happened in those years to the charismatic or evil personality of the Presidents who had exercised their authority in the United States and Argentina. Thus Irigoyen is described as the Saviour of Argentina, the man who took the right decision in order to protect the country, Hoover was seen as the cause of all evil and sorrow, succeeded by Roosevelt, the President who acted in favour of the workers and provided America with new prosperity.

Then the war came. When World War II broke out Italy was allied with America's enemies. Italians in general and Sardinians in particular, who had not hesitated to board the ships to return to Italy in World War I, in order to defend the sacred soil of their country, now found themselves torn between the allegiance to their own motherland and the adoptive one. Some returned for good, some in very strange circumstances. One Salvatore Carta, born at San Vero Mills in 1894, now living at Zeddiani, remembered that he had the duty to prepare the landing of American troops at Alghero, *di mettere il bastone fra le ruote,* to put a spoke in the enemy's wheel. According to his own narrative he was plunged into the water in the company of another Sardinian soldier by the name of Camboni. He said: "they put us in the water in the wrong place. The sea was rough and we reached the shore instead than at Alghero near Cuglieri, further South. The countryside was swarming with fascists and Germans who captured us and made us prisoners." Other returned immigrants also reported that they had to carry out similar tasks and they, too, were made prisoners without being able to accomplish the assignments.

The economic crisis and the war marked the end of definite patterns of behaviour on the part of Sardinian immigrants to America. The Immigration of the first three decades of the century with its well defined contours and its limited scope was transformed into a fluctuating phenomenon characterized by an extreme mobility and flexibility. Before the thirties, immigration had been an event of a most homogenous kind: people went to America because they were poor and they were all so in the same way. They were supposed to work hard in the country of destination in order to save money for the need of families that were waiting for a prompt return home. There were very few deviations from this pattern. Although many immigrants greatly appreciated their life in America, Sardinia remained for them the main centre of preoccupation and desire.

The war altered accepted patterns of behaviour. Those who remained in America, both in the United Sates and Argentina, often succeeded with many efforts to reach higher positions in their soical milieu. Often they were even able to move from the section of the town where they had first established themselves, with their brothers and *compaesani*, to nicer surroundings. Generations began to juxtapose one to the other. Often the children of the first immigrants were able to go to college, and become professional men, expert lawyers, doctors and engineers. Many acquired wealth, through commercial activities of various kinds. They acquired also new pride and perhaps, for the first time, the conscience of belonging to the American continent. At a mental level they began to move between the two lands, one of which was no more a land of exile, a land that could be reached only after one month of painful navigation.

Those who returned to Sardinia underwent another type of change due to the development of Sardinian economy from agricultural to industrial, influenced by the global economic conditions of Italy. The industrial revolution that had reached Sardinia at so late a date greatly affected Sardinian post-war generations. It engendered a new conception of the importance and prestige of work. Much immigration was directed towards the North of Italy and Northern European countries, mainly Germany. Those who went to America could do so thanks to the invitation of their relatives who, in the meantime, had greatly improved both their economic and social conditions and were far from being the most miserable of the most miserable. They soon adjusted to the new ways of life. They also began to move from country to country, from Italy to America and *vice versa*. Either their house in Sardinia or the one they owned in America began to be seen as a *second house*, according to the terminology of the Italian taxation system. This feature, we foresee, will be prevalent in the year 2000. People come and go, have interests and property of many kinds everywhere. The distinction between industrial and agricultural employments is no more so well defined. People may have both or neither. They may leave Sardinia or return to it just in order to study informatics or to enroll in the School of Medicine.

We may record the year 1976 as another very important date in the history of Sardinian immigration: in the United States a crucial emphasis was from then onwards put on ethnicity. If at college in the sixties one asked a student with an obviously clear Italian name: "Are you Italian?", it might sound offensive. A new attitude prevailed in the seventies taking pride of origins, exalting the ecological niches outside of America from where the immigrants had come. It was the time of the Centennial with its reevaluation of the components of American civilization.

The Italian Americans of the 2nd generation had been ashamed of being met by Italians coming from Italy because none of them could speak English. Giovanni Cassitta, born at Sant'Antonio (on April 29, 1904) who immigrated with his family in 1958 and still lives in the United States said during the interview: "In the past it was like that. Now when an Italian comes we try to help him; for the immigrants of my generation, it has been very difficult."

But while the value of ethnicity had reached its climax, strangely enough the Sardinian island with its chains of affections and faithfulness began to lose its primacy in the mind of the immigrant. The connection and sense of belonging became looser. The children of, "parents born here from parents the same," as Whitman put it,[3] got a deeper cognizance of their origins but remained where chance had sent them to. The cult of ethnicity became also the equivalent of a deeper psychological stability, of a greater enjoyment at the opportunities offered by the American continent.

The same happened in Argentina, although perhaps at a less conscious level and less for purely ideological reasons. People felt more at ease both with their sense of belonging to the island where they were born and to the new country. Argentina conferred a second nature to the immigrant. Thus ethnicity really meant also to them a more extended and profound Americanism. What will the end of the process be?

A Sardinian lady from Ozieri, Giovann Pirastru, whom the family took to live in Niagara Falls in 1924, at the age of five, said during our interview: "I love Sardinia very much and I love also the United States. But if I were to choose, I would choose the United States."

Mr. John Peter Manca, born at Sassari in 1947 said: "This is my new American name. I have lived in Sassari until the age of 18, but then I decided to go away. All of a sudden I felt the limitations of island, although I liked it very much. I wanted to see what was there beyond it, on the other side of the world. I always asked questions about what could be found over the ocean."

On the theme of the projection of Sardinian immigration into the year 2000, we like also to quote from an interview with Antonio Cuccuru, 77 years old, a resident of Argentina since 1957, who at the question, "Will your son's daughter, now four years old, be Argentine or Sardinian?'' answered: ''It will depend on destiny.'' We might conclude that in the future the propensity to stay in one land or in another will depend on the lines of one's hands.

Lately some measures have been taken by Sardinian politicians operating within the government of the Regione Sarda to stimulate and support investments of the immigrants returning to Sardinia. In the plans (and minds) of the legislators these measures should convince the immigrants of the necessity of returning to their island and operate as an active force within it. To what extent these measures may succeed, we cannot say. The ground is too shifting and mutable, too divided by heterogeneous segments, often hidden from view. But we appreciate that the Region has undertaken the task of taking good care of the destiny of Sardinians living beyond the separating walls of the sea.

Footnotes

1. These data obtained from observations based on field work are on the whole confirmed by the elaboration of figures offered by the *Annuario Statistico dell-emigrazione italiana dal 1876 al 1925* (Commissariato per l'emigrazione, Roma 1926) on part of authors such as M.Le Lannou, *Patres et Paysans del le Sardaigne*, Tours, Arrault at C.ie, 1941. The census of the Sardinian population for the years 1901 was 791.754; for 1911 was 852.407; for 1921 was 866.681; for 1931 was 973.125.
2. From an interview with Virdis Francesco, born at Bultei on January 8, 1897, immigrated to the United States in 1923.
3. Letter written at Oristano on November 1, 1961, received by Lina Unali while she was at the University of Washington, at Seattle, Washington.
4. Cfr. W. Whitman, *Leaves of Grass*, 'Song of Myself' Sec. 1. on the whole confirmed

Chapter **10**   **BLESSED ARE THE MEEK . . . RELIGION AND SOCIALISM IN ITALIAN AMERICAN HISTORY**
Anthony Mansueto

The relationship of religion to politics, and especially to mass social movements, has become a topic of increasing concern in recent years. This has been especially true with regard to the nations of the Third World, where the expectations of many Communists to the contrary, the religious communities have put themselves in the forefront of the struggle for national liberation and socialism (Berryman). But for us in the United States as well, the relationship between religion and politics has been very much on the agenda. The Republican program of militarism and social austerity finds its principal base of mass support in a rightist social movement of evangelical Protestant inspiration (Davis), while the most credible opposition to this movement has come from political forces rooted in the Black Church, which have formed the core of the "Rainbow Coalition."

Our own Italian American community, and the larger Catholic popular sectors of which it forms an integral part, have stood in an ambiguous relationship to these developments. On the one hand, fully 57% of the Italian American community, and 55% of Catholics generally, supported the Republican Party in the 1984 general elections — somewhat less than the 73% of white Protestant electors who voted Republican, but still a substantial majority (New York Times, 8 November 1984). At the same time, the Italian Catholic governor of New York, Mario Cuomo, has played a critical role in resisting the "right turn" in the Democratic Party, and seems to be creating a new political discourse, deeply rooted in the Christian, and specifically Italian popular Christian tradition, which may play a critical role in ideological resistence to the rightist offensive (New York Time, 17 July 1984). The Catholic hierarchy itself, with its recent and pending pastoral letters (National Conference of Catholic Bishops) has set itself squarely within the ranks of the popular sectors.

Clearly an understanding of the political valence of the Christian tradition is of critical importance if we are to properly assess the situation of the Italian American community in the political life of the nation.

Most studies of Catholic political belief and practice have, unfortunately, focused on doctrinal and institutional questions, or when they have attempted to analyze the religious and political sentiments of the Catholic masses, have had recourse to the methods of survey research (Greeley). Rarely have such studies looked deeply into the role of popular religion in the formation of political consciousness. Because of this a long history of popular struggles deeply bound up with the Christian faith, a history which includes a rich socialist tradition, has remained buried, and important factors shaping the present situation of both the popular democratic and the traditionalist sectors of the Church have been obscured. This essay summarizes the findings of a longer study of Italian immigrant socialism in the United States (Mansueto). It outlines the roots of that movement in the peasant struggles and popular Christian traditions of post-Risorgimento Sicily and the Mezzogiorno, its growth and development during the first quarter of the twentieth century, and its decline in the face of changing economic conditions and the assimilation of second generation Italian Americans to the dominant ethos of North American capitalism during the post-war years. The essay argues that despite the apparent disintegration of the old, popular Christian socialist tradition, important elements of the old culture remain which, with proper leadership, may become once again the basis for a new culture of resistance in North America.

This study is based on oral testimony collected as part of the Italians in Chicago Project during the years 1979—1980, as well as on a small number of informal interviews I conducted independently in the Autumn of 1980 in the towns of Grotte and Piana degli Albanesi, in Sicily, and on testimony gathered from the popular socialist press, particularly *Parola del Popolo*, and a range of popular devotional literature current in the Italian American community. It also draws on a wide range of secondary sources and theoretical works which are discussed more fully in the introduction to the full study (Mansueto).

I

It is impossible to understand correctly either the phenomenon of Italian immigration itself, or the popular movements which grew up in the immigrant communities, apart from the tremendous changes which took place in the countrysides of Sicily and the Mezzogiorno during the years which followed "unification" in 1860. It has been customary among liberal and even some Marxist scholars to regard this process of unification, and the larger Risorgimento which accompanied it, as a great leap forward for the Italian people. This revolution, it is argued, freed Italy from the feudal fetters which blocked formation of a national market, and made possible the economic progress which eventually pushed Italy into the front ranks of the industrial powers. Italy threw off the yoke of Bourbon tyranny and created a liberal, constitutional state, and laid the groundwork for the emergence of a secular and humanistic national culture which would eventually replace Catholicism. Alng with this view of the Risorgimento goes a view of Sicily and the Mezzogiorno as a kind of half civilized borderland, and of the *contadini meridonali* as a species of near barbarians in need of direction from the enlightened North if they are to progress. Typical of this view is the work of Edward Banfield, who chose the region of Basilicata for his study of the *Moral Basis of a Backward Society*.

Marxist historians have dissented from this view less vigorously than one might expect. Antonio Gramsci, for example, regarded the Risorgimento as an "incomplete agrarian revolution." The peasants themselves, while by no means hopelessly reactionary, must be "harnessed to a modern movement" (Hobsbawm, 107) since they are "incapable of thinking . . . as members of a collective and prosecuting . . . systematic action ot change the economic and political conditions" (Gramsci, 66) From the standpoint of most Marxists, the Risorgimento stopped short of carrying out the democratic tasks posed for it by the Italian people, but the fundamentally benign character of the Risorgimento political project: unification, capitalization of land, creation of a unified national market, and secularization are all unquestioned.

According to this view, the emigration which followed hard on the heels of unification was simply a stage in the adaptation of a largely agrarian people to the pressures of industrialization and modernization. The most enterprising and "advanced" elements of the peasantry, impatient with the slow progress of industrialization in backward Italy, made their way across the ocean to the America, to seek out their fortunes in the land of opportunity.

Even a brief examination of the evidence will, I think, convince us that this is incorrect. The economic policy of the Piedmontese bourgeoisie, who dominated the unified state, had three principal objectives: transformation of the South into a base for the "primitive accumulation of captial" necessary for the industrialization of the North, the creation of a unified national market for the products of Northern industry, and capitalization of landed property, which had the result of supplying cheap food, prerequisite for the low wage policies of Northern industry, while at the same time driving the peasantry off the land, creating a large supply of "free" wage labor for Italian — and, as it turned out — North American — industry.

Transformation of the South into a base for primitive accumulation of capital was accomplished largely through the mechanism of fiscal policy. Increased state expenditures led to creation of a large national debt. In 1859 the combined expenditures of the Italian states were ł 570 million, and the combined debt, owed mostly by the Northern States, was ł 1.5 billion. By

1879 the annual expenses of the unified state had risen to   1022, and the combined debt, now being serviced with the help of the Southern states, to t 8.3 billion (Sereni, 59). Neither taxation nor expenditures were distributed equitably. The North controlled 56% of Italy's wealth, and paid only 47% of its taxes. The Cent controlled 17% of the wealth and paid 16% of the taxes. The South, which controlled only 27% of the wealth, carried 37% of the total tax burden! (Sereni, 78). Per capita wealth was, further, lower in the South than in the North (t1372 Lira as against t 2411), making this taxation especially onerous. Distribution of state expenditures was even more inequitable than the distribution of the tax burden. Expenditure per capita in the North was t 25.27, in the Center t 29, and in the South and the Islands it was t 0.38 Lira. While expenditures in the North supported land reclamation, railroad construction and the service of the national debt — and thus accumulation of banking capital — expenditures in the South covered only the costs of the "brigand war" (i.e. repression of the Southern popular movements) and the generous patronage which secured the continued support of the Southern middle classes (Zitara, 60—70). Interest on the national debt, paid largely by the peasants and largely by the South, subsidized the creation of banking capital, which in turn financed Northern industrialization.

A market for Northern manufactured goods was assured by creation of a unified national market. All internal tariffs were eliminated immediately, and external tariffs were cut by 80%. Railroads were constructed which linked Southern markets to the industrial centers of the North. (Sereni, 8). This policy had, not surprisingly, a devastating effect on the South, which before unification had developing textile and sulfur industries. Removal of internatl tariffs opened Southern markets to Northern manufactured goods for the first time, while international competition nearly wiped out, within the space of a decade, the Sicilian textile and sulfur industries. The North meanwhile, profited from this regime of free trade.

Intimately connected with the commerical and fiscal exploitation of the South was the manner in which the new regime "resolved" the agrarian question. Consider the following figures for the *Agro romano*, the rural hinterlands of Rome. Prior to unification 55% of all arable land belonged to the nobility, 30% was in mortmain (i.e. was church or demense land) and 15% was held by the bourgeoisie. After the *land reform* 53% remained in the hands of the nobility, only 7% remained in mortmain, and fully 40% was in the hands of the bourgeoisie (Sereni, 44).

The real significance of this policy can be understood only if we considered the traditional uses of the lands in mortmain. These lands were generally of two kinds: demense lands, and the lands of the church and the so called "*enti morali*" or charitable institutions. Demense lands were administered by the *communi* and served as commons where the poorest peasants could pasture their flocks, gather wood, and forage for the wild asparagus and cactus fruit, mulberries, acorns and chestnuts which formed the greater part of their daily fare. Church lands, like those of the nobility, were essentailly feudal property, held by the peasants in tenancy, but usually on far more favorable terms. The bulk of the lands in mortmain were, further, sold off in large parcels, ostensibly to preven "minifundialization," or simply deeded over to bourgeois usurpers. As Sereni puts it:

> It was the peasant masses themselves who had to carry the burden of the capitalization of landed property. The lands which they had formerly cultivated for the religious institutions on favorable terms were turned over to new owners who exacted far more (Sereni, 139).

Piedmontese agrarian policy thus created a new class of land owners at the expense of the Church and the peasantry, who, it should come as no surprise, soon made common cause against the new regime.

As the underdevelopment of the South progressed, agarian contracts deteriorated. Rents rose and the salaries of day laborers fell. small peasant property all but disappeared, as the total number of landowners in Italy as a whole declined from 4,153,645 in 1865 to 3,351,498 in 1881, due mostly to the expropriation of the mountain small holders for non-payment of taxes (Sereni, 257).

Far from being an "incomplete agrarian revolution," the unification of Italy brought in its wake the expropriation of the few remaining land rights of the peasants of the South and the near liquidation of the small holders of the North and Center. The policy of the Northern bourgeoisies wreaked havoc in the countryside, driving peasants off the land and into the great coastal cities. At the same time, Northern trade and fiscal policy had destroyed the silk and sulfur industries, so that when the dispossessed peasants arrived in Palermo and Naples they found little prospect of employment. A region which had once exported silk and sulfur, wheat, wool and wine, now became a net exporter of people, as poor peasants driven off their land filed first to the cities, and then, when work could not be found there, across the ocean to the Americas.

The peasants did not, however, accept this fate passively. The years following Garibaldi's invasion witnessed the emergence of a powerful movement of resistance to the penetration of capitalism in the the countryside, a movement which gradually took on objectively socialist characteristics. The South had a long tradition of popular resistance which reached back at least to Roman times. The Appenines, the very backbone of Italy, from the high valleys of the Alps south to Calabria, and across the straits of Messina to the mountains of the Sicilian interior, had long sheltered brigands and rebels, who gathered in small bands which subjected the landlords and their state to continuous harrassment. There was the slave Eunus who led an uprising which held the town of Enna, in the parched grain growning uplands of Sicily for two years against the Roman legion, and Quintus Poppedius Silo, who led the resistance forces of the Marsi in Abruzzo, and from whom the novelist Silone took his *nom de querre*. This tradition endured through the middle ages, reinforced by Arab, and later by Greek and Albanian settlers in the remote mountainous regions of the interior, who mounted fierce resistance to the designs of Angevin and Aragonese overlords intent on enclosing their pastures and wheatfields. It was this tradition which gave rise to the famous revolt of the Sicilian Vespers.

The peasants also had a distinct ideological tradition, a tradition which predated Christianity, and which probably had roots in the religions which the Carthaginians brought with them millenia ago, but which had received a profound infusion of eschatological expectation during the later middle ages, when hermits and mendicant friars fired with enthusiasm for the eschatological teachings of Joachim of Fiore and his Franciscan interpreters took their place in the mountains beside the bandits and rebels whom they not infrequently joined. The popular religion of the peasant communities gave meaning to the centuries of struggle against foreign oppression and feudal exploitation, and helped to keep alive the fire of resistance during the long years of despair and repression between revolts.

It was upon this tradition of popular resistance rooted in eschatological Christianity which the peasants drew in the years following unification. It is not possible for us to trace here the whole history of the peasant movements during this period. Suffice it to say that after a prolonged and tortuous process of development, the *contadini meridionali* eventually arrived, in the early 1890's, at an objectively socialist position, and in fact began to adhere in large numbers to peasant leagues, call *fasci*, which were affiliated with the new formed *Partito Socialista dei Lavoratori Italiani (PSLI)*. The movement of the *fasci* is in many ways the most direct ancestor of the socialist movement in the Italian immigrant communities in North America, and we should pause for a moment to examine its principal characteristics, and the course of its development.

The initiative towards the formation of the *fasci* came from two directions. The first Congress of the PSLI in 1892 had committed the party to the "socialist conquest of the countryside" and the leadership of the Sicilian section of the party set about immediately organizing peasant leagues. They came armed an agrarian program calling for a minimum wage, a prohibition on sale of communal lands, transfer of uncultivated demense lands to the peasants, and a general reduction in taxes. But they brought more than a program; they brought an orgizational apparatus which could coordinate struggles on a national scale, disposing in a coordinated manner of strategic and tactical reserves, directing the main blow of the popular movement against the real centers of bourgeois power in the cities, which remained invisible to the peasants. They also brought a new arsenal of tactics — the strike and the electoral struggle — which enabled the peasants to contest with the bourgeoisie on its own terrain. This "gospel of organization" was a new revelation to the peasantry, whose revolutionary traditions had been forged in the struggle aginst feudal oppression, and they hailed the socialists as "angels from heaven" (Hobsbawm,99).

At the same time it was the indigenous organizations of the peasantry which furnished the cadre of the movement and its ideology. Of particular interest in this regard were the lay confraternities which were responsible for the local cults of the saints and which were the carriers of the popular Christian tradition. These confraternities had long served as mutual aid societies, and now began to transform themselves into organizations of struggle. Becasue of this the political culture of the *fasci* was deeply rooted in the traditional idiom of the peasantry. "In our league at Fossa, next to the bearded picture of Karl Marx," writes Ignazio Silone, "There was a picture of Christ, dressed in red, the redeemer of the poor" (Silone, 216). The Waldensian communities, descendents of an old medieval sect long known for its resistance to the *agrari*, also played an important role. In Grotte, a certain S. Dimino, an ex-priest who had founded an evangelical church, which many of the sulfur miners joined, now formed a "Circolo Savonarola" where he taught the miners Christian Socialism. Even a few of the priests supported the movement, among them Father Lorenzo, chaplain of the Church of the Madonna del Balzo, who between giving the peasants tips on the lottery, taught that joining the *fasci* did not mean excommunication, that St. Francis had been the first socialist, and had in fact abolished money (Hobsbawm, 100).

The new initiative of the PSLI and the popular traditions of the rural masses combined to form the basis for the formation of a mass socialist movement. One after another, in village after village, *fasci* sprang up during the winter of 1892—3, and one after another they adhered to the newly formed PSLI (Romano, 14—41, Renda, 5—13).

We should point out here that the Christian peasants of Sicily and the Mezzogiorno proved themselves far more radical in the their vision of social transformation than the supposedly Marxist PSLI. Where the PSLI envisioned only a "minium of equality necessary to guarantee normal social communal and classless society, where all things would be held in common, as Joachim of Fiore and St. Francis had taught them centuries ago. These are the words of a peasant women from Piana dei Greci:

> We want everybody to work as we work. There should no longer be rich or poor . . . It will be enough to put everything in common and to share with justice what is produced. Jesus was a true socialist and he wanted precisely what the *fasci* are asking for (Hobsbawm, 183).

Indeed, the peasants saw in their leagues and the socialist movement to which they had adhered the genuine heir, and perhaps the ultimate fulfillment of the Christian tradition. As Maria Smilorda, an old schoolteacher and Waldensian church leader at Grotte put it, "It is due to the socialism of a century ago that the Gospel has been able to spread" (oral testimony).

In the spring and summer of 1893 the *fasci* won some extraordinary victories, successfully contesting the municipal elections under their own banners, and prosecuting a successful agrarian stike against the landlords of the wheat growing uplands of the Sicilian interior (Renda, 151, 160—83). But in the autumn events took a new turn. The *fasci* adopted a more militant tactic, turning towards direct confrontations with the authorities in the *piazze* in front of the *municipio*, and intitiating a campaign against the onerous taxes imposed by the communl administrations. The *agrari* were fearful that the movement would move swiftly towards insurrection, brought down the government of Giovanni Giolitti, which had taken a cautious attitude towards the movement, and brought to power the old Garibalian radical, Francesco Crispi, who moved to crush the movement. On the night of 3 January 1894 he declared a state of siege, ordered the arrest of the leaders of the movement, and sent 40,000 troops to Sicily to "contain the socialist threat." Massacres and executions and savage prison terms followed. The *fasci* never recovered, and a similar movement, among the *braccianti* of the North and Center in 1897—8 was also put down.

The PSLI, for its part, did little to assist the *fasci*, even as the leadership of its Sicilian section was being thrown into prison. During the autumn the party, along with the Socialist International of which it was a member, had held their Second Congresses. The International rejected a policy of class alliances, arguing that the working class had to take the field under its own banners. The Italian party went further, voting to terminate its work among the Southern peasants, who were mostly *coloni* (tenant farmers), and to concentrate its rural work among the *braccianti* — and this in the wake of a successful agarian strike among tenant farmers under its leadership. This turn was rooted in an understandiang of socialism different from that of the peasants, which saw the roots of socialism in the development of the productive forces under capitalism — and not in the mobilization of traditional forms of resistance, such as those embodied in the peasant leagues, against new forms of exploitation. Socialism is, according to this view, and extension and radicalization of the process of modernization (industrialization, bureaucratization, secularization) which had been initiated by the bourgeoisie. Because of this it was in the cities, among the working class, and not in the backward countrysides that the mass base for socialism was to be found. The PSLI thus abandoned the peasants in their moment of greatest need, in effect sabotaging their movement. This pattern we will see repeated in the relationship of the Socialist Party and Communist Party to the immigrant socialist movement in North America.

Defeat of the *fasci* meant that the course of economic development which had been charted by the bourgeoisie of the North was now secure. As Nicola Zitara puts its:

> The policies of the first 40 years of unification effected the industrialization of Lombardy, Liguria and Piemonte, allowed the development of an advanced capitalist agriculture in Romagna, which had been one of the most desolate regions of the Papal States, and was large with benefits for Tuscany. Into these regions, the ruling classes of which governed the country as a whole, flowed the better part of the disposable resources of the nation, while the Mezzogiorno, at the close of the nineteenth century, was reduced to an outlet for the products of Northern industry. . . . Unity, in assigning to the South a colonial function, made it an underdeveloped nation where conditions are worse than in many parts of the Third World . . . a country the hopes of which could only find refuge in the American dream (Zitara, 76).

Italy lost 1.5 million people in all between unification, and the time when the U.S. closed its doors in 1924. Most left after 1894, and most came from the South. Half were *braccianti* and another quarter *coloni* of various kinds (Sereni, 353—355).

But the *contadini* who left their villages in the dark years after the defeat of the *fasci* did not leave their vision of a new soical order behind them when they boarded the ships for New York. Rather, they brought these traditions with them and adapted them to the new conditions and the new forms of exploitation which they found when they arrived in America. And out of these traditions, arm in arm with their fellow peasants from Poland and Ireland, Russia and the Balkans, farmers from Oklahoma and Jewish merchants and artisans, they helped forge a socialist movement in the United States.

II

The history of post Risorgimento Italy suggests to us, therefore, that the whole phenomenon of Italian emigration ought to be regarded not as the result of some "natural" or "evolutionary" adaptation to an inexorable process of industrialization, but rather as the desperate response of a people whose homeland was being transformed into the colonial playground of an alien occupying power — the Piemontese bourgeoisie. It was, further, a last resort, for which the peasants of Sicily and the Mezzogiorno opted only after the road of popular struggle had been closed off by the defeat of the *fasci*. Today's Italian Americans are, in a very real sense the children of refugees, who fled an exploitation and repression every bit as brutal as that suffered by the peoples of the Third World in the present period.

Also like immigrants and refugees from the oppressed countries of the Third World today, immigrants from Sicily and the Mezzogiorno, and the remote and impovershed mountainous regions of the Italian North and Center, did not discover in the United States a land of opportunity. On the contrary, they found themselves cosigned to relatively backward sectors of the economy, working under coercive, semi-feudal contracts, for wages which were often well below the value of labor power. Rarely employed in what were then the advanced industrial sectors such as stell and machine tools, and concentrated instead in mining, railroad and construction work, or low wage sectors such as the garment industry, forced to pay what amounted to feudal tributes to the *padroni* who organized the labor gangs, and often working under armed guard, the immigrants saved as much as 80% of their earnings, but were still unable to support their families, who had to stay behind in the old country, or else fend for themselves in the crowded slums of the great cities of the Northeast and Midwest. Consider the following example from Vecoli's study of Italian immigration.

> In 1903 a gang of Italians was sent to work on the Little Kanawana River in West Virginia, but upon discovering that the construction site was a swamp covered with several inches of water they demanded to be sent back. The contractors, however, were heavily armed, and told the men that they would have to work until their transportation costs were paid. When the Italians attacked them with axes and clubs, the bosses opened fire, wounding several, while others fled into the forest (Vecoli, 315).

Along with this economic exploitation went political and cultural domination. Immigrant suffrage was controled by complex mechanism which included not only the clientelism of political "machines," but outright violence and intimidation at the hands of the mafia, and, in rural areas, the Ku Klux Klan (Mansueto).

The movement of popular resistance which grew up among the immigrants in the years after 1894, was, like the movement of the *fasci*, deeply rooted in the popular communal institutions and the popular democratic and religious traditions of the immigrant communities themselves. This is nowhere more evident than in the popular base and political strategy of the principal organization of Italian immigrant socialism, the *Federazione Socialista Italiana* (FSI).

The roots of the FSI lie, first and foremost, in the *societa di mutuo soccorso* or mutual benefit societies which were the principal assistantial, revindicative, social and religious organizations of the immigrant communities. These *societa* were organizations of the *paesani* in emigration which developed in order to provide sickness and death benefits to the immigrant families, who would, otherwise, have been left destitute when misfortune struck. They were often at the same time, however, social centers where the immigrants — the men especially — would gather for wine and conversation, and lay religious confraternities responsible for the cult of the patron saint of the village from which the immigrants had come, and as such were the carriers of the popular religious tranditions of the immigrant community. consider the following description of the *Societa della Santissima Crocifissa di Cimina* in Chicago.

> There was a large cross, a table with a Bible, candles, a cup and a dish, for bread and wine. I remember they would say the Our Father, the Hail Mary, maybe the rosary. Then there would be drinking and eating, and cigar smoking. It was a fraternal gathering. (oral testimony).

We see here a radical laicization of the liturgy, and a transposition of the symbolic soldarity of the Eucharist into a real solidarity among friends, without, however, any loss of the transcendent, eschatological hope embodied in the symbolism of the cross, and articulated in the words of the Our Father. This real solidarity among friends, a solidarity mobilized on a day to day basis through the assistential functions of the *societa* in the community's struggle for survival, could not help but begin to take on political dimensions.

Gradually, beginning in the early 1890's the *societa* took on first trade union, and eventually educational and political functions. The *Societa Politica Operaia Italiana* founded in 1894, attempted for a while to establish collective bargaining agreements among the *padroni* and *braccianti*, though it met with little success (Vecoli, 261). In small mining and mill towns in Pennyslvania mutual benefit societies not infrequently transformed themselves into socialist circles or even independent "parties." Typical of such societies was the *Circolo Socialista "Camillo Prampolini"* in Latrobe which, under the influence of Paolo Mazzoli "became a true center of irradiation of a prolific propaganda which later bore fruit in a network of socialist sections, which federated to form the 'Italian Socialist party of Pennsylvania' " (Velona, 19). Other societies retained more humble names, but nonetheless became known as real centers of revolutionary activity. When I asked one old shopkeeper in Chicago's 24th/Oakley district about the *Societa Lovagnini* she looked at me fearfully and said "Oh you're treading on dangerous ground there. They were a benevolent society, but they had some tie in . . . somewhere along the line . . . we used to call them *socialisti* (oral testimony). When she later discovered that I was sympathetic, she reassured me that they were all "very uprighteous men who wanted the same as Jesus did."

Gradually, thanks largely to the work of Giuseppe Bertelli, these societies were united in 1910 into a single federation, the FSI, which was affiliated, albeit tenuously, with the Socialist Party in America. The political strategy of the new federation continued to be concentrated on an effort to integrate itself into the social life of the immigrant communities, becoming indistinguishable from the immigrants' own social and economic institutions and developing a political discourse deeply rooted in popular Christianity. What the FSI understood, better than so many other socialist organizations, is that socialism growns out of the immanent solidarities already present within a community, and that as important as trade union struggles are in defending the immediate interests of the people, it was only by nourishing and refining these already existing solidarities that it is possible to create among the people a fervent faith in the imminent advent of a classless and communal social order. In this sense the FSI was heir to the tradition of the peasant leagues, and part of the same tradition which later produced Tasca, Gramsci, and Silone.

As we have already suggested, at the center of these already existing solidarities were the popular religious traditions. Indeed, nearly all of the immigrant socialists, whether atheists or believers, saw socialism not as a break with the Christian tradition, but as the realization of the Christian ideal of a society based on fraternal love, which the Church itself had long ago betrayed. Issue after of issue of *La Parola del Popolo* debated the religious question, and at Christmas and Easter in particular the paper published socialist interpretations of the life of Jesus . . . and of the terrible suffering endured by his proletarian father and peasant mother. These stories created a fervent cult of the *Gesu socialista*, and a profound revolutionary spirituality which bound the immigrants together in their protracted struggle for a classless and communal society.

Of central importance to this spirituality was the poverty into which Jesus was born. Thus "F.M.", a writer for "*Difesa della Lavoratrice*" (Defense of the Working Woman), in a column reproduced in *La Parola* (14 October 1922):

> Born of the people . . . raised in a carpenter's shop . . . Christ knew . . . the difficult life of those who own nothing by that strength of their arms and saw the abject poverty of the slaves in the roman world, and the iniquity of wealth, made from their blood and their tears (F.M.).

Writers in *La Parola* continuously reminded their readers that the teachings of Jesus were a "system of moral principles without any link to an external cult" (Crivelli). Jesus preached "universal brotherhood" and a struggle against egoism — essentially the same values for which the socialists themselves were struggling (F.M.). At the end of this struggle lies the fulfillment to the promise made by Jesus himself long ago. Socialism is the "kingdom of heaven, the kingdom of justice invoked by Jesus in his immortal prayer. The resurrection of the working people will be the resurrection of Christ" (F.M.).

Perhaps the most marked characteristic of *La Parola's* treatment of the life of Jesus, however, is its intense focus on the crucified and suffering Christ — and the political nature of the crucifixion. Consider the following account of the crucifixion (Giancadula).

> The Nazarene . . . is 33 years old, neither blind nor ill, and has the nerve to publically proclaim that he possesses nothing . . . he hates all the venerable laws of our country, laws which protect the rights of our property owners. He hates the rich. This sinner is guilty of treason. He has preached the pernicious doctrine of peace on earth and human brotherhood . . . it is clear that if the inferior classes come to believe that they are all brothers . . . then Rome will surely perish.
>
> That night while the prosecutor entertained himself with the caresses of his concubines, and enjoyed select wines at a banquet offered in the house of Pontious Pilate, the poor leader of the derelicts, whom men called the ''carpenter of Nazareth'' hung from the cross, with his flesh in tatters and with his dead eyes closed in their bleeding orbits.

Similarly, the socialist periodicals fostered an image of Mary as *"una compagna militante"* who had chosen the painful mountain road, and who endured inexpressible suffering because of her participation in the struggles of her son. She is the ''poor mother pursued by the swords of Herod's retainers'' as she flees into political exile after the massacre at Bethlehem (Crivello).

This effort to link the socialist project to the popular traditions of the immigrant communities meant that the FSI was able to have a profound impact on the political consciousness of Italian Americans, including many who were never members of the federation. We have already heard from one woman who believed that the socialists wanted the same thing as Jesus. Consider now the testimony of Maria Valiani, a garment worker active in unionization drives. Ms. Valiani is in her seventies now, is deeply religious, and devoted to the Virgin Mary.

> The owners of the companies, they don't care. They want to do all the touring and all the spending, and all the enjoyment. And that's no good. Jesus said, . . . He told the rich man ''You shall never enter the Kingdom of Heaven . . . because if you're rich that means you didn't pay your subjects enough.'' And that's why they're suffering. So you're gonna go down in the pit, and they're gonna come to heaven with me.'' So you gotta learn. (oral testimony).

We should pause here to consider briefly some of the implications of our account of Italian immigrant socialism, for our understanding of both the character of the Italian American heritage, and the socialist project. Far from being either backward, fatalistic peasants lost in the capitalist metropolis and seeking solace in festivals and rituals which reminded them of their lost fatherland, or budding entrepreneurs anxious to embrace the competitive values of their new home, the immigrants proved themselves a sophsiticated political force capable of drawing on their own traditions to forge a movement of resistance to the new forms of exploitation they encountered in North America. They proved themselves far more sophisticated, in fact, than much of the Marxist left in the United States. Where Marxists traditionally have believed that the basis for the emergence of mass socialist movements lies in the development of the productive forces under capitalism, which by increasing real social interdependence creates the material conditions for the emergence of collective property forms and socialist consciousness, the FSI realized that the socialist ideal grew organically out of the pre-existing solidarities of the village and neighborhood community, and out of the popular Christian tradition which had nourished popular resistance for centuries. By drawing on these solidarities and traditions, the immigrant socialists were able to develop among the people the aspiriation for the faith in the imminent advent of a classless and communal social order. Thus the extraordinary success of the FSI, — a success that no North American socialist movement since has been able to duplicate.

III

What happened to the socialist movement in the Italian immigrant communities? How is it that a people who build such a powerful movement for socialism could, two generations later lend their support to a Republican Administration which represents the interests of the most reactionary sectors of the North American bourgeoisie? The decline of socialism in America is a problem which has long troubled historians of the popular movements in the United States, and we cannot even summarize in this context the general lines and current status of this debate. But our inquiry suggests that there were some important factors involved in this decline, which historians of the popular movements have hitherto ignored.

We have already suggested that the immigrant socialist movement was integrally bound up with, indeed was the organic expression of, the whole way of life of the immigrant communities. It has its roots in and was nurtured by the pre-existing solidarities of the *societa*, which provided a living sign in the present of the social relations which would prevail in the classess and communal society of the new age. The decline of socialism as a mass movement in the Italian American community was, likewise, integrally bound up with the disappearance of this way of life — that is with the decline of neighborhood and ethnic solidarities, the disintegration of the old popular religious traditions through which the immigrants understood the struggle for a classless and communal social order, and above all with the displacement of the *societa* from the center of community life.

There were a number of factors involved in the disintegration of the old immigrant communities and the assimilation of the second generation Italian Americans to the american Way of Life. Of critical importance, of course was the new economic situation after the Second World War, which opened up new and unheard of opportunities for the immigrant's children, for whom life became increasingly centered around career and consumption. Along with these changing economic conditions came a radical shift in beliefs and values. Increasingly the children of the immigrants began to look for a sense of dignity and purpose not in their family and community, but in their work and above all in their economic success. The expanded opportunities of the post war period gave credibility to the notion that America really was a "land of opportunity" and that the individual really was responsible for his own success or failure. Italian Americans came to share in what Michael Lewis has called the "culture of inequality," which regards prosperity as a mark of moral or intellectual superiority, and poverty a sign of sinfulness or incompetence — hardly the basis for a socialist worldview. Many began to abandon the old ethnic neighborhoods for the suburbs, and those who remained endeavored to give their neighborhoods a more "middle class" character. No longer did people gather in the barber shop or at the lodge of the *societa*, or pass their evenings on the front porch over wine. The Democratic Party replaced the FSI and the mass media the lay confratnity as the principal political and cultural institutions of the immigrant communities. For immigrant men, in particular, the experience of service in World War II hastened the development of an "American" national identity. Indeed, "America" came for these men to embody not only the promise of unheard of prosperity, but also the democratic ideals in the name of which the antifascist struggle had been waged.

The North American bourgeoisie, in other words, by means of the New Deal and its role in the antifascist struggle, was able to establish itself as the representative of the economic aspirations and democratic ideals of the popular sectors, and thus secure its hegemony over the North American popular sectors, including the immigrant communities.

We must ask overselves, however, why it was that the immigrant communities were unable to resist the political and cultural offensives of the bourgeoisie in the post war period. this is a complex question which certainly does not admit of a single answer. One critical factor, however, in the collapse of political and cultural resistance in the Italian immigrant communities, was the liquidation of the "language federations" — the immigrant socialist organizations such as the FSI — by the Communist Party in 1925.

The fact is that the Marxist left in the United States had a long history of chauvinism towards the immigrant communities and the socialist organizations which developed out of them, a chauvinism which was bolstered by their adherence to a productivist understanding of Marxism which looked not to the popular democratic and religious traditions of the oppressed, but to the development of the productive forces for the basis of mass socialist movements. This chauvinism reached back to the old Socialist Party, the dominant elements of which feared that competition from immigrant workers would alienate the better paid Anglo, Irish and German American workers among whom they found their base, and who were alarmed at the radicalism of the immigrant socialists, who stood to the left of the party (Kipnis, 286). In part because of this chauvinism, and in part because of disatisfaction with the Socialist Party's reformist line, the immigrant language federations led the way in creation of the new Communist Party after the schism of 1919.

Conditions in the new party, however, were little better from the standpoint of the immigrant communities, which, taken together, contributed by far the greatest part of the party's cadre. In 1922 only 10% of the party's members belonged to the English speaking section, and by 1925 this figure had risen only to 14% (Glazer, 40). The party was, futher, organized around the semi-autonomous language federations. The leadership, however, did not understand what it had achieved by conquering for itself the allegiance of the immigrant working class. Indeed, in 1925 the party expressed its recognition of the contributions of the immigrants by undertaking a compaign of "Bolshevization" designed to "raise the level of organizational, political and ideological discipline." At the center of this campaign was the liquidation of the language federations, which were the carriers of the immigrant socialist traditions, and the reorganization of the party around a system of factory nuclei. English classes were to be mandatory for all comrades who were not already fluent in the language, and leadership cadre were to be drawn from among the "American" comrades (Glazer, 47—52, 56). Strengthened ideological discipline meant that the orthodox atheistic position on the religious question was much more in evidence, and religious propaganda of the kind developed by the FSI was out of the question.

This campaign had disastrous results. Membership dropped from 14,037 to 7,215 in the space of *one month*, between 25 September and 25 October 1925, as immigrant workers resisting the new line left or were purged from the party. Worse still the party lost its precious roots in the popular communal institutions and the popular democratic and religious traditions of the ethnic working class — roots it has never been able to rebuild.

The liquidation of the language federations had two critical results. First, liquidation of the federations deprived the immigrant communities of the cultural resources and the institutional apparatus they needed to resist the impending cultural offensive of the North American bourgeoisie. Second, the party in effect sent the immigrant communities a strong and clear message that the struggle for socialism had nothing to do with their popular communal institutions and their popular democratic and religious traditions — that it was rather a matter of radical modernization which presupposed the destruction of their institutions, and the disintegration of their traditions. Not surprisingly many of the immigrants abandoned socialism and for all, and sought other outlets for their eschatological aspiration for a classless and communal society: most notably the traditionalist devotionalism, often linked to reactionary political projects, which has been the dominant form of Italian American popular religiosity in the post war period. This traditionalist devotionalism, far from being a celebration of the *status quo* of contemporary capitalism, in fact draws on profound discontent with the individualism and consumerism of contemporary North American society, discontent which, had it not been for the fatal errors-of the Marxist left, might well have been mobilized in the struggle for a classless and communal society.

IV

Where do things stand today with respect to the socioreligious outlook of the Italian American community? Perhaps I can answer this question best by telling a story. This past summer I attended the Feast of Our Lady of Mount Carmel at Greenpoint in Brooklyn. On the surface of things there seemed to be very little in the way of "politics" involved — except, that is for the presence of the area's recently converted anticommunist congressman, Stephen Solarz, working the crowd like an old fashioned ward heeler. The tradtionalist devotionalism of the second generation mixed with the secularism and brash ethnic chauvinism of the third. Middle aged women had themselves consecrated to Our Lady of Mount Carmel, and received scapulars promising that those who wear them need never fear eternal fire, while teenagers hawked the — apparently obligatory — "Kiss Me, I'm Italian" t-shirts. Not a very likely scene for a socialist revival — or even a campaign to replace Solarz with a radical Democrat.

Upon entering the church building, however, I was reminded of the irreducibly popular character of the Christian tradition, even where it has suffered the worst deformations. Along the walls of the tacky pseudo-Baroque sanctuary were rows of liturgical banners. And on those banners: the text of the Magnificat.

> He has brought down monarchs from their thrones,
>   but the humble have been lifted high.
> The hungry he has filled with good things,
>   but the rich he has sent empty away (Luke 1:52—53).

Where else in the contemporary United States could one find a great hall, filled with people, the walls covered with such revolutionary slogans? Even where the original meaning of the tradition is lost, and where its present meanings are often deeply ambiguous, the symbols themselves preserve dangerous memories which, in the hands of those who understand them, can catalyze renewed social ferment.

That feast summed up for me the paradox of our present situation in the Italian American community. On the one hand we are the children of refugees, the product of an emigration set in motion by the imperial designs of the Piemontese bourgeoisie, who made the lands of our ancestors their colonial playground. We are thus bound by our historical memories to the present struggle of the peoples of the Third World. We are a people with a proud tradition of popular resistance, a tradition deeply rooted in popular Christianity — a tradition with a fundamentally socialist character. To be an Italian American, to be faithful to our heritage means, in the most profound sense, to be popular Christian and anti-imperialist and socialist. At the same time, the cultural offensive of the bourgeoisie during the post war period has erased all but the faintest memories of this tradition, so that in a very real sense, for most second and nearly all third generation Italian Americans, our history quite simply does not exist. Even when we are surrounded by the revolutionary symbols of popular Christianity we do not know what they mean. Thus the difficulty in weaning our people away from the pro-imperialist and pro-capitalist project with which they have become entangled.

Standing in that crowded church, however, surrounded by hundreds of my own people, and by those revolutionary banners — the banners of the Magnificat around which the poor and oppressed have rallied for centuries — I could not help but hope that the traditions of our ancestors will once again move the Italian American communities into the ranks of the popular movements and catalyze formation of a new culture of solidarity and resistance.

There is no question, to be sure of such a movement taking on explictly socialist or even anticapitalist content in the near future. But the events of past two years suggest that there *are* currents in the Italian American community which might serve as a center of resistance to the emerging rightist consensus, and contend effectively with the right for the allegiance of the critically important Catholic popular sectors. I am referring, of course to the emergence of Mario Cuomo as *de facto* leader of the center-left of the Democratic party. Without in any sense breaking with the dominant capitalist consensus, Cuomo has begun to elaborate a political discourse which assigns a popular and communitarian content to the democratic trandition — a content objectively at odds with the politics of the right, and ultimately at odds with capitalism itself.

> We would rather have laws written by the man called the world's
> most sincere democrat — St. Francis of Assisi — than laws written
> by Darwin.

> We believe in a government strong enough to use the words love
> and compassion, and smart enough to convert our noblest
> aspiriations into political realities.
>
> We believe in a single fundamental idea that describes . . . what
> a proper government should be. The idea of family. Mutuality.
> The sharing of benefits and burdens for the good of all. Feeling
> one anothers' pain. Sharing one another's blessings.
>
> We believe that we should be the family of America, recognizing
> that at the heart of the matter we are bound to one another, that
> the problems of a retired school teacher in Duluth are our problems.
> That the future of a child in Buffalo is our future. That the struggle
> of a disabled man in Boston is our struggle. That the hunger of
> a woman in Little Rock is our hunger. That the failure to provide
> what reasonably we might, to avoid pain, is our failure.

Cuomo has challenged, at a critical moment in our nation's history, the
dominant, individualistic interpretation of our country's democratic traditions,
and he has done so in a way which draws on and speaks to the popular Christian
traditions and communitarian heritage of the Italian American and other
Catholic communities. In this sense, for all its ambiguities, the emergence of
the current which he represents is a hopeful sign, a sign that we Italian
Americans may yet be able to reclaim our history and recreate within the hearts
and minds of our people a sense of the real meaning of their heritage.

Where the Gospel is preached, and the Our Father prayed, the cause of
socialism is not yet dead.

Works Cited

Banfield, Edward. *The Moral Basis of a Backward Society*. New York: Free
  Press,   1958
Berryman, Phillip. *Religious Roots of Rebellion*. Maryknoll: Orbis, 1983
Crivelli, G. "Socialismo e religione." *La Parola del Popolo*, 21, 28 January
  1922
Crivello, A. "Natale." poem, undated clipping from unidentified magazine
Cuomo, Mario. "Keynote Speech, 1984 Democratic Convention." *New York
  Times*, 17 July 1984
Davis, Mike. "The New Right's Road to Power." *New Left Review* 128 (1981)
F.M. "Cristo." *La Parola del Popolo*, 14 October 1922
Giancadula. "Crucifige! Crucifige!" *La Parola del Popolo*, 14 October 1922
Glazer, Nathan. *The Social Basis of American Communism*. Westport:
  Greenwood, 1961

Gramsci, Antonio. *La questione meridionale*. Roma: Riuniti, 1966

Greeley, Andrew. *The American Catholic*. New York: Harper, 1978

Hobsbawm, Eric. *Primitive Rebels*. New York: Norton, 1959

Kipnis, Ira. *The American Socialist Movement*. New York: Monthly Review, 1952

Lewis, Michael. *The Culture of Inequality*. Amherst: University of Massachusetts Press, 1978

Mansueto, Anthony. "Blessed are the Meek, for they Shall Inherit the Earth: Popular Religion and Political Consciousness in the Italian American Community," Berkeley, California: Graduate Theological Union, 1985, unpublished doctoral dissertation.

National Conference of Catholic Bishops. *Pastoral Letter on Catholic Social Teachings and the U.S. Economy*, 1984

Renda, F. *I fasci siciliani*. Torino: Einaudi, 1977

Romano, S.F. *Storia dei fasci siciliani*. Bari: Laterza, 1959

Sereni, E. *Capitalismo nelle campagne*. Torino: Einaudi, 1968

Silone, Ignazio. *Vino e pane*. Milano: Monadori, 1955

Vecoli, R. "Chicago Italians Prior to World War I." Madison: University of Wisconsin, 1963, unpublished doctoral dissertation

Velona, Fort. "Genesi el movimento socialista democratico e del Parola del Popolo." *La Parola del Popolo*, New Series, December 1958—January 1959

Zitara, Nicola. *L'Unita d'Italia, Nascita di una colonia*. Milano: Jaca Book, 1971

Chapter 11

ITALIAN AMERICANS IN THE YEAR 2000: THE IMPACT OF EDUCATION

William Egelman
Iona College

For the past few years a majority of my research efforts have been focused on the study of Italian Americans in education.[1] With the use of census data I have tracked the changes in levels of educational attainment. The data indicate that Italian Americans, as a group, have shown dramatic increases in the area of education. This paper seeks to analyze why such changes have occurred, and what impact these changes will have on Italian-American identity.

In order to illustrate the changes in educational achievement, data drawn from the 1980 census will be presented and analyzed. Table 1 compares levels of educational attainment for all persons in New York City. Three categories are presented: All persons, Italian Single Ancestry, and Italian Mixed Ancestry. These groups are also divided into specific age categories: 25 to 44 years, 45 to 64 years, and 65 years old and over. Data is presented for both males and females.

In order to get a clearer picture as to the changes taking place, Table 2 focuses solely on the highest educational category: College 4 or more years. The data in this table present a dramatic picture of change. Italian Mixed Ancestry has the highest percent of people in this category for both males and females. Italian Single Ancestry lags behind the All persons category but the rate of increase by age cohort is substantial.

Table 3 gives further evidence of this by detailing the percentage change by age categories. The difference on the college 4 years or more for the younger age cohort as striking. Specifically, Single ancestry males 21 to 44 when compared to Single ancestry males 65 years old and over increased in this category by 445 percent. Single ancestry females increased by 611 percent. These substantial increases may be accounted for by the fact that in the oldest category a very small percentage of Single Ancestry Italians graduated from college (4.0 percent for males and 1.9 percent for females).

Table 1: Years of School Completed For Persons 25 and Over By Sex and Age: All Persons and Persons of Italian Ancestry, New York City, 1980

Male

Years of School Completed	All Persons Number	Percent	Italian Single Ancestry Number	Percent	Italian Mixed Ancestry Number	Percent
Males 25 to 44 years	963,535	100.0	102,578	100.0	26,481	100.0
Elementary Only	103,619	10.8	10,427	10.2	580	2.2
High School Only	410,828	42.6	50,067	48.8	11,231	42.4
H.S. 1 to 3 years	138,563	14.4	14,188	13.8	2,968	11.2
H.S. 4 years	272,265	28.3	35,879	35.0	8,263	31.2
College	449,088	46.6	42,084	41.0	14,670	55.4
College 1 to 5 years	175,571	18.2	19,765	19.3	6,423	24.3
College 4 or more years	273,517	28.4	22,319	21.8	8,247	31.1

Male

Years of School Completed	All Persons Number	Percent	Italian Single Ancestry Number	Percent	Italian Mixed Ancestry Number	Percent
Males 45 to 64 years	668,170	100.0	111,154	100.1	6,088	99.9
Elementary Only	159,025	23.8	28,428	25.6	597	9.8

Table 1: (Cont'd)
Years of School Completed For Persons 25 and Over By Sex and Age: All Persons and Persons of Italian Ancestry, New York City, 1980

	All Persons Number	Percent	Italian Single Ancestry Number	Percent	Italian Mixed Ancestry Number	Percent
High School Only	328,518	49.2	66,873	60.2	3,759	61.7
H.S. 1 to 3 years	130,109	19.5	30,806	27.7	1,510	24.8
H.S. 4 years only	198,409	29.7	36,067	32.4	2,249	36.9
College Only	180,627	27.0	15,853	14.3	1,732	28.4
College 1 to 3 years	71,094	10.6	7,818	7.0	837	13.7
College 4 or more years	109,533	16.4	8,035	7.2	895	14.7

Male

Years of School Completed	All Persons Number	Percent	Italian Single Ancestry Number	Percent	Italian Mixed Ancestry Number	Percent
Males 65 years and over	360,013	100.0	62,174	100.0	1,174	100.0
Elementary Only	166,337	46.2	39,796	64.0	456	38.8
High School Only	125,174	34.8	17,694	28.5	439	37.4
H.S. 1 to 3 years	55,024	15.3	9,509	15.3	208	17.7
H.S. 4 years Only	70,150	19.5	8,185	13.2	231	19.7
College Only	68,502	19.0	4,684	7.5	115	23.8
College 1 to 3 year Only	26,278	7.3	2,221	3.6	115	9.8
College 4 or more years	42,224	11.7	2,463	4.0	164	14.0

Table 1: (Cont'd)
Years of School Completed For Persons 25 and Over By Sex and Age: All Persons and Persons of Italian Ancestry, New York City, 1980

Female

Year of School Completed	All Persons Number	Percent	Italian Single Ancestry Number	Percent	Italian Mixed Ancestry Number	Percent
Females 25 to 44 years	1,080,477	99.9	100,291	100.1	28,220	100.0
Elementary Only	125,851	11.6	11,099	11.1	597	2.1
High School Only	541,666	50.1	63,685	63.5	15,755	55.8
H.S. 1 to 3 years	164,718	15.2	13,096	13.1	3,395	12.0
H.S. 4 years	376,948	34.9	50,589	50.4	12,360	43.8
College Only	412,960	38.2	25,507	25.4	11,868	42.1
College 1 to 3 years	178,671	16.5	12,016	12.0	5,255	18.6
College 4 or more years	123,289	21.7	13,491	13.5	6,613	23.4

Female

Year of School Completed	All Persons Number	Percent	Italian Single Ancestry Number	Percent	Italian Mixed Ancestry Number	Percent
Females 45 to 64 years	826,372	99.9	12,335	100.0	7,744	100.0
Elementary Only	205,307	24.8	31,106	25.2	691	8.9

Table 1: (Cont'd)
Years of School Completed For Persons 25 and
Over By Sex and Age:
All Persons and Persons of Italian Ancestry,
New York City, 1980

Female

Years of School Completed	All Persons Number	Percent	Italian Single Ancestry Number	Percent	Italian Mixed Ancestry Number	Percent
High School Only	460,372	55.7	83,007	67.4	5,544	71.6
H.S. 1 to 3 years	158,742	19.2	34,472	28.0	1,802	23.3
H.S. 4 years Only	301,630	36.5	48,535	39.4	3,742	48.3
College Only	160,693	19.4	9,122	7.4	1,509	19.5
College 1 to 3 years Only	78,412	9.5	4,956	4.0	770	10.1
College 4 or more years	82,281	10.0	4,166	3.4	739	9.5
Females 65 years and over	587,282	99.9	87,664	100.0	1,639	100.0
Elementary Only	289,671	49.3	60,649	69.2	655	40.6
High School Only	228,075	38.8	23,662	27.0	734	44.8
H.S. 1 to 3 years	89,671	15.3	11,961	13.6	357	21.8
H.S. 4 years Only	138,404	23.6	11,701	13.3	377	23.0
College Only	69,536	11.8	3,353	3.8	240	14.6
College 1 to 3 years Only	34,823	5.9	1,700	1.9	149	9.1
College 4 or more years	34,713	5.9	1,653	1.9	91	5.6

Source: 1980 Census Summary Tape File 4B

Table 2: Percent College 4 or More Years For Persons 25 and Over By Sex and Age: All Persons and Persons of Italian Ancestry, New York City, 1980

	All Persons	Italian Single Ancestry	Italian Mixed Ancestry
Males			
25 to 44 years	28.4	21.8	31.1
45 to 64 years	16.4	7.2	14.7
65 years old and over	11.7	4.0	14.0
Females			
25 to 44 years	21.7	13.5	23.4
45 to 64 years	10.0	3.4	9.5
65 years old and over	5.9	1.9	5.6

Source: 1980 Census Summary Tapes File 4B

Table 3: Percent Increase In College 4 or More Years For Persons 25 and Over By Sex and Age: All Persons and Persons of Italian Ancestry, New York City, 1980

	All Persons		Single Ancestry		Mixed Ancestry	
	Males	Females	Males	Females	Males	Females
25 to 44 years — 45 to 64 years	+ 73	+117	+203	+297	+112	+146
45 to 64 years — 65 years old and over	+ 40	+ 70	+ 80	+ 79	+ 5	+ 70
25 to 44 years — 65 years old and over	+143	+269	+445	+611	+159	+318

Source: 1980 Census Summary Tape File 4B

Given these increases one might assume that levels of educational achievement between males and females are converging. Interestingly, this is not the case for any of the groups (See Table 4). While mixed ancestry Italians show fluctuating differences in male-female levels, the total New York City population, and Single Ancestry Italians show a pattern of widening differences in educational achievement. For the oldest group of Single Ancestry Italains the difference in College Graduates was 2.1 percent; however for the youngest group the difference was 8.3 percent. These data appear to indicate that traditional values regarding gender roles may still be impacting upon the educational decision making process for Italian Americans.

What factors contribute to the increases in educational attainment among Italian Americans? There are, I believe, five critical factors which contribute to the changes noted in the data.

1. The bulk of Italian immigration occurred during the latter part of the nineteenth century and the first two decades of the twentieth century. Therefore many Americans who claim Italian ancestry, whether single or mixed, constitute the third or possibly fourth generation. They are the grandchildren and great grandchildren of the immigrants. Their place in America, and in fact, their own self identity is different than that of the earlier generations. Marcus Hansen is one who has discussed the impact of generation on the assimilation process.[3] The first generation (the immigrants) are tied to the old world. Psychologically, and in terms of their norms, values and behavioral patterns the immigrants may live in the new world but their hearts and minds often remained in the old world. The second generation was more tentative with respect to their identity. They wanted to be seen as American, and in many ways may have rejected the old world traditions. On the other hand, they still may have held loyalties to the traditional culture. Therefore, the second generation found itself in an ambivalent situation. The third generation, however, now being secure in American society; that is, they see themselves as Americans and are accepted by others as Americans, are more willing to express an open interest in their ethnic lineage.

    While I do not necessarily agree that Hansen's cyclical theory holds true for the Italian experience, his comments about the third geneation are relevant to this discussion. Italian Americans are now secure in their Americanism. There is little doubt that the current generation and their offspring will be American. This condition makes it all the more likely that Italian Americans today would take greater advantage of the education system than the earlier generations.

2. The factor of generation leads to a second point. A major influence on the early educational experiences of Italian Americans was the primacy of

Table 4: Male—Female Percent Differences, College 4 or More Years For Persons 25 and Over By Sex and Age:
All Persons and Persons of Italian Ancestry,
New York City, 1980

| | All Persons | | | Single Ancestry | | | Mixed Ancestry | | |
	Males	Females	Difference	Males	Females	Difference	Males	Females	Difference
25 to 44 years	28.4	21.7	6.7	21.8	13.5	8.3	31.1	23.4	7.7
45 to 64 years	16.4	10.0	6.4	7.2	3.4	3.8	14.7	9.5	5.2
65 years old and over	11.7	5.9	5.8	4.0	1.9	2.1	14.0	5.6	8.4

Source: 1980 Census Summary Tape file 4B

economic need over educational attainment. For the early immigrants, and Italians are not unique in this matter, child labor was a very important component in the economic life of the family. Most Italian immigrants were involved in unskilled or semi-skilled labor. Although there were some exceptions, most immigrants entered the American labor market at the lowest level with wages commensurate with the status of the position they held. Children worked because they had to work.

As Italian Americans began to increase their earnings, in part due to their own efforts, and in part due to the general upward mobility of the American economy, the need for child labor decreased. The family could afford to allow the children to remain in school for longer periods of time, at least allowing them to attain a high school diploma, and in some cases even go on to college.

3. Economic changes alone cannot explain the changes in educational attainment. The values and attitudes of the subculture one belongs to also plays a very important role in influencing one's behavior. I believe it is safe to say that one value of the Italian American subculture is pragmatism. Italians are a practical people. The stereotypic notions that Italians are "hard workers" and "savers," are not without some merit. As a group Italian Americans will meet the challenges of their environment in a straight forward and practical manner. This is not to say that Italian American culture does not have its "impractical" characteristics too; however, in their everyday lives they appear to be a most pragmatic people.

This practicality is important in the discussion of education. At one time education was an experience for the elite. College was an exercise in intellectual exploration and development. There was little "practical" relevance to education except for select profesions (law, medicine, etc.). During the past few decades there has been a gradual but continuing trend in higher education toward a "vocational" bias. This trend is especially marked during the last two decades.

In general, college today is seen as constituting a more practical experience than in the past, as in "I'm going to college to get a good job." This attitude appears to be pervasive in our society. The Italian American community appears to be aware of the practicality of attending college. College is no longer viewed as an esoteric experience. It is something to urge your children to do in order for them to be economically mobile. There is an economic advantage to going to college which is now recognized.

In addition to the perceived economic benefit to college there is a less obvious but important social benefit. In the Yiddish language there is a work — *Nachus* — I know of no Italian counterpart to it. It is one of those expressions which are most difficult to translate. Its literal meaning is unimportant. The message it conveys is very important. The message is that the successes and achievements of the children reflect upon their parents. If one marries, graduates from college, writes a book, the parents will have *Nachus* in their children. At the same time the parents attain new status in the eyes of the community because of the success of the children.

I believe the same phenomenon exists in the Italian American culture. Buying a "fancy" house in a pretigious area, finding a good spouse, and today going to college brings *Nachus* to Italian American parents. The value of college is now recognized in the Italian American community, and parents whose children attend college gain social status in the eyes of their peers.

4. Evidence indicates that Italian immigrants and their offspring were subjected to a substantial amount of prejudice and discrimination. Italians were seen as being "impulsive," "excitable," "boorish," "ignorant organ grinder," "the buffoon." Their ability to be assimilated into American society was questioned. They were not viewed as good candidates for American citizenship.

These attitudes could not but spill over into the educational sphere. It appears to be the case that Italian American studies were labelled as "non-academic" types. While I have no empirical evidence to support this contention, there was, I believe, an informal tracking system which developed in a number of northeastern urban centers. This tracking system assumed that Italian Americans would either not want to go to college or would be incapable of going on to college. Once such labelling occurred, the system led to a self-fulfilling prophecy may have worked in the following way: Italian Americans were assumed to be inferior; they were tracked into vocational programs; they were not academically prepared for college; they were not motivated by teachers to think of going to college; therefore, they did not go to college. Their not going to college was proof that they were not college material.

I would like to point out that this process could not have been as mechanical as is suggested here. In all likelihood it was a process which occurred time and time again. It was a process involving hundreds and thousands of decisions made by teachers, counselors, advisors, and principals. This tracking process may have been very informal, but, its impact was very real.

This tracking process may now be on the wane. As more and more students of Italian ancestry succeed — go on to college — the perceptions of high school personnel are likely to change. The educational professionals become more open to the idea that Italian American students can master academic programs and are capable of being "college material." The traditional notions regarding Italian American students are challenged and attitudes and perceptions undergo change.

5. The most dramatic increase in levels of educational attainment has been for females. This is due to the fact that historically Italian American females had very low levels of achievement in education. Traditionally, women have been viewed as having a particular niche in Italian culture. Their primary roles were that of wife/mother. Their responsibilities were to take care of the home and tend to the children. These were not roles without some degree of status; however, the culture did not allow most women other options.

As American society's perception of women's roles changed, the Italian American subculture could not be immune to these changes. As egalitarian ideas regarding gender roles increased in the general society, their influence began to be felt in the Italian subsociety. This does not mean that all Italian American women have equal access to higher education. There are still segments of the population that hold to traditional gender roles. The variables of social class and generation are critical in this area. However, one may project that as more Italian Americans enter the white collar/middle class segment of the larger society, and as more and more Italian Americans pass into the third and fourth generation, female educational attainment will continue to increase.

These five factors constitute some of the causes for upward educational attainment. The list is certainly not exhaustive. What then is the potential impact of these changes on the Italian American community and on Italian ethnicity? Will it alter ethnic identity by the year 2000? Darrel Montero[4] in writing about Japanese Americans makes a point that I believe is relevant to the case of Italian Americans. Montero states that Japanese Americans are being pulled in two directions. There is a desire to preserve a strong sense of ethnic identity and the values and elements drawn from traditional Japanese culture. On the other hand, there is also the pull of socioeconomic advancement. As Japanese Americans experience upward mobility, as defined by occupational and educational advancement along with greater geographical dispersion, there appears to be a push away from traditional ethnic culture and a pull toward mainstream middle class American culture.

As Italian Americans experience greater mobility they too may find themselves in the same position as Japanese Americans and other ethnic groups.

Behavior patterns, attitudes, values, beliefs, and self perceptions are all influenced by this mobility. Mobility tends to have a mainstream effect on ethnic cultures. While I do not believe that ethnic identity is likely to disappear, there is little doubt that "Italianisms" will be greatly modified. For example, it is likely that Americans of Italian descent will continue to have a strong sense of family; however, the daily or weekly visits to one's parents may become a thing of the past. This may be especially true given the possibility of greater geographical mobility. In addition, with larger numbers of Italian Americans marrying non-Italian Americans, more couples will be involved in trying to juggle dual heritages. It is becoming more and more the case where Italian Americans are of mixed ancestry. This process may lead to the weakening of both ancestral identities, and the strengthening of the link to mainstream American society.

For those who favor the maintenance of ethnic identities and traditions all is not lost. Italian American culture is now entering its second century. There are a number of third and fourth generation Italian Americans who are aware of their Italian ancestry. These individuals may not be "Italian" in the sense that their immigrant ancestors were Italian; they are however "Italian American." Many of them, I believe, still maintain a symbolic ethnic identity which they value and cherish. They seem to be able to negotiate a dual identity system which makes for a blending of a traditional ethnic culture with the culture of modern urbanized American society.

Footnotes

1. "Italian Americans in New York City: A Demographic Overview," *American Italian Historical Association*, Nov. 9—11, 1984 (with Joseph Salvo); Italian and Irish Americans in Education: A Comparative Study," *American Italian Historical Association*, Nov. 10—13, 1983; Italian-American Educational Attainment: An Introductory Analysis Utilizing Recent Current Population Survey Data." *American Italian Historical Association*, Nov. 1982.
2. "Family Values and Educational Attainment: Intergenerational Change Among Italian Americans," *Eastern Sociological Society*, March 19—21, 1982; "Ethnicity and Education: A Review of the Italian-American Experience," *Brooklyn College Center for Italian American Studies and Greek-American Behavioral Sciences Institute*, April 1981 (with Constance DeVito Egelman).
3. Hansen, Marcus L. "The Third Generation in America," *Commentary* 14 (November 1952), pp. 492—500).
4. Montero, Darrel, "The Japanese Americans: Changing Patterns of Assimilation Over Three Generations," *American Sociological Review* 46 (December 1981), pp. 829—39.

Chapter **12** **A SOCIOLOGICAL PROFILE OF ITALIAN-AMERICANS IN MEDICAL EDUCATION***

Rosanne Martorella
William Paterson College
Patricia Perri Rieker
Harvard Medical School

Introduction

Given the functional importance of the doctor's role to the maintenance of healthy and productive members of society, and the status of medicine as the "model" profession, medical students and practitioners have been studied more than any other professional group. As a result, the training process through which students are transformed into professionals has generated an extensive body of research knowledge. Two of the most common themes in studies of the process of socialization into medicine are recruitment into medical school and the stress or cross-pressures that students face and adapt to during their training. Past studies of the reported stress have tended to emphasize strigent academic demands, prolonged personal sacrifices, and delayed financial rewards as contributing factors. Studies of the profession itself focus on the historical evolution from obscure status to its present position of prominence, power, and wealth in the U.S. (Starr, 1983).

Historically, physicians have tended to be recruited disproportionately from higher socioeconomic levels and until the last decade, women and ethnic minorities have had a very difficult time gaining access to medical schools. While medical schools are legally prohibited from excluding students on the basis of sex, religion, or ethnic identity, many factors are responsible for the small numbers of ethnic minorities in most medical schools. Except for blacks, hispanics and native Americans, medical schools do not even keep statistics on other groups mainly because of the potential for claims of discrimination. Thus, there are no "official" statistics on the distribution or numbers of Italian

*Partial support for this research was provided by William Patterson College and the Italian/American Institute to Foster Higher Education in New York City. We are grateful to Ceryl LaBate for her assistenace.

Americans, for one example, in American medical schools or among the population of practicing physicians.

This paper examines the pattern of participation of Italian Americans within the system of medical education in the United States. Research findings on the percentage of Italian Americans who graduated from medical school in 1981 will be used to compare the distribution of this ethnic group to other graduates. In addition, information obtained in 1983 from a sample of medical students attending a school in the Northeast will provide a psychosocial portrait of this subgroup. These combined data will also serve as a basis for analyzing the structure of medical education and the processes of recruitment and socialization into medicine.

The Structure of Medical Education

Medical sociologists have generated numerous studies of medicine as the model profession and of the recruitment and socialization of physicians. Professions are defined by areas of special expertise, an established code of ethics, and by the ability of its membership to control the content of their own work, standards, and membership. (Caplow, 1954; Friedson, 1970; Goode, 1961; Huges, 1958; Wilensky, 1964). It is not suprising, therefore, that recruitment, which is formally structured around academic qualifications for gaining entrance into medical school, is also supported by a long established network of informal social ties. Both the formal and informal basis of this social structure has functioned to inhibit access of minorities, women, and Italian Americans.

Given the high cost of medical education, physicians are still mainly recruited from the higher socioeconomic levels. In one study, it was reported that in 1960 over half of medical school graduates came from professional or managerial families (Becker, 1972), and that a large proportion of students had fathers or other relatives who were physicians. At Cornell Medical School, in the 1940's, half of the students had relatives who were physicians (Dube, 1978).

Significant changes in the diversity of the student body have occurred in the last decade with increased minority and female enrollment (Clark and Rieker, 1985). However, along with these advances, recent research indicates that most medical students still have parents with higher than average income and education levels, and are themselves recruited from the major universities across the nation (Sullivan, 1982; Gough & Hall, 1977; Gordon, 1979; Hackman, 1979).

Decisions to become a physician occur earlier than most other professions; consequently, students need to be socialized into the values, attitudes, interests, and specialized knowledge throughout their academic development. Students who come from physician families are at a greater advantage given both the early exposure and access to an informal network. Gough and Hall (1977) reported that medical students from physician families attended more prestigious undergraduate colleges and were younger than other students from non-physician families, although the scholastic and MCAT scores of the two groups were similar. Since undergraduate college has been shown to be a significant factor in gaining admission to medical school, students who attend prestigious undergraduate institutions are clearly at an advantage.

Distribution of Italian Americans in Medical Schools in the U.S.

For the academic year 1980—81, each medical school in the country listed in the Association of Amerian Medical Colleges Directory (totaling 126) was sent a letter requesting a copy of their commencement program so that the names of Italian American graduates could be identified. In spite of the probability of error in selecting Italian surnames, no other source of ethnic identification was available to the reseach team; first and last names on a random basis, however, were cross-checked by a linguist. This ample of 1981 graduates ultimately included 91 medical schools, or 72.2% of the total number of schools (Martorella, 1983).

The percent distribution of Italian Americans graduating from the 91 medical schools in 1981 provided a national norm of 5.6%. (According to the 1980 Census, Italian Americans number 12 million, or approximately 5% of the total U.S. population.) The percent of Italian American medical school graduates distributed by region is outlined in Table I along with the percent by state (Figure 1). As Table I and Figure I indicate the highest percentages of graduates were in the Northeast region and states. These data show a higher concentration of Italian American medical school graduates in the urban, industrial and ethnically diverse states (i.e. New York, New Jersey, Connecticut) across the United States. For example, of all the medical graduates in New York City medical schools in 1981, 8.9% were Italian Americans. Currently, Italian Americans represent approximately 14.2% of the general population in New York. In the combined states in the northeast, 10.11% of the medical school graduates were Italian American, while Italian Americans number 6 million people, or 16.1% of the population. The states of Connecticut (18%), New York (10%), New Jersey (9%), Massachusetts (9.8%), West Virginia (8.9%), and Vermont (8%) had the highest representation nationally of Italian Americans as medical school graduates (see Figure 1).

Table II lists the medical schools in the Northeast, according to rank order of prestige, along with percent of Italian Americans graduating from these schools in 1981. In comparing the school's reputed prestige with the distribution of Italian Americans, it becomes clear that the higher the prestige, the lower the percent of Italian American medical school graduates. The top half of the

TABLE I

Regional Distribution of Italian Americans
As Graduates of Medical Schools
United States — 1981

Northeast	10.11%
Middle Atlantic	5.13%
Great Lakes	5.06%
S.W. & So. Central	4.10%
Western	3.85%
Southeastern	2.50%
N.W. & Gr Plains	2.23%

TABLE II

Medical Schools in the Northeast by Rank Order[a]
and Percent Distribution of Italian Americans in 1981

	% Distribution
1. Yale University	na
2. Columbia University	9.6%
3. Cornell University	2.8%
4. Albert Einstein College of Medicine	5.5%
5. University of Rochester	11.0%
6. New York University	8.8%
7. State U. of New York/Upstate	13.3%
8. University of Buffalo	8.0%
9. Albany Medical College	11.0%
10. State U. of New York/Downstate	12.9%
11. University of Connecticut	18.0%
12. New York Medical College	15.7%
13. Loyola College	18.0%
14. College of Medicine & Dentistry/NJ	9.4%

Note: Not all schools participated in this study.
Source: Cole & Lipton (1977:669-71).

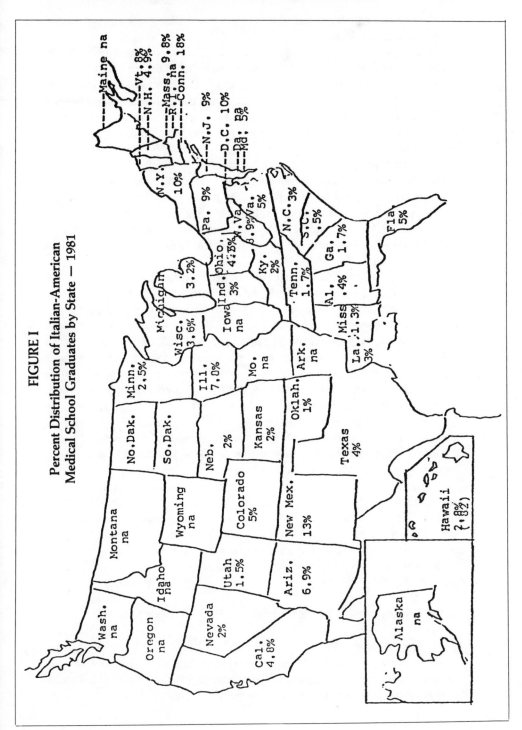

FIGURE I

Percent Distribution of Italian-American Medical School Graduates by State — 1981

Maine na
Vt. .8%
N.H. 4.9%
Mass. 9.8%
R.I. na
Conn. 18%

N.Y. 10%
N.J. 9%
D.C. 10%
Md. 5%
Pa. 9%

W.Va. 5%
Va. 5%
N.C. 3%
S.C. .5%
Fla 5%

Ohio 4.3%
Ind. 3%
Ky. 2%
Tenn. 1.7%
Al. .4%
Ga. 1.7%
Miss. 1.3%
La. 3%

Michigan 3.2%
Wisc. 3.6%
Iowa na
Ill. 7.0%
Mo. na
Ark. na

Minn. 2.5%
No.Dak. na
So.Dak.
Neb. 2%
Kansas 2%
Oklah. 1%
Texas 4%

Montana na
Wyoming na
Colorado 5%
New Mex. 13%

Wash. na
Oregon na
Idaho na
Utah 1.5%
Ariz. 6.9%
Nevada 2%
Cal. 4.8%

Hawaii (2.8%)
Alaska na

most highly ranked schools had a norm of 8.5% of Italian Americans graduates, while the lower half had a norm of 13.9%.

Although geographic, economic, and social factors contribute to this trend, the greater concentration of Italian Americans living in the northeast probably accounts for the higher numbers in those medical schools. In addition, given the costs of financing college and medical education, lower income groups may be at a disadvantage for recruitment into prestigious medical schools as families opt to send their children to the less expensive, and less prestigious state or parochial colleges.

Research on the occupation, education, and income levels of Italian Americans indicates that as a group they lag behind the social status achieved by some other white ethnic groups, despite their economic and occupational advances within the last decade. (Alba, 1985; Egelman, 1985; Krase, 1983; Lieberson, 1979; Lopreato, 1971). The somewhat lower level educational achievement of this ethnic group has often been attributed to an anti-education bias among Italian American families.

However, another factor that has not been explored by social scientists which may play a significant role in the education and achievement levels of Italians Americans is family ties and religious beliefs. Family ties, loyalties, and religious beliefs may influence decisions not only about whether to attend college, but also the location and type of school preferred. Consequently, Italian Americans have often chosen to attend parochial schools and small colleges near home. Such choices may put students in a less competitive position upon graduation. The values of proximity to the family, parent/child loyalties, the ostensible morality of the school, etc., irrespective of financial issues, may be salient part of the decision-making process during the crucial pre-medical period. Thus, Italian American values in general need to be considered in any discussion accounting for the extent of representation in education, and appears more important than the anti-education bias operating in this group.

As discussed earlier, the majority of students admitted to medical schools have professional/managerial parents with high incomes. In addition, they are recruited from approximately 10% of the major universities across the nation, and have higher than average MCAT and ASTIN scores. For example, statistics on the entering classes at Harvard medical school for the years 1980 to 1985 show that the largest percentage of students come from six schools: Harvard/Radcliff, Princeton, Stanford, Yale, MIT and Brown.

A Case Study of one Medical School in the Northeast

In November of 1983, 799 students were sent questionnaires through the Dean of Students' Office at a private medical school in the northeast not included in the list of top ranked schools discussed earlier. Forty-five percent (357 students) of the total medical school population returned the questionnaire.

Italian Americans represented 11.5% (58 students) of the study sample. Of the Italian Americans 22% indicated mixed ancestry. First year students are more highly represented in the sample (first year = 36.8%; second year = 21.1%; third year = 18.4%; fourth year = 23.7%). Data were collected on family backgrounds, pre-medical training, expeiences in medical school, self-esteem, and professional expectations.

Differences were found between Italian Americans and other medical students with regard to their pre-medical education. Italian Americans more often attended schools such as SUNY-Albany, St. John's, NYU, Colgate, Fordham, Syracuse, Northwestern; their college GPA was slightly higher with a norm of 3.4 in comparison to other medical students whose college GPA was 3.3. Italian Americans majored in and took more science courses than other students, and had more college honor courses and advanced placements in high school. Interestingly, their decision to go to medical school occurred later than other medical students with 44% deciding in high school, and 39.9% deciding in college; of the other medical students, 22.8% reported that they had decided in grammar school that they wanted to be physicians. Italian Americans were more likely to be single, but were similar in the ratio of males to females.

The above data certainly reflect the formal recruitment process of medical education today. The slightly higher college averages and the selection of more science and advanced placement courses of Italian Americans may be due to the fact that they attended less competitive undergraduate colleges. In comparison, approximately half of the Harvard Medical school class entering between 1981—84 had GPA's at 3.75 or above, and 75% were science majors.

Family Background — As discussed earlier, researchers continue to report that medical students have higher than average family incomes and have professional and managerial fathers (Gordon, 1979; Gough and Hall, 1977; Hackman, 1979; Lesserman, 1978; Sullivan, 1982; and Zuckerman, 1978). In this sample Italian Americans reported a mean income of approximately $45,000; three of the fifty-eight students reported incomes over the school norm of $64,000. Income and education were directly related for families of Italian Americans, but not for other medical students. However, fathers with less than grammar school education, although a small portion of the sample, reported incomes higher than post-graduate degree holders.

The educational backgrounds of both fathers and mothers is provided in Table III and indicates that in spite of the fact that all medical students have more highly educated parents in comparison to non-medical students, Italian American fathers report fewer college (15.8% vs. 17.1%), and postgraduate (28.9% vs. 33.9%) degrees than other fathers (5.3% of Italian American fathers and 4% of other fathers had only a grammar school education). The same educational differences are observed for Italian American mothers who reported generally lower educational levels with a drastic difference in postgraduate education. Fifty-five percent of Italian American mothers had a high school education or less compared to 33% of other mothers while 10.5% vs. 20.8% had postgraduate degrees. In spite of lower income and education levels of Italian American parents in comparison to the parents of other medical students, as a group they still represent a more highly educated and wealthier elite subgroup of Italian Americans. (This difference could be due to the fact that Italian Americans are being compared with urban, ethnically diverse subgroups including Asians, Jews, and Hispanics.)

TABLE III

Parental Education A Comparison of Italian Americans and Other Medical Students		
	Italian Americans	**Others**
Father's Education		
Grammar School	5.3%	4.0%
Some High School	2.6%	7.4%
H.S. Graduate	36.8%	14.8%
Some College	10.5%	16.4%
College Degree	15.8%	17.1%
Post-grad. Degree	28.9%	33.9%
Mother's Education		
Grammar School	2.6%	2.0%
Some High School	7.9%	3.4%
H.S. Graduate	44.7%	28.2%
Some College	10.5%	16.1%
College Degree	23.7%	18.8%
Post-grad. Degree	10.5%	20.8%

Medical School stress factors and concerns — Table IV shows 34.9% of non-Italian American medical students indicated that their main concern in medical school was the cost of their education, while 29.9% reported the potential workload as the primary main concern. In comparison, 65% of Italian American students reported workload as their main concern while only 15.8% chose financing their education as primary. With the lower than average income levels reported above, one would expect finances to be more problematic than workload. However, several factors might account for this unexpected finding. It may be that parents with less education and non-professional backgrounds feel a great sense of responsibility and honor if a son or daughter, probably the first in their family, becomes a physician. Considerable financial and other kinds of sacrifice are both expected and assumed. In addition, when financing was included as a choice given to students with regard to stress factors, Italian Americans chose study skills, workload, and course content more often than the other medical students. Such concerns could be due to the fact that Italian American students may have come from less competitive academic backgrounds, perhaps making them more anxious about medical school courseload and schedules.

TABLE IV

Stress Factors Among Medical Students
A Comparison of Italian Americans and Other Medical Students

	Italian Americans	Others
Selected Problems		
Course Content	21.1%	15.4%
Study Skills	42.1%	33.6%
Other Students	15.8%	8.7%
Courseload	52.6%	34.2%
Concerns (first choice)		
Cost of Education	15.8%	34.9%
Faculty Attitudes	2.6%	14.4%
Workload	65.8%	29.9%
Competition	2.6%	2.3%
Length of time in School	13.2%	12.8%

Professional Expectations — Students were asked to rank the importance of various aspects of professional achievement. Table V reports responses (that ranged from "unimportant/slightly important," "moderately important," and "very important") to a list of items describing what students might wish to achieve in the future practice of medicine. Differences in expectations were observed between Italian Americans and other medical students in our sample. Italian Americans ranked "helping others" as their most important professional obligation (63.2%), followed by "succeeding in own business" (31.6%), with "being an authority in the field (26.3%) the third most important. The other medical students selected as their first choice, "helping others" (53.7%), followed by "recognition of peers" (26.2%), and "being an authority in the

TABLE V

Professional Expectations of Medical Students
A Comparison of Italian Americans and Other Medical Students

	Italian Americans			Others		
	un/sl imp	mod/imp	v. imp	un/sl imp	mod/imp	v. imp
Authority in Field	23.7%	47.4%	26.3%	29.2%	42.6%	24.2%
Recognition of Peers	18.4%	63.2%	15.8%	19.8%	41.6%	26.2%
Financial Success	36.6%	52.6%	7.9%	45.0%	45.0%	9.1%
Contrib. Sc. Theory	50.0%	28.9%	15.8%	51.4%	25.8%	13.4%
Wr. Orig. Works	47.4%	34.2%	13.2%	51.6%	23.2%	16.1%
Success/Own Bus.	24.2%	28.9%	31.6%	34.2%	34.2%	25.0%
Helping Others	5.3%	28.9%	63.2%	6.7%	30.9%	53.7%

field'' (24.2%). Individual success is business may be an important value to Italian Americans, and function as an underlying goal to be achieved indirectly through medical practice as a type of entrepreneural activity as well.

Although the majority of medical students expect to have a specialty practice along with some research activity, few differences were found in their responses to an open ended question: ''What is your ideal of a successful physician?'' Most students described their ideal physician as being competent and caring. Female students were the only ones to include comments about balancing family life with professional commitment.

Self-Esteem — Students were asked to evaluate themselves (on a scale ranging from below average, average, to above average) on a variety of social, personal, and professional attributes. Table VI shows that approximately 60% of all medical students ranked themselves ''average'' or ''above average'' on nearly all aspects of their self-evaluations. However, Italian Americans ranked themselves higher in comparison to their peers, evaluating themselves as ''above average'' in academic ability, artistic ability, cheerfulness, achievement, originality, political conservatism, social and intellectual self confidence, and in the understanding of others. Other medical students ranked themselves higher on attributes such as defensiveness, leadership, and mathematical ability.

It is beyond the scope of the present study to fully explain the complex determinants of self-image and self esteem. As social scientists, however, we are well aware that many factors beyond actual academic performance, and including family and peers, account for positive or negative images of the self. Other than a few marginal and statistically insignificant differences, Italian American medical students are remarkably similar to other medical students in their confident self-evaluations. Representing the upper ranks of their respective undergraduate colleges, and admitted into a medical school, their sense of self-worth may be reassured by having gained formal access into the most prestigious profession in America today. In addition, given what they report of their backgrounds, it is likely that they may have come from less traditional Italian households. Their family structure appears to have provided a support system and an environment which nurtures autonomy, confidence, and high levels of self esteem. Anxiety about workload and study skills is expected and normal given the rigors of academic work in the first two years of medical school. As they enter their clinical third year, they will soon realize workload can be managed, and that academic knowledge does not always determine clinical skill and judgment.

Italian Americans in Medicine — The Future

Given the data presented above, several components of social behavior can be forecasted. Although a less than normative representation was revealed,

TABLE VI

Self Esteem Among Medical Students
A Comparison of Italian Americans and Other Medical Students

	Italian Americans			Others		
	Below/Av	Average	Abv/Average	Below/Av	Average	Abv/Average
Acad. Ability		18.4%	79.0%	1.7%	18.5%	70.2%
Artistic Ability	23.7%	36.8%	36.0%	29.5%	33.6%	26.2%
Cheerfulness	13.2%	18.4%	65.8%	17.8%	27.5%	54.0%
Defensiveness	29.0%	52.6%	15.8%	28.6%	51.3%	17.8%
Drive to Achieve		13.2%	84.3%	10.4%	20.8%	67.8%
Leadership	5.3%	39.8%	52.6%	10.1%	31.5%	57.4%
Math. Ability	2.6%	31.6%	63.1%	6.0%	23.5%	69.5%
Originality		31.6%	65.8%	4.4%	32.9%	59.5%
Pol. Cons.	23.7%	39.5%	31.6%	45.0%	34.0%	20.0%
Po. Lib.	36.8%	34.8%	23.7%	37.3%	38.3%	23.8%
Self-Conf/Intell.		28.9%	68.4%	5.3%	24.2%	58.5%
Self-Conf/Soc.	10.5%	34.2%	52.7%	16.1%	33.9%	43.0%
Underst. Others		5.3%	92.1%	8.0%	9.7%	75.8%

increased levels of income and education for Italian Americans should lead to professional recruitment. Networking, and the assistance by mentors and counselors could serve well to encourage high school students to select more prestigious colleges and universities for their pre-medical education. However, the mid-80's has proven to be a time of economic retrenchment and greater competition for the higher levels of power and prestige in our society. Hopefully, second and third generation Italian Americans will have internalized the "work ethic" of their ancestors.

Less optimistically, however, several problems remain. The last decade has witnessed the rise of "organizational medicine" in which major corporations have entered the delivery of medicine. This trend has inhibited, to some extent, easy access of young and ethnic doctors. The medical working environment of the future is less individualistic and entrepreneural in nature, and Italian Americans will have to accommodate to this new highly technologized and institutionalized style of work. In addition, Italian American women will encounter higher levels of stress given the conflicting demands of dual roles.

Bibliography

Alba, Richard D.
> "The Italian American Woman." Paper presented at the Eastern Sociological Society. March, 1985. Philadelphia, Pennsylvania. and Gwen Moore, "Ethnicity in the American Elite." *American Sociological Review* 47 (1982): 373—83.
> Association of American Medical Colleges. *Directory of Medical Education*. Washington, D.C., 1982.

Becker, Howard S., Blande Geer, Everett C. Hughes, and Anselm L. Strauss
> *Boys in White: Student Culture in Medical School*. New Brunswick, New Jersey: Transaction Books, 1961.

Clark, Elizabeth J. and Patricia Perri-Rieker
> "Gender Differences in Stress and Relationships of Medical and Law Students." *Journal of Medical Education* 61 (1986): 32—40.

Cole, J.
> "The Reputations of American Medical Schools." *Social Forces* 55 (1966): 662—84.

Egelman, William and Joseph Salvo
> "Italian Americans in New York City: A Demographic Overview." Paper prepared for the American Italian Historical Association meetings. Washington, D.C. 1984.

Gordon, Travis
> "Applicants for 1978—79 First Year Medical School Class."
> *Datagram* 55 (1980): 74—76.

Gough, Harrison and Wallace B. Hall
> "A Comparison of Medical Students from Medical and Nonmedical
> Families." *Journal of Medical Education* 52 (1977): 451—547.

Hackman, Judith D. et. al.
> "The Premed Stereotype." *Journal of Medical Education* 54
> (1979): 308—313.

Haynes, Alfred
> "Influence of Social Background in Medical Education." *Journal
> of Medical Education* 48 (1973): 45—8.

Krase, Jerome
> "Educational Attainment and Educational Values: Italian American
> Students at Brooklyn College." Paper prepared for the American
> Italian Historical Association meetings, Jamaica, New York 1983.

Lesserman, Jane
> "The Professional Values and Expectations of Medical Students."
> *Journal of Medical Education* 53 (1978): 330—6.

Lopreato, Joseph
> "Social Science and Achievement Motivation Among Italian
> Americans," in *Power and Class: The Italian American Experience
> Today*. Francis X. Feminella, editor (New York: AIHA, 1971).

Martorella, Rosanne
> "Italian Americans as Medical Students and Faculty." Paper
> prepared for presentation at the Italian American Institute to Foster
> High Education Conference, Staten Island, New York 1983.

Page, Robert G. and Mary H. Littlemeyer
> Preparation for the Study of Medicine. Chicago, Illinois: University
> of Chicago Press 1969.

Starr, Paul
> *The Social Transformation of American Medicine*. New York: Basic
> Books, Inc. 1983.

Sullivan, Ronald
> "Medical Schools Show Big Drop in Minorities." *New York Times*
> (March 1, 1982): 81.

Chapter 13

FACT IN FICTION:
ORAL TRADITIONS AND THE
ITALIAN AMERICAN WRITER

Fred L. Gardaphe

In the beginning the word was spoken. And because it was meant for ears and human memory, what needed to be remembered needed to be told in such a way as to be easily recalled. For this to happen, the speaker had to use such techniques as rhyme, repetition, exaggeration and vivid description.

Later people took to recording the word on pages with symbols, and although it could make the word live longer, people risked inadequate translation, interpretation, and preservation.

Much later the word could be recorded as it was spoken into machines. This eliminated the need for transcription and thus could insure near perfect transmission of one person's word to another. This also eliminated the need for immediately memorizing the word as it could be consulted later.

This evolution of the word's preservation has profoundly affected social and political interaction. Today, a person's word in court must be substantiated with evidence. Wire-taps, and videotapes have become the new and improved eye-witnesses. This evolution has also had profound effects on the way we view the past.

Today we can literally see and hear the past, where as yesterday we could only sense it through the writer's recorded impressions.

This evolution of the word has changed not only history but story.

Leonard Moss, in his essay: "The Family in Southern Italy: Yesterday and Today" wrote, "The novelist, who is afterall an ethnographer who knows how to write, can shed great light on problems ignored by the historian." (p. 185)

Professor Moss was referring to an idea that reaches back into the origins of language — that history is often preserved in story.

But there is made that a novelist can do than "shed great light" on social problems. Early novelists can tell us much about a culture's storytelling tradition once a culture shifts its emphasis from oral to written communication.

If we see Italian American literature as an extension of our oral traditions we can begin to examine not only what history our literature preserves, but in what manner that history is preserved. That is, we can find much fact in fiction.

Italian Americans have a rich oral culture, one that once was passed on from generation to generation, not by diaries, not by short stories, or novels or other literature, but primarily passed on by word of mouth. This method of carrying on tradition has moved in new directions since Italian Americans have begun to enter into the mainstream of American literature.

Italian American writers such as Pietro DiDonato, John Fante, Jerre Mangione, and Mario Puzo, grew up in a primarily oral culture; many of them were the first of their families to achieve literacy. These and all the early Italian American writers were able to use their skills to preserve many oral stories and experiences of their culture.

All of us have heard stories from our grandparents and had we the inclination we could retell those stories orally or in writing.

In the Chicago suburb where I grew up we had a saying that a really tough guy was one who'd play "morra" for fingers.

"Morra" is a game in which two opponents flash out the fingers of one hand while simultaneously yelling out the total number of fingers they think will be extended. The one who calls out the correct number scores the point. The score is kept with the fingers of the other hand.

Having never known the origins for that reference I received an explanation through a story that my grandfather used to tell. Grandpa used to tell the tale of the two greatest "morra" players in our town's history.

The men are partners of an undefeated "morra" team. When they are asked which of the two is the best each man boasts that there is no one better than himself. Both are so confident that they agree to play against each other and score points by having the loser cut off a finger for each point lost.

This type of storytelling was an integral part of growing up Italian. The older members of my family very often answered questions with a tale. Whether it was at the dinner table, in a garden, or at a wedding reception, they'd look around, survey the audience and launch into a tale that would explain the meaning of an Italian word, why people marry, or why they left Italy.

In the towns of southern Italy, the "cantastorie", or history singers were the guardians of local tradition. Within the family, children learned by listening, watching and imitating. Stories, like those my grandparents told me, educated while they entertained. Perhaps my grandfather, while teaching me how to play morra, was also telling me — through this folktale — not to take any game too seriously.

In this introduction to *Mules and Men* by Zora Hurston, Robert Hemenway discusses the importance of such folktales.

"Folktales illustrate how an entire people adapted and survived in the new world experience, how they transformed what they found into a distinctive way of life. They describe the human behavior the group approves, indicated when the behavior is appropriate and suggests strategies necessary for the preservation of the group in a hostile environment." (Hemenway, xxii)

Early Italian American writers provide us with such portraits of Italians adapting to America

Books were not necessary in southern Italy, nor were they an integral part of Italians adaption to American life. But for their American-born children, literacy became synonymous with "going American."

in American schools, Italian oral culture met the traditions of English literature. Children who went to school for the first time speaking only Italian discovered whole new worlds, first in the English language and then in its literature.

Some of these children, perhaps those who would have been drawn to the canatstorie back in Italy, fell in love with reading. Coming from homes that had few if any books, writers such as Fante, DiDonato, and Mangione, spent many hours in the local library, absorbing the stories they found there.

In interviews, these early Italian American novelists tell of their introduction to the written word. And in their writing, their families and communities are the basis for wonderful tales. Their books became both a bridge between oral and written cultures and a continuation of Italian storytelling traditions.

Writers such as Jerre Mangione and Pietro DiDonato wrote primarily biographical fiction, which simultaneously celebrated the joy of their cultural traditions and related the hardships of adjusting to a way of life where the old values and customs often clashed with those of the new land.

Jerre Mangione's *Mount Allegro*, for example, is the story of a boy growing up in Rochester, New York's little Italy. The work offers vignettes of life in the Italian American extended family, as American born children struggle to reconcile their parents' old world beliefs and uncertainty about whether or not they are "Americans."

"Those who left [Mount Allegro] for good developed strange habits and tastes. They took to drinking fruit juices at breakfast and tea with supper. They wore pyjamas to bed, drank whiskey with soda and learned to play poker . . .

If the children had had their own way, my parents would have dropped all their Sicilian ideas and customs and behaved more like other Americans. That was my childhood dream. Yet, as much as we wanted to live an American life, we did not have the vaguest notion of how to go about it. (Mangione, 208)

This excerpt is but one of the many examples that *Mount Allegro* gives us of Italians adapting to America. It contains many of our first folktales.

Pietro DiDonato's classic, *Christ in Concrete*, the story of a young boy whose father must work under dangerous conditions in a construction job and dies in an unnecessary accident on Good Fridy, is yet another example of how our early literature consists of many expanded folktales.

A second generation of Italian American authors, now in their 30s and 40s have emerged, grappling with the task of rediscovering their heritage and examining it in the light of having become American. Yet for many of contemporary authors their writing still contains a strong sense of the folk tale.

Influenced like their parents by the strong oral culture, the second generation often grew up with few books. Although they went to school speaking English, school provided the opportunity to learn about writing as a new medium for storytelling.

There are close to two hundred Italian American novels that depict the immigrant struggle, second generation conflicts between American born children and their parents and the third generation's search for a cultural heritage. Together these novels flesh out the dry bones of the American past chronicled in the history books.

Only recently have scholars begun to address the importance of the Italian Folktale in America (Mathias & Raspa). However it is my belief that we have been reading them for years and have yet to develop a way of looking at our literature as modern folklore.

In his study, *Orality and Literacy*, Walter Ong identifies characteristics of oral and literate cultures. By applying a few of those characteristics to Italian American literature we can see that early Italian American literature is the first bridge between a primary oral culture and a newly literate culture.

One characteristic of an oral culture that has been identified by Ong is:

> The heroic tradition of primary oral culture and of early literate culture with massive oral residue, relates to the agonistic lifestyle. Oral memory works with heavy characters and the bizzare. (Ong, 49)

Perhaps this is why a novel such as *The Godfather* has had such a strong influence on the way Italian Americans are perceived. It works with stereotypic "heavy" characters such as Luca Brasi, the brute "hit man" and Don Corleone, the patriarchal mafioso. Such characters are often found in the oral stories that get passed on from generation to generation. They become our equivalent of the homespun American folk heroes such as Mickey Finn and Paul Bunyan.

Using Ong's ideas, we can see that Puzo's characters in *The Godfather*, are closer to those of an oral tradition than to a written one. The story is more like a tall tale and perhaps that is why *The Godfather*, more mythical than literary, succeeds as a story and not as a literary masterwork.

Puzo himself admits to his attempts to create a myth in his essay "The Making of *The Godfather*":

> If [*The Godfather*] has energy and I lucked out by creating a central character that was popularly accepted as genuinely mythic . . . (Puzo, 41)

The sentence structure of oral stories, Ong tells us, is characteristically simple. These simple sentences accumulate information rather than imbed it in complex sentences filled with dependent clauses. Such structure facilitates recall. We find this simplicity throughout Fante's work, and especially in the opening of his *Wait Until Spring, Bandini.*

"He came along, kicking the deep snow. Here was a disgusted man. His name was Svevo Bandini, and he lived three blocks down that street. He was cold and there were holes in his shoes. That morning he had patched the holes on the inside with pieces of cardboard from a macaroni box. The macaroni in that box was not paid for. He had thought of that as he placed the cardboard inside of his shoes." (Fante, 11)

Even third generation Italian American writers retain a strong oral residue in their work.

Another characteristic of a primary oral culture is the use of repetition. Though few novels begin with traditional folktale phrases, such as "Once upon a time," many begin with the feel of a story teller calling an audience together. Notice this, especially evidenced by the repitition of key phrases in the opening of Tina DeRosa's first novel:

> This is my mother, washing strawberries, at a sink yellowed by all foods, all liquids, yellowed. This is my mother scalping the green hair of strawberries, scalping them clean, leaving a pink bald spot where the green hair was, and the strawberries grow bumps under cold water, or were they already there, and nobody noticed? These are my mother's hands, skin that has touched thousands of things not touches strawberries, and strawberries are the first thing she has ever touched, but she is not noticing. (DeRosa, 7)

Besides the repetition, the use of present tense, as Ong tells us is a technique that lives storytellers often employ to create a sense of "things happening right before your eyes."

From the first paragraph of Helen Barolini's Chapter One of *Umbertina* we get a sense of orality and of a tradition that is being passed on, one that reached the narrator by word of mouth, one that is passed on through writing.

"She had hazel eyes, fair skin where the sun did not reach and a strong chin. In the village people said of Umbertina that she had character right from the womb. 'She'll be the man of her family,' they said. (Barolini, 23)

"They said . . . with these words we have the sense of orality and the beginning of a story, one that is being passed along to us through the author's writing.

I believe that one gets what he or she needs to write by listening. By listening to the past inside oneself, a writer stays in tune with his or her oral tradition.

An African proverb says, "Ancient things remain in the ear." And good writers listen for them.

Ours is a culture that has moved rapidly from what Ong labels as primary orality to literacy to secondary orality (the orality that occurs in the electronic media experience).

This shift has played an important role in the necessity and use of the literacy that Italian Americans have achieved. But the simplicity of style, the use of dialect, and exaggerated characters that we can find in the writing of first generation Italian Americans, is evidence that we are still close to our oral traditions.

Thanks to these writers we can discover how it feels to make a home in a new country, to create new ways to be American. We can also see the continuation of our oral traditions in their writing. Their writing makes history come alive; it lets us join the children listening at the grandfather's knee.

I end this paper with a short story that I created based on my grandfather's "Morra" tale, which I refered to earlier. I'm including this story because I believe it is the best way to demonstrate the process of moving from an oral to a written tale. It also use it because I cannot presume that other writers were consciously or subconsciously aware of their oral traditions while they were writing, as I am.

In my town when a guy was particularly tough we'd say, "He's so tough he plays 'morra' for fingers." They say that once, two men from town did indeed play this game, and that they kept score by cutting off fingers.

The story of this historic game has been passed down from father to son to grandson. This is the story of how Mario Ranello passed it on to his grandson Frankie.

The event took place in the back yard of a suburban home where a family picnic was in progress. After the meal, Frankie, a boy of ten, was watching the older men of the family playing "morra." He wanted to learn how to play it.

After going from table to table not getting a straight answer: from the women's table, to the old men's table and then to younger men's table, he ran off on his own. He mistook the pronunciation of "morra" for "amore" and thought it had something to do with the song, "That's Amore." He ran to his grandfather for an explanation. And as usual Grandpa answered the question by telling the boy a story.

"Caro Franco, w'at-sah bodder you?"

"Nonno what's that game that Uncle Carlo and Vince are playing. Nonna told me that it was ah-more-ay. Is it something to do with that song? Then he sang, "When the moon hits your eye like a big pizza pie . . ."

And before he could finish his grandfather laughed and said, "That's 'amore.' You know, when you fall innah love and get marry. The game you uncles play is callah morrrr-ay!" Grandpa rolled the 'rs' like a rock into his grandson's ears. And before it hit Frankie thought, 'but the word is the same.'

"Oh nonno, what do you mean? What is the game with the fingers and the yelling of the numbers!"

The old man pulled his grandson closer and said, "Veni qua, I tell you. Is old game. A game we play inah Italy. Is callah More-ay, because when you put out all you fingers they're all the fingers you got. Is-ah no more. Ay? I show you." Frankie took a seat on his grandfather's knee and could feel his wine-garlic-tobaccoed breath on his cheek.

"W'at you gotta do is guess w'at the total number fingers will be. Like this. I t'ro down a t'ree fingers and you t'row down two. But before the fingers show, you got guess what the total will be. If you do then you get the point. You mark the point with you left hand. When you get five points then you play the nex' player. Whoever team wins gets the vino. Capisci?"

"But nonno, how do you know what the total will be?"

"Oh when you firs' play you doan know, you guess. But after you play years an years with the same people, you know. You look deep in they eyes and you can see the number right there, inside they head, big as a bocce ball," he pointed a finger at Frankie's eyes. "I never tell you about Joey Lawyer an Sammie Parenti?"

'Of course,' thought Frankie, 'everyone heard about those winos.' They were two bums who stood all day outside the closed store on Twenty-third and Lake Steet in Dago Corners.

Sammie was the ex-baseball player. People said he used to be a pro until he got thrown out for betting on the games, or drinking or something. And Joey Lawyer, he was the old wino who used to be a lawyer for some big shot. Rumor was, he used to be a sharp, powerful attorney until he took a fall for one of his clients. He was the man with the missing forefinger and pinky on his left hand. And Sammie was the man with the fingerless left hand, who always wore a black glove. The thing to do with both of them was to get them to wave at you and then wave back to them holding a few finger down. Grandpa continued.

"Listen a me Franco. These two guys wasa best-ah more-ay players in town. No one could a beat them. They know just' how everone play.

"One ver' cold day in Jan-wary we was all sittin' in a saloon over Twenty-Third an Lake an someone, I doan remember who was, ask them who wasa the best.

"Now they never play each other, only was on same team, so they doan really know. This day they wasa both full of vino an wasa braggin' how they wasa best team.

"So Mister Rotelli he put a biga juga vino between them an say, 'The best of you two win all this.' Now ol' Joe he wasa so drunk he say he was not 'fraid to play fo' fingers."

"Did you say for fingers?," exclaimed Frankie.

"Oh yes. They say whoever win the point the other would cut off a finger."

The other men were now turning to listen to the old whitehaired Mario tell the story that they themselves had told so often. Mario had been there and told the story better than anyone else. Frankie sat still, mystified by his grandfather's telling.

The old man took a stance next to his chair when he say that he had everyone's attention. Frankie took the chair that had been kept warm by Grandpa. He titled his head up and listened.

Mario's arms were still muscular. His thick wrists lay on each pocket of his baggy flannel pants. His forehead oozed sweat that slowly dripped down to his wine blushed cheeks. His glasses, faded from years of absorbing sweat, dipped when his head bobbed and when they slipped to the end of his nose they revealed a pale strip of skin. His arms left his sides and he waved them in the air.

"'Doo-ayee, trray-ee,' they yell but didn't show those numbers. 'Cheen-kway, kwaah-tro,' they yell again, but nothin'.

"Then they stare deep in the eyes." Mario opened his wrinkled eyelids wide and stared right into the eyes of his grandson. In a raspy whisper he said, "An' there wasa no soun' in the whole bar.

"They hans fly up," (and so did the tightened fists of the old man, slowly in exaggeration he dropped them, flashing four fingers from each hand into Frankie's face). "They both yell 'Ah-toe!' an' they t'row four fingers.

"Everyone wasa on they toes. An' after seein this they all move to they heels. Then, they stop, to sip a lil' vino. Then they look back to Joe an' Sammie. These guys they play fo t'ree 'ours and no one score a point."

Mario's white skirt was now transparent with sweat, revealing the old man's beige t-shirt and cloth scapular. He stopped here, took off his glasses with his right hand and with his left reached into his back pocket, pulling out a large wrinkled red bandanna.

"And then what happened Nonno? What happened next?" Frankie begged.

"Aspetta Franco. You nonno is thirsty. Go bring to me some vino," Mario said swabbing his face with the handkerchief.

Frankie jumped from his seat and ran to the t.v. tray where the opened wine bottle lay in the shade. With both hands he lifted the heavy bottle and lumbered back to his chair. He clumsily poured the wine to the top of his grandfather's withered, purple lipped cup.

Mario took it and without spilling a drop and swallowed off the top fourth of the liquid. He wiped his lips with the back of is hand and shook the drops off his thumb. After chasing the wine with a deep breath, he looked to his audience and continued.

"Well they play fo' t'ree 'ours and Joey's wife she sen' his boy to tell him wasa time to eat. He say he was no hungry. Well they keep play all the night an a day. They just stop to drink more vino. This go one for one, two, t'ree days."

"The whole town 'ear 'bout this game an everyone who was livin back then stop by to see them play. They no eat o sleep fo those t'ree days."

"Ona t'ird day they was people sleepin on a bar an lil' Midget Mikey, he sleep right up on a juke-ah-box. Ol'Nino, he was the bar-tennor an he was worry for where to get more vino. He sold everything in a place. All was left wasa coke-cola."

"They was no more vino for poor Joe an maybe was why he lose the first finger. They yell 'sett-ah' seven-ah times inna row. Everyone know Sammie would a change his t'row the next time. Everone but ol' Joe."

"Some say his brain she dry up without that vino an he not wasa t'inkin' right. Others say wasa no eatin' his wife's pastafagioli fo' t'ree days that make mistake. But no one, not even Joe his self can tell you why he t'row that four for the eight time. But he did. An' Sammie catch him."

Mario flashed the index finger of his left hand into the air and yelled, "The first point wasa win by Sammie an' Joe had to cut offa finger!"

He clutched an invisible knife in his right hand and waved it in the air.

"Well, Joe, he reach ina pocket and without takin' his eyes off-ah Sammie he pull out his curve knife and he reach over an' slice off the little finger of his left hand. Justa like that. The finger fall to the ground like was a dead bird. Boom. An the blood was drippin down, like was a broke faucet . . ."

Mario wiggled the fingers of his right hand down under the stump he made of the little finger on his left hand and dropped the wiggling fingers almost to the green lawn at his feet. With this motion his white shirt left the tight hold of his waistband and flapped a white flag against his blue flannel pants. He inhaled and the breath sounded like a piece of old Parmesan cheese rubbing against a metal grater. He looked into Frankie'e eyes and continued.

"He tell Midget Mikey to go fine him some more vino. Then he say, 'Sammie, the game she stop at five. Eat'sah just begin.' The whole crowd move in to see Joe's finger and he wave it across they faces and the blood was aflyin all over the place. He shout, 'Come on! Le's play!' The score was Sammie uno an' Joe nuttin'."

Mario was tiring. Frankie could tell by the way he heaved his wide chest and took deeper, quicker breaths. But there was more.

Mario reached down, grabbed the paper cup of wine and swallowed it all. He held out the empty cup. Frankie poured the wine without taking his eyes off Grandpa's hands. He noticed that the wedding band on his grandfather's hand seemed to be choking his finger. Mario swiped the cup away from Frankie. He slurped then smacked his lips three times before he continued.

"They play fo' four more days an when was all finish, Joe lose two fingers. He cut off his big finger an little finger. Sammie had alla his."

"The game she probably still go on today if Sammie didn't have to take a pisshad and leave for to go to the buckhouse. Sammie, he walk out the door and maybe he think all the white snow was a bed. Cause he was gone long time."

"After while oldman Rotelli say, 'Ay, I know Sammie drink a lot of vino, but can he still be apissin! Is been an hour. Go see to find him.' Well they fine Sammie lyin down ina snow. He was all purple, but that old rooster wasa still breddin'.

"The doctor he say Sammie was luck he wasa preserved with alcohol cause he get the forsty bite all over an loose all-ah fingers on his lef' han. His right hand was ok, wasa still innah pants. But he could no play ah-more-ay no more."

"They say that was the end of ah-more-ay in town. No one wanna try an beat that game. Some time you see someone play ona street, but is not like used to be. We still play in a family, but for vino, no for fingers!''

"So maybe someday my boy you play. Us old men can play no more but maybe soon you play with you uncles."

With a deep breath and a sigh, Mario reached for his wine and finished the cup in one swallow. When the last drop was lifted from the rim by his purple tongue, he tapped his shirt pocket, pulled out his cigarettes and lit one, all the while staring into Frankie's eyes.

"An so my boy that's what is-ah more-ay."

Bibliography

Barolini, Helen
>   *Umbertina* (New York: Bantam, 1982).
DeRosa, Tina
>   *Paper Fish* (Chicago: The Wine Press, 1980).
DiDonato, Pietro
>   *Christ in Concrete* (New York: Bobbs-Merrill, 1937, 1975).
Fante, John
>   *Wail Until Spring, Bandini* (Santa Barbara, California: Black Sparrow Press, 1938, 1983).
Hemenway, Robert E.
>   "Introduction," to *Mules and Men* by Zora Hurston, (Bloomington: Indiana University Press, 1978).
Mangione, Jerre
>   *Mount Allegro* (New York: Columbia University Press, 1981).
Moss, Leonard
>   "The Family in Southern Italy: Yesterday and Today," in *The United States and Italy: The First Two Hundred Years*, edited by Humert S. Nelli (New York: The American Italian Historical Association, 1976).
Ong, Walter
>   *Orality and Literacy: The Technologizing of the Word*, (New York: Metheun, 1982).
Puzo, Mario
>   *The Godfather Papers* (New York: Fawcett Crest 1972).

14 **THE POETRY AND POLITICS OF ARTURO GIOVANNITTI**
Wallace P. Sillanpoa
University of Rhode Island

Amidst the chorus of voices of the Italian-American past there is one intonation that the present can at times relegate to virtual silence. That voice - vibrant, sometimes strident but always strong - is the voice of personal and organized resistance to the institutionalized injustices of the American economic and political system.[1] It is as though, I suspect, that as succeeding generations of by now mythologized immigrants begin to appropriate the accouterments of full assimilation and social mobility, a collective amnesia can take hold that stills the strains of those ancestors whose cries of protest and visions of a radical alternative prove embarassing and might even controvert accepted mythologies.

Such selective remembering of part of the Italian-American experience has effectively silenced just a voice. That voice, at once lyrical and agitational, belongs to the Italian-American poet and political activist, Arturo Giovannitti. Once hailed as the "Poet of the Workers"[2] and as among the most important of early 20th-Century social poets, Arturo Giovannitti appears today almost forgotten, his name exiled to the indices of social histories, and his verse dismissed to a limbo of the unuttered.

As Professor Joseph Tusiani points out, at least part of the reason for this must be attributed to the disqualifying label that Giovannitti acquired early on: "He was the minstrel of the worker and so he had to remain (. . .); he was poet of the disinherited and such he had to remain (. . .); he was a hero of the cause of nascent unionism and as such he had to be acclaimed (. . .)"[3] Tusiani laments this fact, but he likewise appropriates it in his particular assessment of Giovannitti's verse, as when he writes:

It was because of this label, imposed upon him first by success, and then having become conviction and passion, that Arturo Giovannitti created for himself a monotonous lyric that in poetry

about the work world found both its point of departure and point
of arrival. For this he suppressed whatever other sentiment of his
by now full and pulsating youth.[4]

The reasons for my disagreement with Tusiani on this point will follow.
For now I wish only to point out that Tusiani's essay is one of very few -
if not the sole critical commentary on Giovannitti's English poetry, and it
appears, moreover, in Italian, in a 1978 edition of the by now little known
Socialist paper, *La parola del popolo*, of Chicago. Indeed, securing information
and judgments on Giovannitti approaches the level of archeology since much
that he wrote or that was written about him remains buried in hard-to-find,
and in many cases, extinct periodicals of the Italian-American left - archival
underpinnings of that afore-mentioned historical amnesia. True, after
Giovannitti's death in 1959, family and friends assembled an edition of *The
Collected Poems of Arturo Giovannitti*, published in 1962 by Clemente and
Sons of Chicago with an introduction by Norman Thomas and containing a
1914 preface by Helen Keller to Giovannitti's earliest verse.[5] The collection
does not appear complete, however, and to my knowledge, no one has ever
undertaken the task of gathering and editing all the extant verse Giovannitti
wrote both in English and his native Italian.

Secondary sources referring to Giovannitti's life and activities do exist,
but as previously inferred, these references usually form only a small part of
broader social histories.[6] Warm personal reminiscences of Giovannitti are found
in the autobiographical accounts of many protagonists of early 20th-Century
social struggle, and most especially in Elizabeth Gurley Flynn's, *Rebel Girl*.[7]
As moving as most of these reminiscences are, in the long run they provide
the curious with but hard-to-assort anecdotal reports. Even in more highly
specialized studies such as Daniel Aaron's, *Writers on the Left*,[8] clear though
cursory mention of Giovannitti's writings is made, while John P. Diggins'
discussion of early century radical culture in *The American Left in the Twentieth
Century*,[9] ignores Giovannitti altogether. Consequently, it is of little wonder
that Giovannitti's name is absent from more mainstream studies of American
poetry and culture.

This scantiness of sources - lamentable as it is - does protect this
presentation from any claim to exhaustion or definitiveness. Instead, I fashion
my words as a memorial to contest the near oblivion now surrounding
Giovannitti, man and poet, a memorial that might one day be replaced by a
monument to the man's verse and life. I say this in the spirit of one of
Giovannitti's poems, "Death of a Billionaire," in which the poet derides the
marble and stone erected to honor those "who bade us work and procreate,
And starve and kill and live," insisting, instead, "But glory stalking stealthily
and solemn/ Beyond the tomb, the tablet and the column,/ Will read but one
more name, and will not know it/ For glory is not a tourist but a poet."[10]

And if it be true that every generation writes anew all criticism, literary and cultural as well as political and social, then there is no need to assume that Giovannitti's presence among Italian-American annals will forever remain shroud-like. At best, undertakings such as this modest one can eventually lead to a re-evaluation of the left cultural tradition in Italian-Americana, or at the very least, to an acknowledgement of that tradition's existence. To the prose of accounts of Italian-America's part in the great social and political battles of the early 20th Century, then, Giovannitti adds a poetic timbre - now lyrical, now phatic; now homely, now invective - but a voice, nonetheless, deserving attention.

Arturo Massimo Giovannitti was born in January, 1884, in Ripabottoni, near Campobasso in the Molise region. Within the context of a Southern-Italian agricultural community of the time, his family was considered well-off. His father was a doctor, as was one of his brothers. The other brother became a lawyer. His mother, whose maiden name bore the echoes of a remote French past, was apparently part of an impoverished but proud lesser aristocracy, so familiar to post-Bourbon Southern Italy. Both of Giovannitti's brothers died in World War I after Arturo had already emigrated to the New World. Before emigrating, Giovannitti had completed his secondary education at the *liceo*, "Mario Pagano," pride of the Molise region's educational system. In fact, Giovanni Gentile taught briefly at the "Mario Pagano" in 1899.

Without intending to overestimate the influence of Giovannitti's early schooling, it deserves mention that the "Mario Pagano" was not unlike so many State-run secondary schools of its time. In addition to its typically strong emphasis on the classical and Italian humanist tradition, that is, the "Pagano" was enmeshed in that feverish and troublesome attempt of post-Risorgimento Italy to locate and promote a new national culture. Anti-clericalism, for obvious historical reasons, was rife among an intellectual class in search of a new national and civic identity. Hence, among the poets, Carducci reigned supreme, the early Carducci whose Mazzinian and Jacobin fulminations against a compromised Risorgimento were inextricably tied to an attack on all residues of a feudal and clerical past; not the Carducci, that is, who later capitualted to the post of unofficial poet laureate to the House of Savoy.

Second in importance only to Carducci's poetry for a new lay intelligentsia in formation was that of Lorenzo Stecchetti whose verse of the 1870's and 1880's enjoyed a *succes de scandale* thanks to its unabashedly erotic and blasphemous tones. In light of Giovannitti's own verse decades later, it might be surmised that Stecchetti's denunciatory satires on the moral, religious and social conformity of his day left an impression on the adolescent schoolboy. To the names of Carducci and Stecchetti, those of the poet and parliamentarian, Felice Cavallotti, and of yet another poet, Mario Rapisardi, must be added. These latter scorned loyalist compromises and remained steadfast to both their Republican ideals and their demands for a social justice they found wanting in the new State. Though difficult to ascertain how much of this Republican and Socialist literature was indeed part of Giovannitti's intellectual and social milieu, it can be shown that vociferous groups of radical intellectuals were in evidence in the Campobasso area. Moreover, while at the "Pagano," the young Giovannitti made his first incursion into the world of poetry, winning a national prize for verse written in a classical and humanist vein.

The influence of this early environment is not immediately evident, for in 1901, and at the ripe age of seventeen, Arturo Giovannitti emigrated to the New World leaving behind an Italy to which he never returned.

But the young Giovannitti left to pursue a religious vocation. Strongly affected by a certain Tagliatela, a protestant minister evidently then well known in the Abruzzi and Molise regions,[11] Giovannitti's vocation was certainly heterodox by general Italian standards, grounded as it was in protestant evangelism. Thus, Giovannitti emigrated first to McGill University in Montreal where he completed theological studies and became an evangelical minister. While at McGill, Giovannitti perfected his knowledge of French to a degree that made it his second language. After McGill, the young minister served as assistant in a small Pennsylvania mining community under the direction of its chief pastor, Tagliatela.

By 1906 Giovannitti had abandoned his ministry, moved to New York, and embraced the cause of Socialism. The account of this sudden change offered by Mario DeCiampis is as unqualified as it is terse:

> Arturo came to socialism around 1905 or 1906 when the director of the newspaper, *Il proletario*, was Carlo Tresca; (. . .) when among the ranks of Italian-American socialists there was much talk of Revolutionary Syndicalism. When the switch from cleric to layman occurred, he was already in New York, addressing workers' assemblies and writing for the paper.[12]

From 1905 or 1906 until his death in 1959, Arturo Giovannitti remained in New York, residing for most of his life in the Bronx. He often expressed a passion for his adopted city and its multi-racial, multi-ethnic population, though this affection was equally tempered by a passionate indictment of the New York of Wall Street and Park Avenue. Immediately upon his arrival in New York, Giovannitti became a steadfast member of the *Federazione Socialista Italiana* (FSI) headquartered in MacDougall Street in lower Manhattan, and from that moment on - when not in the forefront - he was certainly a part of every major political and social movement of New York's vigorous left community.

By 1909, and upon mandate of the executive council of the FSI, Giovannitti became editor of *Il proletario*, and in 1911, at the IV Congress of the FSI, he was elected general director of the paper. During these early years,

Giovannitti nurtured strong personal and political ties to the IWW, or 'Wobblies,' and he travelled extensively throughout the United States urging working-class audiences to support the Wobblies' struggle for 'one big Union' that would unite all workers of every race and nationality. Only Industrial Unionism, argued Giovannitti and the IWW, could transcend the debilitating fragmentation of narrow trade unionism, then staunchly defended by the AFL and its old-line, overtly nativist leader, Samuel Gompers. As a result of these travels, Giovannitti soon came to be respected as a powerful and eloquent orator both in his acquired English and native Italian. Also, it was at this time that Giovannitti, together with the IWW organizer, Joseph Ettor, came to be recognized as a leader in the arduous task of organizing Italian-Americans into the IWW.

It was together with Ettor, in fact, that Giovannitti was first thrown into national limelight and earned for himself a permanent place in the history of American labor. Shortly after the 1912 outbreak of the great textile strike in Lawrence, Massachusetts - the 'Bread and Roses' strike - Giovannitti and Ettor travelled to Lawrence to assume direction of the strike at the IWW's invitation. Giovannitti and Ettor proved to be invaluable organizers during that bitter winter of 1912 when the full brunt of the New England owning classes, in league with their allies in government and academia, was unleashed against a terribly exploited, multi-ethnic population of mill workers and their children. The Lawrence strike will always be remembered as the first important labor action in which Italian-Americans were both organized and in positions of prominence. The 63-day-old strike will also be remembered for other reasons. As William Cahn has noted: ''It was a new kind of strike. A singing strike. Song overcame all language barriers.''[13]

In Lawrence, Ettor and Giovannitti were soon joined by the legendary IWW leaders, Elizabeth Gurley Flynn and ''Big'' Bill Haywood, together with Eugene Debs. Their fiery eloquence rallied hundreds and kept spirits high despite State-sponsored recalcitrance and military intimidation. On the night of January 29, police and State troopers clashed with a group of strikers. Ordered to disperse, the strikers found themselves with police on one side and troopers on the other. A shot rang out and the strike's first martyr, a young Italian-American worker, Annie LoPizzo, fell dead. Although ''both men were two miles away during the conflict,''[14] as Mary Heaton Vorse reported to *Harper's Weekly*, Ettor and Giovannitti, together with an unarmed Italian-American worker by the name of Caruso, were arrested and charged with the murder. The government claimed that Caruso had murdered LoPizzo, stirred to violence by the strike leaders, Giovannitti and Ettor. Many students of the strike today concur that the murder was carried out by an *agent provocateur*, probably in the mill owners' pay. In any event, for ten months the three men languished in jail awaiting trial. The trial itself, which ironically took place in Salem, lasted an additional two months. Upon the arrest of the three, however, a Defense Committee was formed that spurred an international mobilization to free the victims. After almost a year in jail, all three men were eventually fully exonerated, but the case remains still a shameful entry in the annuals of American jurisprudence.

While in jail, convinced of his innocence and yet facing a possible capital punishment, Giovannitti composed what is often held to be one of his best poems in English. Entitled, "The Walker," it was his first English poem, soon followed by many others he wrote during his imprisonment. "The Walker," originally published on the pages of the prestigious *Atlantic Monthly*, was almost immediately translated into the world's major tongues including Chinese, Japanese and Esperanto.

In about one-hundred fifty lines of verse - at times end-rhymed, or blank, with resonant internal rhymes and a preponderance of pentameters - Giovannitti evokes the horror, both haunting and desperate, of those locked within the dead confines of wall and bar. From the shadowy atmosphere of cell and silence, the poetic persona of "The Walker" emerges to vent a deep personal anguish:

> I, who have never killed, think like the murderers;
> I, who have never stolen, reason like the thief;
> I think, reason, wish, hope, doubt, wait like the hired assassin,
> the embezzler, the forger, the counterfeiter, the incestuous,
> the raper, the drunkard, the prostitute, the pimp,
> I, I who used to think of love and life and flowers and song and
> beauty and the ideal.[15]

But that same persona detaches itself only to re-emerge into the common mind of fellow prisoners, as in the bitter irony of the poet's outburst:

> Wonderful is the supreme wisdom of the jail that makes all
> think the same thought. Marvelous is the providence of
> the law that equalizes all, even in mind and sentiment.
> Fallen is the last barrier of privilege, the aristocracy of
> the intellect. The democracy of reason has levelled the
> two hundred minds to the common surface of the same
> thought.

And both focus and emblem of that 'same thought' is "A little key, a little key (. . .) of shining brass." That key, symbol *and* effective instrument of release to life, becomes, in Giovannitti's words, the obsession of "two hundred brains all possessed by one single, relentless/ unforgiving, desperate thought."

The poet's dark musings have been triggered by the eerie echo of footsteps in the cell above him, the physically muffled but psychologically thunderous sound of the walker as he passes the night pacing the confines of his cell. The description of torment unleashed nightly by this maddening march, at times redolent of Poe and the phantasmagorical, brings the poet to the very edge of reason. What saves him from the dementia of despair is his verse, expressive of a common humanity that joins him to his unwitting tormentor:

> I hear the footsteps over my head all night.
> They come and they go. Again they come and they go all night.
> They come one eternity in four paces and they go one eternity in
> four paces and they go one eternity in four paces, and between
> the coming and the going there is Silence and the Night and the
> Infinite.
> For infinite are the nine feet of the prison cell, and endless is the
> march of him who walks between the yellow brick wall and the
> red iron gate, thinking things that cannot
> be chained and cannot be locked, but that wander far away in the
> sunlit world, each in a wild pilgrimage after a destines goal.

Opening the poem, these words are later echoed in the poet's gentle plea to his fraternal counterpart at the poem's end: "Stop, rest, sleep my brother, for the dawn is well nigh and/ it is not the key alone that can throw open the gate."

Once again it is Joseph Tusiana who rightfully points out that, unlike Oscar Wilde's "Ballad of Reading Goal" published only fourteen years before Giovannitti's poem and to which comparisons had been made, "The Walker" transcends any implosive descent into personal despair, nor is it ever suggestive of a plea for absolution. As Tusiani incisively states, "The Walker" is "a hymn to life, a paean to the sanctity of the dynamic energy of human life which prison only interrupts but can never half."[16] Furthermore, paraphrasing Tusiani, "The Walker" is pregnant with implications that it is not simply life that awaits outside the prison gate, but the struggle for life; not just beauty, but the defense and propagation of beauty; not just freedom, but the challenge to extend that freedom to countless numbers blinded to life, beauty and freedom by misery and social injustice. Moreover, the continuous shift of poetic persona here - one that detaches itself only to re-immerse itself in a shared humanity and fate - constitutes in "The Walker" perhaps Giovannitti's best (but not only) poetic treatment of the now sustaining, now painful interplay of the existential and the collective; of private sentiment and public self.

For Tusiana, however, "The Walker" is not just a paragon, but the terminus of Giovannitti's English poetry insofar as, after "The Walker," all subsequent compositions, he argues, will split the poetic animus, making for contending categories of poetic expression: those which tremble with private sentiment and those which resound with public bombast.

In strictly formalistic terms, there is much to be considered in Tusiani's assessment, though that assessment seems to betray a Crocean 'poetry/non-poetry' dichotomy whereby the poetic is pre-established as expressive of inner, 'intuitive' sentiment and the non-poetic as anything that rings with overtly political indignation and intent. While helpful, such a measure could only lead to a florilegium of Giovannitti's verse, based on isolated lines determined by *a priori* criteria as to what constitutes poetic authenticity. I have neither the time nor the space here to attempt a full response to Tusiani's challenge. Nor is it my intent merely to advance an acritical and purely encomiastic account encompassing all of Giovannitti's poetry. Simply put, I wish only to present the case of Giovannitti, man and poet, with hopes that an interest may arise where there has been little, and a discussion emerge to fill the silence. Thus, within these limitations, my observations on Giovannitti's poetry to follow must remain general and inclusive.

The Collected Works of Arturo Giovannitti, comprising over ninety compositions, is divided into two main sections. The first section, entitled "Wind Before Dawn," contains poems Giovannitti wrote after his prison poetry from the time of Lawrence. The prison collection, "Arrows in the Gale," was previously published in 1914 with the afore-mentioned introduction by Helen Keller. All of the poetry in the 1962 edition constitutes a wide, but nevertheless incomplete collection of Giovannitti's verse in English.

After Lawrence and the trial, Giovannitti devoted more time than previously to literary endeavors, but never to the exclusion of political involvement. In passing, it is interesting to note that his anti-war play, *As It Was In The Beginning*, enjoyed a successful run on Broadway in 1917. After Lawrence, Giovannitti was also editor of *Il fuoco*, a New York based literary and political journal of the Italian-American left. He wrote in English for *The Masses*, that small but influential journal of politics and art edited by Max Eastman with the help of Floyd Dell and John Reed which Diggins has called "perhaps the heartiest journal in the history of American radicalism."[17] *The Masses* flourished from 1911 until its suppression by the government for anti-war propaganda in 1917, to be replaced in 1918 by *The Liberator* with Giovannitti as a contributing editor following the First World War. Many of Giovannitti's English-language poems first appeared on the pages of *The Liberator*.

Also following World War I, Giovannitti served as general secretary of the Italian Chamber of Labor, and then of the Italian Labor Education Bureau, center for Italian-American union membership, a post he held until about 1940. The Bureau was supported primarily by the Amalgamated Clothing Workers of America and the International Ladies Garment Workers Union for whose publications Giovannitti wrote both poetry and political commentary. Earlier, Giovannitti had been among the very first to react to Mussolini's rise in Italy and encroaching Fascism. As early as 1923, the Anti-Fascist Alliance of North

America (AFANA) had been formed with Giovannitti its secretary. It is again Diggins who reports that "Under the stirring leadership of the AFANA's Secretary, the fiery poet Giovannitti, the war against Fascism began with eloquent passion."[18] Not even Giovannitti's passionate eloquence could cement for long the factious Italian-American left, however, and the AFANA's history proved a sad foreshadow of a similar fate suffered by the Popular Front in the next decade.

Making a leap in time, we learn from Norman Thomas that "Throughout the fifties (Giovannitti) was bedridden by paralysis of the legs but continued to write despite this great handicap. In 1957 he published a collection of his Italian poems under the title, *Quando canta il gallo*, and at the time of his death (. . .) he was editing his English poems (. . .). This champion of labor was himself genuinely a man of letters, a linquist who wrote in verse and prose in Italian, English and French." Of the verse in English, Thomas maintains that Giovannitti "could write with tenderness (. . .) but the note most often sounded was of revolt."[19] Thomas' elegy underscores here Tusiani's critique in this common insistence on two fundamental and defining registers in Giovannitti's poetry, one intimate and lyrical; one public and splenetic.

Since Thomas is not a professional literary critic, he does not expand upon his elegy, citing Giovannitti, instead, as among the "great poets of an aroused working class (who) contributed much to labor's victories but could not find in them the fulfillment of (his) hopes."[20] Tusiani, meanwhile, would find in this twin register the focus of his critical objections. It seems however, that a fully balanced appreciation of Giovannitti's poetic texts can only be achieved ultimately through and by a qualifying appraisal of that verse's context, for in Giovannitti, more so perhaps than in many other modern poets, context - in the sense of a specific social geography - is of fundamental concern.

Giovannitti never construed or constructed his poetry as an exclusively personal expression giving form to a privatized experience. Thomas is right in underscoring the voice of revolt, whether in its overt form of indignation and biting satire, or in its more subdued form of reflection and 'lyrical' recollections, never fully the product of any 'tranqulity.' Most of Giovannitti's poetry is written, therefore, with the disclosure of the street in mind, and not the hush of the drawing room. Moreover, the phatic and sometimes rhetorical ring in many of Giovannitti's poems should be examined within the cultural context in which the poems were born, and in the social context of their intended audience and effect. During the teens, as was noted, Giovannitti was a constant presence at the headquarters of the FSI. But he was likewise often to be found a few blocks away in Greenwich Village, then a boisterous center of bohemian rebellion and cultural ferment that together made up what Diggins has termed, "The Lyrical Left."[21] In Giovannitti's poetry, then, it is essential both to hear and see these underlying twin strains of bohemian revolt and socialist polemic nurtured on, and not necessarily exclusive of, the poet's inner sentiments. In

Giovannitti, that is, one can garner insight into the nature of private pain or reverie as social construct.

Meanwhile, it is the voice of revolt that prevails in a poem like "New York and I." The love/hate that the young poet feels for this "City without history and without legends" concludes with a blast of invectives in polysyndeton whose force can be considered nothing less than Dantesque:

> I shall sing of your slums where you bleed,
> Your machines, iron claws of your greed,
> And your jails, viscid coils of your mind,
> The light of your eyes that dazzle the sun
> And turns your midnights into noons,
> The Street where you buy and resell
> Each day the whole world and mankind,
> Your foundations that reach down to hell
> And your towers that rend the typhoons,
> And your voice drunk with bloody libations,
> And your harbor that swallows the nations,
> And the glory of your nameless dead,
> And the bitterness of your bread,
> And the sword that shall hallow your hand,
> And the dawn that shall garland your head![22]

Decades later, American poetry will again reverberate with such forceful invective in the verse of an Allen Ginsberg or of an Amiri Baraka. Giovannitti, however, consistently tempers his polemic with the suggestion, be it brief or faint, of a possible resolution to the source of his ire, as in the closing refrain to the stanza above. At times his political desires can appear an intrusion, as in the closing lines to "The Unknown Soldier in Westminister Abbey." Here the poet infuses with speech the lifeless body of the nameless soldier who informs us at the poem's end: "I died of a British bullet fired into my head by my captain/ One morning as I stood and shivered and raised my hands in joy/ When from the other trench a voice cried:/ 'Peace, brothers, peace! Hoch die Internationale.'"[23] We may wince at the contrived coda and still appreciate the poem's overall effective denunciation of the class-defined nature of war and patriotism.

It is once again Tusiani who incisively points out that, among American poets, it is more Edwin Markham than Walt Whitman that one must consider a direct influence on Giovannitti. But Whitman is surely there, nonetheless, both as a direct source and as initiator of a poetic and cultural progression that extends from the Manhattan bard's 'americanization' of 19th-Century English verse to Markham's brief and dramatic infusion of social consciousness (e.g., "The Man with the Hoe") into American poetry and Giovannitti's contribution of a decidely 'left-wing' content and polemic. It could be argued, that is, that Giovannitti made use of 'Whitmanesque' idiom in carrying Markham's humanitarian content to a more penetrating political level. To these influences and sources, one should also trace in Giovannitti's work the poetic voices of his adelescent formation in the classical and Italian humanist tradition, together with echoes stemming from that previously mentioned poetic and literary search of post-Risorgimento Italy for a new national and civic identity.

Moreover, Giovannitti's early theological training is everywhere discernible in metaphor and image, as in poems such as "Litany of the Revolution," "The Deum of Labor," and "When the Great Day Came" ("In the Beginning was the Thought, and the Thought was with Man, and the Thought was Man (. . .)"), as well as in the almost eschatological charge of his social, when not socialistic, evangelism. This evangelical conatus constantly appears as the rendering into verse of a secularized religious sentiment whose power is enhanced, not trivialized, by the ironic treatment of its imagery. In "O Labor of America," for example, the injustices of capitalist political economy are deemed a "Babylon," labor's exploitation alluded to as "the last eucharist of sweat," while the "new Jerusalem" of a socialist vision of America is prefiguratively glimpsed: the "(. . .) resurrection has come. Detroit has its hand on the lever,/ Gary maneuvers the brakes/ and Chicago, feeder of the world,/ Rules the switches of the two-fisted earth."[24]

At other times, Giovannitti employs such secularized evangelical sense and symbol in the construction of a self-conscious parody, in a deliberately disturbing transvaluation of traditional Christian imagery which has been corrupted, he implies, under American capitalist piety. In "Litany of the Revolution," for example, the rebellious working classes are urged to unite in a bacchanal "and intone your litany, the Magnificat of Hell, the Te Deum of the damned,/ Man's first chant of victory,"[25] calling to mind, if not Milton's Lucifer, then surely Carducci's Satan. Likewise, in a section of the "Litany" sub-titled, "Veni Creator Spiritus," Giovannitti adopts liturgical rhythms and language not so summon the spirit of any corroboration, but the disquieting force of a challenge: "Come, O Truth, this is your hour,/ rise against the fates, the times,/ the place, the law, the multitude!/ Stand and conquer, smite, devour/ every drowsy certitude,/ every reason, every sense/ that holds forth against your storm/ the dry logic of a norm (. . .)."[26] Still yet, in "The Bum," a fury that can only be called 'prophetic' rages against "This Christian world of sainted thieves,/ And fat apostles of virtue."[27]

Any discussion of Giovannitti's verse must also take into account that the poet's very medium is an acquired one. Remarkably absent, however, is any *overwhelming* sense that this is a poetic language whose rhythms and tropes were not the natural extension of native speech.[28] Furthermore, occasional 'short-comings' in Giovannitti's English take on a certain poignancy when considered in light of his poem, "To the English Language," in which the poet describes metaphorically the acquisition of his literary voice as an athletic contest between him and his conquered medium: "I have put my hands in your hands to grapple with you (. . .)"[29]

Given the agonistic nature of this acquisition, then, it would appear inappropriate to slight Giovannitti if he proved ultimately incapable of forging a truly 'revolutionary' means of expression to suit the 'revolutionary' inspiration of his content. In regard to poetic language, then, one should not leap to any accusation that Giovannitti proved incapable (if not unwilling) to attempt in his English verse what the Futurists were attempting in Italian or various modernists in American poetry of the time. Moreover, the sometimes 'late-Victorian' ring among Giovannitti's cadence and lexicon should be considered in light of the fact that the English of his verse represents a kind of linguistic palimpsest joining 19th-Century American verse to a classical Italian tradition.

In any event, the thematic and metaphoric variety of Arturo Giovannitti's English poetry is certainly worthy of wider discussion. Likewise, a more extensive appraisal of Giovannitti's contributions to the poetic repertoire of American verse is in order. Such deeper examination remains a task yet to be undertaken. Nonetheless, one can make passing mention here of Giovannitti's positive introduction into the American poetic tradition of the figure of the foreign-born immigrant, and of the Italian immigrant in particular, in poems such as "The Last Nickel" or "The Death of Flavio Venanzi." Or of his stirring lines celebrating heroes of the 'other' America, usually unsung, as in "When the Cock Crows," written to the memory of the IWW organizer, Frank Little, lynched by superpatriots in 1920. Or still yet of his introduction into American verse of the 'other,' humble Italy in pieces such as "Samnite Cradle Song," complement to his own celebration of the 'lofty' Italy, object of reverence of a Longfellow or of a Henry James. Always present is the Giovannitti of sharp social satire as in, "Out of the Mouth of Babes," whose pointed barbs would be worthy of a Parini.

Though never experimental in the strict, 'formalistic' sense, Giovannitti's poetic language could at times approach the expressionistic as in the poem, "The Cage," or be fine tuned to the most delicate of lyrical meditations as in the exquisite verse of "The Nuptials of Death," a poem whose hushed intensity is surpassed only by Emily Dickenson's quiet desperations. This rich range of poetic resonance - hones always to a spirit of uncompromising rebellion - needs to be re-evaluated. In language both homeric and homely, this Italian-American 'bard of the proletariat' sems to submit to American culture the challenge to move beyond a critique of convention (*critica di costume* to a more penetrating social critique (*critica sociale*). That challenge remains a viable one.

Finally, Giovannitti should also be remembered for having brought to American poetry of social protest a positively 'Latin' appreciation for the value of sensual delight, mirthful camaraderie and humor amid the seriousness of political struggle. Such a keen sense of the need for laughter in the face of personal and social calamity can be glimpsed in a refrain of the poem Giovannitti composed in celebration of the twenty-seventh birthday of his friend and comrade, Joseph Ettor, as the two men sat in jail awaiting an uncertain fate:

> And so here's to the hope for the trap and the rope
> As the best for us sure is the worst,
> And because I am the older and you are the bolder,
> Here's a health that they hang me the first (. . .).[30]

Footnotes

1   This is not to suggest that the radical tradition within the Italian American experience has been absolutely ignored. I cite as one important contribution the American Italian Historical Association's publication of the proceedings of its Fifth Annual Conference: *Italian American Radicalism: Old World Origins and New World Developments*, edited by Rudolph J. Vecoli, 1972. What I do contest in any discussion today of Italian Americans and 'politics' is a limitation of such discussion to participation in the Democratic and Republican parties to the virtual exclusion of mention of other political activities and traditions.

2   Onorio Ruotolo, ''Uno sguardo al passato e al presente,'' *Il Circolo US, Guaderni di Poesia*, (1950), p. 6. (photocopy of original bearing no number of edition or other bibliographical information other than having been published by Editore Morgillo, 538 West 35th Street, New York. Found among the Elizabeth Gurley Flynn Collection, Tamiment Library, New York University). I assume full responsibility for the translation from the Italian here and in all cited works to follow.

3.   Joseph Tusiani, ''La poesia inglese di Arturo Giovannitti,'' *La parola del popolo*, Chicago (November-December 1978), p. 97.

4   *Ibiden.*

5   ''*Arrows in the Gale* pubblicato nel 1914 (edito dalla 'Hillacre Bookhouse,' Riverdale, Conn.) con bellissima ed estesa prefazione di Helen Keller, la Cieca-Veggente, la donna piu celebre del mondo.'' Onorio Ruotolo, *op. cit.*, p. 6.

6   See, for example: Melvyn Dubofsky, *We Shall Be All, A History of the IWW* (New York: Quadrangle, 1969), *passim.*; John P. Diggins, *Mussolini and Fascism, The View from America* (Princeton, N.J.: Princeton University Press, 1972), *passim.*

7   Elizabeth Gurley Flynn, *Rebel Girl, An Autobiography* (New York: International Publishers, 1955), *passim.*

8 See: Aaron, Daniel, *Writers on the Left*. New York: Oxford University Press, 1961; 1977.

9 See: Diggins, John P., *The American Left in the Twentieth Century*. New York: Harcourt Brace Jovanovich, Inc., 1973.

10 Arturo Giovannitti, *The Collected Poems of Arturo Giovannitti* (Chicago: E. Clemente and Sons, 1962), pp. 117—118. All subsequent citations of Giovannitti's poems are from this volume unless otherwise indicated.

11 See: Mario De Ciampis, "Arturo Massimo Giovannitti poeta giornalista drammaturgo per la causa dei lavoratori," *La parola del popolo* (luglio-agosto 1974), *passim*. Most of the bio-bibliographical information contained in this paper are drawn from this source together with the previously cited article by Onorio Ruotolo. Additional sources not cited directly include: Renato Lalli, "In Giovannitti poeta e 'guerriero' rivivono i sacri ideali della gente sannita," *La parola del popolo* (luglio-agosto 1974), pp. 3—5; Domenico Saudino, "Il ricordo di un compagno," *ibid.*, p. 6; Joseph Tusiani, "Ricordo di Arturo Giovannitti," *ibid.*, pp. 19—20; Carmelo Zito, "Introduzione," *Quando Canta il Gallo* (Chicago: Clemente and Sons, 1957), pp. VII-XIII.

12 *Ibid.*, p. 9.

13 William Cahn, Lawrence 1912, *The Bread and Roses Strike* (New York: The Pilgrim Press, 1980), p. 130.

14 Quoted by William Cahn, *ibid.*, p. 143.

15 Arturo Giovannitti, *Collected Poems*, p. 151.

16 Joseph Tusiani, *op. cit.*, p. 96.

17 John P. Diggins, *The American Left*, p. 80.

18 John P. Diggins, *Mussolini and Fascism*, p. 113.

19 Norman Thomas, "Introduction," *Collected Poems of Arturo Giovannitti*, p. viii.

20 *Ibidem*.

21 John P. Diggins, *The American Left*, p. 73.

22 Arturo Giovannitti, *Collected Poems*, p. 8.

23 *Ibid.*, p. 121.

24 *Ibid*, p. e. The poem cited, "When the Great Day Came," appears on pages 21—23.

25 *Ibid.*, p. 17.

26 *Ibid.*, p. 114.

27 *Ibid.*, p. 69.

28 This is not to suggest that 'shortcomings' in Giovannitti's English are totally absent, especially in certain instances of rhyme where either vocalic value or tonic stress coming from the Italian seem to impose upon the poet's acquired tongue. In one such instance, Giovannitti has the word, "disgust," rhyme with "lost;" in another, "tomb" and "bomb" are paired. Tusiani cites the case of an Italian apocope that hears the English,

"virtue," through the phonetic foil of 'virtu.' Joseph Tusiani, *op. cit.*, p. 95.

29 Arturo Giovannitti, *Collected Poems*, p. 110.

30 Quoted by Elizabeth Gurley Flynn, *op. cit.*, p. 150. The images of wine and song and friendship and hearty sensual delight abound within Giovannitti's poetry. I cite my gratitude for this observation to noted labor historian, Paul Buhle. I am also deeply indebted to Mr. Buhle for having provided me with invaluable documentation on Giovannitti from his private files. Likewise, I express my deep gratitude to Mr. Robert Shafer of New York University's Tamiment Library for his generous assistance in helping me locate information on Giovannitti.

Chapter **15** **REHABILITATING DIDONATO,
A PHONOCENTRIC NOVELIST**
Daniel Orsini
Rhode Island College

In a recent article in *The New York Times Book Review*, Robert S.
McElraine, lamenting that "Throughout most of this nation's history the
industrial working class has been largely ignored in our fiction," concludes
that industrial workers "have never fit the self-image that Americans like to
maintain."[1] According to the myth of the ideal American, to be American
is to be agrarian, successful, and independent; yet here the industrial laborer
fails on all three counts. "If industrial workers are not close to nature and
have to depend on others to earn a living, how can they be Americans?"
McElraine asks only to answer, "Quite easily in reality," since most Americans
have never been either close to nature or self-sufficient. Even so, McElraine
continues, "when we think of a 'real' American, an industrial laborer does
not come to mind."[2]

During the Great Depression of the 1930's, however, the immigrant worker
himself would not have agreed. In one of the best proletarian novels of the
period, *Christ in Concrete*, Pietro DiDonato shows that the Italian laborer —
among other European immigrants — sought to reidentify himself both through
his assimilation with other peoples[3] and through his work. It is true that, by
the end of the novel, DiDonato exposes the futility of that effort. Finally,
DiDonato's protagonist, young Paul, "son of the dead Geremio,"[4] rejects the
American dream. For him, and for DiDonato, capitalism corrupts the work
effort as much as Christianity belies an individual's identity. Consequently,
Christ in Concrete leaves its hero devoid of all identity. At the end of the novel,
although Paul stands at an abyss of self-knowledge, he finds no bridge to an
authentic self. DiDonato alone survives his hero's descent into sudden
disillusionment, and *he* survives ingeniously through the power of his art.

Actually one is tempted to write that DiDonato survives even his chaotic
novel except that, in some profound yet often elusive sense, DiDonato becomes

the novel *Christ in Concrete* just as the selfsame novel becomes DiDonato. That is to say, searching for his protagonist's, as well as for his own, identity, DiDonato constructs a novel that resounds like a ventriloquial voice. Indeed, viewed as a conventional proletarian novel, *Christ in Concrete* employs multiple lyric subjectivities so exaggerated that their effects often become surrealistic. But in fact the narrative offers — and is propelled by — but one lyric subjectivity, that of its solipsistic *authorial* author. Although the novel unfolds through antiphonal points of view in a ventriloquial style, it evokes a world that pulsates mainly through DiDonato's all-encompassing, self-present voice. Enacting every scene with little or no aesthetic distance between the characters and himself, DiDonato charges the novel with life as if he *must*, because apart from his teeming subjectivity neither this world nor these characters could exist. If, as Paul learns, the American dream vitiates selfhood, then perhaps an author alone can regenerate himself, as DiDonato discovers, through such silent speech as composition affords.

Thus, the true subject of the novel is not the history of a particular place or of a particular people but rather the author's own nonempirical ethnic awareness.[5] As a result, when judged from a formalist, ‚New Critical perspective, *Christ in Concrete* appears defective. By contrast, a combined deconstructionist and phenomenological approach to the work may demonstrate both its virtues as a novel and DiDonato's skills as a writer. For DiDonato subverts, even as he transcends, linguistic codes and fictional influence alike, not only through the self-presence of a transparent voice but also through the inner life that he projects out of that voice onto his characters and that is, ultimately, more intuitive than textual, more expressive than indicative.[6] Seeking a form of pure speech, the author finds within himself an empirically resistant voice that conveys those primordial perceptions for which no words, no codes have yet been either invented or discovered.[7] In short, throughout *Christ in Concrete* DiDonato strives to disclose what Husserl calls "a pre-expressive and pre-linguistic stratum of sense"[8] that separates fact from essence, language from being, worldliness from transcendentality.

Of course, such transmundane disclosures do not surface immediately. Despite its far-reaching ains and effects, *Christ in Concrete* begins, simply enough, as a slice-of-life view of the Great Depression. DiDonato's novel is at once an affirmation and a celebration of the working world, of what he himself calls the world of Job. Hence, over and over again DiDonato depicts the "fleshly sense of Job" (97).[9] For instance, when young Paul undertakes his first construction job, he experiences "The feel of flexible steel trowel in pliant warm plushy soon to be stone" as well as the "wet rub of mortar on tender skin" (96—7). On another occasion, after work, Paul "smelled his arms. They smelled of brown and of lime-flowery flesh" (190). In numerous passages DiDonato emphasizes that "workers smelled of flesh brownly" (218); that, as concrete rose beyond "soupy mortar . . . man's flesh lent itself completely to the balanced delirium of building" (238); that, while they were building, workers apprehended "a motion of living, a dazzling nourishing rainbow of earth and man's bone and flesh" (223). Clearly, for DiDonato, "Men of Job were Nature, and health's exuberance was their joy" (223). Through this fleshly experience of work, Job itself becomes "a familiar being" (116), a presence in the world that stirs into life even inanimate objects. Accordingly, at one point, DiDonato notes that, as workers lay brick,

> Waves of amber white simmered through Job. Steel gave off painty metal rance, scaffold breathed of growing forest ash, brick sent out crusty red bake of clay, from mortar traced gray flower of virgin sand, fresh lime and cement . . . . (218)

Obviously, throughout a large portion of the novel, this vital connection between the individual worker and world's work — this "fusion" within both worker and world "of strength into a propelling beautiful new desire" (223) — provides a key reason for DiDonato's celebration of Job. For DiDonato, Job nurtures "a new sense which brought" not only "excitement of men and steel and stone" (116) but also being itself to the world and to its worker.

In this regard, Paùl's development into manhood proves most significant. DiDonato's faith that an individual confronts his essential self — and, more, achieves identity — through work is vividly shown through Paul's transition from childhood into manhood. From his very first workday, when he handles real brick, Paul "photographed it in his soul" (98). Overjoyed, he learns, as he constructs a little wall, that he can become a creator of the world: "He had worried and strained each brick into place; he had real gritty mortar on his hands and shoes and real sharp brickdust on his trousers. He had built that" (98). After his first day's work, Paul feels a new self-esteem: "In his corduroy cap, faded green overcoat, wide blue sailor pants and cemented shoes Paul walked with knowing pride. *With men I have competed and laid brick the long day,*" he boasts to himself, while at their tenement window, watching him return from work, his mother reflects that "My Paul wears the pantaloons of manhood. He walks sorely and belongs no more to the world of children who play and laugh and sing" (113). Thereafter, Paul, like his mother, knows — or believes that he knows — who he is: "He was a bricklayer. He was the father of his father's family" (160). In this sense, Paul's job legitimizes his claim to be an adult. From a sociological perspective, his ability to assume his father's role as family provider remains both the test and the proof of his mahood. However, from a psychological perspective, Job endows Paul with a reward far more important than social status — that is, with the risky, percarious, ecstatic experience of manhood. So DiDonato suggests in a passage concerning that secret that Paul withholds from his mother.

The scaffolds rose a floor a day. With each floor the height
and majesty of skyscraper fascinated him, but he never told mother
Annunziata about the danger of falling or being pushed from a
swinging scaffold or fifty floors above the street. Or of a derrick
cable snapping and sending a girder crashing the scaffold to earth.
It seemed so daring to lay brick at the edge of a wall that ran down
hundreds and hundreds of feet to a toy world below, a wall that
leaned out and seemed about to fall away.

This was steel Job where danger was every present with falling
planks and beams and bolts and white-hot molten steel from
acetylene torch and breaking cable and unexpected drop of hoist
— great dangerous Job who thrilled Paul. (237)

As the latter lines indicate, Paul, now initiated into manhood, can whistle at
Death even as his "breast prided" for himself no less than for all the crew
"Far up in the bone-work of Job" (233). In short, "great dangerous Job,"
which spurs Paul to live with an intensity previously unimaginable to him,
nudges the twelve-year-old into a sphere of Being beyond ordinary existence.

Still, DiDonato does not associate this sphere of Being with intense physical
life alone. For DiDonato, more than social and psychological identification,
Job offers Paul spiritual status. Once Paul becomes "the father of his father's
family" (160), he rises automatically to the rank of his father: Christ Crucified.
To his mother, Paul seems "her carpenter Christ" (113). As a bricklayer's
son who follows "the art of his father," Paul joins "Jesus Christ and all the
saints" (94) on every job. In time, through his work, Paul himself grasps his
tie to the "people, poor people," all "the battered poor" (170) on earth.

So different were people, thought Paul in his bedroom
darkness. After the show of day, after all the incidents and faces
and voices and smells, what was he to think? Did they not all live
atop the other [in tenements] and feel and taste and smell each
other? Did not Job claim them all? With what all-embracing thought
could he bless Amen today?

They, like me, are children of Christ. (140)

And they are, like him, he concludes elsewhere, soldiers of Christ. For half
the novel, DiDonato encourages Paul, and other Italians, in this belief. "Our
own Christ cared naught for gold," one character declares as he and other
bricklayers present a gift — an artificial leg — to a disabled fellow worker,
" . . . now are we to change Christian semblance?" (246) In DiDonato's ideal
world, despite the ceaseless war for living, each man must extend to one another
"the helping hand of Christ's Christians" (171). His workers accept this creed
as a rule of life. In fact, so powerful is their traditional faith in Christ that

at one point Paul and another character wonder whether the spirits of dead bricklayers labor alongside them: "Did they soar about their comrade-worker Christ, or did worker return to Job and press ghostly self against scaffold and wall?" (181) Although the question remains unanswered until the end of the novel, one truth seems clear to most of DiDonato's workers: with "blood and stone" Christians must "go on creating" Christ's Heaven on earth (189). DiDonato views this goal as the very purpose of their lives and in fact links this aim to each worker's identity as man, father, and soldier of Christ.

Or at least he does for the first half of the novel. But then, in a series of bitter turnabouts, DiDonato rejects every form of identity — social, psychological, and spiritual — that he has thus far defined. In effect, DiDonato methodically deconstructs the vaunted hope no less than the apparent subject of his novel — namely, the American dream of freedom, opportunity, and success. The American dream, he asserts halfway through the novel, is a fraud. "Discovered by an Italian — named from Italian — But oh, that I may leave this land of disillusion!," one jobless bricklayer grieves in the final section of the novel. There, commenting on the Great Depression, DiDonato records that "the active world of Job shrunk and overnight men were wandering the streets trowel on hip and lunch beneath arm in futile search of wall" (273). As a result, deprived of work, men soon forget their bond in Christ. "This land has become a soil that has contradicted itself," Nazone, Paul's godfather, complains. Now it appears to him "a country of Babel where Christians are beginning to wander about in hungry distress cursing each other in strange tongues, ripping their hearts, and possessing no longer even fingernails with which to scratch their desperation" (279).[10] Earlier, before the onset of the Depression, Paul himself had experienced such painful disillusionment. Regarding executives and clerks as a breed of men different from the laborers, he can register only contempt for them: "it seemed a revelation [to him] that these glaze-skinned, soft, white-fingered men who looked like painted mustached women dressed in men's clothes owned the great buildings and the city" (240). Eventually Paul finds that even his fleshly joy in work turns rancid. Having experienced the plight of the immigrant worker in America, Paul knows that "Before the grace of morning properly rises over earth, before Christians can gather their senses and stretch upward to God's heaven in joy of living, they are bent and twisted into unfeeling reds and grays of Job" (187). And, in time, he understands that "Job would be a brick labyrinth that would suck him in deeper and deeper, . . . [that] there would be no going back. Life would never be a dear music, a festival, a gift of nature"; on the contrary, it would mean "the same fierce silence and loss of consciousness" (188); the same enslavement by the corporation, that "greedy greenhorn carrion" (183); the same crucifixion that killed both his father and his godfather and that maimed his uncle.

Granted, after the latter tragedies, Paul still believes that One exists who will save his people, all the workers of the world: "It is our Lord Christ who will do it," he declares, for "He made us, he loves us and will not deny us; he is our friend and will help us in need!" (293). However, when his godfather is killed, "rocketed away from Paul and the scaffold through deathed nothing and smashed to the street bridge twenty floors below" (286), Paul asks Annunziata, "Who nails us to the cross? Mother . . . why are we living!" (298) Anguished and comfortless, he realizes in the defeat of his father's proletarian, and of his own spiritual, ideals that "not even the Death can free us, for we are . . . Christ in concrete" (298). Sensing his apostasy, Annunziata pleads with him: But "In the next world is our salvation — and He is coming — He is coming," his mother promises him. Yet that hope can no longer console him: "I want justice here! I want happiness here! I want life here!" (304) he cries in despair. He feels "cheated" (303), he tells her, and, to be sure, in the end a reader can only count young Paul's losses, not the least of them being those patterns of identity — social, psychological, and spiritual — that previously DiDonato had formulated for him. Without faith in a Heavenly Father or a Heavenly Son, through whom the social transformation of the world may unfold, Job ceases to be purposeful. Nor can Paul's identity as "the father of his father's family" survive the death of his father's dream, the creation of the workers' new Heaven on earth. Finally Paul is made to seem no more than an unfree, bitter, and misguided nonentity.

In short, *Christ in Concrete* ends by subverting its own religious and secular predispositions. Although early in the novel DiDonato extols Christian hope no less than American democracy as the underpinnings of his workers' ideal society, later he repudiates both a failed Church and a corrupt nation. This, on her death-bed, Annunziata, "With numbing hand . . . beckoned" her "Children wonderful" (311): "love . . . love love . . . love ever our Paul," she counsels them. "Follow him" (311). But how and where? And to what? No answers are forthcoming. And apparently that is the point. Since Paul has been denied — "cheated," as he exclaims, of his social as well as his spiritual identity, he is left with the need to define himself not as a Christian or as an American but as an essence. Throughout Paul's story DiDonato suggests that during the first forty years of this century the European immigrant — here, specifically, the Italian immigrant — had asked a singular question: How can the world's workers, recognizing their identity in Christ, build God's Heaven on earth?[11] Yet it was the wrong question. Rather, the immigrant worker should have asked *this* question: How, in a godless world polluted by humankind, can the individual still know and achieve his identity? In his own way DiDonato does answer this question, but his answer proves as elusive as it is ingenious. Actually his answer forms a whole subtext that becomes in time more crucial to his novel's meaning than the treatment of either his social or his religious themes.

I have said that, by the end of the novel, Paul has lost his faith both in God and in society. In despair he cries, "Now! Now! I want salvation now! For I know oh I know that we cannot live forever . . ." (304). Nevertheless, Paul realizes also that, in spite of anguish, "we must go on," not to a capitalistic society that battens on the poor[12] or to a fictive Heaven but to "a world of our own" (304). Yet, although he grasps that life is of this world, he lacks the power — or so he feels — to reinvent that world on his own terms. Hence, he wishes "That he could sleep silently, sleep away from all knowing" (306). By contrast, DiDonato himself, perceiving not only that life is of this world but also that one's own identity originates in his consciousness of the world, confronts, recreates, and in time commands that world in order to waken into further knowing. Early in *Christ in Concrete* DiDonato makes a remark — surprisingly enough, through the conventionally religious Annunziata — that states the main problem that he must resolve in this novel. " . . . would the will could disfact that which happens" (99), [13] DiDonato has Paul's mother saying. Elsewhere, after denouncing Paul's Job as "a brick labyrinth that would suck him in deeper and deeper" (188), DiDonato, in his role of general narrator, addresses even more directly the problem of "disfacting" the mazelike world. "No poet would be there to intone meter of soul's sentence to stone," he complains,

> No artist upon scaffold to paint the vinegary sweat of Christian
> in correspondence with red brick and gray mortar, no composer
> attuned to the screaming movement of Job and voiceless cry in
> overalls. (189)

This passage is, no doubt, ironical, for all along DiDonato has been that poet, that artist who will celebrate the worker in the world — will celebrate him and will do something more than that. DiDonato will identify the Italian immigrant as an essence. DiDonato shows that, although consciousness is always directed toward objects in the world, and although those objects are inevitably corrupted by humankind, the individual can nonetheless know and achieve his identity. It is all a matter of perception — *i.e.*, not of seeing alone but of reseeing — and of artistic strategies as well. Accordingly, what DiDonato attempts throughout his novel is to capture Paul's ethnic identity and through it his universal stature as a human being. In other words, he does for Paul what Paul cannot, as a protagonist, do for himself. However, to glimpse and then to display Paul's selfhood, DiDonato contrives an often subversive narrative style. In effect, since this world remains socially and hence perceptually corrupt, and since he does wish to explore Paul's pure or essential identify — ethnic as well as universal — DiDonato must skillfully reconstruct the phenomenology of Paul's experience even as he deconstructs the language that is ordinarily its medium of expression.[14]

Thus, he observes, and recreates with meticulous detail, the objects, characters, and events of Paul's daily life — whether feast, religious ritual, family, or friendship. However, in order to convey young Paul's — and by extension his own — essence, DiDonato deliberately fragments his authorial perceptions, almost from the very first pages of his novel, in several ways. First of all, he disfigures conventional grammar and syntax through his use of dialect as well as through the omission of definite and indefinite articles. For instance, at one point a bricklayer nicknamed "The Lucy" scolds his fellow workers: "Have you no respect for women? Put your tongue in tail or you'll go to Sing-a-Sing" (104). Elsewhere Luigi, Paul's convalescent uncle, praises his nurse: "I like-a you. You be too good-a by me." Then he adds: "I like-a every people" (192). At still another point, "Old Philomena recounted of Geremio's father, Pietro the wild . . . 'He was the one ever wanting to eat and drink finely, arouse the village with bedlam prank, and do for people's ripe daughter'" (256). Typically, in the latter passage DiDonato omits all articles, as he often does, not only in lines of dialogue but also in his omniscient narrative commentary. For example, one morning — DiDonato relates —

> Paul was first on empty deserted Job. He studied the wall bonds and touched scaffold and brick and joint and stone of wall. Job was sharp with expanding fresh smell of lime cement, new-cut wood, iron's red paint and brackish night dew.
> Though stiff the morning, sun was rising with tawny glow and told of warm workday. (105)

Obviously, at times these narrative strategies — the solecisms along with the ellipses — make DiDonato's style sound archaic, hackneyed, and mannered. Even his occasional lack of punctuation can seem merely idosyncratic, if not chaotic, and may jar or annoy a reader, as in his description of Luigi's dream:

> . . . Geremio is smiling with that overtopping twinkle and motions for him and hands him a brick hammer so that he can break stones with the men and Luigi wants to feel and embrace him because he knows that he is proud and lonely and has done something and for some reason it is known that Geremio is not supposed to mix with people and Geremio glides away from him and shakes his head smilingly like a stranger and Luigi feels the blueshirt's foreboding black eyes and spontaneously swings the little brick hammer as though he were wound up at the big stone that he recognizes and the hammer handle becomes smaller and smaller and the big black eyes blow up bigger and he no longer has any hammer and is frantically beating the stone with his hands

> and the stony face looms larger *larger* and rolls over on him and
> does not hurt him and he starts to laugh to think that somewhere
> that he couldn't place that stone had frightened him and when he
> laughs louder the men break out in storms of high-pitched laughter.
> (69)

The plethora or words here is calculated and, of course, emphasizes the flow of Luigi's consciousness. And to a greater or lesser extent that is the effect of all these devices. By fracturing conventional grammar, punctuation, and syntax, and also by using — and exploiting — dialectal cliches, DiDonato strips away the facade of his immigrants' American identity in order to reach their authentic Italian identity and thereafter their universal status as human beings.[15] For this reason, he catalogues not only the people of Paul's world but also the sundry phenomena of that immigrant world, including its objects, events, acts, images, and symbols. Yet through such narrative strategies as those mentioned above he voices rather than writes these catalogues. In short, DiDonato discovers, for himself, and for his readers, that the way to a representative Italian identity is through speech acts construed as phonocentric[16] — that is, through words conceived as elemental, self-present, and hence pure sounds which he employs not to write about, but rather to speak of, the vivid worldly consciousness of his characters. All in all, if recurrently DiDonato's diction proves awkward and even un-English, these effects appear intentional. DiDonato aims to capture an essence peculiar to the Italian race, and for hims that identity is betrayed less by dialectal or ethnic cliches — which are, after all, an Italian's lively *spoken* responses to the world — than by the homogenized, anonymous, statis *written* symbols of a foreign tongue. Now, it is true that, since DiDonato does record his story in novel form, a reader might assume that, if writing can corrupt vision, then his text inevitably falls prey to that pollution. Yet this is precisely DiDonato's point: By fragmenting language — *i.e.*, by deliberately disseminating, then dispersing, then negating his words — he strips the text of its textuality. Just as he exposes gaps of meaning halfway through the novel in a representative immigrant's social and religious philosophy, so he eventually reveals the perils of writing — of *ecriture* — with its built-in codes, heresies, and prejudgments. Simply enough, DiDonato favors even garbled speech over writing because the latter remains for him merely one other form of inflexible, suffocating concrete. Finally he prefers the living truths of his own disfigurement of language.

However, it should be noted that DiDonato distorts his fictional world not only through the artistic strategies mentioned above but also through a narrative style — and a point of view — that can best be called ventriloquial. DiDonato does not merely vivify his characters; he becomes his characters. The world of *Christ in Concrete* is truly the creation of its author's innumerable voices. Whether he imitates, in a long passage, Paul's sense of the "quiet-quiet" (60) that pervades his sleeping house; or mimicks, in his own affected authorial voice, a bricklayer's curse at "Malcreance of pleasure!" (220); or simply echoes the "Tung-atee-ring-a-tung!, and tambourine held high" (266) of a musician, DiDonato invests each character with the power of his own self-present ventriloquial voice. Everywhere a reader can detect the poetic rhythms, syntax, and locutions of Pietro DiDonato rather than of his characters.

Thus, at various stages in the novel, his untutored immigrants deliver these lofty remarks: Geremio apostrophizes "Home where midst the monkey chatter of my piccolinos I will float off to blessed slumber" (14); Annunziata whispers, amid "the fraught sleep of hunger" (84), that "In the home of Geremio senses have become swollen vessels and eyes ceaseless falls" (85); Nazone announces, alliteratively, that "The boy [Paul] is man-child of master mason and born in the mortar tub" (93); Luigi wonders why he might not "fly . . . to a distant refuge . . . to wing to the Saviour from under a sky clean-clean and broad" (123); an anonymous character asserts that "Christ is happy when poor's table weeps red in laughter of wine!" (251); and Paul, exulting at first that "home I come with father's hands . . . we shall rise" (104), declaims in the end that "My toil has been used against me" (303), that "we must go on to a world of our own" (304). DiDonato plays — and speaks — all these roles seemingly to protect his characters from misrepresentation. It is as if he needs to encapsulate the very intentions of their speech — which becomes his speech — because, without its living unfoldment in his own mind, his subject — the essence of his Italian characters — would evaporate.[17] The novel is really a soliloquy in the mind of one man — an artist — who recognizes, intuitively or otherwise, the primacy of speech over writing. DiDonato's ingenious transcriptions of Italian consciousness appear a concession to communication — a compromise meant to counter the distortions no less than the uncertainties ingrained in written speech.

In other words, DiDonato expresses shrewdly through his own multiple voices, and preserves purely in silent speech, the identity of his subject, and he accomplishes this aim because he refuses to indicate his meanings with the corrupt "trace" of convention-bound language — specifically, that of writing, of *ecriture*.[18] That is why he usurps all his characters' roles and mangles traditional syntax and grammar. His linguistic subversions and obsessive ventriloguisms are not just a stylistic signature. Rather, they illustrate DiDonato's attempt to say the unsayable — to *speak* it — even as he writes it. But he speaks it silently and hence projects its truth upon the world through his own seemingly unmediated self-presence.[19] Furthermore, through his omnipresent consciousness, DiDonato manages both to exploit and to surpass his authorial author's pervasive self-reference.[20] DiDonato's world mind, mimicking Divine omniscience, represents a metaphor — in the novel, a re-emergent hope — of universal or cosmic consciousness. The novel demonstrates, perhaps inadvertently, that DiDonato's final faith resides not only in the self-present speech of his ancestors but also in its ultimate referent, the transcendent God Whose meaning-shrouded utterance he imitates in his all but casual yet most subversive ventriloquism. Despite the novel's putative apostasy, DiDonato reconstructs Paul's fragmented world, wittingly or unwittingly, through the power of his own implicitly religious imagination, itself the offshoot equally of consciousness and of the self-presence of origin.[21] As an author who aspires to speak, not write, DiDonato acts here to bind the parts of Paul's, and his, world, to join them together — as Annunziata might say — like carpenter or bricklayer Christ. Yet surely the novel's hero is not the Italian worker as bricklayer but as artist, a different kind of craftsman and savior.

And what, for DiDonato, is the Italian essence? The answer at first disappoints and then surprises us. Initially, DiDonato's view of Italian identity strikes a reader as merely broad, general, and stereotypical. Almost all the Italians in his novel appear earthy, emotional, suffering, religious, hopeful, life-affirming. Needless to say, we have met these Italians before. The outworn codes of literature, film, and opera proliferate with such ethnic types. Besides, on the surfaces, DiDonato never connects the latter traits to their universal source in our common humanity. We feel that Paul — defeated, disoriented, incoherent at the end — fails his human, let alone his ethnic, heritage. The conclusion, marked by Paul's social despair, is decidedly a letdown. Paul, believing nothing, seems nothing, a sort of transitional man devoid of identity. By contrast, even as Paul fails his human potential, DiDonato — an intuitive novelist all along — manifests, through his prodigious narrative voice, an ethnic pride, joyfulness, optimism, and ingenuity that link him to all humankind. Yet, while such traits *are* universal, their expression, cast in a lyric key, sounds racial. Indeed, DiDonato's lyric key proves so abundant, his cadences suggest an overflow of thought and feeling in every circumstance. Through his emphasis on dirgelike yet often seriocomic speech, DiDonato portrays what the British poet Hopkins, following Duns Scotus, would have called the "thisness" of the subject: a song — an aria — more than a sound, a sound more than a word; but a sound that resists phenomenological reduction.

As a result, what we remember about DiDonato's Italians is not their dialect or their olive-oil cooking or their tarantella or their brown flesh or their lustiness; rather, we recall their saturnine joy. Through the force of his authorial author's exclamations, expletives, litanies, repetitions, babble, DiDonato echoes an inner rhythm that, in his own words, "kept radiating his senses farther and farther beyond his immediate physical identification, as though he, a planet of flesh, were sending out the power of his senses over time and space" (285). Significantly, these lines appear just prior to DiDonato's heightened description of the bricklayer Nazone's fall from a scaffold "through deathed nothing" (286). "Oh, the surprise," DiDonato's omnipresent narrator groans even as he proceeds to stylize "the terrible meaty gnash [that] sounded up to Paul" (286). "Oh, Jesus, the misery he poured up!" he continues his dirge.

> Christ-Christ hold him back! Give strength to the air!
> Christ don't let him drop so fast! Christ have him float gently!
> Have him land safely! Christ oh Christ he's spinning
> faster and faster and getting smaller and smaller!
> Don't! No! Christ! No! Noooooo . . .!

The music in that passage — the fierce vowel refrain, the subversive lyric bliss[22] — remains as mannered and as triumphant and as revealing as any feature, trait, or definition in the novel. After the rippling sound "o" especially, DiDonato need no longer identify his Italian characters. Defying conventional linguistic and fictive codes, he has spoken to us — speaks to us — beyond the boundedness of words. That is why he both overshadows and — by extension — rescues Paul from oblivion. Paul, we feel, will survive his despair, but he has languished in the wrong key. As Paul's counterpart, DiDonato himself suffers in the right key — a key of perverse creative bliss — and, by so doing, captures the Italian essence, for the 30's, for the 80's, indeed for the year 2000. At the end of the novel, DiDonato, unlike Paul, knows who he is, and knows also who Geremio, Nazone, Luigi, Annunziata, Cola, and all the rest are. These Italians are no whiners or defeatists or pawns or even victims. These are people who sing in the face of chaos.

Footnotes

1. "Workers in Fiction: Locked Out," *The New York Times Book Review*, 1 Sept. 1985, p. 19.
2. McElraine, p. 19.
3. In *Immigrant Minorities and the Urban Working Class* (New York: Associated Faculty Press, 1983), Scott Cummings asserts that "arguments proclaiming an end of minority identification and the ultimate success of the assimilation process must be viewed with suspicion" (p. 52) since minority status both generates and perpetuates urban liberalism "and uncovers the mythology of assimilationist thinking" (p. 61). However, in *From Immigrants to Ethnics: The Italian Americans* (New York: Oxford Univ. Press, 1983), Humbert S. Nelli argues that, for the Italian immigrant in the New World, the ethnic community served only as "a staging ground where most newcomers remained until they absorbed new ideas and values that facilitated their adjustment to urban America" (p. 60). Still, as Alan M. Kraut shows in *The Huddled Masses: The Immigrant in America Society, 1880—1921* (Illinois: Harlan Davidson, 1982), "New immigrants

did not undergo their metamorphosis passively. Each newcomer made choices among a limited number of options that would shape his relationship to his new country and determine the rate and extent of assimilation'' (p. 113).

4. Pietro DiDonato, *Christ in Concrete (New York: Bobbs-Merrill, 1937)*, *p. 73. Subsequent references to pages of this edition are in the text.*

5. *For opposing views concerning the feasibility of this aim, see Jacques Derrida, Speech and Phenomena*, tr. David B. Allison (Evanston, Illinois: Northwestern Univ. Press, 1973), especially ch. 6. For Edmund Husserl, ''The ideality'' of an object ''can only be expressed in an element whose phenomenality does not have worldly form. *The name of this element is the voice*,'' i.e., the silent voice (p. 76). Nevertheless, Derrida maintains that ''this transcendence is only apparent'' (p. 77) because ''Being-primordial must be thought on the basis of the trace'' (which comprises all the absent meanings whose differences from the present signified lend the latter its seeming identity) ''and not the reverse. This protowriting is at work at the origin of sense'' (p. 85). As this paper will demonstrate, I favor Husserl's belief in a ''metaphysics of presence.'' In other words, the Reality of Presence always *is*, like a line stretched out into infinity. Thus, the ''history'' of Presence — e.g., DiDonato's novel — constitutes the ''trace'' of *that* Reality, a preconscious as well as a spatiotemporal supplement to it.

6. Derrida discusses the difference between expression and indication in *Speech and Phenomena*, pp. 27—59.

7. In this regard, see Vernon Gras's trenchant essay, ''Understanding, Historicity, and Truth,'' from *Papers on Language and Literature*, 17 (1982): ''Derrida's 'deconstruction' roots itself in the historical existence of man defined negatively as endless language play . . . Why emancipate man from his mythologies if no genuine dialogue with Being can ever take place? . . . when our conversation with Being is cognitive and revelatory even though partial and temporal, it does seem worthwhile to write about writing'' (p. 53). And also possible, I would add, to create a metalinguistic novel like *Christ in Concrete*.

8. *Speech and Phenomena*, p. 31.

9. Yet Kraut emphasizes that Italian Immigrants ''— even in the second generation — were frequently unfamiliar'' with ''the idea that work can be a central purpose of life'' (*Huddled Masses*, p. 81). ''To the southern Italian, work was something one did to acquire sufficient money to be comfortable and not for personal fulfillment or satisfaction'' (p. 106).

10. In *The Italian in America* (New York: Exposition Press, 1957), Lawrence Frank Pisani explains that ''In many years the number of Italians leaving the United States was more than half the number coming in,'' though ''Many of these were men who were adhering to their original plan to

put together a reasonable sum of money which would enable them to get ahead in their native country'' (p. 66). However, in ''The American Italians: Upraised or Uprooted?,'' Andrew Rolle asserts that ''most [Italian] immigrants considered their life in America permanent, and sent for brothers, sisters, wives, and families in Italy.'' [See **Contemporary American Immigration**, ed. Dennis Laurence Cuddy (Boston: Twayne Publishers, 1982), p. 34] Nevertheless, as Nelli mentions, in America ''Movement out of the ethnic districts slowed during the 1930's because of the Depression'' (*From Immigrants to Ethnics*, p. 175).

11. Kraut contends that ''Statistics on change in religious practice are notoriously unreliable'' but adds that the children of European immigrants often ''abandoned religious customs and rituals which conflicted with economic or social demands of American life'' (*Huddled Masses*, p. 122). Yet, by writing his novel, DiDonato demonstrates that, though many immigrants may have spurned traditional religious expressions, individual Italians retained — and redirected — their spiritual fervor nonetheless.

12. Cummings suggests that ''The captains of industry, the foremen, the shop-keepers and merchants, the company store bosses were not only daily reminders of class inequality, they were also seen as the architects of minority oppression'' (*Immigrant Minorities and the Urban Working Class*, p. 124).

13. Rolle believes that, eventually, Italy's migrants ''no longer could find those metaphysical parts of themselves they had left behind'' (*Contemporary American Immigration*, p. 35). Understandably, then, throughout *Christ in Concrete* DiDonato attempts to rediscover — and to recreate — the Italian immigrant as a transcendental construct.

14. For DiDonato, this twofold procedure remains necessary if he is to illuminate the essence of his Italian immigrants. In other words, ultimately DiDonato proves less interested in the phenomenal world of his novel than he does in the noumenal sphere of Paul's transcendent being. In this respect, he aptly embodies that type of metaphysical writer whose ''speaking is not adequately characterized as referential: to be sure he may name familiar entities, but what is distinctive in his activity is a pre-referential making present of what was not *there*, what was in the manner of no-thing prior to its being gathered to itself and set forth in his speaking. Thus the world that is presupposed by reference and representational thinking is brought to light in the reciprocal plays of linguistic response to being.'' See James E. Swearingen, ''The Poet and the Phenomenon of World,'' in *Papers on Language and Literature*, p. 66.

15. Recently, in an important essay, ''Viewpoint: A New Meaning of Meaning,'' George Steiner declares that such elusive authenticity remains impossible to achieve apart from a writer's application of the transcendental

prerogative. In short, Steiner upholds a thesis that DiDonato illustrates throughout his novel, namely, that "Meaning is an attribute of being." See *The Times Literary Supplement*, 8 November 1985, pp. 1262, 1275.

16. I refer here, of course, to silent speech, which, for Husserl, stands as "a pure phenomenon." See David B. Allison's "Translator's Introduction" in *Speech and Phenomena*, pp. xxxix-xl.

17. DiDonato aims to achieve a text that exists — to use a phrase from Roland Barthes — "beyond the gross form of things." However, unlike Barthes, DiDonato seeks, within his illuminated consciousness, determinate Being itself rather than only the "absolute *flow of becoming*." See Barthes' "Theory of the Text" in *Untying the Text: A Post-Structuralist Readerf*, ed. Robert Young (Boston: Routledge & Kegan Paul, 1981), p. 45.

18. DiDonato strives to avoid the theft of his meaning, which is "always the theft of speech or text, or trace." To compare his linguistic strategies with those of a modern master of the theater, see Jacques Derrida's analysis of Antonin Artaud's "rigorous textuality of shouts . . . reaching beyond empirical language," in *Writing and Difference*, tr. Alan Bass (Chicago: Univ. of Chicago Press, 1978), pp. 175, 191.

19. Husserl maintains that the key to self-presence is "pure expression" rather than mere "indication." See *Speech and Phenomena*, p. 21.

20. In other words, through his subversive prose, DiDonato identifies himself as that type of artist who "institutes rather than represents world by . . . originary disclosure." See Swearingen, p. 67.

21. Throughout his novel, DiDonato demonstrates that the signifying function of the "I" *as expression* depends upon the life of the speaking subject. In other words, "I am" means that each time I relate to, and participate in, I AM, I become what I have always been, i.e., I "express" myself. To study Derrida's confusion on this point, see *Speech and Phenomena*, p. 96.

22. As Roland Barthes asserts, "pleasure can be expressed in words, bliss cannot. Bliss is unspeakable, inter-dicted." See *The Pleasure of the Text*, tr. Richard Miller (New York: Hill and Wang, 1975), p. 21.

Chapter **16** **THE FORMATIVE YEARS OF AN IMMIGRANT SCULPTOR: POMPEO COPPINI[1]**

Carol Bradley
Florence, Italy

This paper specifically aims to recompose Pompeo Coppini's formative years in Italy in order to better comprehend his contribution to art in America. It is also my personal hope that this presentation might act as my emissary and so help to activate my plan for creating a computerized source center for materials related to all forms of Italian immigrant art, for only in this way will it be possible to fully investigate and comprehend the artistic heritage that Italian immigrant artists and artisans have bestowed on our country.

In the last decade of the 19th century the emigrating masses from Italy were largely unskilled and often illiterate, but there were those, as the sculptor Pompeo Coppini, who represent that comparatively small number of immigrants capable of offering some specialized professional service to their host country. Pompeo in his autobiographical book, *From Dawn to Sunset*,[2] while providing an extensive, vivacious documentation of his American years, from his arrival in 1896 to his death in San Antonio in 1957, makes only brief references to his formative years in Italy. A period which, from his birth in 1870 to his departure for America in 1896,[3] was particularly turbulent — economically, socially, politically and artistically.

While Pompeo entered America through New York, he was able to give substance to his dreams only after he migrated to Texas in 1901[4] where he was well received. There the sculptural programs became for Pompeo a door re-opened on his past, the visual embodiments of his patriotic idealism, artistic style and technical skills. In fact, his American works were directly inspired by all those factors which had led to the formation of the Italian Kingdom in 1860—61. This is particularly clear in Pompeo's comments were he denounces the use of utilitarian monuments — non-representative or abstract monuments that by eliminating all visual, material references to events destroys the art form itself. Pompeo underlines his belief in content, in the message of the monument, when he writes that art "unless inspired by religion, history or patriotism, unless assuming the responsibility of being the exponent of a glorious past, and the demonstrator of the gratitude of the living for the greatest contributing events that made for our progress and advanced civilization, is not a great art.(. . .) art, without an uplifting mission, is not really a fine art, but a simple commercial decoration of the shallow ornamentation of our homes, or public places, missing thus its high philosophic and moral ideal of educating mankind and failing to become the perpetual teacher of virtue and truth. An art that has no effect on the betterment of the soul, and on the building of better character, by a strong message that portrays the better events of the past as a philosophical teaching, or that brings emphasis to the greatest deeds of our contemporary people, is to my way of thinking as degenerating as are those who like it that way". Whether applied to Italy or America, for Pompeo, the artistic concepts of "progress and (an) advanced civilization", of art as the "perpetual teacher of virtues and truth", are ideas that are a part of a "national inheritance", the result of a "magnificent, romantic and tragic history".[5] Pompeo matured these ideas in the wake of the *Risorgimento* in Italy, but it was in America that he relived these romantic words and embodied them in every monument he created.

These thoughts demonstrate how strongly Pompeo felt about his art, but to fully comprehend what this immigrant transposed to America, it is necessary to review his past through a brief tour of those places and events that informed his view point. For Pompeo the tour begins in Florence, the city where his family settled shortly after Pompeo's birth in Moglia (province of Mantua). Florence, as Pompeo knew it, was a city in development. Already during the period 1865—71, when Florence served as the capitol of unified Italy, it has undergone major urbanistic changes. For example, the architect, Giuseppe Poggi, striving to give the city a more modern appearance began his ambitious remodelling project by tearing down the city walls and replacing them with wide, inviting boulevards encircling the city and culminating in a broad open piazza on a high hill dominated by the church of San Miniato. Though from this point, the Piazzale Michelangelo, the profile of the city below retains much of its Medieval-Renaissance character, as one descends to the heart of the city, the discontinuous fabric of the city signalled by abrupt juxtapositions of the old and new testifies to the cultural changes that matured in the 1880's. One of the most contested and polemical of these town-plan modifications was in the central area called the "Mercato Vecchio", the Old Market. On the debate concerning the reconstruction of this area, Silvano Fei writes that the governing class, hoping to encourage the economy in Florence as well as demonstrating an enlightened social awareness, desired this new center as the seat of prestigious financing companies and banks.[6] Thus the elimination of that over populated, unhygenic area while taken by some to demonstrate only a positive example of progress in the city, for others represented a political retaliation by destroying the area where radical groups tended to congregate. After a decade of discussion and various changes, on the 20th of September 1890, the new piazza Vittorio, now called the Repubblica, was inaugurated. The long arcades which are connected by a triumphal framing the equestrian statue of Vittorio Emanuele II. In this context, the commemorative statue, states Fei, could be interpreted as the triumphalistic emblem of Florence converged on King Vittorio; from this newly organized epicenter, from this privileged position of the King emanated the confirmation of order, security and decorum.[7] The sculptor of the equestrian monument was Emilio Zocchi,[8] one of Pompeo's first teachers in Florence.

At the same time that the central Piazza Repubblica was being constructed, in the nearby piazza of the Duomo, another major work, the facade of the Cathedral, had only recently been completed and inaugurated. Earlier centuries had made continuous but unsuccessful efforts to complete the church; the 19th century, too, proposed numerous projects, none of which satisfied the aesthetic requirements of the times. A final attempt was begun in 1859 when a new contest was opened under the auspices of the Grand Duke of Tuscany and though the Grand Duke went into exile the same year, the work was carried on. Pompeo, present at the inauguration of the facade in 1878, witnessed the unveiling of a laudatory program exemplifying through Florence's major protector Saints, illustrious artists and benefactors, a compendium of her history, of her religious, artistic and civic culture. For the young sculptor Pompeo, the facade of the Cathedral and the statue of Vittorio Emanuele might have seemed to be two mirrors, one, historical turned towards the past, towards those geniuses of Tuscan national history, the other, turned towards the present, reflecting the myth which from the date of the King's death in 1878 was rapidly receiving widespread acclamation, thereby necessitating the appearance of equestrian statues of King Vittorio, whether as an integral element or a necessary adjunct, in all the major piazzas of Italy. Turning back in time but continuing to investigate the Florence that Pompeo knew so well, reference must be made to the facade of the Uffizi Gallery. The facade of alternating columns and niches was designed by Giorgio Vasari in the 16th century. However, a typographer, Vincenzo Batelli, in 1835 maintained that Vasari did not plan the niches as mere empty architectural decoration and so proposed that the facade be completed by filling these spaces with statues of illustrious Tuscan men.[9] Filippo Moise writing on this project in 1836 recommends to the sculptors to use their works so as to represent the religion of their own times. Moise proclaimed that with their statues the artist must represent history with the intent of forming better citizens for the future. Further he declared that for the artist sculpture represents a "civic mission" and he continues by encouraging the artists to emphathize with the virtues embodied in their subjects; for, he decreed, works communicating simple sensations rather than a profound love for their subject would not be acceptable.[10] Moise's recommendations regarding the artist's mission were complemented by that — mission — of the public for in them was invested the role of patron, financing the project through public subscription. Indeed, the program of the statues for the niches is a roll-call of Tuscany's illustrious. Among those represented are Orcagna, Nicola, Pisano, Giotto, Leonardo da Vinci, Donatello, Michelangelo, Machiavelli and Dante. Dante as a major Tuscan literary figure was of course assured a place in the Uffizi facade, but for the post-Risorgimental period his role had expanded for Dante was also emblematic of a larger nationalistic movement aimed at rejoining the Austrian occupied territories of Trento and Trieste to Italy. These geographical areas, the Irredentists claimed, were linguistically a part of Italy and should therefore be redeemed as the word irredentist implies. On June 22, 1890, the association *Pro Patria* held a congress in Trento and the Austrians retaliated by dissolving the society. Further irritation was in store for the Irredentists when on October 8, 1890, Crispi, at Florence, spoke against the movement declaring their goals a "cry for war".[11] Matteo Imbriani, in turn, proposed to raise a monument to Dante in Trento thus focalizing attention on the irredentist position. The Dante monument also served as a reply to the Austrian population which had raised a monument in Bolzano to their 13th century hero-poet, Walther von der Vogelweide.[12] The tension between the Irredentists and Rome was raised to new heights. Though Pompeo saw the Dante momument in place only when he returned to Italy for a visit in 1908, he in the 90's as as active member in the Irredentist movement, was surely caught up in the enthusiasm for the project and he probably followed the development of the monument, during the 90's, in the studio of his Florentine friend Cesare Zocchi,[13] who had won the monument competition.

Without a doubt revolutionary causes, as that of the Irredentists, were enthusiastically championed by our young, energetic and high-spirited Pompeo. It is therefore no surprise to discover that he also participated in secret political societies. Indeed Pompeo was merely continuing the family tradition of an earlier relative Lorenzo who fought in the 1859 battle which attempted to liberate Venice from the Austrians and that of his own father who participated in a similar battle of 1866. In 1882, the political-fraternal movements in which Pompeo was active, the irredentists, the Republican party and the Free Masons, considered themselves as the true perpetuators of the ideal's formulated and fought for during the Risorgimento; thus, these groups were to the Prime Minister, Depretis, highly suspect. Irredentism could be considered as an anarchic movement because it was closely identified to the anti-monarchical and anti-clerical Republican party thereby causing its followers to be considered as a highly undesirable group. Another rallying point for Pompeo was the Republican Guglielmo Oberdan, who, in 1882, became a heroic figure for the Irredentist group after he, Oberdan, prepared a futile attempt on the life of the Austrian Emperor Francis Joseph. Oberdan was caught and hung. His cause, as other similar causes, are recorded in Pompeo's book; he writes of his participation around 1890 in the ''Guglielmo Oberdant Republican Intransigent Club'' saying that he helped publish inflamatory pamphlets and defied the law by speaking in public on the liberation of Trento and Trieste from Austria. During one of these meetings at Florence, the police — the ''Carabinieri'' — raided the hall and Pompeo, at that time in the military — the ''Bersaglieri'' — barely escaped. He denied all charges made by the captain of his company, but he was punished and sent to a garrison of ''Carabinieri'' at Grosseto in the Maremma.[14] A contemporary Republican, Giovanni Spadolini, former Prime Minister, actually Minister of Defense, has written in his book, *The Republicans after the Unification*, that in the 1880's in Tuscany — in the zones of the Maremma and Lunigiana — republicanism coincided with a negation of the present order, with an authentic refusal for the Italian political orientation whether of its internal or foreign policies, of its ideological directions or of its social intentions. Spadolini continues by saying that the men who adhered to the Republican party were disdainful of power, were indifferent to privileges, were of unquestioned honesty, were unmoveable in their spirit of sacrifice and faithful without exception, thus inflexibly faithful to the ideals of the past.[15] Pompeo's character was formed in these groups, first in Florence and then later in Sicily at San Buca Zabut (now Sambuca di Sicilia) where he was sent by the military in 1894 to help dispel riots being staged by the starving workers.[16] Secretly Pompeo was convinced of their cause. Indeed Pompeo continued to fight for his ideals through a ''clandestine'' Free Mason group when, after his return from Sicily, desperately in need of work, he sought jobs in the marble shops of Tuscany located along the Tyrrhenean sea. It was at this period that he first worked in Pietrasanta for the Palla family, the shop where he in 1950 completed one of his last projects, a marble statue for his hometown Moglia. With this heroic size monument, *Martyrs of War*,[17] represented by a nude seated figure which closes in on himself in desperation, Pompeo sculptured a final message for future generations — an admonition to respect the brotherhood of all people. Pompeo, still very young when he first worked at Pietrasanta, held to his strong beliefs on the rights of the proletariats. For this reason, Pompeo, who says he belonged to a Mason Lodge with the Orient in Palermo again found himself, with his Lodge, in political difficulty, as they opposed the ''mismanagement'' of the government by Crispi, at that time Prime Minister and Grand Master of the Mason Lodge with the Orient in Rome. To Pompeo a career in Italy as a sculptor must have seemed to hold few possibilities. Therefore, it was probably at this time that he began to consider emigration perhaps lured by the American statuary trade with the same marble shops in which he was employed. Without a doubt, Pompeo Coppini by developing his sensitivity to those fraternal ideals attuned to heroic causes and peoples — received a very unique preparation for all the battles he would later fight in his committment to monumental statuary honoring heroic New World counterparts — both national and of his adopted homeland

Texas. His public commissions included among others his first work in Texas, a Jefferson Davis for the Austin Confederate monument, a George Washington for Mexico City and Terry's Texas Ranger for Austin, another equestrian, Gen. John Hunt Morgan for Lexington, Kentucky and the allegorical doors for the Mason Lodge in San Antonio with scenes, on one door, of Washington presiding over the Blue Lodge in Alexandria and in the act of signing the Declaration of Independence. On the other door there is General Sam Houston presiding at the formation of the Grand Lodge of Texas and the signing of the Declaration of Independence of Texas. Also in San Antonio is the Alamo Heroes Cenotaph with figures that represent "The Spirit of Sacrifice".[18]

Turning again to Pompeo's formation in Italy, we note that children's literature, which might be considered as an unusual source, also serves to give insight into Pompeo's early years. As Alberto Rosa comments this literature was fundamental in the political, cultural and moral education of the period. For Rosa, two particular books stand out as witnesses to an Italy in stress,[19] to the trauma that the new state was experiencing. One, a book by Edmondo De Amicis called, *Cuore, Hearts*, may not be familiar to all, but that of Carlo Lorenzini, Collodi, *The Adventures of Pinocchio* is well known. Rosa sees in the pages of these books a key to a more complete understanding of the infantile Italy, rebellious and egoistic, battling, through adolesence towards adulthood. Pinocchio was also Tuscan and the story of his education from his birth, an anomalous unformed piece of wood, through his transformation to a human being is, says Rosa, a reflection of the struggling young state.[20] Pinocchio passes from one episode to another; he is often stubborn and naughty, but he earns of survival even during the moments of greatest sacrifice. No less than Pinocchio, Coppini was a part of that national reality and adventure.

To complete the tour of Pompeo's Tuscany it is necessary to focus on some of the artistic ideas contributing to his formation. Existing documents in the Florence Art Academy record Pompeo's presence in the years of 1887 and 1888.[21] Thus, the sculptors who m ose influenced Pompeo's education were those artists who participated in the mid-century aesthetic changes in Tuscany. For many, 1860 — the formation of modern Italy — also signalled a similar cultural advancement for in 1861 the first Italian national exhibition of sculpture and painting was held in Florence. Turning back to the statues of the Uffizi facade it is clear that after the 1840's the artists had begun to move away from neo-classical abstracted forms towards a more naturalistic vocabulary. These qualities in varying intensities can be seen in the Uffizi facade statues by Emilio Demi, *Dante*, Emilio Santarelli, *Michelangelo* and Giovanni Dupré, *San Antonino*.[22] This naturalistic trend was even more fully explored by the sculptor Adriano Cecioni who wrote that art is "nature in the act of being surprised in her normal and abnormal moments."[23] Because of a major interest in the momentary, the fragmentary, a total anti-academic position, in its extreme manifestations this is an art form which is antithetical to a monumental style.

Though the naturalistic trend become a dominant factor in much of the ensuing decades, an exclusive interest in fleeting external phenomena was to be somewhat conditioned by the artistic competitions available in the 1880's. First the death of King Vittorio in 1878 and then that of Garibaldi in 1882 provided new monumental sculptural opportunities. Pompeo's teachers Emilio Zocchi and Augusto Rivalta[24] had matured their styles in this period. Rivalta, especially, tended towards the new descriptive language and an interest in pictorial qualities which were easily reproduced in bronze. However, his celebrative equestrian statues to Garibaldi in Genova[25] and Vittorio Emanuele in Livorno[26] show that though Rivalta was committed to those external realities they were not intended as an end in themselves. Celebrative statuary had a mission; ideally it should be permeated by all the idealistic qualities which the movement represented. Thus, for Rivalta's generation an equestrian monument of these two central figures represented the highest challenge that sculpture could offer.

Unfortunately Pompeo was too young to take part in any of the competitions in Italy for these monuments. In fact he left the country just at the moment when many of the statues were being inaugurated in various piazzas around the country. Arriving in America, Pompeo migrated to Texas where he came into his own and where, with his indomitable Italian spirit he helped to form the sculptural landscape in the only image he deemed worthy of existing by creating art to hold "high the philosophic and moral ideal of educating mankind".

Pompeo was only one of many immigrant artists who have sought and who will seek a place in the cultural development of America. Through their individual perserverances they have filled the landscape from coast to coast with "American art". For this reason alone future studies of both their formative years and their later multiformed contributions will continue to fascinate researchers; however, finding the necessary documentation to fully comprehend this Italian heritage is difficult and frustrating. Therefore, hopeful in facilitating this task for future students, I several years ago proposed a project — a computerized information center dedicated to Italian immigrant artistic documents and sources. As I stated previously, my information center project has not yet been realized, but is needed, not only for those who have already contributed to the "melting pot", but also for those Italian artists who will arrive even beyond the year 2000.

Footnotes

1. My thanks to the American Association of University Women for the 1982—83 Fellowship and to the National Endowment for the Humanities for a 1984 Travel to Collections Grant which permitted me to pursue my research on Italian immigrants.
   Pompeo Coppini, born Moglia (Mantua) May 19, 1870. Married Elizabeth Di Barberi of New Haven, Connecticut, 1898. Became U.S. citizen 1901. Died San Antonio, Texas, September 28, 1957. See Carol Bradley, "Pompeo Coppini" in *Dizionario Biografico degli Italiani*, (Roma, 1983), XXVIII. While many plaster models of Coppini's work are still conserved by his only student, Waldine Tauch, at the Coppini Academy, San Antonio, Texas, Dr. Tauch, in 1983 following my recommendation to safeguard the material, donated other recommendation to safeguard the material, donated other documentation — papers and scrapbooks — to the Barker History Center, University of Texas, Austin, Texas.
2. Pompeo Coppini, *From Dawn to Sunset* (San Antonio, Texas, n.d. 1949).
3. Coppini sailed from Genova, Italy for New York, February 21. 1896 aboard the S.S. Kaiser William II with intermediate stops at Naples and Gibralter. Coppini writes that he landed "at Castle Garden, now the Aquarium, the morning of March 5, 1896", (Pompeo Coppini, pp. 37—38). Another immigrant artist, Joseph Stella, in his petition for citizenship, states that he arrived at New York, March 4, 1896 on the S.S. Kaiser Wilhelm der Grosse, see: "Joseph Stella" in *The Golden Door, Artist-Immigrants of America 1876—1976* (Washington, 1976) p. 131, notes 1, 2.
4. Coppini left New York for San Antonio, November 1901, where he modelled a statue of Jefferson Davis for Frank Teich who had been given the commission for the Austin Cofederate Monument (Pompeo Coppini, p. 90).
5. Pompeo Coppini, p. 90.
6. Silvano Fei, *Firenze 1881—1898: La Grande Operazione Urbanistica* (Roma, 1977), p. 16f.
7. Silvano Fei, p. 150.
8. Emilio Zocchi, born Florence, March 5, 1835. Died January 10, 1913. Studied at the Florence Art Academy with Giovanni Dupre. The monument was moved to the entrance of the park, the "Cascine" in 1932.
9. Piero Barbera, *Ricordi Biografici di Vincenzo Batelli Tipografo Fiorentino* (Firenze, 1872), p. 8.
10. F(ilippo) Moise, *Sopra un Progetto d'Esecuzione di 28 Statue in Marmo Rappresentanti Illustri Toscani da Collocarsi nelle Nicchie delle Fabbrica degli Uffizi in Firenze* (Firenze, 1836), p. 9f.

11. Saverio Cilibrizzi, *Storia Parlamentare Politica e Diplomatica d'Italia* (Milano, 1925), II, pp. 394, 396.
12. Dennis Mack Smith, *Storia d'Italia, 1861—1969* (Bari, 1975), p. 222.
13. Cesare Zocchi, born Florence, June 7, 1851.
    Studied with his cousin Emilio Zocchi who had a studio in the Florence Art Academy. Died 1922. The Dante Monument was inaugurated October 10, 1896.
14. Pompeo Coppini, p. 19.
15. Giovanni Spadolini, *I Repubblicani Dopo l'Unita* (Firenze, 1963), p. 54f.
16. Pompeo Coppini, p. 26f.
17. Date of inauguration April 22, 1951. *Omaggio di Moglia a Coppini* (numero unico, Moglia, 22 aprile 1951).
18. See: Pompeo Coppini, index. Carol Bradley, *Dizionario Biografico. The Supplement to Who's Who* (Chicago, March—may 1959), p. 2413.
19. Alberto Asor Rosa, *Storia d'Italia* (Torino, 1975), 4(2) p. 925f.
20. Alberta A. Rosa, p. 939.
21. Carol Bradley, *Dizionario Biografico*.
22. *Dante*, inaugurated 1842; *Michelangelo*, inaugurated 1842; *San Antonino*, inaugurated 1854.
23. Adriano Cecioni, born July 26, 1836, Fontebuona (near Florence). Student of Aistodemo Costoli at the Florence Art Academy. Died May 23, 1886. Adriano Cecioni, "Dell 'Importanza Tecnica nell'Arte", April 18, 1873, in *Opere e Scritti* (Milano, 1932), p. 11.
24. Augusto Rivalta, born Alessandria (Piedmont) 1837 or 1838. Studied with Dupre at Florence. Died Florence April 14, 1925.
25. Inaugurated 1893.
26. Inaugurated 1892.

Chapter **17** **ITALIAN-AMERICAN COMMUNITY ORGANIZATIONS: PROBLEMS AND PROSPECTS FOR FUTURE STUDY**

Jerome Krase
Sociology Department, Brooklyn College

In the United States, when people speak about "community" problems they are often referring to "ethnic" problems. And, furthermore, when one discusses these problems in a local context, the proper designation for them are problems of the ethnic neighborhood community. It must be remembered that a large proportion of the problems which result from living in an ethnic neighborhood is due to the "minority" group aspect of local community life. Regardless of the degree to which the particular group is either despised or idolized by the dominant society, minority status is part of the psychological, cultural and social structure of the neighborhood. This situation also effects the socialization process of the young, organizational performance, as well as intra-group and intergroup interaction.

The local ethnic neighborhood community is seldom, or for very long, an unadulterated replication or simple relocation of a foreign society. Even when a whole village emigrates to a new country and settles together, the uprooting and replanting process significantly effects the social reality of local life. This subsociety, both in anticipation and in confrontation with the new environment and its challenges, is modified by the basic need of all social systems to adapt to changed external environments. For most peasant subcultures the adaption process usually results in a loss of local control over members; especially the young. Such communities also experience difficulty in dealing with challenges presented by large, impersonal bureaucratic organizations with which it deals in an modern urban environment. In order for the community to become fully integrated into the new system it must develop new ways to deal with its own members and to interact with the outside society. Historically, in America, this has been a special problem for Mediterranean-American ethnic communities located in large urban settings. In some cases, the adaptation has been a retreat from interaction with the outside whenever possible. This places such communities at a distinct disadvantage in ethnic group competition which is an important part of the city scene.

Kurt Lewin and others have argued that some element of self hatred is all but inevitable in the ethnic minority community (1953). Of course the reality and degree of self deprecation is not an analytic proposition, but is determined by the definition of the subgroup in the lexicon of the dominant society. Unfortunately for Mediterraneans, in Anglo-American society, that definition has been, and continues to be, negative. The degree of lost self esteem is also influenced by the extent and quality of extra-community interaction, and the strength of the local group to counter negative definitions *via* its own cultural mechanisms for self and group preservation. Seldom, however, are ethnic communities able to either completely segregate themselves from the outside or to be totally effective in in-group propaganda. This propaganda often takes the form of super-group chauvinism and counter-attacks on the mores and conditions existing in the dominant society outside. Defensive activities in themselves can have negative effects as definitions become less positive and more contra-positive. It is a tenuous image which is based on being less bad than how others perceive you.

Negative self and group images also make it more difficult for the group to interact effectively with the outside world. Additionally, it causes divisions within the ethnic subcommunity to increase. In some cases one part of the community blames another part for their collective troubles. Such problems reduce the possibility of ethnic community solidarity. The ethnic neighborhood invariably becomes self conscious and defensive which often reduces its ability to deal with local issues and makes it more vulnerable to outside intrusion.

To exemplify the debilitating aspects of contra-negative self images, I can note many of my own experiences in attempting to assist local ethnic community groups to deal with social problems such as juvenile delinquency and substance abuse. Quite often the response to problems within the community brought to their attention by "outsiders," such as myself, is the strident defense of the group's reputation, the countering that the problem is not as bad as claimed because the group is not "understood," that the group does not need outside help, or that the problem is the responsibility of those outside. This is a reaction of "shame." Shame frequently prevents ethnic communities from facing reality and being able to deal with its problems. Organizationally, the Italian-American community is not likely to form an organization called the Italian-American Anti-Drug Abuse Society. Positive themes are much more likely to generate attention, such as the high culture, art and historical figures.

Howard Becker had noted in his studies of deviant behavior that the insider-outsider mentality is a result of the negative social labelling process by which minorities, i.e., cultural deviants, define themselves in opposition to the group doing the labelling. (1963) Emile Durkheim, of course, established much earlier the tendency of threats from the outside to increase the solidarity of the group and for it to narrow and strengthen its own social boundaries. (1964) My own research (1982) and that of Gerald Suttles (1972) have shown that, in response to attack, neighborhoods defen symbolic as well as territorial boundaries. Closure of the community is related to self-esteem. Morris Rosenberg, in an early study, found that in the case of religious minorities, when they are less than 25 percent of the local population, they have a lower self esteem and higher rates of depression and psychosomatic symptoms than when they are more than 25 percent of the local population. In greater concentrations they are less likely to develop feelings of fear, anxiety and insecurity as they have a greater sense of belonging and acceptance. (1962)

Although successful defense can be seen as positive, Tamatsu Shibutani and Kian M. Kwan argue that there are some structural dysfunctions which result. (1965) The ethnic neighborhood is a "haven of refuge" or "safety zone." Although wage earners and others go into the outside world and more or less conform to "foreign" dictates, inside the neighborhood they can follow the more traditional ways of life. The ethnics feel comfortable only among their peers and cannot relax with outsiders because they do not know what to expect. This problem of psychological discomfort or stress is exaggerated by the lack of facility with the dominant language. The result of this lack of communication and understanding places the ethnic on guard, even inadvertently, against those with whom they do not share a common ethnic bond. "Within each community, then, there tends to develop a special universe of discourse. This is a matter of great importance, for human experiences are classified in terms of words," according to Shibutani (p. 285). Ethnocentrism and self-segregation results from defense.

The ethnic community can become self-limiting and self-defeating by fostering and maintaining mutual categorization and misunderstanding between the in- and out-group. Closure is a barrier to intergroup relations and perpetuates and increases social distances, while at the same time protecting self-esteem and traditions. The lack of cultural and other variety within the community limits personal and social development. The individual is excluded from the kinds of discourse and interaction which would increase the possibility of success outside of the closed environment. The young are especially disadvantaged in this regard. It is virtually impossible to prevent intrusion through the electronic media and public school systems and therefore inter-generational conflict is assured. The young are enticed by "forbidden fruits" and the older fear the loss of control. Both experience degrees of personal disequilibrium as a result. In many third-generational ethnic neighborhoods the cultural bases for surviving folkways have long since wasted away and are mere cultural artifacts. The community may still remain closed, while lacking meaningful cultural substance, and sustenance. Neighborhoods such as these may exhibit many of the stereotypical indicators of psychological and social pathology such as high school drop-out rates, substance abuse, and broken or troubled families. Members of such "disorganized" ethnic communities can be just as xenophobic as their more stable counterparts. Over time, ethnic communities have a tendency, according to Judith Kramer, to become status communities with a high degree of cultural and social parochialism (1970).

Specific values of ethnic communities may also have negative value in the wider environment, or at least been seen as negative by outsiders. Traditional values, despite their sanctity, are often in conflict with modern ideals such as individual freedom, equality of opportunity, democracy and freedom of expression. Most notably in many ethnic communities are the restraints placed upon women in all areas of life, and especially in educational and occupational opportunity. Traditional ethnic communities may also continue support for castes or caste-like economic and social systems. In these instances, individuals and families are trapped in historically, culturally and sometimes religiously supported socio-economic structures, which for the most part determine their current and future status within the community. For both women and other persons upon whom these traditions of conformity and obedience weigh most heavily, the option to grow and change in the locality is unavailable and one must choose, if the opportunity is presented, between remaining with the group or moving out. One need only contemplate the social and psychological problems confronted by the individual who makes either choice.

To many people, ethnic enclaves appear to be idyllic scenes of happy, healthy people. Invisible to most observers are the poor, troubled families, neglected elderly and others who, it is assumed, are either non-existent or served by family and other traditional support systems. The view of the ethnic neighborhood as "trouble-free" is often the result of individual, family and group pride which reduces the frequency with which problems are brought to the attention of outside public or private agencies. It is also unlikely that needed professional help is easily available to the community. Ethnic professionals are seldom full-time residents of ethnic neighborhoods as socio-economic advancement is accompanied by geographic mobility. Distrust of outsiders and other local attitudes decrease willingness to call for professional assistance.

One can add to the litany of overlooked problems of ethnic neighborhoods the preservation of folk attitudes toward health care and psychological problems, which are just as likely to be dangerous as they are beneficial to local people. For example, in many Italian-American neighborhoods the *machismo* ethic of males prevents workers from seeking medical treatment for physical problems. As for psychological assistance to troubled young people, traditional parents are unwilling to seek professional guidance, or in some cases, even to admit to the existence of family difficulties. Health and psychological problems are frequently seen as indicators of family failure and produce communal shame.

Most ideas about ethnic neighborhood communities in America place the person in the center of a series of concentric circles, or spheres, which represent the boundaries of levels of social organizations in which the individual holds a status. Reaching down to the individual level of social life in ethnic studies is much like peeling an onion; when you arrive at the center there is nothing left. Looking at ethnic neighborhoods from the point of view of the persons living in them, a different perspective on the communities' functions and malfunctions is provided. Rather than the individual being "protected from the outside" by each successive layer, we see many institutions and structures, each making their own, often conflicting, demands. This represents an exceedingly complex, rather than simple, environment in which the community is as much an antagonist as it is a protector and supporter of the individual. For example, the person who wishes to deal with the outside world must create for himself or herself elaborate arrangements for negotiating successive barriers, a clear channel through the barriers, or a separate identity for social intercourse with the outside. Even the family as a primary group has several levels based on parallel kinship, gender, and age groupings as part of the complex topography which results in the negative as well as the positive functions of the Italian-American Neighborhood.

There have been many studies of the associational life of Italians and their communities in the United States. Some are interesting and, perhaps, controversial assessments of the overall structure and operation of the Italian-American community as a whole, and others have focused on Italians in specific locations. Most researchers have generally described the ethnic group and their neighborhoods as exhibiting "traditional" organization forms, with regional and historical variation. In general, the Italian-American associations are characterized as being "behind the times." Even after many generations, Italians in America, it has been argued, show a cultural lag in adopting more modern bureaucratic and objective structures for dealing with problems.

Some people hail this situation as a preservation of Italian immigrant values and cite the advantages of intense local and primary group relations for neighborhood and family stability in a constantly changing, and confusing modern environment. This view romanticizes immigrant and working-class communities. Others lament the lag as a major causative factor in the relative inability of the Italian-American community to compete with other, better organized, ethnic groups. This view, on the other hand, sees Italian-American cultural habits and traditional community forms as major impediments to effective competition in the social, economic and political arenas.

The reality of modern America is that the good "old fashioned" virtues are generally applauded, but that groups who persist in doing things on their own and solving their own problems without government or other outside help, will be at a distinct disadvantage. Many of today's problems are not simply family affairs. Italian-American neighborhoods are no longer insular and immune to the problems which face the whole of society. Urban Italian-Americans are, in this context, the worst off of groups, as they face stiff opposition, as well as, competition from other organized ethnic groups.

It was nor my purpose here to either praise of condemn the Italian-American penchant for personal leadership, informal networking or traditional organization. My intent was to note that such cultural and subcultural factors have important effects on the ability of the community to recognize, approach and solve social problems. One must emphasize in this regard that ever since the turn of the 20th Century, treatment and prevention of even the most local of problems have increasingly become the domain of extra-community formal organizations. These groups range from private philanthropies, through government created and maintained bureaucracies. This fact makes it essential that we assess the problems and prospects of the Italian-American community organizations for today and toward the year 2000.

References

Becker, Howard S.
>*Outsiders*. New York: The Free Press, 1963

Durkheim, Emile.
>*The Division of Labor in Society*. New York: The Free Press, 1964. George Simpson (trans.)

Kramer, Judith R.
>*The American Minority Community*. New York: Thomas Y. Crowell, 1970

Krase, Jerome.
>*Self and Community in the City*. Washington, D.C.: University Press of America, 1982.

Lewin, Kurt.
>"Self Hatred Among Jews," in Arnold M. Rose (ed.), *Race Prejudice and Discrimination*. New York: A.A. Knopf, 1953, pp. 321—32.

Parks, Robert E.
>*Human Communities*. Glencoe, Illinois: The Free Press, 1952.

Rosenberg, Morris.
>"The Dissonant Religious Context and Emotional Disturbance." *American Journal of Sociology* 68, 1 (July) 1962, pp. 2—5.

Shibutani, Tamotsu and Kian M. Kwan.
>*Ethnic Stratification*. New York: MacMillan, 1965.

Suttles, Gerald D.
>*The Social Construction of Communities*. Chicago: University of Chicago Press, 1972.

Chapter **18** THE DEVELOPMENT AND
MAINTENANCE OF
NEW YORK CITY'S
ITALIAN-AMERICAN
NEIGHBORHOODS

Robert C. Freeman
Montclair State College/Fordham University

Italian-Americans started entering the United States in large numbers a little over a century ago, settling largely in the major cities of the northeast. Today, the entrance of their descendants into the American middle-class is denoted by the emergence of such nationally-prominent and instantly recognizable personalities as New York Governor Mario Cuomo and ex-Vice Presidential nominee Geraldine Ferraro in politics; the outgoing Yale President A. Bartlett Giamatti in higher education; and actors Al Pacino and Robert DeNiro and filmmakers Francis Ford Coppola and Martin Scorcese from the world of cinema. Understandably, such a development gives rise to the public perception that Italian-Americans, as a group, have "made it" in American society. Typically, an ethnic groups' upward mobility into the middle-class involves a spatial movement away from the urban center; at the same time, the "Little Italy" remains one of the more conspicuous locales in nearly every sizeable North American central city.

Rather than attempt to identify those who still reside in such urban neighborhoods (those trapped by poverty? the elderly immigrant generation? recent immigrants?), this paper will look back at the development and growth of the urban Italian-American neighborhood; explore some recent developments in these neighborhoods, and will look ahead at the prospects for "Little Italy" in the year 2000. This analysis will focus upon tha most heavily Italian of all U.S. cities, New York City.

The Italian Presence in New York City

Italian-Americans continue to display an unusually high degree of urban concentration. Velikonja (28) determined that nearly 92% of all Italian stock in the U.S. in 1960 resided in urban areas, against a figure of slightly under

70% for the general U.S. population. The urban agglomeration of Italians has been particularly strong in the Boston-Washington megalopolis, which Velikonja found contained 70% of the identifiable Italian stock in America. Furthermore, over 72% of all the resident Italian aliens in the U.S. as of early 1968 were registered in the Northeast, a figure which had changed little over preceding years (31). Velikonja found that 10.3% of the population of the New York-New Jersey Consolidated Area was Italian stock, and that their proportions were higher in many selected subdivisions of this area, such as Brooklyn and Staten Island, where the Italian stock comprised over 14% of the population (34). On the 1980 Census, one out of seven New York City residents was of Italian ancestry; this figure jumps to 27% of the City if one omits the black and Hispanic population components. About 8% of all Americans of Italian ancestry currently live in New York City, and nearly one-quarter live in New York State (Egelman and Salvo 2).

Recent decades have seen little dispersal of Italian in- migrants to rural areas, and a marked preference for a few select metropolitan areas (Velikonja 37). Over the last two decades several of South Brooklyn's Italian neighborhoods, particularly Bay Ridge and Gravesend, have become the destination of many of the Italian immigrants to New York City. There, in a cruel variation on a theme oft-repeated in immigration history, the newcomers' work ethic, clothes, and language difficulties are mocked by a second-generation Italian-American population seeking to maintain social distance from the so-called "Gheeps" (Kessner and Caroli 219—21). Nevertheless, today's Italian immigrants are much more likely to be skilled or semiskilled workers than was the case in earlier decades (Ianni 107)[1].

New York City, then, has been and continues to be a major focal point for the Italian-American population of the U.S. Being hardly a "typical" American city, however, the findings of this paper regarding Italian-American neighborhoods are probably generalizable to the rest of the country only with considerable qualifications attached.

The Housing of Early Italian Immigrants in New York City

The Italian immigrants who came to New York City in the years of large-scale immigration (roughly 1880—1920) were mostly from southern Italy and found work as unskilled construction workers. They were heavily involved in the construction of New York City's subways, railroads, and aqueducts, as well as major buildings like Grand Central Terminal (Kessner 58).

The earliest large residential concentration of Italians in the City was in the "immigrant zone" on Manhattan's Lower East Side, although the uptown colony in East Harlem had already been established by the mid- '80's (Kessner 129). It has been suggested that the worst housing conditions in early twentieth-century American cities were found in the Italian districts (Northam 262). These areas were generally characterized by large populations, high densities, and high mortality rates.[2] Russian Jewish neighborhoods, although densely settled, had lower death rates while Irish ghettos tended to be less crowded.

Descriptions of New York City's Italian immigrant neighborhoods tended to be colorful and occasionally melodramatic. Foerster's description of one Italian neighborhood on the Lower East Side may be as evocative as any:

> Who that has sauntered through these colonies can forget them? Who . . . can describe them? An ant hill is like them or a beehive — but too soon all analogies break down! [This district] disputes with few other blocks the dismal honor of being the most populous spot on earth. Its tenements rise four or five stories into the air but each story bursts, as if the inward pressure were too great, into a balcony. The street below is at once playground and place of business: one threads one's way betwixt push carts and stands, past little children and quite as little old women . . . (382)

Such neighborhoods attracted reformers and curious outsiders. Residents of fashionable Harlem in the 1890's were known to meander over to East Harlem on religious holidays and feast days to survey the exotica of that Italian neighborhood: marionette shows, organ grinders, and pushcart peddlers. The poorest Italians, though, scrounged leftover food in the area's garbage dumps and ashbarrels (Osofsky 82—3).

In lower Manhattan, Italians lived in "old law" (pre-1901) tenements, also known as "dumb-bell" tenements. These were mostly five or six stories high, with each floor usually divided into four apartments. The front apartments on each floor consisted of four rooms each, while the rear two apartments had three rooms apiece. Of the fourteen rooms per floor, only four received direct light and air from the street or small yard at the back. The bedrooms at the back of the apartment, a closet-sized 7 x 8½ feet each, were generally almost dark, except for those on the highest stories which received somewhat more light from the 28- inch indentation of the wall called, with grim irony, the air-shaft (DeForest and Veiller 8). Two water closets were located on each floor in the public hallway; each was used by two families, and lighted and ventilated by the air shaft. For such accommodations around the turn of the century a family paid $12 to $18 per month for a four-room apartment, and $10 to $15 monthly for a rear apartment.

The Tenement House Act passed by New York State in 1901, a landmark in New York City tenement house reform, provided for a water-closet for each family, widened the air shaft, provided for windows in the hall on each floor and took steps to upgrade fire escapes and the fireproofing of halls and stairs (De Forest and Veiller xv). Tenements erected after the passage of this legislation thus became known as "new law" buildings.

Formation of Italian-American Neighborhoods

One of the more remarkable features of Italian-American neighborhoods is their seeming permanence: while German, Irish, and Jewish neighborhoods in New York City have largely disappeared, replaced by black and Hispanic and the recent Caribbean immigrant populations, a number of reasonably vibrant Italian neighborhoods remain, particularly in the City's outer boroughs. One enclave in the central Bronx has remained predominantly Italian since it was settled near the turn of the century, while adjacent one-time Irish and Jewish neighborhoods have long since gone through transition to a racial minority population. However, it should be remembered that the view of the Italian neighborhood as a static unit obscures significant population movement: the replacement of out-migrating younger people by immigrant newcomers and even, in some (few?) cases, the return of grown children who had previously moved away to the suburbs.

Unlike the situation in the outer boroughs, however, the Italian neighborhoods in Manhattan have either disappeared or seem to be heading in that direction. Originally, these districts housed day laborers who, by clustering in a central location, gained access to the principal markets of unskilled labor. Pratt (162—71) found that Italian immigrants settled close to their place of employment, thus minimizing transportation expenses.[3] Additionally, many of these men worked long and/or awkward hours, thus making preferable the short pedestrian journey to work; furthermore, since daily hiring was often practiced by employers in the fields of day laboring and portering, residence near downtown maximized access to alternative job opportunities in case the work relocated to another site or unemployment befall the worker (Thompson 21). Other factors were instrumental in drawing Italians together in the American city: poor immigrants sought out cheap housing, which was most often found in the "immigrant zone" near downtown; once a neighborhood acquired something of an ethnic identity, it attracted even those members of the group without kin or friends in the area, who gravitated there because of the familiar dialect and folkways and institutions, and also because they had likely met with discrimination on the part of landlords in other sections.[4]

Of course, for any particular worker, the choice of residence was quite often dictated by the location of kin or *paesani* with whom the newly-arrived often stayed as a boarder, taking a job at the workplace of the host either until he was able to obtain his own accommodations or else returned to Italy. The process of chain migration whereby a lone Italian male financed the passage to America of family and friends after securing a foothold in the American labor force resulted in the clustering of Italian immigrants in New York City (as elsewhere) on the basis of home village (MacDonald and MacDonald 230—1)[5]. Such clustering was often on a block-by-block, or even building-by-building basis, and was overlaid with the formation of mutual aid societies often named after the home village and with membership restricted to those who hailed from that village (Foerster 393). Gabaccia (105) has described the softening of Italian localism as social networks expanded due to involvement with peddlers' markets, business partnerships, youth gangs, church-related activities and festival societies. Immigrants from a family-dominated society who had once thought of themselves as, at most, Sicilians or Calabrians developed an awareness of a common membership in a larger political unit (Nelli, 1983:60). Such a blurring of regional distinctions, however, never quite materialized for that great divide between northern and southern Italian, a chasm founded upon such factors as social class and skill level and amplified by the ramifications of the generally earlier entry of the northerners into the American labor force (Gambino 66; Mormino 230).

Neilli (1970:6) has argued for another transformation of the Italian-American community in the U.S. metropolis: villagers raised in an ethos of "amoral familism" (Banfield) in southern Italy developed a sense of warmth and intimacy in the New World urban enclave. What is erroneously thought of as "old world intimacy" is actually a new world response to the urban environment. Perhaps relevant here is Gabaccia's description of the way in which males and children from a lower Manhattan district, by socializing with other residents the block of streetcorners and in cafes and backyards, were able to minimize the potential harm to their social networks caused by frequent moves from building to building in search of better housing (77). These Elizabeth Street immigrants enjoyed neighborhood social life and appreciated the district's relatively low rents, while yet disliking the physical reality of their living quarters (Gabaccia 85).

I have briefly discussed above some of the factors involved in the formation of, and some of the internal dynamics of, Italian immigrant neighborhoods. As was mentioned, these old Manhattan neighborhoods have now largely disappeared for a variety of reasons: e.g., the Mulberry Street "Little Italy", the symbolic heart of the City's Italian-American community, is threatened by the expansion of the neighboring Chinatown community currently receiving a large immigrant influx; the South Village Italian community has become a thriving artists' community; the Italian community in East Harlem underwent the twin shocks of redlining and the construction of housing projects on a large scale in the '40's and '50's which forced the relocation of some Italian residents, drove from the projects those whose incomes rose above the mandated income ceiling, and induced other non-project dwellers to leave the neighborhood as landlords neglected their properties in expectation of the impending bulldozing of their block to make way for more public housing (Freeman 10—11). Although the particular mix of factors involved in any neighborhood's demise may be unique to it, a common feature would seem to be a simple lack of sufficient numbers of incoming Italaian immigrants to fill up the vacancies left by those who departed for better housing in more decentralized locations.

Nowadays, the most vibrant "Little Italys" in New York City are found in The Bronx and Brooklyn. Here, the relatively greater degree of home ownership, as opposed to tenement dwelling, intensifies commitment to the locale. This investment, combined with the financial hardship entailed by a move to the suburbs at a time of relatively high interest rates, means that the residents of such neighborhoods are inclined (at least, initially) to fight to hold on to their neighborhoods in the face of threatened neighborhood transition, which is perceived as bringing with it higher crime rates and lower property values. The threat of turnover is fairly widespread among the City's Italian-American neighborhoods for, besides the possibility of a minority influx, "yuppies" and other gentrifiers have come to find the charm, low rents, specialty stores, centralized location, and relative safety of these areas to their liking.

In the following section I will discuss the importance of home ownership for Italain-Americans; following that, I will describe how three New York City Italian-American neighborhoods are coping with the threat of neighborhood change.

Italian-Americans and Home Ownership

If it is possible, as a sociological rule of thumb, to characterize immigrant Jewish aspirations as being education-centered, particularly for the younger generation, then one may fairly ascribe the same importance to home ownership for Italian immigrants. Few accounts of the Italian immigrant experience in the U.S. have ignored the exalted place that home ownership held in their hierarchy of values. Williams noted that when an Italian finally purchases his own home

> He has attained the prestige that the coming to America promised him, a prestige worth all the sacrifices and losses entailed (46). Yans-McLaughlin sees property ownership conferring a kind of familiar, secure, and concrete status which immigrants appreciated . . . Land was an important symbol of wealth, security, and status in the old country. Immigrants seeking petit bourgeois status could believe that they had attained it when they purchased a home (177).

Indeed, the struggle to be able to afford a home was so arduous for the earlier immigrants that the relative alacrity with which recent Italian immigrants have been able to purchase a new house in South Brooklyn has engendered a certain amount of resentment among the second- and third- generation Italian-Americans living there (Kessner and Caroli 219).

The drive to acquire a home was sufficient to entice the normally protective Italian male to allow his wife and daughter to seek part-time and summer employment to help pay for the future dwelling. Homes were also paid for by boarders fees, by sharing living costs with relatives, and by putting sons to work as soon as they were legally able, rather than sending them on to college (Yans-McLaughlin 175). In St. Louis, Mormino found that many Italian homes on "The Hill" were paid for out of bootlegging profits extracted from basement wine-making enterprises during the days of Prohibition (225).

Historically, the home ownership rates of Italian-Americans has been impressive. By 1930, for instance, nearly 60% of the 1341 homes in St. Louis' Italian "Hill" district were occupied by their owners, as against a city-wide average of 32%; a decade later, after the Depression years, this area still had a homeowner rate twice that of the city (Mormino 169). However, even within the St. Louis city limits, Mormino found that there were great differences in neighborhood character and housing in the two main Italian districts; the stability of "The Hill", which was settled largely by northern Italians who built their brick bungalows and remained in the neighborhood, contrasted vividly with the transience, high vacancy rates, crime, and bad housing characteristic of the Sicilian-dominated "Little Italy", home to a less skilled population. Such a finding points to the importance of the "fit" between the occupational skills of the immigrant group and the structure of the labor force at the time of arrival as a key factor in the eventual settlement pattern of the group.

The Housing Market and the Threat of Neighborhood Change in New York City's "Little Italys"

A number of recently- published participant observation studies of Italian-American communities in New York City provide us with some insight into the workings of the housing market in these areas threatened by racial transition. These studies will be reviewed here:

Greenpoint-Williamsburg (Brooklyn)

Susser's study of this ethnically-mixed but largely Italian area found that most of the homes were divided into two or three apartments, and that the sole income for some households came from the renting out of apartments. Although the author found that the homeowners did not usually collect welfare, many of them apparently applied for food stamps (91). Rent and credit arrangements were quite flexible and often negotiated on the spot, the fee being raised or lowered according to the ethnicity and resources of the potential tenant (92). Leases were easily broken, and rent was sometimes owed for up to six months at a time (91).

In order to maintain some kind of control over the market for prospective tenants, many resident-landlords in Greenpoint-Williamsburg gave first preference to relatives, followed by advertisements in church bulletins and ethnic organizations (e.g., the Italian-American League). Few racial minorities sought apartments with resident landlords; blacks claimed to want to avoid the inevitable rebuffs. Discrimination in renting was justified on the grounds of the expected hostile reaction to black renters by white tenants and neighbors. When a building where a black family was renting an apartment was burned down, the neighborhood grapevine associated the arson with the presence of blacks in the building (93).

Landlords in this neighborhood routinely turned away families with children either by explicitly stating ''adults preferred'' on announcements or, more indirectly, by prohibiting washing machines. Local newspapers ran ads for apartment vacancies with the qualification ''no welfare''. The tenants market could also be pre-screened for landlords by their listing with real estate agents who explicitly advertised themselves as catering to a specific ethnic group (95).

As elsewhere, the personal stake resident landlords have in their property here promoted greater concern with building maintenance, tenant relations, block upkeep, and neighborhood affairs than was the case with the absentee landlords; it also, however, fostered more housing discrimination. The result was a pattern in Greenpoint-Williamsburg whereby blocks of white ethnic homeowners were well-maintained, while other blocks in the area containing a greater proportion of absentee landlords were more poorly maintained and comprised a somewhat heavier proportion of minorities (97). The absentee landlords typically held on to their property until it could be sold or profitably developed; in the meantime, their outlay for maintenance was minimal.

The South Village (Manhattan)

As described by Tricarico, a major event in the recent history of this neighborhood was the passage of a municipal zoning amendment in 1971 which legalized the residence in lofts in a designated area by officially-certified working artists. Subsequently, lofts became a hot real estate item. Although the South Village Italian neighborhood was not within the designated area, it nevertheless felt the impact of the SoHo (South of Houston St.) phenomenon for there was a sharp increase in the demand for apartments and storefronts in the South Village. Local land values and the rent structure soared, and South Village landlords started listing their apartments with a SoHo address and demanding comparable rents. Young people who wanted to be part of an interesting art ''scene'' flocked into the neighborhood; they were further attracted by the reasonable rents (although higher than that paid by the Italian families) and ''ethnic'' ambiance. To a great degree, the Italians in the area were protected from the higher rents by the rent control laws. With apartments in great demand, however, landlords pressured Italians into leaving by cutting back on services.

The South Village renaissance was hardly oriented toward the Italians, catering instead to the newcomers with a variety of antique, jewelry, and gourmet food shops; boutiques; art supply stores, and sculpture galleries. Many traditional Italian-owned enterprises, such as candy stores and social clubs, were unable to bear the rent increases; others that were able to change sufficiently to accommodate the new clientele were rejuvenated. In summary, Tricarico insists that the Italians have been pulled out of the South Village by upward mobility and assimilation, rather than pushed out by the SoHo phenomenon (17).

Canarsie (Brooklyn)

Rieder's sensitive portrayal of (as his subtitle suggests) the "Jews and Italians of Brooklyn against Liberalism", offers important insights into the housing, politics, and community life of Canarsie's Italians in the 1970's. The Italians of Old Canarsie have moved into the skilled blue-collar and lower white-collar occupations, with only about ten percent in professional or managerial work, most of these being women employed as typists, secretaries, and bookkeepers. Dual paychecks helped raise 1980 family income to between $12,000 and $18,000, while less than 25 % had incomes over $25,000 (36).

Neighborhood change was perceived as a threat by Canarsians in the 1970's. While all but seven of the 33 census tracts which make up Canarsie's core had fewer than a dozen black residents in 1980, transition was taking place in peripheral neighborhoods and in nearby housing projects. In a tract adjacent to one project, the number of blacks increased from a dozen to 400 in the decade '70-'80. Resistance to black infiltration was openly proclaimed by Italian leaders in the Republican party, the North Canarise Civic Association, and the Conservative Party (81). The atmosphere created was such that, as one realtor said

> [Among blacks] only troublemakers demand a house in Canarsie.
> But they usually get the message (83).

A number of Canarsians had fled from black "invasion" previously in other Brooklyn neighborhoods, and had learned from experience that after the initial "good element" of minorities had moved in, less-desirable ones followed. Although such a sequence can mostly be attributed to the panicking of white homeowners, it was regarded by them as inevitable. In Rieder's view, this had led to a kind of preemptive strike pattern by the whites whereby middle-class blacks are excluded from neighborhood housing as a means of keeping out the "sure-to-follow" lower-class.

Canarsians organized local drives to protect the neighborhood's "stability"; less formally, vigilante peer groups defended neighborhood "turf" from any intruding minorities, sometimes employing violent means in the process. Merely keeping information about housing vacancies out of the big daily newspapers was deemed inadequate. As one civic leader said

> We have to replace the whites who are leaving or getting old. Let's advertise in the Jewish, Italian, and Chinese papers (194).

Still, fewer whites and more blacks sought openings in Canarsie, necessitating the recruiting of emigre Russian Jews who had initially settled in the Brighton Beach section of Brooklyn. A Jewish leader in Canarsie admitted.

We use the Russian Jews to fill up the Canarsie spaces with whites (94). Captains in the Democratic Club, members of civic groups, and residents got word to home sellers that they would procure buyers for them, and pressured them not to put up "for sale" signs. These groups advertised for prospective buyers in temples and through informal communications channels. A home seller was instructed to contact a group of homeowners who had formed a home-buying service; the latter would see to it that a "proper" sale would be effected.

On another front, strings were pulled to get Russian Jewish immigrant children bused into Canarsie schools to compensate for the declining white enrollments there. Canarsie parents, afraid that the enrollment drop would intensify pressures to bus in black children, thus once again turned to the Russian immigrants as their "trump card".

By 1980, Rieder perceived that a relative racial calm had descended upon Canarsie, as well as a resigned acceptance of integration. Undoubtedly, this development was at least partly due to the high interest rates of the period which made it more difficult for the whites to move.

These recent community studies provide us with a picture of transformation and determined neighborhood defense in New York City's "Little Italys". The South Village is being transformed as old community institutions (political clubs; street corner groups) either wither away or, as in the case of the neighborhood economy and parish social settlements, become oriented to the newcomers (Tricarico 159). The two Brooklyn communities examined here are utilizing ethnic recruitment, block associations, and home-finder's services as a way of controlling the housing market.

What, however, about the "Little Italy" of the year 2000? Will the transformation seen in the South Village be the typical pattern for the outer borough Italian-American neighborhoods, too? Will blight and abandonment strike the Italian communities of Brooklyn as it has other areas in that borough? Such complex questions force us to look, for openers, at recent migration trends:

It is probably safe to suggest that relatively homogeneous Italian neighborhoods in Manhattan are a thing of the past. Miranda and Rossi found evidence in 1970 census tract data for a movement of New York City's Italian stock population into residential areas of eastern Queens and Staten Island (26), and a general out-movement from Manhattan. Even traditional Italian neighborhoods in Brooklyn like Red Hook and Bushwick showed steep declines in this analysis (41). It appears that this out-migration consists of the upwardly-mobile second- and third- generation who, in addition to being "pulled" to middle-class, low- density neighborhoods, have also been "pushed" by economic decline in the central areas and the fears Rieder described. As for neighborhood integration, the research of Miranda and Rossi supports Rieder; the sole exception to the general pattern of an inverse relationship between the concentration of Italian-Americans and blacks in the City's neighborhoods was in those areas where the Italians lived below the poverty line (42—3).

Ominous conclusions about the fate of Italian neighborhoods in the outer boroughs may be reached using other models. The description of the housing market operations in the communities studied by Susser and Rieder conforms closely to one of the three ideal-type neighborhood market patterns presented by Solomon and Vandell in an analysis of neighborhood decline. In this particular type of neighborhood, a key actor is a landlord who views his property as part of his personal or household economy, rather than as a capital asset. Tenant-landlord relations are seen as reciprocal, personal, and social, without a formal lease and with landlord residency. Rents are below market price because of reciprocity and concern with homogeneity and satisfaction. In addition, tenant selection is based on similar backgrounds and mutual self-selection; resident owners are unsophisticated in accounting principles; rehabilitation investment is determined by landlord residency or desire to upgrade the neighborhood, and there is little usage of borrowed capital, except from family and friends.

In such a neighborhood, Solomon and Vandell propose that the principal cause of decline is a breakdown in the reciprocity relationship, either as a result of lack of sufficient desirable tenants in the market (e.g., Canarsie), forcing some landlords to take in tenants of less compatible backgrounds; or because landlords operating under the above principles leave and are replaced by those operating under more orthodox economic rules of behavior; or because certain factors, such as cheap capital available outside the neighborhood or externally imposed regulations, may force landlords to begin behaving in a more orthodox economic manner, replacing friendliness with more impersonal regulations, and resident landlords with absentee landlords. Rent levels go up because of the landlord's increasing responsibility for repair and maintenance and his realization of the opportunity costs of his own labor. The tenants, now less committed to the property, maintain it less well and feel less responsibility for rental payments, and begin to move out with more frequency as a result of landlord evictions or in search of better housing. Friends and relatives of the landlord become less likely to make loans as they come to feel less committed to the ever-weakening neighborhood bonds. The landlord is forced to seek outside funding in the conventional money market, but lenders here see the risks involved and demand higher rates and stricter terms, forcing the landlord into the "underworld" of real estate finance. As potential returns from the property fall below the financing cost, the landlord's desire to finance improvements or to repay loans diminishes, resulting in "milking," mortgage delinquency, and abandonment. (85—6).

Will this be the fate of the Greenpoints and Canarsies in the year 2000? The declining numbers of incoming Italian immigrants, combined with the out-migration from these areas of young Italian-Americans, would seem to suggest so. "Little Italys", however, are nothing if not hardy entities, and have probably persisted on the urban scene for far longer than the early Chicago School theorists had thought possible. Their dreams will be the cause of mourning for some, and delight for others; their struggle to resist the seemingly inevitable tides of change will be watched closely by all observers of the contemporary American city.

Footnotes

1. A little under 24% of the persons of Italian ancestry in New York City in 1980 were foreign-born; a touch over 13% of all New York City Italians in 1980 had come to the U.S. since 1965 (Egelman and Salvo 14).
2. It was reported that 1000 Italians occupied a single tenement on Baxter Street, in lower Manhattan, in 1881, and that many of these suffered from malaria (Iorizzo and Mondello 53).
3. This also held true in the outer boroughs. For instance, the mid-Bronx Italian enclave was largely settled in the late 1890's by laborers working on the roads which were being laid in that area. Usually, the opening of the elevated railways, and later the subways, was a necessary feature in opening up a district in the outer boroughs to immigrate. If there was work for day laborers in the area (and road and railroad construction in the outer boroughs was booming by the 1890's), Italian immigrants could be expected to locate there. As a result, the model delineated by Cressey, whereby immigrant groups decentralize as they engage in upward social mobility, holds only to a limited extent for New York City (Kessner 157). Such outlying Italian-American neighborhoods as East Harlem and Brownsville grew almost from the start of the large immigrant influx of the latter nineteenth century. After the establishment of such districts, new immigrants often simply skipped Manhattan's Lower East Side "immigrant zone" and headed directly for one of the outlying neighborhoods in

northern Manhattan, The Bronx, or Brooklyn. Nelli (1970) has noted a similar pattern for Chicago's Italian colonies.

4. Landlords seemed to find that while the Italian tenant was desirable because of the promptness with which he paid his rent, he was also dirty and destructive, in time reducing a house to his own level, so that it is really fit for no other class of tenant. The Neapolitan may be considered as the most filthy, as he seems to have hardly a sense of decency at all . . . (*Real Estate Record* of 1893, quoted in Jackson 88).

5. For instance, East 107th Street in Manhattan was the heart of the colony of immigrants from the village of San Fratello, Sicily; the Aviglianese settled in E. 112th Street from the East River to First Avenue (Iorizzo and Mondello 103).

Bibliography

Banfield, Edward C.
　　The Moral Basis of a Backward Society. New York: The Free Press, 1958.

DeForest, Robert W., and Lawrence Veiller
　　eds. *The Tenement House Problem*. Vol. 1. New York: The Macmillan Co., 1903.

Egelman, William, and Joseph Salvo
　　"Italian Americans in New York City: A Demographic Overview". Meetings of American Italian Historical Association. Washington, D.C., Nov. 1984.

Cressey, Paul Frederick
　　"Population Succession in Chicago: 1898—1930." *American Journal of Sociology* 44.1 (1938): 59—69.

Foerster, Robert F.
　　The Italian Emigration of Our Times. New York: Russell and Russell, 1919.

Freeman, Robert C.
　　"The Role of Political Factors in the Decline and Renewal of 'Little Italy': Some Examples from New York". Meetings of American Italian Historical Association. Washington D.C., Nov. 1984.

Gabaccia, Donna R.
　　From Sicily to Elizabeth Street: Housing and Social Change Among Italian Immigrants, 1880—1930. Albany: State University of New York Press, 1984.

Ianni, Francis A.J.
　　"Familism in the South of Italy and in the United States", *Perspectives in Italian Immigration and Ethnicity*. Ed. S.M. Tomasi. New York: Center for Migration Studies, 1977.

Iorizzo, Luciano J., and Salvatore Mondello
          eds. *The Italian Americans*, Rev. ed. Boston: Twayne Publishers,
          1980.
Jackson, Anthony
          A Place Called Home. Cambridge, MA: MIT Press, 1976.
Kessner, Thomas
          The Golden Door. New York: Oxford University Press, 1977.
                    and Betty B. Caroli. *Today's Immigrants*. New York:
          Oxford University Press, 1982.
MacDonald, John S., and Leatrice D. MacDonald
          "Chain Migration, Ethnic Neighborhood Formation, and Social
          Networks". *An Urban World*. Ed. Charles Tilly. Boston: Little,
          Brown and Co., 1974.
Miranda, Edward J., and Ino J. Rossi
          eds. *New York City's Italians*. New York: Italian-American Center
          for Urban Affairs, Inc., 1976.
Mormino, Gary Ross
          *The Hill Upon the City: An Italo-American Neighborhood in St.
          Louis, Missouri, 1880—1955*. Diss. No. Carolina, 1971. Ann
          Arbor: UMI, 1977.
Nelli, Humbert S.
          Italians in Chicago, 1880—1930. New York: Oxford University
          Press, 1970.
                    . "Italians in Urban America". *The Italian Experience
          inn the United States*. Eds. S.M. Tomasi and Madeline H. Engel.
          New York: Center for Migration Studies, Inc., 1977.
                    From Immigrants to Ethnics. New York: Oxford
          University Press, 1983.
Northam, Ray M.
          Urban Geography. New York: John Wiley & Sons, Inc., 1975.
Osofsky, Gilbert
          Harlem: The Making of a Ghetto. 2nd ed. New York: Harper &
          Row, 1971.
Pratt, Edward Ewing
          Industrial Causes of Congestion of Population in New York City.
          New York: Columbia University, 1911.
Rieder, Jonathan
          Canarsie: The Jews and Italians of Brooklyn Against Liberalism.
          Cambridge: Harvard University Press, 1985.
Susser, Ida
          Norman Street: Poverty and Politics in an Urban Neighborhood.
          New York: Oxford University Press, 1982.

Solomon, Arthur P., and Kerry D. Vandell
>"Alternative perspectives on Neighborhood Decline". *Journal of the American Planning Association* 48 Winter 1982: 81—98.

Thompson, Bryan
>*Cultural Ties as Determinants of Immigrant Settlement in Urban Areas*. New York: Arno Press, 1980.

Tricarico, Donald
>*The Italians of Greenwich Village: The Social Structure and Transformation of an Ethnic Community*. New York: The Center for Migration Studies of New York, Inc., 1984.

Velikonja, Joseph
>"Italian Immigrants in the United States in the Sixties". *The Italian Experience in the United States*. Eds. S.M. Tomasi and Madeline H. Engel. New York: Center for Migration Studies, Inc., 1977.

Williams, Phyllis H.
>*South Italian Folkways in Europe and America*. New Haven: Yale University Press, 1938.

Yans-McLaughlin, Virginia
>*Family and Community: Italian Immigrants in Buffalo, 1880—1930*. Ithaca: Cornell University Press, 1977.

19 "INVOLVED AND 'THERE':
THE ACTIVITIES OF ITALIAN
AMERICAN WOMEN IN URBAN
NEIGHBORHOODS"

Judith N. DeSena
State University of New York at Farmingdale

Women, as a topic of sociological inquiry, have been given increasing attention over the past decade. However, women have not been a focus in studies on urban neighborhoods. More specifically, research on urban neighborhoods has not included an examination of the role of women. Furthermore, studies on Italian American neighborhoods[1] have been based on a male perspective and treat women as merely "there,"[2] they are part of the scene, but are not part of the action.

This paper focuses on the activities of women in a blue collar neighborhood in Brooklyn called Greenpoint. It examines the role of women in general, and Italian American women in particular as they participate in and create many of Greenpoint's informal structures. This research is part of a larger study on neighborhood defense in Greenpoint. The data presented are from interviews with twenty-eight women who were residents of Greenpoint and of Italian, Irish, and Polich descent. The focus is on informal activities instead of formal structures. The involvement of women in general, and Italian American women in particular in neighborhood activities is evident by the existence of an informal housing network and local surveillance by civilians in Greenpoint.

This paper begins with a description of Greenpoint, followed by a review of literature. Women's activities in Greenpoint are then presented. This includes a discussion of an informal housing network previously mentioned, and local surveillance. Finally, the implications of this research for theory are examined, since neighborhood women are involved in a variety of local dynamics.

Description of Greenpoint

Greenpoint is a peninsula at the northermost tip of Brooklyn. It is bounded on the north and the east by Newtown Creek, and on the west by the East

River. The Brooklyn-Queens Expressway (Meeker Avenue) and North 7th Street are Greenpoint's southern boundary (this is the boundary cited by the New York City Planning Commission in 1969).

Greenpoint lies across the river from Manhattan. In fact, the Citicorp building is visible from Greenpoint's main shopping strip (Manhattan Avenue). Its waterfront overlooks Manhattan's east side. Manhattan is easily accessible from Greenpoint by car. Greenpoint is also connected to neighborhoods in Queens, namely Long Island City, Sunnyside, and Maspeth by the Pulaski Bridge, the Greenpoint Avenue Bridge and the Kosciusko Bridge, respectively.

Greenpoint has been described as a working class neighborhood. In 1980, the population of Greenpoint was approximately 39,310. Like the population of the City that it is part of, Greenpoint's has been declining. Between 1970 and 1980, Greenpoint lost approximately 11,900 residents. Since the early 1900's Greenpoint has been a white ethnic neighborhood comprised mostly of Irish, Italian, and Polish families. The Irish were the largest group through the 1920's. A significant influx of Polish immigrants occurred in Greenpoint after World War II.[3] More recently there has been an additional wave of Polish refugees who fled martial law in Poland.

In 1980, residents of non-Hispanic, white ethnicities made up 75% of Greenpoint's population.[4] Since 1950, however, northern Greenpoint has seen an influx of Hispanic residents, who in 1980 comprised 21% of the neighborhood's population. Although the Hispanic population increased between 1970 and 1980, the Puerto Rican population grew very slightly in this ten year period.[5] In 1970 there were 5,014 Puerto Ricans living in Greenpoint. In 1980, the Puerto Rican population was 5, 166, the largest Hispanic group in Greenpoint (63% of Hispanics). The increase in Greenpoint's Hispanic population has been among Latin Americans, Colombians and Ecuardorians. The remaining 4% of Greenpoint's population was made up of Asian (2.5%) and black (.50%) individuals. One percent identified themselves as "other". Therefore in 1980, 75% of Greenpoint's population was made up of whites (non-Hispanic), while the remaining 25% was made up of minority residents.

In 1980, 44% of Greenpoint's population were high school graduates.[6] The proportion of graduates in Greenpoint is much lower than that of Brooklyn as a whole, and substantially lower than the proportion of high school graduates in New York City.

Average median family income in 1979 in Greenpoint was $14,464.00. In 1980, Greenpoint residents held a variety of occupations. The largest group was in technical and sales occupations (32%), and only 9% held professional or managerial occupations.

While a majority of Greenpoint's housing was built before 1939, many structures were built before 1900. More than 60% of the residential buildings are made of wood.[7] There are a few streets in Greenpoint made up of brownstones and brick townhouses, remnants of Dutch settlement from the 17th century. Residential structures in Greenpoint are not higher than six stories, and 71% of them contain four or fewer dwelling units per structure.[8] The percentage of owner occupied buildings with rental units is unusually high.

The Role of Neighborhood Women

Urban sociology has ignored women.[9] Research on Italian American neighborhoods, in particular is based on a male perspective and focuses primarily on men.

Whyte's study of Cornerville, an Italian slum in the North End of Boston, is an example.[10] Whyte selected Cornerville because he was interested in studying a slum district, and Cornerville best fitted his sense of what a slum district should look like. He focussed on the interaction of "corner boys" (The Nortons), "college boys" (the Italian Community Club), "racketeers," and "politicians."

The intensive examinations of these groups enabled Whyte to uncover the status of group members, and the social structure of Cornerville, which held individual members in their places. This study also helped to dispel a widely held idea that slums were disorganized. The area's physical decay did not reflect its social structure.

Whyte notes in response to a critique of his research, that because of local customs, he could not become involved with young women in Cornerville. He would have been expected to marry a women whom he dated steadily.[11]

Like Whyte, Gans studied an Italian American community in Boston.[12] Gans studied the West End, which was bulldozed between 1958 and 1960 and replaced by luxury housing, in contrast to Whyte's North End which still exists as an Italian American area. Gans' research began in an effort to test the validity of the approach used by professionals to help low income populations improve their living conditions. He argued that professional "caretakers" (city planners, social workers, etc.) impose their middle class values on low income populations, by making policy decisions, regarding the future existence of slum districts. His research, therefore, focused on the lifestyles of a working class Italian American subculture in West End, a Boston neighborhood that had been previously declared a slum. Gans concludes from his study that "caretakers" were wrong about the West End, since it was not really a slum. West Enders' way of life constituted a distinct, complex, and independent working class subculture. Thus, for Gans, the values and lifestyles of this population should first be understood and considered by "caretakers" before policy decisions are made. These conclusions, however, were too late to have an impact on West End, for it has been redeveloped under the federal renewal program, and no longer exists in the way that Gans studied it. Like Whyte in the North End, Gans found a viable social structure in the West End and not a disorganized slum. Furthermore, like Whyte, Gans also collected more of his data from men than women. Gans states that he was unable to gain access to women's groups.

Suttles also examined Italians as well as Mexicans, Puerto Ricans, and Blacks in the Addams area of Chicago.[13] Territory has been divided among these four groups and residents are fragmented. In the Addams area an "ordered segmentation" has been created that allows for orderly relationships among groups. Turf is clearly defined. Groups only combine in instances of opposition to outside threats. Ethnic groups are separated by location, institutional arrangements (religion, recreation), and communicative devices (language, clothing). Street corner gangs maintain ethnic boundaries. Like Whyte and Gans, Suttles also focuses on men.

Lofland argues that in studies on urban sociology, women are merely "there."[14] They are part of the background, but are not included in the action. Lofland points to the emphasis on formal elements of community as a model of social organization as a factor in creating the "thereness of women." Lofland argues that the use of this model moves researchers away from women's activities. This study on Greenpoint captures the activities of women because of its focus on informal practices.

Moreover, most researchers have been men. This creates a problem of access into various research situations. Gans notes, for example, that communication between the sexes is limited in a working class neighborhood. Thus, gaining access to women's groups or obtaining interviews with women are difficult tasks for male researchers. Women will be the focus of urban research when more urban researchers are women, or when male urban researchers realize the possibility of "taking the role of the other." According to Daniels, researchers can penetrate a social setting even when they do not fit into roles that are traditionally acceptable.[15] In her study of U.S. army subgroups, Daniels describes the tactics and strategies she employed in order to overcome the resistance of military officers to a sociologist, a civilian, and a woman. Howell, in his study of Clay Street, spent a great deal of time with two respondents who were women, Bobbi Jean Shackelford and June Moseby.[16] He attributes his being married and having a child as a major factor which enabled him to gain access to women neighbors. Howell lived in the neighborhood and his wife and child were often with him when he visited Bobbi Jean and June. As Howell explains, his family was friendly with their families.

In addition, Horowitz's study of a Chicano community in Chicago suggests that being a women is advantageous in field work.[17] She frequented street corners and park benches with male gang members in order to understand their process of growing up. She gained access to these gangs because, as a women, she did not threaten them. Because of her sex, she also had access to the young women.

Criticisms have been made by professionals from other fields who rely on this literature. Wekerle notes that detailed research on women in urban settings might provide information for planners and designers, which would enable them to create environments that are more responsive to women's needs.[18]

Greenpoint's Informal Housing Network

It is difficult to rent an apartment or purchase a house in Greenpoint. Local realtors have said that "there isn't a one, two or three family house available." The local newspaper lists only a few apartments and houses for sale, while the length of its "APTS. WANTED" and "HOURSES WANTED" columns increase. It seems that residents are particularly cautious about renting their vacant apartments. Not only do they want to control rigidly the type of tenants they may get, but they also want to determine who will be informed about the availability of an apartment.

It appears that women play a major role in Greenpoint's informal housing network. They seem to "pass along the work," regarding the availability of housing to family, friends, and neighbors. Women have replaced the role of realtors. The following anecdote reported by a local woman illustrates this point.

> I was in a butcher one day and we were talking, and I just happen to mention that my niece was looking for rooms, and this woman says, "Hello," she told me who she was, and that she had rooms. So there right in the butcher shop, not that I ever got the rooms. But (if I wanted) rooms for a friend of mine or for anybody I would spread the word around in the society (a woman's religious organization). That would be the first place, right I's say, "Girls, anybody hears of rooms let me know." They would tell someone.

This account suggests that women's activities are largely informal and occur in places like a butcher shop. It further suggests that when women are members of formal organizations, the organizations tend to be made up of mostly women. Male researchers are therefore unable to reach them. Moreover, it supports the idea that women's activities are "behind the scenes." Greenpoint's informal housing network is a sound example.

Surveillance

Another way that women are involved in Greenpoint is through local surveillance. Surveillance in Greenpoint can be divided into two categories, informal and formal. Informal surveillance refers to activities where individuals "watch" the block. These individuals are not sanctioned by any authority to "block watch," nor are they tied to any local organization for this purpose. Formal surveillance, on the other hand, operates by a Civilian Observation Patrol (COP). The Civilian Observation Patrol is a local organization whose purpose is to train and coordinate individual block or small area (a number of blocks) patrols. In both cases, the objective is to protect the neighborhood (*i.e.*, neighbors, children, property, etc.) from criminal disturbances.

Neighborhood women, particularly Italian American women, act as informal surveillants, witnessing and reporting suspicious events and crimes to the police. As one woman described,

> I walked up Calyer Street towards Manhattan Avenue, I got as far as Guernsey Street and I'm crossing Guernsey Street and I see these two men coming, and one with a television on his shoulder, and I said, "Gee, they could have robbed that television." So I turned around to see if I could get the license plate number. There was no license plate number on the front of the car. So I make believe I forgot something and turned around like that, (as if I were) the cop, and I walked back, and I crossed Guernsey Street back again, and I turned around just as they were pulling away. And I got the license plate number of the car, and it was Bonneville, and I forgot about it. I did write it down but I forgot about it. But later on in the evening a neighbor, now I happened to be walking up the Avenue again and I saw (a neighbor) sitting and few other people sitting on the stoop down Guernsey Street. And they called to me there to ask me a question of some kind. When I was leaving I said, "By the way if anybody lost a television on this block I know where it is, I'm a detective." The next morning (the neighbor) calls me, she says, "Do you still have the license plate number," she said. "The lady across the street was robbed yesterday and they took her television." So the two of them went around to the police station and I undersand they did get them.

Women in Greenpoint are also involved in formal surveillance. They are members of an organized civilian patrol. The Civilian Observation Patrol (COP), a voluntary organization in Greenpoint, first began as part of a block association. It developed in response to numerous complaints by members of block associations about auto thefts and break-ins. The result was a system, where two residents ride around a particular segment of the neighborhood in their own cars, which are equipped with CB radios. If they encounter any criminal activity or any event which appears suspicious, they relay the event to their "base station." A base station consists of a CB radio in someone's home and a resident to respond to calls. If a call is relayed to the base station, the base station operator responds by alerting police of the incident. According to a COP member, most base station operators are women, while most car patrols are made up by men. Patrol membes do not become directly involved with neighborhood disturbances. They act as additional "eyes and ears" for the local police. Patrols usually operate on weekend nights and follow a schedule that was developed by members.

In Greenpoint, women are important members of the civilian patrols. As mentioned earlier most operate base stations, as opposed to policing the area in cars at night. However, it was reported that one of the active patrols included a day patrol which is made up of local women. The day patrol is a foot patrol. Teams of women walk around the area with CB radios and relay disturbances to their base station. They patrol an area around the Greenpoint Savings Bank on the first few days of each month, during which time, senior citizens receive and cash their Social Security checks. This patrol tries to prevent robberies. Moreover, there is an organization in Greenpoint called Friends of McGolrick Park, whose membership is made up mostly of women. The major objective of this group was to restore and beautify MCGolrick Park. The group encountered some problems with drug addicts congregating in the park. To help alleviate this problem they formed a day patrol which is comprised solely of women. The patrol is called Park Anti-Crime Teams (PACT). PACT was originally a member of a larger COP which acted as an umbrella organization for smaller COP'S, but withdrew its membership. This group felt that they were being discriminated against because they were women.

> They look almost a year in training us before we could get out on patrol. They didn't like the idea of two women in a car, they wanted a man. And I always felt that they had no right to make a decision. (Then at a fundraising event they wanted us) to sell raffles . . . and all hell broke loose and my whole group left and we formed our own (patrol).

Conclusion

In Greenpoint, Italian American women appear to be local power brokers. They make decisions regarding who is informed about available housing. They also negotiate between tenants and landlords and essentially decide who lives in Greenpoint. Moreover, women are disproportionately represented in all forms of civic, religious, and neighborhood improvement organizations. They are also much more likely than men, to actively participate in grass roots protests or efforts of pressure aimed at government or elected officials. As this research indicates, the role of Italian American women continues to expand. Their involvement in neighborhood activities persists even though they are assuming more responsibilities outside the home, such as seizing educational opportunities, and/or entering the labor force.

The neighborhood has traditionally been viewed by Italians as an extension of the home.[19] Italians in urban neighborhood create symbolic boundaries which define their turf, and engage in block watching activities. Street festivals, such as the "festa" are quite common in Italian neighborhoods, as well as the practice of neighbors gathering on steps and sidewalks in front of their homes. However, as Italian American women continue to enter the labor force, and to achieve success and social mobility by increasing their levels of education[20] they will experience greater pressures. Competing issues of work, home, and family combined with constraints of time will lead to a re-ordering of responsibility for domestic tasks within the household. Involvement in neighborhood activities is among these tasks. The decisions made by Italian American households are crucial to the future of the "Italian Village." The viability of ethnic neighborhoods in general will be decided by "choice." Households can choose to give up the neighborhood by not participating in activities and by ignoring local practices, such as an informal housing network. On the other hand, they may organize their domestic tasks in such a way that neighborhood activities are viewed as important. This decision will help to maintain the existence of ethnic neighborhoods.

Given the crucial role that women play in ethnic neighborhoods, you would expect them to be a major focus of studies on urban neighborhoods. However, this is not the case. The stereotype of Italian American women views them as being "indoors."[21] Unfortunately scholars have adopted and promoted this view, which helps to explain why women's activities have not been included in studies on urban neighborhoods. Scholars begin their research with the idea that women are indoors and therefore, not visible. Their research is directed away from women from the outset. This paper suggests the opposite. Women of Italian descent are active participants in neighborhood life. Scholars must look past stereotypes, traditional roles and formal organizations in order to recognize the importance of women.

The role of Italian American women will continue to expand. In many ways their heritage has been conducive to a modern role because Italian culture provides support for women through the family and religion.[22] Scholars must recognize their expanding role and realize that women have power in neighborhoods and with regard to the future of neighborhoods. They can no longer be disregarded or not seriously considered in research on urban neighborhoods.

Footnotes

1. William Foote Whyte, *Street Corner Society* (Chicago: University of Chicago Press, 1955); Herbert Gans, *The Urban Villagers* (New York: The Free Press, 1962); Gerald Suttles, *The Social Order of the Slum* (Chicago: University of Chicago Press, 1968)

2. Lynn Lofland, "The Thereness of Women," in *Another Voice*, ed. Marcia Millman and Rosabeth Moss Kanter, (New York: Anchor Books, 1975)

3. Ida Susser, *Norman Street* (New York: Oxford University Press, 1982)

4. Information on total population and race were obtained by examining block data from the 1980 Census. The white and black counts do not include Hispanic persons. Hispanics were counted as a separate category.

5. This was obtained by examining tract data from the 1970 Census on Puerto Rican Birth or Parentage.

6. Information on education refers to person over 25 years old. It was obtained from the 1980 Census.

7. *Greenpoint: Striking a Balance Between Industry and Housing* (New York: New York City Planning Commission, 1974)

8. *Greenpoint: Striking a Balance Between Industry and Housing*

9. Sylvia Fleis Fava, Janet Abu-Lughod, and Noel Gist, *Urban Society*, seventh edition, (New York: Harper and Row Publishers, forthcoming)

10. Whyte, *Street Corner Society*, 1955

11. William Foote Whyte, "Comments on Robert E. Washington's Review on *Street Corner Society*," in *Reviews in Anthropology* 5, 1978

12. Gans, *The Urban Villagers*, 1962

13. Suttles, *The Social Order of the Slum*

14. Lofland, "The Thereness of Women"

15. Arlene Kaplan Daniels, "The Law Caste Stranger in Social Research," in *Ethnics, Politics and Social Research*, ed. Gideon Sjorberg, (Cambridge, Massachusetts: Schenkman Publishing Company, 1967)

16. Joseph T. Howell, *Hard Living on Clay Street* (New York: Anchor Books, 1973)

17. Ruth Horowitz, *Honor and the American Dream* (New Brunswick, New Jersey: Rutgers University Press, 1983)

18. Gerda Wekerle, "Women in the Urban Environment," *Signs: Journal of Women in Culture and Society*, 5, (1980)

19. Donald Tricarico, "The Italians of Greenwich Village: The Restructuring of Ethnic Community," in *The Family and Community Life of Italian Americans*, ed. Richard N. Juliani, (New York: American Italian Historical Association, 1983)

20. Jerome Krase, "Italian American Female College Students: A New Generation Connected to the Old," in *The Italian Immigrant Women in North America*, eds. Betty Boyd Caroli, Robert F. Harney, and Lydio F. Tomasi, (Toronto: The Multicultural History Society of Ontario, 1978)

21. Jerome Krase, "The Italian American Community: An Essay on Multiple Social Realities," in *The Family and Community Life of Italian Americans*, ed. Richard N. Juliani, (New York: American Italian Historical Association, 1983)

22. Venetta — Marie D'Andrea, "The Social Role Identity of Italian American Women: An Analysis and Comparison of Families," in *The Family and Community Life of Italian Americans*, ed. Richard N. Juliani, (New York: American Italian Historical Association, 1983)

Chapter **20** CELEBRATION, CONFLICT &
RECONCILIATION
AT SAINT ANTHONY'S
Edythe Quinn Caro
White Plains, New York

Saint Anthony's Mission served the Italian-American community of Silver
Lake, New York from 1922 to 1952, with Italian priests, Italian-language
masses, and festivals. In 1952, the New York Archdiocese reorganized Saint
Anthony's as a parish with an Irish-Catholic monsignor. The resulting strife,
as Southern Italian-Catholic folk religiosity collided with Irish-American
Catholic orthodoxy, stifled the religious/cultural practices and strained the faith
of the Italian-American people. In recent years, the people and pastor have
become reconciled, but the golden era of the ethnic mission cannot be recreated.
In presenting the history of Saint Anthony's Mission and Parish, I will offer
an almost textbook-perfect example of the conflicts documented in Silvano
Tomasi's book, *Piety and Power*[1], which probes the conflict between the
American—Irish Catholic Church and the religious needs of the immigrant
population, especially the Italians. However, in my case study, there is one
important difference. Tomasi discussed "The Role of the Italian Parishes in
the New York Metropolitan Area from 1800—1930."[2] The history of Saint
Anthony's only begins in 1922, with its golden age of celebration from
1934—1952, the eighteen years following the span in which Tomasi's research
is placed. The conflicts of 1952—1969 occurred unenlightened by the
cumulative experiences of the previous seventy years.

In order to understand the role of Saint Anthony's Mission to the Italian-
American community, I will very briefly describe the Silver Lake neighborhood
community which I identify as an Italian-American "hilltown". In Westchester
County, New York, Silver Lake is located in the northwest corner of Harrison.
Silver Lake is a small, densely-populated neighborhood community, roughly
little more than one-half of one-square mile, with approximately 4,000 people
of whom 75 percent are of Italian-American descent. From 1894, when the
first Italian immigrants arrived in Silver Lake, the community has thrived as

an American-Italian hilltown, because Silver Lake offered: an environment conducive to family values; a topography similar to the ancestral villages; land for homes and gardens; agarian employment on the nearby estates, which was later converted to the current private businesses in landscaping and construction; and a supportive religious institution on which to focus communal life and ethnic celebrations.

Surprisingly, the founding of Saint Anthony's Mission, occurred quite late in the community's history, not in 1900, but in 1922, and as much as a response to the people's needs as a reaction to the presence of a local Baptist mission to the Italian people. Silver Lake Memorial Baptist Chapel, with its missionary beginnings in the early 1900s, dedicated in 1909, and surviving today as the Memorial Community Church of West Harrison, Baptist, is classic case of the Protestant Pentacostal mission to the Italian immigrants.

The New York Archdiocese was undoubtedly aware of the presence of the Baptist Chapel and its success among the Italian immigrants. In 1922, Catholic Charities purchased from Harrison an unused one-room schoolhouse for conversion to a mission church. The Mission was administered by the Stigmatine Fathers, a North Italian order, who staffed Our Lady of Mount Carmel Church in nearby White Plains.

Father Joseph F. Rosa was the first rector assigned to Saint Anthony's Mission. A descendant of an old, cultured family of Trento, Father Rosa had received an outstanding education. An even more valuable asset was his acknowledged ability to get along with everyone.

From the beginning, the Mission attempted to satisfy the needs of the people it served, beginning slowly and adding services and religious societies as experience and resources allowed. Mass, of course, was in Latin; but the gospel, sermon and announcements were given in both Italian and English, first in one, then repeated in the other language. While from the beginning the congregation was heavily Italian, it also included Irish, Germans, Lithuanians, and others.

Monsignor Joseph Raimondo, pastor of Saint Gregory The Great Church in downtown Harrison, had served as an altar boy a Saint Anthony's Mission. He recalled:

> I always remember the many candles. I was brought up in a candle-lighting kind faith. The people responded that way. They used to say the rosary; you know, they had that devotion.[3]

When Monsignor Raimondo commented affectionately about the people of Silver Lake, "They always had celebrations in their bones there," he was identifying a central theme of this Italian-American community.[4] The Italian-American community celebrated the Feast Day of Saint Anthony, June 13, with a *festa*. From all accounts, the early Silver Lake festas closely resembled the celebrations in New York City, though, of course, on a smaller scale, including the procession with the saints' statues, the people running up to pin dollars on the statues' ribbons, the Italian bands, food booths, fireworks, and the greasy pole competition.

Several years after establishing the Mission in Silver Lake, Father Rosa left to concentrate on his duties at Mount Carmel, where he became pastor in 1934—35. Two other young Stigmatine priests, Father Louis Fontana and Father Louis Zuliana, served as rectors at the Mission.

In 1934, Saint Anthony's Mission entered a new era, what would be almost two decades of growth and spiritual and social success. This golden age of celebration at the Mission of Saint Anthony's was the result of one priest's dedicated service combined with the work of his loyal mission members. In 1934, Father Richard Zambiasi came to Our Lady of Mount Carmel Church and was assigned as rector of Saint Anthony's Mission. As with Father Rosa, Father Zambiasi brought the advantages of education and experience. Also, as with Father Rosa and the other North Italian order priests who served before him, he never exhibited an attitude of superiority or alienation towards the religious folkways of the Southern Italians he served. Throughout the oral histories, no incident of disparagement is recollected. Although Father Richard, as he was always informally and affectionately called, was 55 when he took over the demanding position of rector in the still-fledgling mission, he worked with the vitality and spirit of a much younger man. Under his care, the Mission immediately began to flourish, as explained by an oral history respondent:

> When Father Richard came in 1934, from that time on, things
> began happening. Organizations and things. We had weddings in
> our church if we wanted them and funerals too with him. [5]

In 1937, Father Richard organized the men of the parish into the Holy Name Society. Although the primary purpose of the Society was spiritual, its practical purpose was the welfare of the parish. According to a history of the Society, in 1938, the members worked to renovate and enlarge the mission church and to improve the social hall:

> The members raised funds, solicited skilled and manual labor
> and begged materials for alterations . . . They sacrificed their
> Saturdays, Sundays, holidays and evenings so that we might have
> a building large enough to accommodate our parishioners in their
> worship.(6)

Not only did parishioners donate time, labor, and materials, non-church goers and non-Catholics assisted too, making it a community effort. An oral-history respondent of Northern Italian heritage, explained his family's involvement:

> We didn't participate with Church. None of us from the North
> are church-goers. But when they called for volunteers for
> construction and work, who was there? Us from the North. We
> built all the walls; we built all the steps; we built everything.[7]

For the Italian women of the congregation, their parish societies satisfied
more than their religious needs. The Church was their social outlet. Whether
meeting in their homes or in the church, coming together for religious society
business was a form of recreation, a diversion from the routine of family and
housework, as one female respondent explained:

> At one time, that time, I think the Church was the only source
> of pleasure, entertainment. Outside of the home was the Church.
> That was only thing they had.[8]

From the early 1940s through 1952, the Holy Rosary Society and the Holy
Name Society sponsored the festas. As Father Rosa had done in the first
processions, Father Richard marched with his people. The procession climbed
the hilly streets from the church. As before, people would pin money on the
ribbons, receiving prayer cards and buttons as mementoes.

The sense of belonging, of pride and loyalty had taken deep root in the
Mission, imbuing it with the same values a parish generates. To this day, the
people still recall how much of this spirit was due to the love and encouragement
of Father Richard Zambiasi. His special qualities which made this union of
priest and people flourish are best described by the people whom he served.
A female respondent recalled:

> He was a very meek, humble man; not a pusher. He was not
> like some people who are authoritative. He was gentle. He got
> everything done. People loved him. He'd hardly have to ask. He'd
> just mention something and they'd do and do it for him.[9]

A male respondent remembered:

> He'd want something done, the place painted; that's all he'd
> have to say. We'd often take him out. We'd get together, quite
> a few of us, six, seven, eight of us and take him.[10]

At the height of his Mission's success, on Oct. 7, 1951, Father Richard
Zambiasi, C.P.S., celebrated his Golden Jubilee in the priesthood. In light
of what was to follow within six months, many of the speeches given at the
anniversary dinner were to be sadly ironic. The Golden Jubilee Booklet
concluded with this wish: ''May you be given health, strength, and length of

days in overflowing measure to minister to the good, and devoted people of Silver Lake.''[11] The Booklet also contained this statement in its history of the church:

> No prophet is required to foresee that this community faces a bright future with so many new houses mushrooming up all over Silver Lake. With the progress of Silver Lake, Saint Anthony's will prove its worth and may that day come when a new edifice will rise to serve the spiritual needs of the church.[12]

What was happening? Corporations were moving into new suburban headquarters on the Harrison-White Plains border. The newly-developed section of Parkway Knolls, adjacent to Silver Lake, became the bedroom community for these corporate families and others leaving the city for suburbia. White collar workers and professionals moved into new, single family houses next to the old, blue-collar, ethnic neighborhood of multi-family dwellings. The new residents included many Irish Catholics in need of a parish and parochial school. Of course, there had always been Irish Catholics in the congregation, but by custom and population, Saint Anthony's had been predominately Italian.

Although my research for church records continues, based on the situation at the time and the effects of diocesan action, in all likelihood, the New York Archdiocese must have carefully studied the situation, appraising the current status, evaluating the potential. Here was a small, unassuming Italian mission with no rectory, no parochial school, and with an older rector assigned from a White Plains parish, from an Italian religious order. Within the missionn boundaries was a growing Irish-Catholic population, anxious to affiliate and to secure parochial education for their children. However, to feel comfortable, they would require a more Americanized environment and Irish-Catholic atmosphere to which they were accustomed. Probably sensing that further growth in numbers and revenue for the Church was with the newcomers, the Archdiocese made several abrupt changes which would forever affect the character of Saint Anthony's and of Silver Lake.

In May 1952, His Eminence, the late Francis Cardinal Spellman designated Saint Anthony's a parish and assigned an Irish Catholic priest, Father Francis J. Boyle, as the first pastor. The era of service from the Stigmatine Fathers ended. The era of celebration in the Italian Mission closed. Father Richard Zambiasi was gone. Immediately! Father Boyle celebrated his first Mass in Saint Anthony's on Sunday, May 25, 1952.

Possessing an entirely different temperment than Father Zambiasi and coming from the traditions of American-Irish Catholicism, Father Boyle's actions and opinions seemed in direct, drastic and unflattering contrast to his predecessor. The bitterness, conscious or not, still lingered in this respondent's voice when he said:

> A lot of people missed Father Zambiasi. They could have kept
> him on. It was too much of a thing to do to that man. Some people
> left the church on account of that; went to White Plains.[13]

The majority stayed — unhappily. The older women in the Holy Rosary
Society had problems dealing with Father Boyle and the Holy Name Society
dispersed. Said one woman in response:

> We didn't have the Italian priest and the Italian people resented
> the fact that he [Msgr. Boyle] was a priest they couldn't talk to.[14]

Something had happened to the once-loving union of clergy and
congregation. Something vital in the partnership — one of the partners — had
changed with little notice. This wasn't the union entered into 30 years earlier.
The new partner didn't understand the old loyalties or have reason to honor
them; but rather was involved in trying to establish new loyalties, sometimes
in new directions.

The Mission of Saint Anthony, although a satellite of Our Lady of Mount
Carmel Church in White Plains, had closely resembled an ethnic parish in its
role in the community. In *Piety and Power*, Silvano Tomasi credits the ethnic
parish "as the first line of defense behind which the immigrants could organize
themselves and preserve their group identity."[15] No longer benefitting from
a culturally and religiously supportive congregation, the Italian-Americans in
Silver Lake were abandoned in an American-Catholic parish which was
predominately Irish.

The most dramatic clash between Father Boyle and the Italian community
occurred over the celebration of the *festa*. When he came in May 1952, the
festa was already scheduled for June. The *festa* occurred on schedule and Father
Boyle marched. But the experience turned him against the celebration. A
respondent remembered:

> He couldn't see people parading up and down the street,
> begging for money. Those were his exact words; I remembered
> him saying it. You know, he couldn't see it. And then it stopped.
> And with that I think the closeness sort of drifted.[16]

By striking down the *festa*, Father Boyle had struck at the very heart of
the Italian-Catholic community. The *festa* was central to religious tradition,
both in Italy and in Italian-American communities here. Here was the brief
but poignant opportunity to make the sacred, i.e., sainthood and religious ritual,
a part of the common celebration of life. the profane. The saint, through his/her
statue, was included in the parade, with the band, celebrated with fireworks.
At the same time, the profane, the common, i.e., favorite foods, music,

parades, and games, was raised to a level of sacredness by association. By attacking this celebration, the Irish pastor attacked the religious tradition of the Italian people.[17] However, the attack struck at more than just the religious tradition, it threatened the immigrant community's continuity with the homeland, as explained by Rudolph J. Vecoli:

> The cult of the patron saint was perhaps the strongest emotional bond, outside the family, which tied the immigrants to each other and to the distant *paese*. Not surprisingly then, the festa was the most vital and vivid expression of Italian immigrant culture in America.[18].

Father Boyle's protest echoed similar protests voiced over the years, as Irish-Catholic religious sobriety clashed with Italian-Catholic festive behavior. Regular protests arose from Church officials regarding the ethnic celebrations and demonstrations of the ethnic/national parishes. From *Piety and Power*, " . . . in the 1880's Archbishop Corrigan had forbidden public processions of Italians, and Irish pastors had simply defined them a disgrace."[19]

The impact of losing the festa affected other church relations, as a respondent recalled:

> If they went to church, they went just for their own devotion, really.[20]

Another major loss to the Italian community was the cessation of the Italian language in church services. Monsignor Boyle did not speak Italian and he did not allow any of his assistants to perform services in Italian. Despite all the differences and conflicts, most of the Italian-American members of the congregation continued to attend. A respondent explained:

> I think the people hungered for religious setting in their lives so they did things in spite of him.[21]

With the support of the Archdiocese and the Parkway Knolls section, the parish progressed, with the financing and building of a parochial grade school, and with personal success for Father Boyle who was advanced to the rank of domestic prelate, with the title of right reverend monsignor, in Dec. 1957. In the mid-1960s, he received permission to build a new church on a different site. His ambitious plans further strained relations with the Italian-American community, who thought the building was much too costly for the economy of the community.

All this time, what the Italian people most wanted was a return of the festa. Several times they asked Monsignor Boyle and he said no. Finally in 1969, he agreed as long as they didn't carry the statue in procession. A respondent who had been festa chairperson and worker for many years, enthusiastically recalled:

> They had been wanting it for such a long time. It was almost like the magic word and the people swarmed from every nook and cranny in this town and offered to help. I think it was a need to get back into the Church, maybe from a guilt for not going to Church as often as they could; and maybe this was their way of being a part of the Church, of being drawn into it the easy way.
>
> They remembered the festa before, remembered the camaraderie and the fun and getting to know one another. It brought it back to years ago when the town was small, the intimacy of a small community, I think. It was fantastic. It still is.[22]

Other major changes in parish life were brought about by the recommendations of the Vatican Council II. In 1968, Saint Anthony's formulated a Parish Council, composed of religious and lay members. Working in committees, the parishioners set goals for various aspects of parish life and worked to achieve them.[23] This opportunity for involvement in parish affairs came at a time when the Italian-Catholic parishioners were ready for such participation. They were better educated and experienced in businesses, organizations and politics than their immigrant parents. No longer were the men simply laborers and the women only homemakers.

In 1975, in accord with the policy of the Archdiocese Monsignor Boyle retired from the active pastorate. (He died on Nov. 23, 1980.) Monsignor Francis X. Duffy was assigned as pastor. Following in the heavy footsteps of a man whom a major faction of the congregation strongly disliked, and also being of Irish descent, Monsignor Duffy received a strained welcome. A respondent explained:

> People were very angry because they wanted an Italian priest and had had one Irishman who didn't understand them and now were getting another. It took people a while to warm up to him. When they could see he was a different type of man; that he had compassion, they accepted him better.[24]

Although a naturally reserved man, Monsignor Duffy displayed sensitivity and respect which the Italian-American community appreciated. Since the late 1970s, an Italian-language Mass is celebrated on the first Sunday of each month at 8:00 a.m. Associate pastor, Father John M. Muscat, a native of Malta, off the coast of Italy, usually says the Mass, but Monsignor Duffy fills in when needed. Monsignor Duffy explained that the Italian-language Mass will continue to be offered as long as there is a need and the parishioners express a desire for it.[25]

Although there are still difficulties normal to any relationship, a reconciliation between clergy and the Italian-American community of Saint Anthony's has taken place and perhaps can best be summed up in this celebration of the festa, as described by this respondent:

> A few years ago, we got together. We said, ''The festa's great but there's one thing missing, the religious part of it.'' So then Monsignor Duffy made a lovely little ceremony . . . After the last Mass on Sunday, the choir, the altar boys and parishioners parade with the banners. They sing. They come down from the church to the statue. We all gather around and there's a benediction.[26]

Despite the obvious improvement in relations, I must stress that this has not been a reconciliation between equals. The Irish-Catholic hierarchy is still in power and American-Irish Catholic tradition still dominates in the church and elementary school. The Church has returned to the Italian-American people only this small, diluted portion of what had once been a whole, vital celebration and tradition. However, with the end of conflict, with the return of some ethnic celebration, the Italian-American congregation has cause to the enjoy the benediction.

Looking back at this history of Saint Anthony's, one may define classic conflicts. The 1952 conflict in Saint Anthony's in Silver Lake illustrated problems common within the American Catholic Church a half century earlier. However, in the typical historical scenario, the Italian immigrants intruded upon a already-established Irish parishes, or within the jurisdiction of Irish-Catholic authority. In Silver Lake, in 1952, the Irish-Catholics invaded an already-established Italian-Catholic mission. However, as in the past, the hierarchy supported the Irish-Catholic population over the Italian-Catholic tradition.

The difficulties associated with ethnic conflicts and with the Italian ethnic subordinate to Irish influence and domination which were rampant in the 1880s through 1910 materialized like an anachronism in the 1950s in Silver Lake. The old lessons, learned with great difficulty, that the Italian-American parish was a positive expression were forgotten; and the Church shifted to an Irish pastor, an Irish-oriented parish, with the Italian-American population relegated to second class membership. For many years, until Monsignor Duffy demonstrated that an Irish-American pastor could provide sensitive leadership and until the Vatican gave congregation members a more active role in parish affairs, the parish suffered dissent. Dr. Tomasi pointed out that cases of such dissent were usually not based on ideological disagreements. ''Rather, political decisions and administrative policies caused rebellion by their disregard of the cultural traditions and social organization of ethnic groups.''[27]

Footnotes

1. Silvano Tomasi, *Piety and Power*, The Role of Italian Parishes in the New York Metropolitan Area, 1880—1930 (Staten Island, N.Y., 1954).
2. Tomasi, *Piety and Power*.
3. Monsignor Joseph Raimondo, #115.
4. Monsignor Joseph Raimondo, #108.
5. Elsie Krewet Bambace, Silver Lake, Harrison, N.Y., Interview, April 15, 1982, #164.
6. "Society News," "The Church of Saint Anthony Parish Monthly," Vol. 1, No. 6, (Silver Lake, Harrison, N.Y.: June 1951), p. 2.
7. John Riguzzi Sr., Silver Lake, Harrison, N.Y., Interview, Jan. 25, 1982, #513.
8. Rose Cannistra Grosskopf, Silver Lake, Harrison, N.Y., Interview Feb. 2, 1982, #520.
9. Elsie Krewet Bambace, #2-020.
10. Sam Galasso, Silver Lake, Harrison, N.Y., Interview, May 26, 1982, #2-296.
11. Golden Jubilee, 50th Anniversary of Rev. Richard A. Zambiasi, Oct. 7, 1951, (Silver Lake, Harrison, N.Y.).
12. Golden Jubilee.
13. Sam Galasso, #2-300.
14. Rose Cannistra Grosskopf, #2-020.
15. Silvano Tomasi, p. 3.
16. Rose Cannistra Grosskopf, #2-024.
17. Frank Salamone, Personal Conversation, White Plains, N.Y., Oct. 1985.
18. Rudolph J. Vecoli, "Cult and Occult in Italian-American Culture: The Persistence of a Religious Heritage," in Immigrants and Religion in Urban America, ed. by M. Miller and Thomas D. Marzik (Philadelphia: 1977), p. 30.
19. Silvano Tomasi, p. 143.
20. Romana Cannistra, Silver Lake, Harrison, N.Y., Interview, Feb. 2, 1982, #2-027.
21. Rose Cannistra Grosskopf, #2-173.
22. Rose Cannistra Grosskopf, #2-244-268.
23. "Twenty-Fifth Anniversary of The Saint Anthony's Church," "Benefit Dinner Dance" [Program], (Silver Lake, Harrison, N.Y., Dec. 10, 1977).
24. Rose Cannistra Grosskopf, Conversation, 1982.
25. Rev. Msgr. Francis X. Duffy, Silver Lake, Harrison, N.Y., Conservations and Interviews, 1981—1984.
26. Rose Cannistra Grosskopf, #2-344.
27. Silvano Tomasi, p. 147.

Chapter 21 WORKING FOR SOME RICH PEOPLE: AN ORAL HISTORY OF HIGHWOOD, ILLINOIS

Adria Bernardi
Memphis, Tennessee

Highwood, a community of 5,500 on Chicago's North Shore, is predominantly a community of Italian immigrants and their families. It is the "poor cousin" to such jewels as Lake Forest, Highland Park, Winnetka and Kenilworth, which are some of the wealthiest communities in America.

As a youngster, I remember asking my grandparents, who lived in Highwood, where certain friends of their worked. "For some rich people," they said.

The Italian immigrants of Highwood worked for *i milionari* (the millionaires), as stone masons, gardeners, plasterers, landscapers, ditchdiggers, and chauffeurs. They worked "nel golf;" in the golf courses of the numerous country clubs along the North Shore. Others moonlighted, picking up extra money at the Moraine Hotel, once an exclusive hotel on Lake Michigan. More than one man took his first job at the McCormick estates, tending the grounds. Grocers in Highwood counted the wealthy of the surrounding suburbs as their "big accounts," including them in their delivery routes. Successful landscaping and construction businesses established by Italian immigrants served the wealthy in surrounding communities.

Women also found work on the North Shore. Even during the Depression when most had nothing, the wealthy still needed laborers to wash and iron their clothes, clean their houses, cook their food, and sew their drapes. The Italian women of Highwood provided that labor.

Italians first began to arrive in Highwood before World War I. Many of the immigrants came to Highwood, not to settle permanently, but to pick up seasonal work during periods of layoffs, shutdowns and strikes at mines in Colorado, Texas, Illinois, Missouri and Iowa. The greatest influx of Italian immigrants to Highwood occurred during the 1920s when many men permanently left jobs in Midwestern mines.[1]

The reputation of Highwood as a place to find work grew, and Highwood became a stopping point for many. One woman describes her feelings about staying in Highwood. After years of moving among mining communities, she told her husband that she would not leave Highwood.

There was no work for women. There was no work for the men, neither. The mines, the coal mines, sometimes, they stopped and my husband was one of those men that liked to move from here, go over there, and while he was over there, he get tired, like to go over there. You know those men that like to move all the time? Mine was one. There was not work all the time because there was strike and they don't work for so long. . . .

He came over here to work in the "golf". After we came in Highwood, he want to move from here, too. I say, "you can move, but, I don't move any more. Me, I stay here because if you don't work, I could make my living because I was work for five dollars a day. Washing floors, washing clothes, wash ceiling, wash windows, all over around here."[2]

In one way or another most jobs in Highwood were tied to serving the wealthy of the North Shore, or to serving those who worked for the wealthy. One man describes this relationship:

People that had money, their businesses were in Chicago, and the labor, they just took care of the town. There's been a lot of building going on for many years. And then, even Lake Forest, it took a lot of manpower to build all those new homes that they built. Lake Forest has always been taken care of but there's always been building going on . . .'[3]

There are several other aspects which make Highwood's Italian-American community unique and which make it worth studying as yet another variation of the Italian-American experience in the United States.

A working class town, it remains isolated from other immigrant communities and other working class communities. Firstly, Highwood is surrounded by affluent communities to the north and south. Secondly, while there are families from many part of Northern and Southern Italy, the majority of Highwood's Italian immigrants came from the province of Modena in north central Italy; most of them from a certain area of the Modenese Appenines called the Frignano. There is also a significant number of families of Bolognese origin. Thirdly, there exists today, more than eighty years since the immigration of Modenese to the U.S. began, a strong bond between Highwood and the communities in the Frignano.

This paper is based on interviews conducted with about forty members of the Highwood community. The purpose of the paper is to present a portrait of the Italian-American immigrants of the city *via* oral history and to preserve the stories in the words of those who lived these stories. It represents one chapter of a book currently in progress. What follows are selections from the interviews that will give an overview of Highwood's Italian immigrants and their work for "some rich people" and some impressions about their relationship with the moneyed communities.

"I Milionari"

Several people interviewed had ties to the Harold and Cyrus Jr. McCormick (of International Harvester) estates in Lake Forest. Others worked for the powerful in the Chicago business world, including Stanley Harris of the Harris Bank and Trust, A.B. Dick's family, and General Robert E. Wood, chairman of Sears and Roebuck.[3]

Tony Casorio, 91, worked as a gardener at the McCormick estates from 1912 until 1928, except for the period of time he served in the U.S. Army during World War I. In 1928, he was offered work by Charles Fiore, an Italian immigrant with a private landscaping and gardening business. Mr. Casorio was reluctant to leave McCormick.

> When I got married 1921, McCormick sent limousine here take me to the church. Limousine and a chauffeur, big machine you know . . . (t)he chauffeur, he wait right outside until we get married then he pick me up and take me back in here. Then before I got married, they had a big party on the place, a very big party, you know and invite all the people, maids and people who worked in the house . . . This was why I didn't like to leave McCormick.[4]

Mr. Casorio overcame his reluctance to leave McCormick, when he was offered $55 dollars a week and the opportunity to learn more about gardening techniques. In 1935, Mr. Casorio left his work with Fiore Nursery, the business of a Highwood Italian immigrant, and began working as the gardener at the home of Stanley Harris. He spoke fondly of the Harris family, saying they were "nice people," just as he spoke well of the McCormicks, saying they were "wonderful people." He worked at the Harris home until he retired and said he felt like "one in the family."[5]

As the chief gardener, Mr. Casorio sometimes hired others.

I was the only Italian but when I needed a hand I used to hire some
of those Italians, boys. Sometimes, I had my son, my brother-in-
law, you know . . . Italian, always Italian, that's all you get in
Highwood, was just Italians . . .[6]

While Mr. Casorio's work at the McCormick estates launched him into
a lifetime career of gardening, another man's work on the McCormick estates
led to another, hardly predictable path: automotive mechanics. Louis Bernardi,
94, worked at the McCormick estates for several seasons beginning in 1910
when he was also seasonally employed in Illinois coal mines and in a Rockford,
Ill., factory.

(I worked) in the garden doing everything. Helping the gardener,
sometimes helping the chauffeur. Then, it was in the summer or
the fall of 1915, the company sent over from England a truck, the
chauffeur was supposed to drive it. But the chauffeur was
downtown (Chicago) all the time, taking the people. So the
superintendent called me and asked me what information I had in
the mechanical field.[7]

Mr. Bernardi relates how the superintendent sent him to a mechanic school
run by two Italian race car drivers in Chicago. This education allowed him
to serve as a mechanic in the American armed forces during World War I
and make a living in Highwood as a mechanic in his own garage.

Henry Piacenza here describes part of his duties as a chauffeur and gardener
for some "rich people here in Highland Park":

" . . . they belonged to a club down in Chicago. The University
Club. We used to go down quite a bit, either movies, opera or
something like that, you know. I used to drive quite a bit. . . ."[8]

"Nel Golf"

Work at the North Shore's numerous country clubs brought many Italian
immigrants to Highwood for the first time. For men working in Midwestern
mines, working "**nel** golf" provided an alternative to layoffs due to mine
closings, strikes and shutdowns of the 1910's, '20s and '30s.

Dominic Lattanzi, 89, came to the U.S. in 1913. Before that his father
and uncle had worked in mines in Spring Valley, Illinois during the winter,
and worked seasonally at Lake Shore Country Club in Glencoe. Mr. Lattanzi
later worked at the club.

In the fall and the spring, I was over here in Lake Shore Country Club, because in the summer, they no hire so many people, just a few of the old people. My father was working there. He was there first. And they called three or four from Highwood. The one cut the grass with the horse. They had the pull-horses, you know . . . I make the bunker, cut the grass, clean up for a couple of months in the spring, one month in the fall.[9]

Adelmo Bertucci[10], born in Pievepelago, Modena, was for many years the superintendent of groundskeeping at Old Elm Country Club in Lake Forest. He worked there when the club was being built. He began to work regularly at the club in 1915. He worked as foreman and later as superintendent of groundskeeping. In that position he was able to provide jobs for others in Highwood.

I got to direct all the work. I got all the men to take care of, a job there, a job there . . . I know some poor people who came from Pievepelago and I tried to give them the job, to hire. They didn't know how to speak nothing. So I give them the job to work until they know about the language and so on.[11]

People in Highwood who had private businesses also benefited from the demand for work created by the country clubs. For example, Louis Bernardi, the automobile mechanic, seasonally overhauled the machinery at Old Elm and Knollwood Club in Lake Forest, where he knew the superintendents of groundskeeping.

Le Serve

There is a stereotype about Italian women, especially Southern Italian women, being sheltered in the home, never being "permitted" by their domineering husbands to leave the house to work.[12] The ideas expressed in certain interviews follow this pattern.

. . . (s) he was taking care of the kids. That's all I want her to do. I don't want her to do any work. Take care of the house. Take care of the kids. And that's all. And I Casorio, done all the work, whatever I could do, to just to get along.[13]

The flip side of this experience, however, and the more common one among Highwood's Italians, is that many of the women of Highwood, for significant periods of their lives, worked outside the home. Many others worked in the house as a result of contact outside the home. This included laundering, washing, ironing and having boarders in their homes.

"Practically all the Italian ladies worked," said one man in during an interview.[14] The wealthy suburbs of Chicago's North Shore provided a natural workplace for women who opted to work. Women worked in laundries at the Highland Park Hospital, Fort Sheridan, and in private laundry businesses. Many women worked as "le serve," or maids, in the homes of the wealthy.

There was a precedence for going to work in the homes of **i signori**. From the mountains of Modena, many single young women, went to work in the winter in big cities such as Firenze, Milano, Pisa and Livorno, where they worked as maids in private homes or in hotels. They would work away from home in the winter, returning in the spring or summer to their homes on the farm.[16]

Mary Baldi, 87, immigrated as a child to the coal mining town of Dalzell, Ill. She moved to Highwood in 1920 with her husband and family. She worked cleaning houses and doing laundry in her home. Below she describes how many women in Highwood worked in the homes of the wealthy.

> Most all the Italian women went out doing this. . . . They were good, hardworking girls. At that time, it was hard to get anybody and there were all these Italian immigrants from Italy, didn't know how to speak, but still they knew how to work.[17]

> During the interview, I asked Mrs. Baldi if there was any other type of work that she could have done.

> Not me, I don't know about the others. A lot of them took in sewing, they took in laundry at home and then later on they started making language, manicotti, and all that . . . I guess that was the main thing, cleaning house and ironing and laundry . . .

> I used to take in washings after coming home. In the night, I had washings to do. You know, it was too much for a man . . . most of the time there was no work. I remember my husband working with me at a millionaire's home, the Loeb home, they live on Sheridan Road. That's one of the wealthy persons that I was telling you about. Jewish. And he'd help me. I think they gave him about a dollar a day. Going down there and washing windows and doing a lot of things.

> I worked in Highland Park, in Glencoe, in Ravinia, and as far as Winnetka. They mostly were Jews. Sometimes I even go in two

places in one day, to keep up my customers, 'cuz I liked them, and I guess they liked me. They liked my work. I was a hard working women . . .[18]

"Il Labor"

A major area of employment for the Italian immigrant men in Highwood was the construction trades, particularly stone masonry, with skilled laborers continuing to immigrate from Italy after the Second World War.

For the early immigrants, the decade preceding the Stock Market Crash, was a time of expansion for the nation, including the North Shore.[19] Many of the skilled and unskilled laborers responsible for building many of the homes and public buildings of the North Shore were Italian immigrants from Highwood.

Viterbo Ponsi, a stone mason, worked on projects throughout the North Shore. Like others interviewed, Mr. Ponsi learned his craft when he was a young man in Italy.[20] His interview reflects the common perception that during the 1920s work as abundant. After the disaster of 1929, however, there was little work. He said: "Until '29 it was pretty good. I even went (back) to Italy. I didn't have any troubles. A lot found the work . . ."[21]

His recollections of the Depression were shared by most interviewed:

At that time there, I had taken work for two days . . . if I could do it for one day, or two, oh, I was happy. How many times I would leave here . . . on foot, we went as far as Glencoe and then even to Winnetka[22] to see if there was work . . .

Nothing, nothing, nothing. *Ma che*,[23] they didn't give anything. There were six years, terrible, maybe more, seven or eight. But how many houses were lost. The good years started after the fair of '33. Then you started to see some work. Then came the war . . . *ecco, e venuta la guerra e tutti lavoravano.*[24] . . .

He recalls the impact of the Market Crash" on some of the area's wealthy.

I don't know how many *signori* killed themselves here in Lake Forest. One here in Ravinia Park. He had a huge house . . . Tonight be millionaire, in the morning zero, nothing. *Niente*. The Big Depression. Disaster.[25]

The Hotel On The Lake

One business which employed many people from Highwood was the Moraine Hotel, an elegant hotel that overlooked Lake Michigan. Some had a second job there. Others worked full time. Phillip Pasquesi, 84, worked as a houseman, responsible for doing anything and everything that was asked of him. He worked there during the 1920s and recalls:

> It was beautiful. Rich people used to come for summer resort. They were rich people and I was working there. Chicago, mostly from Chicago. All these Jews . . . was people they got the store, big stores, downtown. They had the whole family and they come to the Moraine Hotel in the summertime because it was too hot in Chicago . . . During the day, these people, they're businessman, they used to take the train and go down in Chicago. And the family stay up here. The family used to go down to Lake Michigan when it was hot, swimming and things like that. Oh yes. They had it pretty good.[26]

Tony Casorio worked at the Moraine Hotel as a bus boy for about four years while he was employed as the gardener at the Harris home.

> I was working night, Sunday, holiday . . . And I used to come, many time, many night, I used to come with a hundred dollars in the pocket. A couple thousand dollars a month just in the Summer . . .[27]

The Opera-Goers and Gli Artisti

Just as work on the North Shore allowed the Italian immigrants of Highwood to rub elbows with the elite, for several weeks each summer, Highwood fell under the spell of another elite, the *gli artisti*, the artists. From 1915 and until 1932,[28] grand opera was sung in evening performances at Ravinia Park, less than five miles from Highwood. Italians from Highwood not only attended the opera regularly, but many worked for the stars and struck up friendships with the performers, many of whom boarded in Highwood.

In interviews, people talk of the performers and performances with affection. The great operatic stars, Giovanni Martinelli, Rosa Raisa, Virgilio Lazzari, Elisabeth Rethberg, Lucrezia Bori and Claudia Muzio, performed at nearby Ravinia Theater. One woman recalled that for several weeks each summer, "Highwood was full of artists . . ."[29]

Tony Casorio remembered one of the fringe benefits of working on the McCormick estates: free opera tickets.

> In McCormick, over there, they used to buy a big book and give tickets all the five, six tickets to all the employees, monthly man, the ones that working by the month . . .[30]

Another benefit to the opera season was the work it created for some people of Highwood. One woman recalls working for Gennaro Papi, one of Ravinia's conductors, cooking meals for him in his Glencoe home.[31] Some chorus members, *i choristi*, boarded with Italian families in Highwood.

Italian food was another drawing card for the performers, many of whom were Italian. "Those ladies would cook dinners for the stars if they wanted an Italian dinner," one woman explained . . ."[32]

Olympia Fabri and Pia Gibertini of Highwood, both had private dining rooms where they served opera performers. Martinelli frequently ate at Mrs. Fabri's. Although stars like Bori, Mojica, Raisa and Rethberg ate at the Gibertini's, most of their customers were members of the chorus. They ate meals there before their performances, then often returned to the dining rooms for food and wine following their performances. In addition to the artists, wealthy customers, including the Swifts and Armours of Lake Forest dined in Highwood's private dining rooms.[33] Mrs. Pia Gilbertini, who, in addition to her private dining business, ran a boarding house that served Italian laborers recalls:

> Some of the names that used to come, some of the Armours, Swift and Company . . . but they were always nice. Ten o'clock they always left. They came with their wives . . . I never had Mr. (Samuel) Insull but I had some of his friends and I had many of my boarders that used to work for him. They thought they were eccentric . . . and little by little they went broke. Everything so very expensive. He had a bunch of men working for him and maybe in his appearance, probably he was a little (eccentric). But I know that he was a big, rich man. Very rich. He had, I think, the biggest bunch of people working for him there.[33]

Whiskey Junction and The Image Abroad

To its own, Highwood is a town of simple living, hard working people. To outsiders, it has had quite another image in the past — that of a tavern town, a "wide open" town, a "wet" oasis on a basically "dry" area that stretched about 30 miles from Chicago to Waukegan, Illinois.

Just as food and drink brought the opera stars and customers in evening clothes, to Highwood's private dining rooms, Highwood's flourishing tavern trade, brought outsiders in. Highwood has been known as "Whiskey Junction."[34] It was called the "toughest town in America" by President Theodore Roosevelt.[35]

During Prohibition, Highwood had a reputation for being one place where the thirsty could buy alcohol, and where gambling and prostitution went on.

Italian immigrants, particularly single men, frequented "blindpigs", where wine was sold for a dollar a bottle. Many patrons came from outside Highwood.[36]

One man was asked about the reputation of Highwood to those who didn't live there. He said:

> Highwood really was, well, Highwood was known as a tavern town. They came in here and then they do (did) alot of things in Highwood. And not only gambling.[37]

And according to another:

> . . . They used to come here (from outside Highwood) . . . Most of them used to come here and gamble, too. They used to play for big money too. Oooh. They used to have roulette, they used to have everything. It was just like what they have in Las Vegas now.[38]

Ft. Sheridan, an army base adjacent to Highwood[39], has always played a major role in Highwood's economy, especially its tavern trade. One man explained:

> . . . Highwood always had a bad, bad, bad, bad reputation. In fact, we had the Ft. Sheridan so close and when he opened up the tavern the soldiers used to come in town here and every night they had some kind of a fight, you know, between the soldiers and other people. It was pretty bad. Soldiers and the Italians. You know when people get drunk. It's just like somebody they used to call 'em "wop" or a "dago" or something like that and they start to fight. And then there was a time here when we had the soldiers, they used get the girls. Not (from) Highwood, but used to get girls from outside. And they used to do business with the soldiers. Used to come from all over the North Shore . . .[40]

During interviews, people frequently defended Highwood, responding to slights accumulated over the years and touting the progress made by the Italians and Highwood. At the close of the Second World War, one resident responded to a letter in a local paper which she interpreted as a swipe at Highwood's reputation. She wrote:

> . . . I have nothing but contempt for anyone who would . . . stoop to make a snide remark about 'tavern conscious Highwood.' The jibe struck deep . . . For a long time, although taverns are legal

businesses, Highwood has been the butt of jokes and insults on that subject and we residents have borne them in silence. But I, for one, cannot contain myself.

Do we crap on taverns? No, we don't even know they exist. But apparently some outsiders who have no earthly concern in Highwood affairs, are 'tavern conscious.' At least they are the ones who support them with their patronage . . . This however, would not be readily understood by the outsider who wrote this prize sentence: "We in Highland Park don't consider a tavern very homelike."[41]

Conclusion and Further Study

Comparisons between Highwood and its surrounding neighbors came up frequently during the course of my interviews. They sometimes sneaked into the conversation as an aside, for example, in an interview with the city's current mayor, who was discussing why he wouldn't give a certain city employee a raise: "I can't afford to pay what Highland Park pays. They're a wealthy community. So let's compare apples with apples."[42]

This research points to many more questions than answers. Future interviews and subsequent research should further explore Highwood's relationship to the surrounding wealthy communities. For instance, how do the Italians of Highwood look at the wealthy Jews and "WASPS" of surrounding communities? How do they look at the Hispanics who now live in Highwood, working for the "signori," the way Highwood's Italian immigrants once did? In terms of upward mobility, have Highwood's children benefited from its close proximity to wealthy suburbs? Fifty years since the biggest influx of Italians into this community, do they still feel defensive in the face of the wealth of the surrounding communities?

Based on the interviews done to date and personal conversations, I think it is fair to say that there is an ambivilence among Highwood's Italians about wealth and the wealthy, and about different lifestyles. There is still exists a sense of "we" and "they". The strains in relationships caused by upward mobility, by no means peculiar to Highwood's Italians, should be examined because of Highwood's unique relationship with wealthy communities.

The attitudes of the people of Highwood toward the overwhelmingly Jewish community of Highland Park[43] is perhaps one of the most interesting relationships to be examined. Highwood is tied to Highland Park, which surrounds it, as it is to no other North Shore community.

In several interviews, the Jewish community is singled out for comment, the common sentiment expressed is that the Jews were the ones with money. "And when I think of all the money they had and they were so damned cheap . . ." and "I think the Jewish people have the money," said one interviewee.

Are the attitudes of the Italians toward "'sti Judei," these Jews, as they are called by Highwood's Modenesi, any different than those of people who work for others as servants or are the Italians of Highwood anti-Semitic, just as others have been anti-Italian?

In conclusion, I offer a little poem recited by a women who was interviewed.[44] It reflects the sentiment of the Italians in Highwood toward their community, a community which may never be as wealthy as those of "the rich people," but one which is a source of deep pride for people who came to this country with nothing.

Casa mia, casa mia,
Per piacina che tu sia,
Tu mi sembra una badia.

This I have loosely translated to mean:

My home, my home,
However small you might be,
you are a castle to me.

Footnotes

1. Census figures for 1920 and 1930 indicate a dramatic decline in the population of Illinois coal mining towns where many Highwood residents once lived. During this period Highwood experienced a dramatic growth, from 1,446 in 1920, to 3,590 in 1930. (figures from U.S. Census reports)

	1920	1930
Ladd IL	2,040	1,318
Nokomis IL	3,465	2,454
Cherry IL	1,265	636
SpringValley IL	6,493	5,270
Dalzell IL	903	577

2. Interview with Adele Dinelli, 2/24/84. Unless indicated otherwise, all interviews are in possession of author and were conducted in the Highwood area.
3. Interview with Everett Bellei, 5/27/84.

4. Interview with Joseph Muzzarelli 4/23/80 part of the Italians in Chicago oral history project and is in possession of Italian Cultural Center and University of Illinois at Chicago library. Interviews with Louis Bernardi, 7/14/84; Tony Casorio, 2/25/84; Eritrea Pasquesi, 8/26/85.
5. Casorio
6. Casorio
7. Casorio
8. Bernardi
9. Interview with Henry Piacenza, 2/24/84. Mr. Piacenza is deceased and was 88 at the time of his interview.
10. Interview with Domenico Lattanzi, 6/27/84.
11. Mr. Bertucci is deceased. He was 98 when interviewed 2/24/84.
12. Bertucci
13. For a discussion of this and review of other sources see Virginia Yans McLaughlin, "Patterns of Work and Family Organization: Buffalo's Italians," *Journal of Interdisciplinary History*, 2 Autumn (1971), page 306.
14. Casorio
15. Interview with Everett Bellei, 5/27/84.
16. Interviews with Massima Vanoni, 10/9/84; Teresa Saielli, 12/31/83; Domenica Mocogni, 2/27/84; and Eritrea Pasquesi.
17. Interview with Mary Baldi, 1/5/84.
18. Baldi
19. Below are figures indicating population growth of North Shore communities between 1920 and 1930. U.S. Census figures:

1920	1930	
Highwood	1446	3590
Lake Forest	3657	6554
Highland Park	6167	12203
Wilmette	7814	15233
Winnetka	6694	12166
Glencoe	6295	6825

20. Interviews with Rosa Fiocchi, 10/17-18/85; and Domenick Linari, 4/19/85.
21. Interview with Viterbo Ponsi 2/28/84.
22. A distance of about 10 miles.
23. Nonsense
24. "There you go, the war came and everybody worked."
25. Ponsi
26. Interview with Phillip Pasquesi, 8/27/85.
27. Casorio

28. Ronald Davis, *Opera in Chicago*, pages 198-202.

29. Interview with Teresa Saielli, 12/31/83.

30. Casorio

31. Saielli

32. Interview with Gina DeBartolo, 6/30/84.

33. Interview with Pia Gilbertini, 9/18-19/85, Tucson, Ariz.; and Maria Manfredini, 10/15/85, Princeton, Ill.

34. Interview with Fidel Ghini, mayor of Highwood, 1/3/85.

35. *Chicago Tribune Magazine*, June 6, 1965, page. 18.

36. P. Pasquesi

37. Interview with Guy Viti, 5/27/84.

38. P. Pasquesi

39. Ft. Sheridan was founded in 1887 after Chicago businessmen donated land to the U.S. government to build a military base following the Haymarket Riot of 1886.

40. P. Pasquesi

41. "Highwood Citizen Speaks," *The Highland Park Press*.

42. Ghini

43. Jews first moved into the North Shore suburbs, including Highland Park, after World War I, although the movement to the suburbs from Chicago was greatest after World War II. Irving Cutler estimates that Highland Park is 50 percent Jewish today. See "The Jews of Chicago," *Ethnic Chicago*, Peter d'A. Jones and Melvin G. Holli, eds. Grand Rapids, Mich.

44. Gibertini

Chapter **22** **CURRENT PATTERNS OF SOCIALIZATION AND ADAPTATION IN AN ITALIAN AMERICAN COMMUNITY**
Concetta A. Maglione Chiacchio
Rutgers University, New Jersey

Introduction

This research is a qualitative study of the current third and fourth generations of an Italian-American community. The current patterns of socialization and adaptation and the people's folk system are investigated.[1]

The community, referred to here as Hewittown, is an Italian-American enclave which has remained intact for over one hundred years.

Hewittown was formed when Italians, many from a town outside of Naples known as Casandrino, migrated to the United States at the turn of the century. Many came to work either at a wire factory located in the community or at one of the potteries nearby. Hewittown is located in a major New Jersey city and comprises an area of one hundred square blocks of Italian-American concentration. Residents consider a twelve block area to be the "heart" of the community. According to the 1980 census, 7,101 persons lived in Hewittown which comprises 10% of the total of 72,143 for the city.[2] Although the community is a composition of other ethnic groups, it is referred to as Italian.[3]

The Italian immigrant to Hewittown confronted a new environment and culture. The process of socialization and adaptations of these immigrants were affected by cultural influences and external conditions. They developed a subculture as a response to the broad social environment of the mass American society.[4] Each succeeding generation confronted and adapted to a different experience. Certain patterns of behavior exhibited by the people of Hewittown are adaptive strategies that developed as a means of adjustment to the environmental situation. They are responses to the opportunities and deprivations they encountered.

To understand the current socialization pattern of the Italian-American third and fourth generations, and to ascertain how Hewittowners adapt to their environment, this research investigates the transformation of socialization and the process of intergenerational continuity. The people's folk system is examined to determine how Hewittowners perceive and interpret the social relationships in which they are involved.

Ethnicity

Some theoretical considerations on the topic of ethnicity are required. The literature concerning the nature, trends and changes of ethnicity is abundant from the melting pot theory to the celebration of neo-ethnicity.[5] From the wealth of research on ethnicity the following perspectives are offered to provide a frame of reference pertinent to this investigation. According to the "melting pot theory", immigrant cultures would merge to provide a blended unique American culture. The fact that Hewittown remains an identifiable Italian-American subculture proves that the melting pot did not happen for this group. Ethnicity is dynamic in that it changes and transforms.[6] In *Beyond the Melting Pot*, Glazer and Moynihan discuss the transformation of socialization in that ethnic groups are continually recreated by new experiences. Assimilation operated on immigrant groups in different ways to make them distinct. For each immigrant group and for each generation of their descendents there were different experiences.[7]

In *Assimilation in American Life*, Milton Gordon distinguishes between the cultural and social dimensions of ethnicity. The author refers to the ethnic group as a type of group in America set apart by race, religion, and/or national origin. According to Gordon, the ethnic group or subsociety serves three functions: (1) it serves psychologically as a group identification; (2) it provides a network of groups and institutions that allows an individual to confine the individual's own ethnic group throughout all stages of the life cycle; (3) it refracts the national cultural patterns of behavior and values through the prism of its own cultural heritage. Gordon views the American assimilation pattern as one of continuous acculturation and structural separateness. According to Gordon, the ethnic subsociety can exist even after it has lost most of its distinctive cultural attributes.[8] Parsons explains an ethnic group as a "transgenerational type of a group" with distinctive characteristics.[9] A distinctive identity with a distinctive sense of history, and an emphasis on what the individual *is* rather than what the individual *does* characterizes the ethnic group. An important general core of the group is a common culture. Isaacs discusses a "basic group identity" as an "affective link" for members of an ethnic group.[10] It is an identity an individual acquires at birth.

While Gans, Hansen, and Steinberg are concerned with ethnicity and the total assimilation process, they provide valuable insight pertinent to this study of the current generations of Italian-Americans.[11]

Gans suggests the term "symbolic ethnicity" to describe the ethnic revival in the past decades.[12] Symbolic ethnicity is a nostalgic allegiance to the immigrant culture in that it is an expression of love and pride for tradition that can be felt without becoming part of everyday behavior. This romanticized expression may be identified by an interest in the history of the homeland, and certain practices such as the preparation of ethnic foods and participations in traditional events. Steinberg suggests that when the core elements of traditional culture are altered, ethnic identity elevates to a "symbolic plane" in which people want to "feel ethnic because they are losing the prerequisites for being ethnic".[13] Hansen examines group identification as it affects second and third generations and offers "the principle of third generation interest".[14] The author discusses the "third generation return hypothesis" as it relates to Swedish immigrants and explains that third generations want to remember what the second generation wants to forget. Second generations may experience problems of marginality and want to reject their heritage, whereas the third generations are more secure in being American and develop an interest in their heritage.

Methodology

Ethnographic methods of anthropological research were employed which included the following fieldwork techniques: participant observation, interviews, administration of questionnaires, informal association, use of meetings and gatherings, the study of records and documents, and photography. Primary informants consisted of twenty families who were interviewed in depth on numerous occasions. Secondary informants were interviewed less frequently and included individuals of various community institutions and those contacted during informal associations and meetings and gatherings. Interview schedules covered the following categories: family profile including conjugal roles and childrearing, educational attitudes and achievement, religious and political views, and community involvement. Personal background and values questionnaires were administered.

Primary informants included twenty families of third and/or fourth generation Italian-Americans of Hewittown who were identified to represent the various occupations held by the residents of the community. (Table 1 illustrates the occupational categories represented in this study. Table 2 illustrates other characteristics of the family informants.)

Interviews were taped recorded to preserve the information in context and to capture the informants' expression and intonations. This researcher elicited participants' responses to spontaneous aspects which were unanticipated, but significant. Upon completion and during data collection the recorded interviews were completely transcribed. For some informants, the interviews resulted into

Table 1
Occupations of Hewittown Family Informants

	Husband	Wife
Managerial and professional specialty occupations	4	3
Technical, sales, and administrative support	4	4 (5 part time)
Service occupations	4	2 (1 part time)
Precision production, craft and repair occupations	4	0
Operators, fabricators, and laborers	4	1

genealogical searches for answers to questions that never occurred to them prior to the research. Others considered the family profile interview sessions especially therapeutic. One informant thought that the sessions were better than marriage counseling. The twenty primary families in this inquiry include a total of 40 adults and 33 of their offspring. Other primary and secondary informants make a total of 116 people interviewed by the researcher. Considering the other numerous contacts made by this researcher at meetings and gatherings, an approximate total of 150 people of Hewittown were consulted for this study.

Oral histories were recorded from older members of the community to provide a diachronic perspective and a better understanding of the shared knowledge of the community. (Figure 1 illustrates the Italian origin of the sample families in this study.)

Analysis

The basis for collecting the data in this research of the current generations of Italian-Americans of Hewittown was guided by three central concerns:

(1) the current pattern of socialization exhibited by the third and fourth generations;

Table 2
Characteristics of Research Families

Age	Husband	Wife
22—27	0	1
28—33	5	4
34—39	5	5
40—45	6	6
46—51	3	4
52—57	1	0

Place of Birth	Husband	Wife
Hewittown	13	20
Other	7	0

Annual Family Income	Number of Families
$10,000 — $20,000	4
$20,000 — $30,000	5
$30,000 — $40,000	6
over $40,000	5

Residence	Number of Families
Homeowners	16
Renters	4
Other real property owned	4

(2) the pattern of adaptation of the current generations:

(3) the people's folk system.

Certain patterns were recognized which were then organized under cultural themes.[15]

Three themes recur in the data regardless of the discussion topic. An overriding cultural theme is that the people of the community are "close" and "care" about each other. They watch out for each other and are there to help.

FIGURE 1

Origins in Italy

X - Provinces of origin in Italy of the Hewittown Research families. (13 families claim origin in or near Naples, 8 families claim origin in or near Rome.)

* - Based on the birthplace of maternal and paternal grandparents or great-grandparents.

On an explicit level respondents express, "this is where your heart is," or "this is where you will always belong." They also express a feeling of being "safe" and "protected." When asked to elaborate on this phenomenon, they describe contradictions. Respondents express a guilt about moving away and those who move away maintain ties with the community. This recurrent theme has enabled this researcher to identify a folk system referred to as "symbolic affection."

Another recurring theme is the centrality of the family and the reference to the family. There is a very strong allegiance to the family. The family is described in all aspects of life and the term "family" describes social relationships in other institutional activity such as the expression "we are all like one big family." In the family status is acquired and maintained.

A third repeated theme is that individual aspirations were not pursued or attained. Recurrent in the discussions is the importance of education, however, most respondents explain that they did not direct their education to occupational choices or long range goals. They tell about grandparents and parents who had to lessen their goals and aspirations in order to pursue what they could realistically attain. For Hewittowners, the centrality of the family and the need to remain close to the subculture of the community may interfere with the accessibility of personal goals and aspirations.

Group Orientation

A residential group which sets itself off by a distinct identity, reputation, and boundaries may be analyzed in terms of physical structures and cognitive maps.[16] The physical structure consists of the locations of such things as facilities and specialized activity. Cognitive maps are used by the residents to describe not necessarily what the community is like, but what the people think it ought to be like.

Hewittown residents impose different physical boundaries on the community. Although a community is a place on the city map, it may also be a "social construct" that exists in people's minds.[17] The city map illustrates Hewittown as a broader area from what the residents define as their community. (Figure 2) Residents agree that a twelve block area of Italian concentration is the "heart" of the community. Bordering streets of adjacent residential areas are referred to as "outskirts." The bordering streets with an Hispanic or Black populace are referred to as "fringes." One informant living on the "fringe" explains that residents use the terms "them" and "us" to distinguish between those individuals who live in the center of the area. One respondent also demarcates areas with the community by referring to distinct "sections" of Hewittown.

Hewittown is one residential area of the city surrounded by three suburban townships. Although the bordering streets meld into other residential

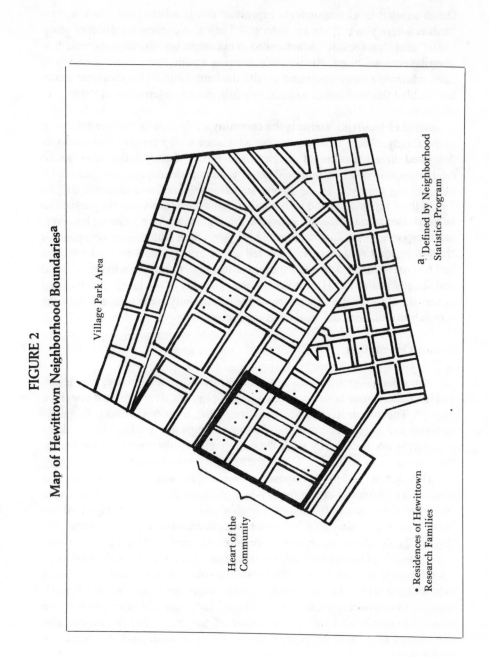

FIGURE 2

Map of Hewittown Neighborhood Boundaries[a]

Village Park Area

Heart of the
Community

• Residences of Hewittown
Research Families

[a] Defined by Neighborhood
Statistics Program

neighborhoods, Hewittowners are emphatic about the divisions, both physical and social.

The concern of encroachment by other minority groups is expressed by the current generations.[18] The influx of new Italian immigrants also present uncertainty. They pose a threat to the community's identity in that they are seen as not having a sense of caring for the neighborhood.

The early immigrants formed a colony out of necessity in order to feel protected and safe. The younger generations maintain an "affective tie" to the immigrant generation. The need to maintain a protected community has perpetuated throughout the years and has evolved into a romanticized expressive solidarity and "closeness". The term "symbolic affection" is suggested to describe the folk system exhibited by Hewittowners. This "ethos" of expressed closeness is a romanticized view of how the people want to perceive their social reality.[20] This documented ethos of "symbolic affection" is a consequence of the interaction of both cultural and structural forces that guided Hewittowners' behavior.

Hewittowners claim their expression of solidarity as a special quality of the community. The early Italian immigrants of Hewittown defended themselves against the mass American society. Current generations still express the need to protect the area from the encroachment of other ethnic groups in order to preserve the community's Italian-American identity. New Italian immigrants present a threat to the residents in that they lack a loyalty to the community that may alter its identity. The residents of Hewittown claim their community as a special place. This claim is based upon its historic accomplishments and the fact that it still exists as a very distinct community among others.

Conclusion

Ethnicity is dynamic, but it is also persistent.[21] For Hewittown the traditional institutions and values have remained relatively stable and intact. The residents of the community have sanctioned the centrality of the family and the concept of the neighborhood as an extension of the family through the generations. The institutions are changing, but certain traditions are maintained.

The neighborhood boundaries are shrinking with the influx of non-Italians and other ethnic groups which may suggest its future demise as an Italian-American ethnic community. However, also operating in tandem, are renewed interests and trends that may stabilize the ethnic group identity. A *rinascimento* (rebirth) is envisioned by residents, community leaders, and city officials.

Presently, Hewittown includes residents who may remain in the community because of their economic situation as well as the artists, professionals, and others with economic means who choose not to leave. For those who do remain, the ethnic neighborhood is significant and is part of their everyday lifestyle.

Affective ties and traditional institutions and values remain also for those who leave the community. Hewittown extends its boundaries as respondents express, "they brought Hewittown with them." The suburban grandchildren participate in community events and the teenagers congregate with the Hewittown peer group when they visit with grandparents or great-grandparents. For others Hewittown may have symbolic significances described by Gans as a "symbolic ethnicity" of nostalgic allegiance to the immigrant culture and tradition.[22]

For whatever significance this ethnic community holds, or will continue to hold for individuals, residents say it will be remembered. Hewittown's future as an Italian-American ethnic community depends on the younger generation. Currently it is in a dynamic balance of transformation and persistence.

Footnotes

1. See Nobua K. Shimahara, *Adaptation and Education In Japan* (New York: Praeger Press, 1979) 1. Adaptation is the utilization of resources to attain goals. It is a dynamic strategy for solving human problems. A *pattern* of adaptation consists of the traits *or* observable features that characterize the adaptive behavior. For an explanation of "folk system" as a people's concept of their social reality built up by their experiences and interpretations of these experiences, see Paul Bohannon, *Social Anthropology* (New York: Holt, Reinhart and Winston, 1963) 51 and John U. Ogbu, *The Next Generation: An Ethnography of Education In An Urban Neighborhood* (New York: Academic Press, 1974).
2. The City Department of Housing and Development provided demographics which were obtained from a 1980 Diennial Report, Neighborhood Statistics Program based upon the 1980 U.S. Department of Census Report.
3. Gerald D. Suttles, *The Social Structure of Communities* (Chicago: The University of Chicago Press, 1972). A relative concentration of a single ethnic group in comparison to other residential areas establishes the identity of a community.
4. Harry Jebsen, Jr., "Assimilation In a Working Class Suburb: The Italians of Blue Island Illinois" in Pat Gallo, ed., *The Urban Experience of Italian-Americans*, Proceedings of the Eighth Annual Conference of the American-Italian Historical Association held at New York, November, 1975 (Staten Island: American Italian Historic Association, 1977) 64—84. Jebsen discusses how ethnic groups came to the American industrial centers and formed ethnic enclaves within the cities. The "colonies" provided the immigrant a sense of belonging within the mass society of America.
5. For a thorough discussion of ethnicity see, for example, George DeVos and Lola Romanucci-Ross, eds., *Ethnic Identity, Cultural Continuities and*

Change (Palo Alto: Mayfield Publishing Company, 1975); Milton M. Gordon, *Assimilation in American Life* (New York: Oxford University Press, 1964); Nathan Glazer & Daniel P. Moynihan, *Beyond the Melting Pot: The Negroes, Puerto Ricans, Jews, Italians, and Irish of New York City* (The M.I.T. Press, 1963); Glazer and Moynihan, eds. *Ethnicity: Theory and Experience* (Cambridge: Harvard University Press); Orlando Patterson, *Ethnic Chauvinism* (New York: Stein and Day Publishers, 1977); Stephen Steinberg, *The Ethnic Myth* (New York: Antheum, 1981).

6. See Glazer and Moynihan, *Beyond the Melting Pot*; Richard N. Juliani, "In Search of Ethnicity, Professor Chronicles Immigrants," *The Spires*, February 1984; 4, 10.

7. Glazer and Moynihan, *Beyond the Melting Pot* 13—17.

8. Gordon 27, 37—38.

9. Talcott Parsons, "Some Theoritical Consideration On The Nature and Change of Ethnicity," in N. Glazer and D.P. Moynihan, eds., *Ethnicity: Theory and Experience*, 53—83.

10. Harold R. Isaacs, "Basic Group Identity: The Idol of the Tribe" in N. Glazer and D.P. Moynihan, eds., *Ethnicity: Theory and Experience*, 29—52.

11. Herbert J. Gans, "Symbolic Ethnicity: The Future of Ethic Groups and Cultures in America," *Ethnic and Racial Studies* 2 (January, 1979): 1—18; Marcus L. Hansen, "The Third Generation In America" *Commentary* 14 (November, 1952): 499—500; Steinberg, *The Ethnic Myth*.

12. Gans, 1—18

13. Steinberg, 63

14. Hansen, 499—500

15. James P. Spradley, *Participant Observation* (New York: Holt, Reinhart, Winston, Inc. 1980) 1 41. Spradley defines a cultural theme as "any principle recurrent in a number of domains, tacit or explicit, serving a relationship among subsystems of cultural meanings."

16. Suttles 22. This is apparent when residents give discrete boundaries for a neighborhood or area despite there being no sharp divisions between adjacent spaces.

17. Gordon 163

18. Joseph A. Scimecca & Francis X Feminella, "An Exploratory Study of Italo-Americans on the Left" in F.X. Feminella, ed., *Power and Class: The Italian American Experience Today*, Proceeding of the Fourth Annual Conference, October, 1971 (Staten Island: American Italian Historic Association) 12—19. The authors suggest that Italian-Americans will begin to identify with other minorities. Refering to what Richard Hofstader describes as "status anxiety" the authors suggest that Italian-American will begin to identify with other minorities when they feel secure with their own status as an ethnic group.

19. For a discussion of sub-systems, see Albert S. Alissi, *Boys In Little Italy: A Comparison of Their Individual Patterns, and Peer Group Association* (San Francisco: R. & E Research Associates, 1978). The "deviant sub-system" includes foreign born Italians who exhibit behavior inconsistent with others in the neighborhood. They may receive negative reactions from residents.
20. Bohannon 51
21. Glazer & Moynihan, *Beyond the Melting Pot*; Juliani.
22. Gans 1—18.

Chapter **23** NASSAU COUNTY'S ITALIAN
AMERICAN WOMEN:
A COMPARATIVE VIEW
Mary Jane Capozzoli

This paper is a study of Italian American Women in suburban America.
It's purpose is to focus on the unique elements of the Italian heritage and how
the heritage affects the lives of these women. The subjects of the study all
live in Nassau County, in the state of New York. Three hundred and one Italian
American women and one hundred and eleven non-Italian American women
are included in the study. The analysis focuses on differences and similarities
in work experience, religiosity, and gender relations.

The Italian American women were predominantly of Catholic background
with only 5 percent non Catholic. For the non-Italian women, 55 percent were
Catholic, and 45 percent were non-Catholic. The two groups were similar with
respect to marital status (most were married), mean age, average number of
years married, age at marriage, and average number of children.

Scholars have found that Italian family members often live closer to one
another than do family members of other ethnic groups. It is also asserted that
their neighborhoods are more stable because, as Gans points out, Italian
Americans are less likely to move.[2] When asked where most of their relatives
lived, four-fifths of the Italian women said either in their immediate vicinity,
in the county, or in New York State (usually New York City). Only 57 percent
of non-Italians kin lived in the vicinity, county or state. Only one in five of
the Italians had relatives living outside of New York State, as compared with
two in five for non-Italians.

Stronger kinship ties were revealed indirectly, when it was found that,
while some 60 percent of non-Italians were born in the City, 80 percent of
the Italian women were born there: one in four of the former were born outside
the State, one in ten of the latter.[3] Such figures indicate less geographic mobility
among Italian families, and may also indicate a desire to live near their
birthplace in order to be closer to parents and other relatives.

Being Italian has also been shown to be influential in analyzing women's work. Virginia Yans-McLaughlin found that Italian-born women who are gainfully employed are less likely to work outside the home than other married women.[4] Richard Gambino[5] points out that when Italian women work, they choose part-time jobs or work that includes few concerns after the work day is completed. Such jobs cause minimal disruption of the family and do not threaten the male's role as breadwinner. Of all white working females, Italian women generally have the lowest proportion in professional or technical careers and the highest in manual or in operative labor categories.

Regardless of ethnic background or marital status, over half of all the women in this study worked. Three quarters (74%) of Italian-American women interviewed had worked part-time at one time in their lives, as had the non-Italian women. The evidence suggests that the values of the Italian-born regarding women working has changed over time.

The occupational status of these two groups of women is quite similar. The largest number of both groups were in one of the following occupations: teacher, secretary, clerk, nurse.[6] When their status is compared, however, differences emerge. While those in the lower white-collar (e.g. clerical) category were equal, there were fewer Italians (33%) than non-Italians (41%) in the high white-collar positions (Table 1). More Italian women were blue collar workers, usually in the semiskilled category, with a preponderance in the garment industry, whereas none of the non-Italians women were employed there.

Table 1

Occupational Status of Nassau County Women

	Italians		Non-Italians	
	No.	%	No.	%
High white-collar	59	33%	28	41%
Low white-collar	96	54	37	54
Blue-collar	23	13	7	6

A review of the daughters' occupations indicates a similar pattern. For both groups, the leading occupations are teacher, secretary, and nurse. Comparable proportions are housewives, are in school or college, or are employed outside the home. But while Table 2 indicates that almost equal numbers of Italian daughters were found in the high and low white-collar categories, most non-Italian women clustered in the high white-collar group. Slightly more Italian daughters had blue-collar jobs as compared with non-Italian daughters.

Table 2

Occupational Status of Daughters

	Italians		Non-Italians	
	No.	%	No.	%
High white-collar	52	45%	22	61%
Low white-collar	57	50	13	36
Blue-collar	6	5	1	3

A greater difference between types of jobs and status level is found by comparing the occupations of the mothers of women questioned for this survey. Among non-Italians the prevalent job types were teacher, secretary, and bookkeeper; for the Italians, they were sewing-machine operator, seamstress, and working in one's own business. Not surprisingly these differences were reflected in the proportion of women holding white-collar and blue-collar job (Table 3). While 3 percent of Italian mothers were in the high white-collar category, 27 percent of non-Italian mothers were professional workers. The difference was less in the lower white-collar category. Over two-thirds of Italian mothers were blue-collar workers, while less than one-half of non-Italian mothers (32%) were employed in blue collar jobs.[7]

Table 3

Occupational Status of Mothers

	Italians		Non-Italians	
	No.	%	No.	%
High white-collar	3	3%	11	27%
Low white-collar	32	27	17	41
Blue-collar	81	70	13	32

In discussing their working lives, women were also asked about paying board at home. Both groups indicated that the practice was customary. However, Italian women (86%) more often contributed to the household than non-Italians (61%). The latter included middle-class families in which daughters did not contribute. The difference may also suggest, however, a stricter adherence to the Italian working-class tradition of the family economy; or it may imply that Italian daughters were more easily controlled by their parents, less able to assert their independence. Perhaps they, more than other women, felt a greater responsibility to the family.

When asked about moving out of the house before marriage, Italian women exhibited greater dependence. Whereas one in three non-Italian moved away, fewer than one in twenty Italians of the second and third generation left the home before getting married. In discussing this issue, two of the non-Italians explained it quite differently from the way Italian women had. Marilyn, aged 59, said she, "Never planned to live at home with my parents . . . That wasn't my cup of tea."[8] And Betty: "I wasn't aware that I should be home. It was part of my expectations that I would live on my own."[9] In contrast, a 35 year old Italian-American woman from Valley Stream noted: "Only one type of girl left home and she wasn't a good girl. Now we're going to get down to being Italian. It wasn't done."[10]

The restrictive and protective environment of the Italian home is also reflected in the number of women who attended local colleges. Only 14 percent of Italian women went to colleges outside of the New York Metropolitan area. The figure for non-Italians was much higher (44 percent). Differences between the two groups are still evident among the children of these women. Daughters of second- and third-generation women are still less likely to go away to college (40%) than their non-Italian counterparts (56%).

It should be noted that most Italian women in this sample never attended college. Earning a living tended to be the first priority for the Italian-born; hence a utilitarian vocation was valued over education. Such skills could often be acquired without formal education. Daughters were expected to prepare themselves for their future as wives and mothers. Life in America and the decision to stay there helped reshape these commitments, along with the changing economy.[11] Miriam Cohen has shown how family support of education for women in New York City came about in the period between the two world wars. The second-generation daughters completed high school so they would be prepared for clerical positions. However, Cohen also noted that on the whole these women were more educated than their male counterparts, who still sought blue-collar employment in construction and other trades. Most of these occupations did not require a high school diploma.[12]

With respect to the educational level of the Italian women in the study, generally they were a highly educated group; however, they were somewhat less educated than the non-Italian women (Table 4). Nearly three-fourths (72%) of the Italians were high school graduates, which was approximately the same (75%) for non-Italian women, but only two-fifths of Italian women took courses beyond high school, as compared with over half of the non-Italians.[13] For Italians, it seems, higher education was not a priority; completing high school was enough.

For the daughters of these women, the level of education had improved markedly over the previous generation, even if they had not caught up to the non-Italian groups. Half of the daughters had attained at least a college degree, as compared to two-thirds of the other group. Non-Italian daughters were more likely (21% to 17%) to have taken some college as compared to the Italians, and it appears that twice as many Italians stopped with a high school diploma. Again, the importance of obtaining education beyond the high school level appears to be less crucial for Italians.

Table 4

Women's Highest Level of Education

Level	Italians (%) (N⁵301)	Non-Italians (%) (N⁵111)
Grammar school only	1%	0%
High school: Attended	0	0
Graduated	21	11
Business/trade school	6	5
College: Attended	17	21
Graduated	32	35
Postgraduate: Courses	11	11
Degree	12	12

Any attempt to highlight the distinctiveness of being Italian would not be complete without an examination of religious practices. For Italians, religion plays a different, and less crucial role then it does for other Catholics. Andrew Greeley notes that Italians, when compared with other Catholics, were the least pious. Although they considered church attendence less important, they believed that their children should be baptized and receive religious instruction in preparation for First Communion and Confirmation. Most Italian-born immigrants distrusted the Catholic Church in this country. Few sent their children to parochial schools. Their tradition of feasts honoring patron saints, and their belief in such superstitions as the evil eye appalled other Catholics. Gambino asserts that with the move to the suburbs religion may have played a greater role in the lives of Italian-Americans as they became "Hibernianized."[14]

In the interviews women were asked how religion affected the way they were raised. Non-Italians women who were also Catholic were twice as likely as Italians to say that religion had played a major role in their lives, using such phrases as, "Most vital part of my life," "center of our lives," "strongly affected by upbringing." In contrast, Italians said religion had a "moderate" influence on them, that attending mass was the visible part of religion in their childhood.[15]

In fact, the Italian response as a whole tends to be indicative of the secondary role that religion characteristically played in Italian life. Italian women were not at all apologetic about the fact that religion was not a major factor in their lives. Ida recalled: "Religion was never a big thing in my house. My parents were really not very religious."

When asked how often their family had attended church when they were children, nine out of ten women, Italians and non-Italians alike, reported regular attendance at church. Almost without exception, they said they and their children went to religious instruction and received First Communion and confirmation. One gets the impression from the interview, however, that non-Italians continued going to church after adolescence, while many Italians reported parental pressures to attend easing off at that time.

When questioned about church attendance in their own families, Italians reported a much lower frequency than non-Italians: almost nine out of ten (88%) among the latter, six of ten (63%) among the former. Similarly, infrequent or no attendance was much greater (17%—20%) for Italians as compared with non-Italian Catholics (5—7%).

A similar pattern is revealed in figures gathered from women concerning church attendance in their daughter's families. Both groups reported regular church attendance (65% non-Italian, 53% Italian), although again, the proportion was lower among the Italians. Italians were also slightly more likely to attend church irregularly (7%) than other Catholics (5%). Non-attendance was again higher for the Italians (40% versus 30%).

However, Italians still practice many religious traditions from their ethnic heritage. In keeping with the emphasis on home and family, attending feasts to honor patron saints was reported by the parents of many Italian women (71%), although less so in their own families (44%). No similar activity was reported in interviews with non-Italians. Belief in the evil eye was common in over one-fourth (29%) of Italian women's parents, but only one in eight non-Italians recalled superstitious beliefs in their own family. One Italian woman in twenty reported this belief; no non-Italians did. Religious symbols — crucifixes, statues, saints' pictures — were found in a majority (53%) of Italian women's homes and in those of their mothers, but among the small number of Catholic non-Italians interviewed, the proportion was only one in four, although one in three said their mothers and had such symbols.[17]

Not surprisingly, because of their distrust of the institutional church, as well as their more personal and home-oriented attitude toward religion, Italian women and their mothers were less involved in church organizations than their

Catholic counterparts. For example, while half the non-Italians interviewed belonged to church organizations, less than one-quarter of the Italians did. Among mothers of the former, two-fifths were members of religious groups; one-fifth of Italian mothers were. Among daughters of these groups, participation rates were still higher for non-Italians. Only 8 percent of Italian daughters were involved in church associations, 13 percent of other Catholic daughters were.

My findings tend to confirm those of other scholars[18] in that Italians are not generally "joiners" as compared to other white ethnic groups. Asked if their mothers belonged to any sort of group, three-fifths (64%) of non-Italian women said yes, but less than one-third (31%) of Italians said their mothers were group members. Moreover, non-Italian women were also more likely to be group members (82%) than the Italian women (68%). The former more often belonged to more than one organization (55%) than the Italian females (36%). This was also true for the daughters of both groups.[19]

In patterns of work, education, religion, and group affiliation, distinctions between Italian women and others have been indicated. But the influence of Italian values on women is most apparent in their personal behavior, specifically, in their attitudes toward gender roles.[20] The protection and supervision of women, a customary practice in Italian families, which frequently stifled their independence and sense of identity were perpetuated beyond the first generation. This is especially apparent when contrasted with the experiences of eighteen non-Italian interviewees ranging in age from 35 to 80.

The tone of the interviews with Italian women was quite different from that with other women, largely because of the Italians' stronger sense of ethnic identity. When interviewees were asked how their ethnic background had affected the way they were raised, Italian women more often acknowledged their ethnicity, their Italianness, and emphasized respect, obedience, and the importance of family. For example, Debbie, 28, noted:

> The importance and respect for the family was always emphasized. You had to go see your grandparents every week. God forbid if you missed a birthday or a holiday.[21]

In contrast, non-Italian women sought to deemphasize their ethnicity. A Manhattan-bred woman of 63, discussing her German-Russian-Jewish heritage, said, "I don't think it affected anything. I don't think we were raised very differently." An Irish Catholic, 47, raised in Queens, admitted that she had never paid much attention to ethnic and religious backgrounds.[22] A German-Irish woman wrote:

Had trouble answering some of these questions. Not the answers
but found difficulty in relating to the questions — I believe because
I'm *not* ethnic enough.[23]

Besides denying the importance of ethnicity in their upbrinding, non-Italian
women more often emphasized their freedom, not the restrictions that governed
their youth, adolescence, and early childhod. Even when they mentioned rules,
restrictions, or instances of inequality, non-Italian women tended to be more
matter-of-fact about them than did the Italian women. Again and again, Italian
women used the world "strict" to describe their upbringing, often becoming
emotional and resentful in discussing it.

Non-Italians characterized their growing up in more detached terms.
Evelyn, a senior citizen, noted: "My parents were very lenient. I did just about
as I wanted." A Garden City woman, in her 40s, reported: "I was given a
great deal of freedom to grow. We were never held down to any great
degree."[24] What is noticeable about these interviews is that none of the women
mentioned conflicts over the sexual division of labor. Even women who
admitted differences in treatment between boys and girls told bow they received
concessions from their parents in other ways. Marilyn, for instance,
acknowledged that her brothers could stay out later than the girls but added
that they could more easily get the use of the family car.[25] It is significant
that none of these women used the word "sheltered", as did the Italians, in
talking about their upbringing.

While parental attitudes for both groups concerning dress, smoking,
drinking, and hair-dyeing tended to be similar, restrictions on the use of makeup
were more frequent in the case of Italian interviewees, whose families were
more apt to express negative feelings about it. Naturally, therefore, more
Italians used makeup without parental consent than did the non-Italians. More
than twice as many of the latter recalled no parental restrictions about the use
of cosmetics. In general, parental reaction to the use of makeup was also less
violent. Phyllis, for example, said, "I don't think there was any arguing about
any of these things," referring to makeup, smoking, hair-dyeing, and so forth.
But the use of makeup by Italian women seemed to change traditional values
about how a woman ought to appear; that is, the "natural" look was supposedly
the mark of a woman's respectability. Because it was a more serious matter,
therefore, going against parental wishes by using makeup provoked a greater
reaction in Italian families than in others, where one did not find the counterpart
of the Italian daughter being hit for wearing lipstick.[26]

Supervision of dating was also more common among Italian women. While
unheard of among the non-Italian group, chaperonage was a fairly common
practice among some first- and second-generation Italian women. Moreover,

many of the first and even second generation also reported having dated only their husbands. That is probably why one finds that many Italian women dated secretly, in contrast to the non-Italian group in which such behavior was non-existent. On the other hand, although both groups had curfews, the proportion was higher among Italian women. Such regulations were more strictly enforced among Italian families; an Irish woman remarked: "Never, ever was anything said if you came in late." In contrast, an Italian woman from Westbury reported that when he came home 15 minutes late, her father dislocated her jaw.[27] While these cases represent two extremes, they illustrate the importance of obedience to rules in an Italian home.

Dating was more subtly controlled by Italian parents who also tended to make it known that they preferred that their daughters date and marry Italians. Hence, while a majority of both groups indicated that they could and did date young men of any and all ethnic or religious backgrounds, Italian women were more inclined to say that their parents preferred an Italian boy. The non-Italian group reported that their parents tended to favor young men who were of the same religion. A somewhat similar pattern was revealed in responses concerning the importance of the young man's religion and ethnicity in marriage. Both groups said their parents favored a husband of the same religion, but Italian women gave ethnicity a higher priority than did the other group. These findings are supported by a comparison of the ethnic and religious backgrounds of mates of Italian Catholics and other women. Among the latter, 36 percent married men having the same religious and ethnic backgrounds as their own, while 67 percent of the spouses of Italian women were also Italian Catholic. But while ethnicity seemed to be more important for Italian women, marrying within the same faith took precedence among other women. Almost half (48%) of the latter indicated that they had married a man having the same religion: 91 percent of the Italian Catholic women married Catholics.[28]

Finally, in order to explore Italian protectiveness at its most personal level, women were asked if they received information about sex before marriage; they were also asked about birth control and abortion. Slightly fewer Italian women (67%) than non-Italian (73%) said they had received information about sex before marriage, and both groups reported the same sources: mothers, friends, books. But while non-Italian women were just as likely to be informed by their mothers as by their friends, this was not the case with Italians, suggesting that Italian mothers and daughters were more reluctant to discuss sexual matters. Unfortunately, such reluctance often meant providing no information at all. Many Italian girls therefore relied on friends. Similarly, many Italian women were less likely than others to be informed about menstruation, a greater proportion of them learning about it only after it had happened.

Even more uncommon were discussions of birth control and abortion. Compared to non-Italians, a smaller proportion of Italian women admitted that they or their mothers had practiced birth control. Three non-Italian women told of having obtained some form of birth control devices before marriage. In addition, compared to the non-Italian group, birth control was less likely to be discussed with friends or relatives, according to Italian women. The subject of abortion was more taboo among Italians, but more Italian women knew relatives or friends who had had abortions; several of the women had had one or more themselves, this situation is understandable if we realize that the non-Italian were more apt to use birth control and that over 40 percent were Catholics who would not consider having an abortion.

In conclusion, there were important differences in the lives of these Italian and non-Italian women. That Italian traditions of families and male superiority were especially influential in shaping such differences in behavior suggest that living in suburbia did not bring about complete assimilation. For instance, Italian women tended, even after marriage, to live nearer their kin. They paid board at home more frequently and smaller percentage of them moved out of the house or left homme to go away to college.

Religion tended to be less important in the lives of Italians compared with other Catholic women. The former did not attend church as often and were less likely to belong to church organizations. But, on the other hand, they often followed religious traditions and practices carried over from Italy and they were more apt to display religious objects — crucifixes, pictures of the Virgin Mary, images of saints — in their homes than other Catholics.

Another indication of the home and family orientation of Italian women is the fact that fewer mothers of Italian women were members of groups. Within the home, Italian women seemed to be more controlled — more sheltered, protected, restricted — than other women. Italian daughters were more apt to feel that they were treated differently from their brothers, particularly in the matter of chores and the relative freedom allowed each gender.

Restrictions were also greater for Italian women in matters of makeup and dating. Compared to non-Italians, their parents seemed to put more pressure on them to date and marry Italians. All of which indicate that these women probably possessed a greater ethnic awareness than other women: they were more apt to think to themselves as Italians first and Americans second.

From all such evidence it appears that Italian mores were influential in shaping the lives of the women interviewed. Living in a suburban county did not give rise to full assimilation. Yet, over the course of three generations, Italian mores have changed. As the behavior of the Italian-American woman become similar to that of other American suburban women, some of the traditional values and behavior patterns will disappear.

Footnotes

1. Other statistics include:

	Italian	Non-Italian
Mean number of years lived in Nassau	30	34
Mean age	55	57
Average number of years married	30	30
age difference between mates	3	3
age of mates at marriage	26	24
Woman's age at birth of first child	26	26
Woman's age at birth of last child	32	32
Woman's child-bearing span	6	6
Mean number of children per family	2.4	2.6

2. Herbert Gans, *The Urban Villagers* (New York, 1962), pp. 15, 289.
3. These figures were calculated without the foreign-born. Of both groups, 10% were born in Nassau County.
4. Virginia Yans-McLaughlin, *Family and Community* (Ithaca, N.Y., 1977), pp. 53, 364.
5. Richard Gambino, *Blood of My Blood* (Garden City, N.Y., 1974), pp. 14, 176, 179.
6. Among Italian positions, salesperson was tied for fourth.
7. Since the women were asked about their mothers' occupation, responses do not reflect the situation in 1981. Most were retired or dead. The largest category for non-Italian mothers were unskilled, while for most Italian mothers it was semiskilled.
8. Interview with M.P., Manhasset, N.Y., 8/31/81.
9. Interview with B.A., Manhasset, 8/5/81.
10. Interview with A.Z., Valley Stream, 9/15/81.
11. Gambino, *Blood of My Blood*, pp. 245—247, 338.
12. Miriam Cohen, "From Workshop to Office: Italian Women and Family Strategies in New York City, 1900—1950" (Ph.D. dissertation, University of Michigan, 1978), pp. 218ff., 287.
13. According to the 1980 census, 76% of Nassau women aged 25 and over had completed high school (*General Social and Economic Characteristics: New York*, 2:34—951).
14. Andrew Greeley, *Why Can't They Be Like Us?* (New York, 1971), p. 68; Gambino *Blood of My Blood*, pp. 232—234, 241.
15. Questionnaire #78; interview with: G.R., Oceanside, 9/23/81; P.E., Garden City, 9/21/81; S.O., Merrick, 4/20/81. Pat, who had attended Catholic school, said religion had "thoroughly" affected the way she was

raised and that she and her friends had thought of becoming nuns. They had played with their holy-water fonts and used Necco wafers for "communion." No such response was recorded for the Italian American women.

16. Interview with I.S., Plainview, 6/25/81; interview with M.M., Merrick, 5/7/81.
17. While Italians mentioned their observance of saints days, non-Italians Catholics did not.
18. Gambino, *Blood of My Blood*, p. 324.
19. Group membership: 35% among Italian daughters, 71% among non-Italians, who often belonged to several groups.
20. Francis X. Femminella and Jill S. Guadragno, "The Italian American Family," *Ethnic Families in America*, eds. C.H. Mindel and R.W. Haberstein (New York, 1976), pp. 79—80.
21. Interview with D.A., Westbury, 7/9/81.
22. Interview with B.K., Merrick, 9/8/81; interview with M.R., Plainedge, 7/25/81.
23. Questionnaire #24.
24. Interview with E.C., Merrick, 10/27/81; interview with M.D., Garden City, 7/29/81.
25. Interview with M.P., Manhasset, 8/31/81.
26. Interview with P.B., Massapequa, 9/9/81; interview with S.M., Wantagh, 6/31/81.
27. Interview with M.R., Plainedge, 7/25/81; interview with J.B., Westbury, 9/24/81.
28. The largest ethnic group (22) in my sample was Irish. Half of the husbands of Irish women were also Irish, and all of the Irish women had married Catholic men.

INDEX